OPERATION BREADBASKET

OPERATION BREADBASKET

AN UNTOLD STORY OF CIVIL RIGHTS IN CHICAGO, 1966–1971

Martin L. Deppe

Foreword by James R. Ralph, Jr.

The University of Georgia Press   *Athens*

© 2017 by the University of Georgia Press
Athens, Georgia 30602
www.ugapress.org
All rights reserved
Designed by Erin Kirk New
Set in 10.5/13 Minion

All images in this book are from the author's collection
unless otherwise noted.

Most University of Georgia Press titles are
available from popular e-book vendors.

Printed digitally

Library of Congress Cataloging-in-Publication Data
Names: Deppe, Martin L., author.
Title: Operation Breadbasket : an untold story of civil rights in Chicago,
   1966–1971 / Martin L. Deppe.
Other titles: Untold story of civil rights in Chicago, 1966–1971
Description: Athens, GA : The University of Georgia Press, [2017] | Includes
   bibliographical references and index.
Identifiers: LCCN 2016020563| ISBN 9780820350462 (hard bound : alk. paper) |
   ISBN 9780820350479 (pbk. : alk. paper)
Subjects: LCSH: Deppe, Martin L. | Operation Breadbasket (U.S.)—History. |
   African Americans—Illinois—Chicago—Economic conditions—20th century. |
   Grocery trade—Illinois—Chicago—History—20th century. | African
   American business enterprises—Illinois—Chicago. | African
   Americans—Civil rights—Illinois—Chicago—History—20th century. | Civil
   rights movements—Illinois—Chicago—History—20th century. | Civil rights
   workers—Illinois—Chicago—Biography | Methodist
   Church—Clergy—Illinois—Chicago—Biography. | Chicago (Ill.)—Race
   relations—History—20th century.
Classification: LCC F548.9.N4 D46 2017 | DDC 323.1196/0730773110904—
   dc23 LC record available at https://lccn.loc.gov/2016020563

In memory of my parents, Florence and Frederick Deppe,
whose lives were a witness to what America should be

In recognition of my Steering Committee colleagues:
"Your ministers fight for jobs and rights"

In honor of my grandson, Robin Frederick Powell Deppe,
and all young African Americans, for whom this story is a gift
and a challenge

I came home and said to Martin, "I think that Jesse Jackson and Operation Breadbasket have something that is needed in every community across the nation."

—CORETTA SCOTT KING

CONTENTS

ABBREVIATIONS

AFL-CIO	American Federation of Labor and Congress of Industrial Organizations
A&P	Great Atlantic & Pacific Tea Company
BCA	Breadbasket Commercial Association
BMM	Black Men Moving
CA	*Chicago American*
CALC	Clergy and Laity Concerned (about the Vietnam War)
CBL	Contract Buyers League
CCCO	Coordinating Council of Community Organizations
CD	*Chicago Defender*
CEO	chief operating officer
CFM	Chicago Freedom Movement
CME	Christian Methodist Episcopal (Church)
CMEC	Chicago Merit Employment Committee
COINTELPRO	Counter Intelligence Program coordinated by the FBI
CORE	Congress of Racial Equality
CST	*Chicago Sun-Times*
CT	*Chicago Tribune*
CTA	Chicago Transit Authority
CTS	Chicago Theological Seminary
CTW	Concerned Transit Workers
CUCA	Coalition of United Community Action
CUL	Chicago Urban League
EEOC	Equal Employment Opportunity Commission
FBI	Federal Bureau of Investigation
FSA	Freedom Scavenger Association
HUD	U.S. Department of Housing and Urban Development
KOCO	Kenwood Oakland Community Organization
NAACP	National Association for the Advancement of Colored People
NCU	National Consumers Union
NGO	nongovernmental organization

NYT	*New York Times*
PBBF	personal Breadbasket files of author
PPC	Poor People's Campaign
PUSH	Operation PUSH (People United to Serve Humanity)
SC	Steering Committee (of Operation Breadbasket)
SCLC	Southern Christian Leadership Conference
SNCC	Student Nonviolent Coordinating Committee
UCL	University of Chicago Library
UFW	United Farm Workers (of California)
UN	United Nations

FOREWORD

Operation Breadbasket is the least well known of the important civil rights organizations that emerged in the mid-twentieth century. The Congress of Racial Equality (CORE), organized in 1942; the Southern Christian Leadership Conference (SCLC), founded in 1957; and the Student Nonviolent Coordinating Committee (SNCC), established in 1960, are all leading players in histories of the modern civil rights movement. But with the exception of the venerable National Association for the Advancement of Colored People (NAACP), no civil rights organization has had such a substantial impact over such a long period of time. SNCC collapsed within a decade of its founding; CORE and, to a lesser extent, even the SCLC are shells of their earlier, and most impactful, incarnations.

Operation Breadbasket in Chicago grew dramatically in its early years, then transformed into People United to Serve Humanity (Operation PUSH) in 1971, and morphed again into the Rainbow PUSH Coalition in 1996. Now in its fiftieth year, the Rainbow PUSH Coalition is still relevant in American politics and activism.

Breadbasket's story is intimately tied with the ascending prominence of Jesse L. Jackson Sr., the youngest of the remarkable group of talented activists who worked closely with Martin Luther King Jr. Jackson has been one of the most visible American leaders for decades, but his impact has not been fully grasped. He is the decisive figure in understanding the reverberations of the modern civil rights movement of the 1960s into our own time.

That Operation Breadbasket remains relatively obscure in historical scholarship and that the significance of Jesse Jackson's activism has not been fully recognized both flow in part from the contours of the writing on the black freedom struggle. Conventional narratives have tended to focus on the most heroic years of the fight for racial justice, from 1955 to 1965. They suggest a fading of the civil rights movement in the aftermath of the campaign for voting rights in Selma and, certainly, by the time of King's assassination in Memphis in April 1968. In traditional accounts, the primary story of the second half of the 1960s is the rise of the black power movement, which, with its emphasis on black pride and black community control, grabbed center stage from the nonviolent, integrationist civil rights movement.[1]

An outgrowth of Martin Luther King's evolving and maturing approach to America's racial injustices, Operation Breadbasket does not fit comfortably into the standard accounts; it is something of a historical orphan. It was founded too late to be part of the heroic phase of the civil rights movement, and it was too closely linked to King and the nonviolent movement to be readily incorporated into the black power story.

It is Breadbasket's outlier status that makes Martin L. Deppe's new book so timely. Until now, the best available account of Operation Breadbasket has been Gary Massoni's important study, which was published more than a quarter century ago (and written more than forty-five years ago). Massoni, one of Jesse Jackson's top aides, offered a detailed history of the first few years of the organization, as well as an illuminating organizational analysis.[2] Even Jackson's biographers, including Marshall Frady, so focused on their charismatic subject, have not greatly deepened our understanding of the organization over which he presided.[3]

Deppe's book is the first study to cover comprehensively Breadbasket's history until its break with the SCLC in 1971. It carefully details Breadbasket's selective patronage campaigns. The use of black consumer power—the key early Breadbasket strategy—had deep roots in Chicago and elsewhere. The first major "Don't Buy Where You Can't Work" campaigns were launched in Chicago in 1929, and this approach was then regularly employed by black Chicagoans.[4] One of the central tactics of black communities as they launched the modern civil rights movement was the withholding of black patronage. That strategy worked in Montgomery, Alabama; Nashville, Tennessee; Birmingham, Alabama; and elsewhere.[5] The Reverend Leon Sullivan popularized selective patronage to advance black employment in the late 1950s and early 1960s in Philadelphia.[6] In 1962 the SCLC established its own program in Atlanta using black buying power, Operation Breadbasket, which was modeled on Sullivan's efforts.

In the fall of 1965 Dr. King and the SCLC joined with the Coordinating Council of Community Organizations (CCCO) to form the Chicago Freedom Movement. The multipronged Chicago movement was King's and the SCLC's response to growing distress over the racial oppression faced by northern blacks. The Chicago movement's goal was to end slums, and King believed that a Chicago chapter of Operation Breadbasket, supported by the organizing power of churches, could assist in that mission. In February 1966, a group of ministers was brought together by King, and before long, under the direction of Jesse Jackson, this program revived the tradition of selective buying in black Chicago.

Martin Deppe, a white Methodist minister presiding over a largely African American congregation, was one of the first clergymen to join the new organization, which quickly made a mark with successful campaigns against dairy companies that sold their products in black communities. In the summer of 1966, Breadbasket successfully pressured soft drink bottlers to hire more black workers. By the fall, it had started winning victories against major supermarket chains, compelling them to stock products produced by black businesses and to funnel some of their assets into black-owned banks.

Deppe details the first campaigns of Operation Breadbasket and then follows the story of selective buying for the next five years. Relapses by targeted employers often muted the initial declarations of victory, but Deppe and his associates did not relent. They reapplied pressure to advance black employment and economic interests. In the end, Deppe demonstrates, there was substantive progress as a result of Breadbasket's efforts.[7]

Over time, Breadbasket broadened its approach to economic justice. In 1969, it was a leader in a campaign to end hunger, which afflicted people of all backgrounds across Illinois. Jesse Jackson canvassed the state and received a standing ovation when he called for action in the Illinois Senate in Springfield, Abraham Lincoln's hometown.

Operation Breadbasket also promoted black economic development. By the late 1960s, it had become an engine for black entrepreneurship, hosting an annual Black Expo that highlighted black businesses. By harnessing the dynamic powers of capitalism, Jackson and members of his staff believed that African Americans in Chicago and beyond could advance their material standing in a society in which money matters so much.[8] Breadbasket's program of deploying and developing black economic muscle was, it can be argued, a concrete application of the resonating call for black power.[9]

A great virtue of Deppe's study is that it is an insider's account. Deppe was involved in many of the episodes he recounts, especially the selective patronage efforts. He was a committed member of the Breadbasket Steering Committee. There is an immediacy to much of his writing that brings to life the aura and excitement as well as the tensions and challenges that marked Breadbasket's history.

His study also offers important insight into the leadership of Jesse Jackson. As the coordinating director of Operation Breadbasket in Chicago, Jackson, only a couple of years removed from college and his own migration from the South to the North, quickly proved his value to Dr. King and the SCLC. During the summer of 1966, he also served as one of the chief captains of the Chicago Freedom Movement's open housing campaign. By early 1967, King was lauding Breadbasket's work as shining evidence of the Chicago movement's success.

Energetic and charismatic, an incisive thinker and a quick actor, Jackson remarkably brought together a number of black Chicago's most accomplished ministers to work together to advance the collective interests of the black community. In the summer of 1967, King appointed Jackson to be the national director of Operation Breadbasket, an appointment that formally catapulted him into the inner circle of the SCLC's leadership.

Deppe highlights Jackson's evolution from local to national leader, especially as Jackson stepped into the vacuum of leadership left by King's tragic assassination. Jackson possessed the confidence and the rhetorical skill to help point the way forward. He was, Deppe reveals, a master motivator and a man with an uncanny understanding of the currents of the times. But as Breadbasket grew and his stature soared, Jackson also had a tendency to overstretch and lose sight of details.

One of Jackson's greatest strengths—much like King's—was his ability to attract talented people to work with him. Leading black businessmen like Cirilo McSween and Al Boutte offered decisive support. Jackson also developed a first-rate staff, consisting of men and women, blacks and whites, all dedicated to Breadbasket's mission. One of the major contributions of Deppe's study is its coverage of the important roles played by Willie Barrow, Hermene Hartman, Gary Massoni, Calvin Morris, Al Pitcher, Ed Riddick, and David Wallace, among others.

Deppe also highlights the contributions of the thousands of people who made Breadbasket so vital—from those who engaged in its boycotts to those who helped organize and enliven the Saturday morning meetings, including an inspiring orchestra and choir, to the volunteer ministers who led the selective patronage campaigns. Breadbasket was Jackson's organization, but it was more than a one-person show.

One major consequence of this detailed portrait of Operation Breadbasket—its personnel, its mission, its activities, and even its internal tensions and shortcomings—is a questioning of three interrelated conventional interpretations of the modern civil rights movement. The first concerns the view that the Chicago civil rights movement—which was arguably one of the most vigorous local movements in the North in the 1960s—rapidly declined after 1966.[10] This perspective pivots on the fortunes of the Coordinating Council of Community Organizations, which—as its name suggests—was the nerve center for civil rights activity, especially against school and housing segregation in Chicago from 1962 to 1967. A wide coalition of community, social service, and activist groups, the CCCO held regular meetings of delegates from its constituent groups, developed over time a central staff, and launched protest campaigns. By the end of the Chicago Freedom Movement, it had fragmented, and in 1968, within a year after the resignation of its convener, Al Raby, it dissolved. The CCCO's passing, the traditional interpretation has suggested, marked the end of the civil rights movement in Chicago.[11]

Deppe's experience and his study suggest an alternative interpretation. With the rise of its rousing programs every Saturday morning at its headquarters on the South Side, Operation Breadbasket became the hub of civil rights efforts in the city, assuming the role formerly played by the CCCO and accenting economic justice. More so than the CCCO, Breadbasket was anchored in the black community, especially the black church. Still, it welcomed white progressives like Deppe and those who had supported the CCCO.[12]

That the Chicago Freedom Movement failed is the second important line of interpretation that Deppe's book challenges. Over the years, most analysts have argued that Mayor Richard J. Daley and the complexity of a northern metropolis bested Martin Luther King and his allies in their quest to build a better Chicago. These commentators typically point to the immediate aftermath of the Summit Agreement in late August 1966, which brought the freedom movement's open-housing campaign to a close, as evidence of defeat.[13]

It is true that the city of Chicago did not address housing discrimination and segregation with the vigor that the Chicago activists had hoped, but a number of scholars have highlighted oft-neglected initiatives and the long-term impact of the movement. The sustained and significant work of Operation Breadbasket that Deppe chronicles supports this emerging alternative interpretation of the Chicago Freedom Movement.[14]

Finally, the story of Operation Breadbasket upends the conventional periodization of the black freedom struggle: a civil rights heyday followed by a black power era. And it confirms the importance of a broad geographical perspective—extending beyond the South—on that struggle.[15] Breadbasket cultivated the mission and spirit of Dr. King well after his death. As Deppe reminds us, the clergy behind Breadbasket's selective patronage campaign embraced the motto "Your ministers fight for jobs and rights." Breadbasket, grounded in the black church, adhered to nonviolence even as Jesse Jackson sculpted his organization to reflect an urban, northern ethos that emphasized black pride and community development.[16]

One of the most significant Breadbasket initiatives was its leadership in the 1969 campaign to open up jobs in the building trades to African Americans. Jackson and Breadbasket partnered with the Reverend C. T. Vivian of the Urban Training Center, who had been one of Martin Luther King's chief lieutenants during the monumental campaigns in Birmingham and Selma, as well as the Black P Stone Nation, the Conservative Vice Lords, and the Disciples, three of the city's most powerful African American gangs. To press their case, the Coalition for United Community Action shut down construction sites across the city and, ultimately, compelled Mayor Daley to support a plan to hire more African American workers into the skilled trades.[17]

In short, a King-inspired organization, faithful to its founding principles, Operation Breadbasket summons scholars to develop an even more nuanced and complex framework for understanding the black freedom struggle after 1965.

We are indebted to Martin Deppe for this book, a rich blend of personal recollections and historical research, which tells with vigor an overlooked story and invites a reconsideration of one of the most momentous eras in America's history.[18] Moreover, the story of Operation Breadbasket—with its tested approach to promoting economic justice—remains relevant to those who seek a better world in our own time.

JAMES R. RALPH JR.

PREFACE

> God never intended one people to live in superfluous and inordinate wealth, while others know only deadening poverty. God wants all of his children to have the basic necessities of life.—Martin Luther King Jr.

My journey to Operation Breadbasket began as early as my teen years growing up in Glen Ellyn, a western suburb of Chicago. A black family, the Thomases, lived just across Geneva Road, the village boundary, in a small house in the woods. My younger sister, Cathy, walked to school with Mary Thomas, and they became chums. Occasionally the girls played together at our home after school. One day the Thomases' dog was poisoned and then their deer; finally, they were burned out in an arson attack. My family collected food and clothes for them. One day, while I was sorting items on the front porch, a car slowed down and the driver shouted at me "n—lover" before speeding away. While my parents sensed the dangers of white retaliation for our efforts, they did not back down. That was my initiation into America's racism.

In October 1963, as a young preacher on the West Side, I was serving as the treasurer of the Inner City Fellowship; we had a bank balance of $50. Overnight, literally, I found myself collecting bail money for fellow Methodist pastors who had been arrested in Jackson, Mississippi, for going to church in interracial groups. Over four days, half asleep in an old stuffed chair set up at the front door of the parsonage, I received from Methodists all over the Chicago area $17,000 in cash and checks. Our local attorney arrived with money belts. We strapped the money to his legs and arms, and he was off to O'Hare Airport for a flight south to arrange the release of our colleagues and several Tougaloo College students jailed with them.

I was simply thrust into the civil rights movement. For me, this was a nudge from the One who leads us in paths we do not expect to take.

My turn to go south came a few months later. On January 19, 1964, I walked up the steps of Capitol Street Methodist Church in Jackson, Mississippi, with a black Tougaloo student, Thomas Armstrong, and a white seminary student from Naperville, Illinois, Rolly Kidder. Three ushers met us, with a police officer standing a few yards away. When I introduced my friends, an usher stepped forward and shook hands with Rolly and me, but not Thomas.

To him, he said, "You will have to leave. The official board has declared this a segregated church. There will be no entrance by force. I'm just carrying out board policy." I replied, "My understanding of the Methodist Church is that it is open to all. Jesus said, 'Come unto me all you who labor and are heavy laden.'" The usher repeated his position. I asked, "Who is Lord of the church?" He responded, "God is Lord of the church, but these people have built this church."

When Rolly quoted, "In Christ there is neither Jew nor Greek, male nor female, slave nor free," the usher grew belligerent and beckoned the policemen. We had to back off on prior instructions that there was no available bail money. We knew, from reports of other jailed black students, that Thomas would not be safe alone in jail overnight. As we turned away, Rolly said to the ushers, "I hope you will be free someday."[1]

Dr. Martin Luther King Jr. was in the background of that witness. I had heard him preach at the Chicago Sunday Evening Club in January 1963, months before the March on Washington and his "I Have a Dream" speech. It was Youth Night, and I took my Methodist Youth Fellowship group into the jam-packed Orchestra Hall to hear him preach "Paul's Letter to American Christians," revising the First Corinthians letter to fit the American scene. I was struck by Dr. King's challenge to use our economic resources and our capitalism "to eliminate poverty from the earth," so that all God's children could have "the basic necessities of life."[2] It was a moving event, and I bumped into a former seminary colleague, Rev. Don Jones, then serving at Park Ridge Methodist Church in a nearby Chicago suburb. With him was his Methodist Youth Fellowship group, including a young Hillary Rodham (now Clinton).

In the summer of 1964, with the Mississippi Freedom Project (known as Freedom Summer) in full bloom down south, I was transferred from a church on Chicago's West Side to a church in the Auburn-Gresham neighborhood on the city's South Side. My wife, Peg, eight months' pregnant; our toddler son, Andrew; and I drove south on the Dan Ryan Expressway, past the massive row of Robert Taylor Homes, which we called "skyscraper slums," and turned west on 87th Street, stopping at the Gresham Methodist Church on the corner of Emerald Avenue.

The tree-lined Auburn-Gresham neighborhood, just south of all-black Englewood, where my parents had courted thirty-five years earlier, was at that very moment convulsed in racial turmoil. The housing complexion was changing block by block. Led by real estate redlining, and the accompanying fear of change and dropping home values, the community changed from 40 percent black to 90 percent black within one year. Embarrassed to flee, many whites moved out at night. Fearful new black residents moved in at night. Before long, I had transferred out 550 white members from our church, many of them still traumatized by the bizarre stampeding around the sanctuary of several irate members as the first black person was received into membership at the altar. This had occurred only weeks before my arrival.

Most of the new residents were buying their first homes, coming from rented apartments, including the skyscraper slums. They were excited, enthusiastic, hope-filled, hard-working younger families, many with small children. In the usual pattern, the new residents began dropping their kids off for church school. Simultaneously the white members withdrew their children from the Sunday school. So, for several months we had a virtually all-black children's program at 9:30 a.m. followed by an all-white worshiping congregation at 11:00 a.m. I couldn't believe this was Chicago, not Mississippi.

A long-time Sunday school teacher and retired public school teacher came to me one Sunday and whispered, "Pastor, I just can't teach these children. You will have to replace me." I replied, "Myrtle, I haven't got anyone else. Please give me some time." She agreed reluctantly. A few months later she buttonholed me after church and declared, "Pastor, I want to stay. I have come to love these children." Myrtle and her sister never left our church or their home in that community. Along with a few other long-time faithful white members, they were welcoming faces as we built a predominantly African American congregation. Today, the New Gresham United Methodist Church at the corner of 87th and Emerald continues small but strong.

When Dr. King and the Southern Christian Leadership Conference came to Chicago in January 1966, I was still serving at the Gresham church. His advisors had said, "Don't go north, Martin, we're having success here in the south."[3] But as King traveled the country raising funds for SCLC and the civil rights movement, he was shocked by what he saw of the condition of black people in segregated ghettos in northern cities. After he was heckled from the crowds when he tried to speak in Watts after the horrific riot in that Los Angeles community in August 1965, he felt called to address this newly exposed evil.

Around the same time, Dr. King received an invitation from Chicago's civil rights leaders to bring his SCLC to Chicago to assist in the three-year-long struggle over our segregated public schools. After much consideration of alternative sites, King chose to come to this "metropolis on the lake." Even when a group of powerful black pastors in Chicago told him to "stay out," he refused to be swayed. King sent SCLC staffers to begin organizing in the fall of 1965, and he himself came in January 1966, taking up residence with his wife,

Coretta, and their children in a shabby West Side flat. He spoke to over thirty thousand people at Soldier Field, energizing them into action. That number included me and a group of members from my Gresham congregation.

One of Dr. King's first efforts was to bring together the pastors in the black community at the South Side Jubilee Temple, CME (Christian Methodist Episcopal), on February 11, 1966. King's invitation was forwarded to me by my bishop, Thomas Pryor of the Chicago Area of the Methodist Church. It was astonishing that the bishop chose not to honor this invitation with his own presence; it was even more astonishing that he chose a white pastor from a black congregation rather than one of our many black pastors to represent him.

At this event, which turned out to be the founding meeting of SCLC's Operation Breadbasket, I found myself sitting behind a stout, broad-shouldered man. He stood, turned around, and introduced himself to me as Rev. Martin Luther King Sr. I soon learned that he was known throughout the movement as "Daddy King." His son began to speak. In that moment, when Daddy King turned to greet me, my journey to Breadbasket was complete. But my life with Operation Breadbasket had just begun.

INTRODUCTION

Keep a slice of the "bread" in your community.—Breadbasket slogan

In the summer of 2006, in a rather nostalgic mood, I headed to the basement of my Chicago bungalow in search of the old Breadbasket files. Finding a batch of yellowed folders, I proceeded to leaf through them gingerly, recalling my Breadbasket years. At nearby Sulzer Library, a Chicago regional public library, I soon began to review civil rights literature, searching specifically for material on the Southern Christian Leadership Conference (SCLC) and its Operation Breadbasket, as well as writings by and biographical accounts of Dr. Martin Luther King Jr. and Rev. Jesse L. Jackson. To my dismay, I found the Breadbasket story largely absent.

Much of the relevant literature argues that Dr. King's northern campaign with the Chicago Freedom Movement was a failure. Even the distinguished Pulitzer Prize–winning historian Taylor Branch is both dismissive and inaccurate regarding Breadbasket. *At Canaan's Edge: America in the King Years 1965-68*, the final book of Branch's three-volume tome, covers half of Breadbasket's six years, but he simply ignores the Breadbasket story and its importance in the life and legacy of Dr. King. He may have thought that Breadbasket was essentially "Jesse's thing," but my own experience with Dr. King was that he was an involved "godfather" who attended meetings, took notes, and asked penetrating questions of the Steering Committee whenever he could be present. Branch writes that in a March 1967 speech, Dr. King praised the "standout progress in the drive to integrate the workforces of all-white companies under Jesse Jackson."[1] Dr. King knew well, and Taylor Branch should have known, that none of the companies with which we negotiated were all white either in employment or in clientele.

Sadly, Branch is just one of many historians and observers who have disregarded the Breadbasket story. In my explorations I found multiple gaps and factual inaccuracies. It is my intention to demonstrate that these omissions and fragmentary accounts do an injustice to the actual imprint of Breadbasket on the movement, on the community, and on the history of race and economics in America.

The only comprehensive account of Operation Breadbasket is an early insider view by a staff member, Gary Massoni, in his "Perspectives on Operation Breadbasket" (1971). Massoni hoped "that Breadbasket can learn from an evaluation of itself and thus maximize its potential for creative social change." Regrettably, this did not come to pass, since Breadbasket fell apart soon after Gary's dissertation was finished. Even today, David Garrow's book *Chicago 1966* (1989), which includes "Perspectives on Operation Breadbasket," is unavailable to readers in the Chicago area, except for one copy in a reading room at the Harold Washington Library. Part 1 of Massoni's dissertation is a well-written and accurate summary of the Breadbasket narrative. Part 2 gives a perceptive analysis of the structural and authority issues as Breadbasket transitioned from a movement to an organization and from a consensus model to the charismatic leadership of Jesse Jackson. I am indebted to Gary for his excellent work, and I trust my account honors his efforts by broadening the narrative with additional context, stories, and interpretive insights.

An account of the northern movement, Thomas Sugrue's *Sweet Land of Liberty*, relegates Chicago Breadbasket to one sentence in 543 pages.[2] Dr. Timuel Black, a contemporary African American historian, writes that Breadbasket was "the forerunner of what became known all over the world as Operation PUSH (People United to Save Humanity)."[3] While unintentional, this reduces Breadbasket to a footnote.

In an excellent history of the SCLC and Dr. King, Adam Fairclough touches on Operation Breadbasket, acknowledges the founding role of King and the youthful leadership of Jackson, and summarizes the operation with reference to negotiated and direct action victories over Country Delight and A&P Food Stores. He writes, "After its inception in February, 1966, Chicago's Operation Breadbasket went from strength to strength." This fine book ignores, unfortunately, a significant piece of the SCLC story.[4] A second history of the SCLC, by Thomas R. Peake, leaves out entirely the successes of Operation Breadbasket, not recognizing it as one of "several key programs operative in 1968." While Peake gives Breadbasket a few spare glances in the most general terms, he recognizes Jesse's later Operation PUSH as a King legacy.[5]

James Ralph Jr. gives one of the most captivating if brief accounts of Operation Breadbasket, indicating that the Breadbasket program "went unnoticed" and was "small scale, but successful.... More than any other organization, Operation Breadbasket carried the spirit of the Chicago insurgency after CCCO declined" and "retained its focus on the bread-and-butter issue of expanding black opportunity" as well as providing "a secure organizational base for the ascent of Jesse Jackson" in Chicago and nationally.[6]

Jeanne Theoharis and Komozi Woodard's edited collection *Freedom North: Black Freedom Struggles Outside the South, 1940–1980* omits Operation

Breadbasket completely in its eleven chapters on black liberation. While Theoharis recognizes that the northern movement had its own roots, save for a single reference she inexplicably disregards the Chicago Freedom Movement and six years of Breadbasket followed by PUSH, which carried the Breadbasket model up to and beyond the 1980s.[7]

In a major critical account of the CFM, historians and participants Drs. Alan Anderson and George Pickering document Dr. King's and Rev. Jackson's verbal reports of Breadbasket successes to the CCCO meetings during 1966. They quote Dr. King commenting that Breadbasket was the movement's "most concrete program," which had "tangible results," and the "public needs to know about it." "We must not despair. We are getting undramatic victories." The authors acknowledge that "Breadbasket was the success story of the Chicago campaign."[8] But since the scope of their book is limited to the story of the Chicago Freedom Movement and its collapse in mid-1967, they do not recognize that their conclusions are called into question by the life of SCLC's Operation Breadbasket beyond that date.

In his personal account about politics in Chicago, the late Dempsey Travis, a real estate agent and movement participant, acknowledged Breadbasket's early successes: "Jesse Jackson persuaded milk and soft drink firms to open or upgrade some 295 jobs for qualified blacks." It is true that Jesse was our charismatic coordinator, but without the buying power of the community and the leadership of pastors and congregations, these early covenants would not have been consummated. Travis is inaccurate regarding the Saturday meetings, which did not commence with the start of Breadbasket, but rather almost a year later. At the same time Travis avers that "Operation Breadbasket, arm of SCLC, yielded the earliest and most solid achievements for the Chicago Freedom Movement under the leadership of the charismatic and youthful Rev. Jesse L. Jackson." And: "Dr. Martin Luther King, Jr. left monuments and civil rights blueprints in Chicago that are still being used [in 1987] to build towers of racial equity and fairness."[9]

In *Bearing the Cross*, David J. Garrow's 1986 Pulitzer Prize–winning account of Dr. King and the SCLC, I found the most penetrating analysis of Breadbasket. Garrow pays attention to the contradiction between Jesse's efforts to foster black development and King's increasingly "socialist" views as he called for "a radical redistribution of economic and political power" and "a radical redefinition of work." Garrow leaves the Breadbasket assessment vaguely open, but he certainly acknowledges its place in the center of King's programs and vision.[10]

Dr. King's own commitment to Operation Breadbasket is another secret not exposed by the existing literature. I found no reference to King's comment in his report to the SCLC board of directors in August 1967, where he declared,

"The most dramatic success in Chicago has been Operation Breadbasket." Noting the expanded covenant agreements (beyond jobs to services and products), King said, "These several interrelated aspects of economic development, all based on the power of organized consumers, hold great possibilities for dealing with the problems of Negroes in other northern cities. The kinds of requests made by Breadbasket in Chicago can be made not only of chain stores, but of almost any major industry in any city in the country. And so, Operation Breadbasket has a very simple program, but a powerful one. It simply says, 'If you respect my dollar, you must respect my person.'"[11] King's famous final sermon on April 3, 1968, is remembered for the concluding vision of his being on the mountaintop and seeing the "promised land." Yet in that same speech, Dr. King challenged his Memphis audience to engage in a Breadbasket-style boycott to help "redistribute the pain" beyond the thirteen hundred striking city garbage workers.[12] I have found no reference in the literature to this final affirmation of the Breadbasket model by Dr. King.

The silence on Operation Breadbasket has been compounded over the years. A Goodman Theatre production of *Magnolia*, a play by Regina Taylor set in Atlanta in January 1963, which I previewed in March 2009, illustrates the problem. In a background piece in the printed Chicago program entitled "Chicago and America in the time of *Magnolia*," the only references to Chicago are the founding of the Chicago Freedom Movement in 1965 around school segregation, the extension into housing discrimination in 1966, the riots in the aftermath of Dr. King's assassination in 1968, and the election of Harold Washington as the first African American mayor of Chicago in 1983. Not a word about the twin legacies of King in Chicago: Breadbasket and the Leadership Council for Metropolitan Open Communities. This glaring omission keeps repeating.

Aside from Massoni's dissertation, the only insider account is a 2013 memoir by a volunteer with Breadbasket's fledgling African American entrepreneurs. Dr. Robert McKersie, then a business management professor at the University of Chicago, has a chapter called "Jesse Jackson, Operation Breadbasket, and Minority Enterprise."[13] While he has written a helpful account of the growing economic development side, he does not seem to recognize the centrality of Breadbasket's main thrust, captured in our motto "Your Ministers Fight for Jobs and Rights."

Power to the Poor: Black-Brown Coalition and the Fight for Economic Justice, 1960–1974 (2013) by Gordon K. Mantler is the first account I have seen of the larger economic justice struggle of that time which incorporates Operation Breadbasket. While his references are limited, Mantler recognizes Breadbasket's concerns beyond jobs and economic development, namely, welfare, hunger, and cultural identity. He gives an excellent account of the farmworker fight and documents the sadly truncated cooperation between the black and Hispanic movements.

Finally, David Chappell's *Waking from the Dream* gives a fine overview of post-King civil rights achievements. While he has a grasp of the forest, he misses many trees, omitting Operation Breadbasket completely either as a legacy of Dr. King or as a piece of what he calls "Jesse Jackson's rebirth." For Chappell, Jesse seems to come out of nowhere, alighting onto the covers of *Newsweek* and *Time* magazines and suddenly leading PUSH.[14]

Reflecting on this neglect and the widespread view of the Chicago movement as a failure, I decided to test my appraisal with the other Breadbasket pastors and staffers still alive. With their encouragement and sharing of files, I set out to close this gap in the story.

I dove into the project with abandon. The resulting account fills a glaring omission in the historical record. Beyond that, this book was written to share with my family, friends, and colleagues a glimpse of one of the most vital and memorable involvements in my life. The Breadbasket years remain a high point of my ministry.

Beyond the personal story, however, lies the ignored but transformative Breadbasket story, which flows into the larger history of black economic and political power in Chicago.

A young Barack Obama chose this northern metropolis as the place to begin his career and, in November 2008, he gave his presidential election victory speech to a vast crowd in the city's famous Grant Park. Rev. Jesse Jackson launched a lifetime of civil rights leadership in Chicago; Harold Washington was the city's first African American mayor; and Chicago was chosen by Dr. King to confront America's urban crisis. Yet this Chicago has been curiously ignored as a significant player in the historic civil rights movement. A missing piece of this history is the untold story of the SCLC's Operation Breadbasket, 1966–1971. I aim to demonstrate that the Breadbasket narrative is a noteworthy piece of the movement that has stamped a vital imprint on the life of African American communities to this present day. I have rediscovered it to be a fascinating story as well.

A *breadbasket* can be defined as putting food on the table in the form of a steady job. It is an answer to the prayer "Give us today our daily bread." Chicago Breadbasket began with a group of pastors who were concerned for the livelihoods of their people and came together at Dr. King's call; we then organized into teams, collected employment information about corporations selling products in the community, and met with the businesses' executives to negotiate for a fair share of jobs. We Breadbasket pastors started with the milk industry. When one official refused to share information and declared he was "not about to let Negro preachers tell him what to do," we launched a "Don't Buy" campaign. It was "To the pulpits!" where we asked our congregants not to drink that milk until further notice. After we picketed local stores carrying that milk for four days, the same official phoned us to capitulate; his firm opened forty-four jobs, including fifteen truck driver jobs, to be filled in thirty days. Then it was back to the pulpit to share the good news of justice, and a team of pastors began the hard work of monitoring the agreement.

Breadbasket was a major legacy of Dr. King, the SCLC, the Chicago Freedom Movement, and the civil rights movement itself. Following the lull and letdown after the Voting Rights Act of 1965, our early Breadbasket negotiations netted new jobs for African Americans in the milk and soft drink industries. These small successes helped assuage opposition to Dr. King's controversial move north and helped offset the August 1966 Summit Agreement between King's movement forces and Mayor Richard J. Daley's machine.

The Chicago Summit is consistently called a failure and relegated to footnotes in the literature. But Breadbasket outlasted the Chicago Freedom Movement and needs to be viewed independently. While Dr. King brought the program to Chicago and watched over it until his death, Breadbasket continued under the leadership of Jesse Jackson, Breadbasket clergy, congregations, and consumers. Coretta Scott King acknowledged this legacy when she later praised Breadbasket as "one of the finest monuments to my husband's memory."[15] The heritage continued when Breadbasket morphed into Operation PUSH in late 1971, and it survives as the Rainbow PUSH Coalition. But my memoir/history is limited to the life of SCLC's Operation Breadbasket in Chicago, 1966–1971.

Breadbasket directly impacted the economic vitality of the African American community. Through negotiated "covenants" between Breadbasket ministers and industry executives, including targeted "Don't Buy" campaigns, we added over twenty-two hundred new and several hundred upgraded jobs in milk, soft drinks, food chains, and superstores Walgreen and Sears. These jobs were added across all employment classifications. Other jobs were opened through contracts for black products and black service providers. Supported by consumer clubs in the churches, this new economic power and independence enabled black people to participate freely in the market.

From Breadbasket records, I have estimated that in Breadbasket's six years some forty-five hundred jobs were filled by black Americans, bringing in approximately $29 million annually. Adding income from black products and service contracts involving scavengers, janitors, advertising, auto dealerships, construction, and banking, the African American community gained an estimated $57.5 million annually by 1971, a previously undocumented number.[16] These dollars are equivalent to $391.8 million in the 2016 economy. The involvement of these segments of the community, along with consumers, signaled Breadbasket's response to the challenge of increasing black power by offering creative programs that truly empowered Chicago's black community.

The impact of Breadbasket's campaigns reached beyond the signed covenants. From inside sources the Steering Committee heard about corporate board meetings where those present wondered "when will Breadbasket target us?"[17] It seems logical that some preemptive actions toward economic justice in related industries came out of this perceived threat.

Breadbasket developed a successful direct action model to help crack systemic discrimination in the American economy. Using Rev. Leon Sullivan's "Philadelphia plan," which threatened a consumer withdrawal campaign targeting corporations that refused requests from local clergy leaders to implement fair housing practices, Dr. King introduced a similar program to SCLC Atlanta in 1962 and then to Chicago's South Side clergy in February 1966. We then shaped and expanded the concept with the combined power of the pulpit and the cooperating consumers in the pews. Early successes made Breadbasket a player in the economic scene in Chicago almost overnight. Then, Breadbasket went beyond jobs and economic power to develop a cultural and social arm called Saturday Breadbasket, which evolved into a national phenomenon.

While Breadbasket sought to affect the private economic sphere, the efforts of the civil rights movement in the public sphere had bogged down drastically by mid-1968, as evidenced by the demise of the Poor People's Campaign. In reality, King's assassination strategically undermined his final effort to effect fundamental change on behalf of the nation's poor through legislative action. Significantly, however, Breadbasket did not end with King's death, but continued as an effective instrument for economic justice right through the white backlash of the late 1960s. Breadbasket's successor, Operation PUSH (People United to Serve Humanity), went on in the 1970s and '80s to secure jobs and services for African Americans from major corporations across the nation. Thus, Chicago Breadbasket developed a model that is arguably still usable when economic justice for all remains a deferred dream of poor people anywhere.

Breadbasket also helped launch Jesse Jackson into his role as a national civil rights and political leader. At Dr. King's request, Jesse agreed to coordinate the new clergy project, and before long its demands caused him to drop out of Chicago Theological Seminary (CTS). His boundless energy, idea-a-minute towering presence, and magnetism provided glue and loyalty among the Steering Committee pastors. Based on our early achievements, he was promoted by Dr. King to national director with the expectation of forming Breadbasket chapters across the nation. Although this goal was not realized except for a limited number of branches, most notably in New York, Cleveland, Los Angeles, and Kansas City, Jesse's home base in Chicago grew exponentially.

While the name "Jesse Jackson" became synonymous with Breadbasket, the reality was more complex. Tensions developed as Jesse's charismatic personality overtook our collegial style and as we moved from a movement to an organization, and from a jobs focus to a broader economic empowerment focus with demands for black products and services, and then into electoral politics. An early biography of Jesse by the journalist Barbara Reynolds details his Breadbasket involvement, but it remains a flawed account flavored with personal hurt.[18] In this book, I attempt to fill out the picture of young Jesse, demonstrating his gifts, graces, and growth as well as the flaws of self-promotion and insecurity that both helped and hindered his remarkable climb into national and international prominence.

In December 1971, after falling out with the leadership of the SCLC, Jesse took the entire Breadbasket structure and staff into his own organization, Operation PUSH. In 1984, following the first of two respectable runs for president of the United States, Jesse organized the National Rainbow Coalition, then merged these groups into the Rainbow PUSH Coalition in 1987. Jesse used his considerable negotiating skills in bringing hostages home, including some captured U.S. soldiers held by Serbia's repressive regime in the 1990s. PUSH's Wall Street Project secured jobs for African Americans, and its Excellence in Education program made some progress in assisting minority high school students across the country. Without a doubt, it was Operation Breadbasket that catapulted Jesse Jackson's career.

Much of the untold story is about Breadbasket participants: the clergy, staff, congregants/consumers, cooperating entrepreneurs, and countless volunteers in the office, in the choir, and on the picket line. Breadbasket is their story, from the SC stalwarts to the staff, from the business supporters to the volunteers, from Jesse Jackson himself to the teenager on the A&P picket line. As Rev. Clay Evans told me, "Operation Breadbasket is Dr. King's legacy, but our legacy too. Operation Breadbasket is something I leave behind which made a difference."[19]

Breadbasket became a cultural mecca, a platform for black trailblazers in politics, entertainment, art, sports, and business. With orchestra and choirs guiding the spirit, preachers from major pulpits stirring the crowds, and guests from across the spectrum of black America, Saturday Breadbasket was the place to be. The original Friday sc center had shifted to a Saturday cultural phenomenon. In addition, Breadbasket's celebration of Black Christmas and Black Easter and three successful Black Expos (1969–1971) all helped move Breadbasket beyond economic justice work to a celebration of personhood, incorporating a new image and a new self-definition of "somebodyness." Over time, Saturday Breadbasket morphed into Rainbow push Coalition's Saturday Morning Forum, which continues the original Breadbasket heart-beat as of this writing.

Further, Breadbasket midwifed reforms in social policy. The Illinois Campaign to End Hunger exposed malnutrition as a serious problem in and beyond Illinois, drawing grudging involvement from the White House. In Chicago this campaign helped birth school breakfast programs and a pub-lic food program for poor neighborhoods across the city. Statewide, it was instrumental in stopping legislation that callously reduced state welfare allot-ments to the very poor as a so-called budget-saving measure. Breadbasket teachers exposed racial discrimination in the schools and impacted long-term educational reform, and Breadbasket doctors and nurses led in securing improved health care. We also interacted with gangs and attempted to quell gang violence, but with less success. Overall, Breadbasket made an imprint on several areas of communal life beyond putting bread on the table.

Breadbasket also influenced politics in Chicago and nationally, assisting in the election of black mayors in Cleveland and Newark and promoting a black American, Shirley Chisholm, in her run for president in 1972. While Jesse's campaign for mayor of Chicago fell flat, periodic voter registration efforts and political education classes planted the seeds that culminated in the elec-tion of Chicago's first African American mayor, Harold Washington, in 1983.

In sum, Operation Breadbasket carved out a method of forcing corpo-rate powers to change their ways and to operate more justly. This economic empowerment of the black community in and beyond Chicago was a step-pingstone in the long history of black America. Breadbasket stands with the NAACP, CORE, SNCC, and other movement groups and alongside towering figures such as Harriet Tubman, Frederick Douglass, W. E. B. Du Bois, Rosa Parks, Medgar Evers, John Lewis, Fred Hampton, Martin Luther King Jr., and Harold Washington as an integral part of the story that led to the first African American president of the United States. Barack Obama's election in November 2008 was a tribute to this long line of splendor and the entire history of the civil rights movement.

This narrative is both memoir and history. As a memoirist my stance is that of an active participant in the Breadbasket Steering Committee. That voice uses

the first person and includes the "I" and "we" references and personal observations from within the operation. The second voice is that of a historian who
seeks to tell the tale as objectively and truthfully as possible based upon the
available documented evidence. The resultant account is an interplay of the
two voices and two layers of analysis and insight, giving the book, hopefully,
a unique but balanced flow. Finally, my assessments take into consideration
my personal participation on the inside; the reflections of other Breadbasket
colleagues, also on the inside; and the critical analysis of outside scholarly
observations, all three.

My own yellowed files have been augmented with materials shared by other
Breadbasket pastors. While the original files inherited by Operation PUSH
have been lost, I did extensive research in the *Chicago Defender*'s archives and
in the voluminous papers of Breadbasket participant Dr. Alvin Pitcher at the
University of Chicago Library, interviewed several Breadbasket participants
still among us, and explored the larger civil rights movement literature.

In chapter 1, "Beginnings," I sketch the initial meeting with Dr. King and
review the historical context of racism in Chicago. That story was altered with
the emergence of the Chicago Freedom Movement. I lift up the forerunners
to Breadbasket and highlight the early meetings that gave birth to Operation
Breadbasket. In "The Team" (chapter 2), I trace Jesse Jackson's journey to
Breadbasket, lay out our six-step praxis, describe our clergy team, and define
our purpose.

"Early Campaigns" (chapter 3) chronicles the work with the milk and soft
drink industries, the move into food chains, and the emergence of the black
business circle. Chapter 4, "Evolving Campaigns," describes Breadbasket's
demands beyond jobs, with the addition of black-owned products and
services, and then shares the success story of our covenant with Jewel Tea
Company. Finally, it looks at the empowering of black-owned banks and the
Breadbasket connection to the United Methodist Church.

"Expansion" (chapter 5) describes the rapid growth of the black business
circle, adding economic development to our jobs focus, a move to share the
Chicago model with other cities, and the evolution of Saturday Breadbasket,
which morphed into a cultural venue for black pride and leadership. I look
at Jesse's mushrooming role, the Black Expos, and the efforts to establish a
network of Breadbasket chapters across the nation.

In chapter 6, "Interruption," I talk about Dr. King's assassination in
Memphis; I share my thoughts and participation in the daily events from
April 4 through Easter Sunday, April 14. Other special remembrances fol-
low. The chapter concludes with Breadbasket's regrouping and the Poor
People's Campaign. "Breaking the Chains" (chapter 7) explores the exhausting

three-month boycott of A&P foods, which culminated in our most comprehensive covenant. I tell about the construction "spoke" opening up major contracts and describe Breadbasket's participation in a larger community empowerment coalition.

Chapter 8, "The Hunger Campaign," recounts the story of our statewide effort to end hunger. Without the power of consumer sanctions, Breadbasket used public hearings to expose poverty and to shame both the public and politicians into action. "Proliferation" (chapter 9) reviews Breadbasket's black holidays, Dr. King's birthday celebrations, the jail ministry, Fred Hampton's assassination, school reform, violence in neighborhoods, and Jesse's and Breadbasket's major thrust into politics. I also examine Breadbasket's sporadic support for the United Farm Workers' grape boycott and the Contract Buyers League.

"Internal Issues" (chapter 10) details the major shift from collegial to charismatic leadership and addresses the debate over jobs versus entrepreneurship, structure and accountability issues, black capitalism, the South Side versus the West Side, tensions with Jesse's half brother Noah Robinson, SC struggles, and the interplay between Jesse Jackson and the SCLC's Ralph Abernathy. Chapter 11, "Decline and Transformation," examines our confrontation with Walgreen Drug Stores, which led to our last significant victory in economic empowerment, and our last campaign against National Tea. I include an account of our last days and the inauguration of Operation PUSH. Finally, an afterword summarizes the economic empowerment numbers of this six-year sensation.

The Breadbasket story is part of the 1960s movements for change. Participants felt a sense of pride and confidence that what we were doing would indeed change our society for the better. It was an age of awakening, enlightenment, sisterhood, and brotherhood. It was a richly diverse movement of blacks, browns, and whites; adults, teens, and children; Protestants, Catholics, and Jews. It was a movement of inclusivity, of democracy aborning, where "the arc of human history bends toward justice," to paraphrase Dr. King. We had freedom of speech and protest, and we took the risks associated with arrest and opposition. We believed "de battle am in our hands," in the words of an old spiritual. The Breadbasket symbol was a clenched fist with wheat (bread) emerging out of the pinkie finger and dollar signs (jobs and economic development) coming out of the forefinger and thumb. One flyer showed a loaf of bread being cut, with a dollar sign on each falling slice, over the words "Keep a slice of the 'bread' in your community." That tells it all.

The Steering Committee of local pastors was remarkable for its dedication, vigor, and creative intelligence. It was majority Baptist but also included Roman Catholic, Episcopal, United Church of Christ, Lutheran, Methodist, and independent clergy. "Your Ministers Fight for Jobs and Rights" was our motto. The physical presence and, later, guiding spirit of Dr. King, the charismatic leadership of Rev. Jackson, a brilliant staff, committed black entrepreneurs, and energized volunteers made for a powerful team in the Breadbasket adventure.

Researching, interviewing participants, and writing this book have been labors of love. I offer this story as part of the effort of God's people to right the wrongs of slavery and its long aftermath in our nation's history. I trust this book will authenticate a historically significant and compelling story.

A word about language: as the Breadbasket narrative began, the descendants of African slaves were still called "Negroes" or "colored." However, as the civil rights era peaked, nearly the exact period of Breadbasket, 1966–1971, the language changed. By the fall of 1967 the term "black" (often capitalized) emerged as a self-chosen affirmation, followed soon after by the term "African American." Aside from direct quotations, this book uses the primary identifiers that are authentic to our current era, namely, black and African American.

A word about the history of the change: The self-definition of African Americans shifted when Stokely Carmichael, the new chair of the Student Nonviolent Coordinating Committee (SNCC), shouted "Black Power" during the Meredith March in Mississippi in June 1966. For months, Carmichael and the members of SNCC had been calling themselves black people, but now they began to use it publicly. It took another eighteen months before the *Chicago Defender* began to shift from "Negro" to "black" in all articles. Our Breadbasket covenants used the word "Negro" through the end of 1967. But change had occurred on the street, and Jesse Jackson's ear was sensitive to this transformation. In October 1967 Jesse intoned, "Every black man, woman, and child must recognize and assert his worth and confidence, his pride and yet humility. Black is beautiful and it is so beautiful to be black."[20] By November 1967, the words "Negro" and "black" were being used interchangeably in the *Chicago Sun-Times*, the *Defender*, *Jet* magazine, and our Breadbasket SC minutes.

I recall my own difficulty with language in those days. What word should I use? It was a question of respect. Looking back four decades, Jackie Jackson, Jesse's wife, asked rhetorically, "Why were whites so scared as blacks redefined themselves? Blacks were just imposing their own pride."[21] I, for one, simply wanted to acknowledge that pride. For too long white people had used the N-word to hurt and demean a whole people. It was time to receive, affirm, and applaud this new self-identity. For some of us, stumbling over words was a matter of transition, sensitivity, and respect. It would be a long while before the use of specific words degenerated into accusations of "political correctness."

This language change had its lighter side. In calling for a boycott of Certified Food Stores at the Amphitheatre in October 1967, Dr. King told the crowd, "Negroes who fail to assist in the boycott will be turning their backs on an essential thrust toward complete freedom of black people."[22] I was confused more than once about which word to use in the sc discussions and in my written reports. I am sure my colleagues were smiling on the inside.

OPERATION BREADBASKET

CHAPTER 1

BEGINNINGS

No, no, you lead it, Dr. King!—Audience outburst at King's request for a local clergy leader

Birth Meeting of Operation Breadbasket

Sitting in Fellowship Hall of Jubilee CME Church on February 11, 1966, I had no idea that the meeting about to start would become a historic moment in Chicago, the founding of SCLC's Operation Breadbasket. Clearly my bishop had no idea of this when he asked me to attend in his place. Dr. King had received a positive response when he tested the Breadbasket concept with a smaller group just days earlier. Written invitations over King's personal signature had led to this meeting. Because he had been alerted to the distrust between the local civil rights leadership (the Coordinating Council of Community Organizations, CCCO) and the city's African American pastors, he hoped to mobilize the gathered pastors with a project all their own.[1]

The hall was jammed with at least three hundred pastors, among them a few whites like me.[2] Rev. Martin Luther King Sr. sat just in front of me. He had come from Atlanta as a sign of support but also to underscore the significance of his son's vision for expanding Breadbasket to his adopted northern city. Only later did I learn that Daddy King was active in Atlanta Breadbasket.[3]

After prayers and introductions Dr. King gave an overview of the Breadbasket model, beginning with Rev. Leon Sullivan's groundbreaking selective-buying campaign in Philadelphia and the SCLC program in Atlanta, which had just turned its attention to the trucking industry. He indicated that in three years the jobs gained in Atlanta had added $15 million in income. He assured us that African Americans in Chicago had the buying power to make the difference between profit and loss for almost any business operating in the black community. In a conversational style King offered a simple rationale ("if you respect my money then you must respect me"), described the use of the pulpit to support demands for economic fairness, and laid out a five-step methodology: (1) fact finding to determine a company's employment data, (2) recommendations for changes in hiring and for upgrading jobs, (3) education and negotiation, and, if necessary, (4) economic withdrawal with picketing and leafleting, and (5) reconciliation and signing an agreement.

The pastors listened attentively, seemingly quite impressed. Dr. King challenged us to join in and do our part in the emerging Chicago Freedom Movement by creating a Chicago-based Operation Breadbasket. When King began to talk logistics, the nuts and bolts of organizing the program, questions came from the floor. When he asked for one of us to lead the project, there was almost a chorus of "No, no, you lead it, Dr. King!" He was astonished. The pastors indicated they would not follow one of their own, and he chided them. It became obvious that the group felt enormous competition and a lack of trust in each other. I sensed that we were watching a historic drama involving the role of black leadership, which was still very much squeezed into the singular institution of the church.

Dr. King backed off the leadership question and presented an organizing statement that focused on "the problem of Negro unemployment and called for more Negroes to be hired by bakeries, dairies, coffee plants, soft-drink bottlers, chewing gum plants, radio and television stations, newspapers, magazines, utility firms, and oil companies."[4] After making a few minor changes, the assembled clergy gave unanimous consent to the declaration. From this birthing moment a group of approximately sixty pastors, myself included, agreed to serve as the Steering Committee. Rev. Clay Evans invited the group to meet at his church in the following week, and thus began the familiar Friday afternoon meetings in the drab basement of Fellowship Baptist Church at South Princeton and 45th Place. This location quickly became the spiritual and strategic center of Operation Breadbasket.

It was no accident that we met at Rev. Evans's church. He had come to Chicago from Brownsville, Tennessee, and had lived in segregation. "I found racism here in Chicago too, though in more subtle forms. I wanted to be identified with a movement to change the situation, and Operation Breadbasket felt like a good fit for me and what I wanted to see happen." Rev. Evans saw Dr. King as a great leader who "felt if he could bring change to Chicago, it would be possible across the North."[5]

Racism Chicago Style

> There are no ghettos in Chicago. —Mayor Richard J. Daley

The challenge for any project dealing with job discrimination was confronting the systemic racism built into the main structures of every northern urban center. Long before Dr. King and SCLC came north, Jim Crow was here, having followed the Great Migration of black folks during World War I, with an evolving color line in housing, schools, jobs, and politics. As a young lad, I became acutely aware of segregated housing, for example, when our family drove to the South Side to visit my grandparents. Often we drove through all-black neighborhoods on the way.

The color line, which barely existed at the turn of the twentieth century, grew pronounced during the migration. Seeking to control this influx of non-white people, the real estate powers applied restrictive covenants beginning in 1917. Chicago's race riot in 1919 was simply the most notorious event locking the African American population into a "Black Belt." The African American population grew continuously and then exponentially in the second migration during World War II. When the restrictive covenants were declared constitutionally unenforceable in 1948, antiblack riots, or "border wars," broke out, and later redlining tactics helped to freeze black Chicago into sharply defined West Side and South Side ghetto areas.[6]

The increase in Chicago's African American population is striking. Prior to 1900, black people made up 1 percent of the city, by 1920, 4 percent, and by 1940, 8 percent. With the second migration the African American population jumped to 14 percent in 1950, almost a half million people. Through the 1950s and 1960s the increase was approximately 30,000 a year. As the Breadbasket story began in 1966, African Americans were 28 percent of Chicago's populace, just under 1 million souls, with roughly 350,000 on the West Side and 650,000 on the South Side.[7]

The color line in housing was mirrored by a neighborhood school policy, which was in fact a containment policy. When the black population skyrocketed in the late 1940s and 1950s, school overcrowding led to double shifts and finally to mobile classrooms in the ghetto areas. The Chicago Urban League reported class sizes in black schools to be 25 percent higher and per pupil spending 33 percent lower than in white schools.[8] As the crisis grew, the city's leaders continued to mouth the civic creed that our schools were open and equal. Their flat denials of a problem only exacerbated the situation, and soon the spirit of the civil rights movement caught fire here in Chicago.[9] It began in the fall of 1961 with parents and small community groups that were fed up with the overcrowding and second-rate conditions of the ghetto schools. Before long they began to picket the mobile classrooms, calling them "Willis wagons" after the school superintendent, Benjamin Willis.

As picketing continued at four or five schools over the next months, parents, local community groups, and citywide human rights organizations finally came together in the spring of 1963 to form Chicago's first civil rights umbrella group, the Coordinating Council of Community Organizations or, as we called it, "Triple CO." Included were Englewood and Chatham–Avalon Park community groups, the Woodlawn Organization (TWO), the Chicago Urban League (CUL), local chapters of the NAACP, the Congress of Racial Equality (CORE), and the Student Nonviolent Coordinating Committee (SNCC). At this point Mayor Daley's claim, on the eve of the July 1963 national NAACP convention, that "there are no ghettos in Chicago" became a ludicrous denial. He was booed off the Grant Park stage the next day for that remark.[10]

In August 1963, a fellow pastor on Chicago's South Side, Rev. Phil Dripps, invited several colleagues to join him, parents, and members of his small parish in picketing at their neighborhood school at 73rd and Lowe. I remember carrying a picket sign as we circled one of the Willis wagons in the schoolyard while clearly staying on the public sidewalk. In a pastoral letter to my congregation on Chicago's West Side, I reported: "Do not be misled by press reports or by Willis's comments. The issue is not mobile unit classrooms, although they are small, quite limited in facilities, and located between an alley and a railway. The issue is segregation. . . . Anyone willing to 'wear Christian clothes' and stand with our Negro brethren in this situation should contact me immediately."[11] Just days before, 100 people, including comedian and activist Dick Gregory, had been arrested for trespassing. The die was cast. Protests and marches continued, including a school boycott with 225,000 children staying home on October 22, 1963; 175,000 in February 1964; and another 100,000 in June, after Dr. Willis's contract was extended. Marches, negotiations, charges, and countercharges continued through the summer of 1964. Marching picked up again in the summer of 1965, leading Al Raby, the CCCO convener, to claim that some 6,000 people were regularly involved.[12]

While the federal War on Poverty poured millions of dollars into urban areas, including Chicago, with a clause requiring the "maximum participation of the poor," Mayor Daley was able to cajole President Lyndon Johnson into accepting Daley's self-appointed Chicago committee of seventy-five members as sufficient to meet the terms of the federal grants. Seven representatives of poor neighborhoods, chosen by Daley, were a façade at best.[13]

As a concerned pastor serving a largely African American congregation, I telegrammed Mayor Daley in May 1965: "I protest vigorously the action of your office on behalf of Superintendent Willis. Controversy has only begun and will increase as the school administrator continues to resist quality and equal education for all. The Christian conscience of our community is sad today." A few months later forty-seven Methodist ministers convened to review the school crisis and issued a statement charging that thousands of students had been denied "adequate quality, integrated education by the refusal of the mayor and the Board of Education . . . to implement policies leading to justice for all." Our request that the school board terminate Superintendent Willis's contract brought no response.[14]

The movement got a boost when Dr. King came to Chicago in late July to join Raby and the CCCO for weekend rallies and a downtown march under the banner "We Can't Wait."[15] Our exhausted movement was reenergized for the time being. More important, this joint effort was a significant influence on what would soon solidify into the SCLC–CCCO collaboration that birthed the Chicago Freedom Movement.

Breadbasket was a response to the color line in employment. In the Great Migration some fifty thousand black people came north to assist in the war effort, about ten thousand of whom were given semiskilled or even skilled jobs, but they were fired after World War I ended. Once again blacks were held under a job ceiling above which only whites could enjoy management, professional, clerical, and skilled jobs. Blacks were expected to take unskilled jobs, including manual and domestic work.[16] In the Great Depression the job ceiling for blacks dipped again. Low-level hotel and restaurant jobs went to white women.[17] The low point in black unemployment is revealed by the unemployment census of January 1931, which showed that 58.5 percent of employable black women and 43.5 percent of employable black men were without jobs.[18] By 1940 black unemployment was still at 22 percent, and those who held jobs were "clinging precariously to the margins of the economy."[19]

The job ceiling was breached again in World War II with high-sounding statements about regarding "each Negro employee as an individual, with potentialities and limitations, who takes his or her place in your firm on the basis of merit as a worker."[20] This civil creed sounded wonderful. However, after the war the invisible ceiling descended again. This contradiction went unrecognized. Nevertheless, some progress was made by black people during this general period of economic prosperity. "Negro family income increased by 50 percent between 1950 and 1956 while white family income increased by only 28 percent."[21] This helped to reduce the gap in median income between whites and blacks.

Another effort began in 1947 in the state capital when the Illinois House adopted a fair employment practices bill, which was blocked in the Senate. This became an annual pattern until 1961, when both houses finally passed the bill. The newly empowered Fair Employment Practices Commission "added a new weapon to the arsenal of those fighting discrimination."[22]

The job ceiling had remained entrenched as of 1960, when 67 percent of minorities worked below the ceiling while 67 percent of whites worked above the ceiling. Among craftspeople, 23.6 percent of whites held jobs versus 12.3 percent of blacks. The managerial gap was even greater: 12.8 percent versus 2.6 percent. The building trades were lily-white, locking out qualified black workers. By the mid-1960s there were sixty thousand unemployed African Americans in Chicago with a rate twice that of white Chicagoans.[23] Put starkly, "about one-fifth of the entire black labor force, in 1966, a peak prosperity year in [the] Midwest Metropolis, was employed at incomes below the poverty line (set at $3,000 a year for a family of four in 1966)."[24]

Racial discrimination was exacerbated in the postwar years by the loss of manufacturing jobs across America caused by deindustrialization as well as the movement of factories out of cities. This "problem of jobs" was a double whammy for black Americans seeking to make a living.[25] In this weighty context, Operation Breadbasket was born in 1966.

The last color line in Chicago's style of racism was subservience in machine politics. The city's colorful mayor William Hale "Big Bill" Thompson (1915–1923, 1927–1931) had established black patronage, trading a few select seats for votes. By the 1960s the black aldermen, under the wing of William Dawson (1933–1942), who later served as a congressman until his death in 1970, came to be known as the "Silent Six." They were in Mayor Daley's hip pocket. No Democrat could get elected citywide or countywide without the votes they produced. The color line was fully operative in politics, as Dr. King discovered even before his arrival in Chicago in January 1966.

The National Situation

The movement in Chicago emerged within the larger context of key national events. With the victory for school desegregation in *Brown v. Board of Education* in Topeka, Kansas, in 1954, the Montgomery bus boycott of 1955–1956, and the founding of the SCLC in 1957, the civil rights movement took off across the Deep South. Sit-ins commenced in 1960 and Freedom Rides in 1961. Spontaneous local organizing coalesced with national efforts. The use of fire hoses on the children of Birmingham by the notorious "Bull" Connor in 1963 helped mobilize public support, leading to the Civil Rights Act of 1964; and police brutality at the Edmund Pettus Bridge in Selma in 1965 brought a national reaction that galvanized advocacy for a major civil rights campaign, culminating in the Voting Rights Act. As change moved across the old Confederacy, expectations rose among African American people everywhere. Yet northern cities gave little sign of improvement.

Urban unrest emerged in street disturbances in 1963 and again in 1964. That summer, rioting in Rochester, New York, left 4 dead, 350 injured, 1,000 arrested, and 204 stores looted. Dr. King became aware of this mood of despair and hopelessness as he traveled the northern cities speaking and fundraising for the southern campaigns. After Selma in March 1965, he began to consult his colleagues about taking the movement north, but all hell broke loose in the Watts neighborhood of Los Angeles on August 11, 1965. On the third day of the disturbance, with 30 people already dead, Dr. King flew in. When he stood to speak in the burned-out heart of Watts, someone shouted, "Get out of here, Dr. King! We don't want you." Another voice intoned, "All we want is jobs. We get jobs, we don't bother nobody. We don't get no jobs, we'll tear up Los Angeles, period." The crowd finally calmed down and listened. King concluded, "There will be a brighter tomorrow; white and black together, we shall overcome."[26] The Watts protests illustrated all that Dr. King feared, and only increased his passion for breaking the urban despair throughout the country.

The harsh reality of Watts was profound. Life in the non-southern ghettos, whether in Los Angeles, Detroit, or Chicago, was severely circumscribed by overpriced slum housing, segregated poor-quality schools, and jobs that disappeared to mechanization or to the suburbs, resulting in high unemployment. In most cases the police maintained tight and brutal control, which reminded recent migrants of Jim Crow at its worst. In the two years before the outbreak in Watts, 65 African Americans were killed by LA police, 27 shot in the back, 25 of them unarmed, 23 of them suspected of nonviolent crimes. Watts ripped open the racial wounds that were just beginning to heal down south after the voting rights victory. The results of the protests were shocking: some 30,000 people participated over the course of six days with 34 deaths, 1,032 injured, 3,438 arrests, 268 buildings destroyed, and more than $220 million in damages.[27]

Civil rights activist Bayard Rustin noted the deliberate attack on property, a lack of remorse, a celebratory and unrepentant mood. He stated that the outbreak in Watts "was carried on with the express purpose of asserting that they [black people] would no longer quietly submit to the deprivation of slum life."[28] Even President Johnson stated privately, "The Negro . . . [is] still nowhere. He knows it. And that's why he's out in the streets. Hell, I'd be there too."[29] The urban crisis was now front and center in the nation's psyche.

Chicago Freedom Movement, 1965–1967

> "What is our problem?"
> "Tell us."
> "It is that we are powerless—how do we get power?"
> "Tell us, Martin!"
> "By organizing ourselves. By getting together."
> "That's right!"
> "We are *somebody* because we are *God's* children."
> "That's right!"
> —Martin Luther King Jr. and a West Side church audience

Over multiple visits to the Windy City during 1965, Dr. King and his aides examined Chicago as a target and explored several constituencies for needed support: the African American churches, civil rights groups, several Saul

Alinsky–trained community organizations, labor, white North Shore liberals, ecumenical groups, and youth. Detractors included King's close ally Rustin, who warned him, "You don't know what Chicago is like. . . . You've got the Daley machine to deal with, you've got the powerful black ministers who are going to be jealous of you coming in here. You've got problems . . . which you don't have in the southern communities that you are accustomed to. . . . You are going to kill yourself in Chicago. You're going to be wiped out."[30]

Indeed, Daley had blocked the ccco from making any inroads in desegregating the public schools. And the local churches were divided, with many pastors tied to Daley through the Silent Six. On the other hand, Dr. King was impressed that some 42 percent of Chicago's African Americans were either first- or second-generation Mississippians. He was convinced that he understood southern black people.

The final test was Dr. King's three-day visit in July 1965, to which I received an invitation from the ccco. Unfortunately, a prearranged family vacation had me in northern Wisconsin during that historic weekend. The events included six neighborhood rallies, preaching engagements, an evening rally in suburban Winnetka with some ten thousand people in attendance, and an address to the Catholic Interracial Council, all of it culminating in a Grant Park rally and a march to City Hall with a crowd estimated between eight thousand (police) and twenty-five or thirty thousand (Dr. King). To the assembled throng King declared, "Chicago is a city of both tremendous shame and shining glory. We are here to issue a call to conscience, that Chicago might forsake her shame and rise to the challenge of our age and creatively pursue the paths of glory." Dr. King's mind was made up: he would bring the movement north to the great midwestern metropolis by the lake.[31]

While Chicago continued to claim that it was a harmonious city with no slums, fair employment, and equal education, the black population knew otherwise. Dr. King and his staff believed that despairing slum dwellers would come together, as they had down south, when they were organized to right the wrongs suffered at the hands of a cruel system. But Dr. King profoundly underestimated the power of the Daley machine. Dorothy Tillman, a young civil rights volunteer from the South and later a long-serving alderwoman, related that Chicago's black leadership held a press conference and "told us to go back down south where we came from. And that blew my mind."[32] The Daley-King tango was just beginning.

First on the scene was Rev. James Bevel, King's brilliant and eccentric aide and a key strategist of the Birmingham and Selma campaigns. He became a program director of the West Side Christian Parish, from which base, with ten additional staffers from Atlanta, he began to organize the residents beginning in the fall of 1965. The concept of ending the slums emerged out of this effort. Also at this time, Bevel advised other groups, including a Kenwood-Oakland community group that included a young volunteer seminarian from CTS, Jesse Jackson. Jesse quickly latched on to Bevel as a mentor. In October a joint retreat of CCCO and SCLC leadership surveyed the enormous task ahead, drawing them beyond the original Willis wagon protests.

On January 7, 1966, with the CCCO's convener, Al Raby, a Chicago public school teacher, standing beside him, Dr. King announced a "war on slums" to "bring the unconditional surrender" to the forces maintaining the slums. King promised to spend two or three days a week living in a West Side apartment. He indicated that the fight would address the intertwined issues of inadequate housing, education, and the lack of "jobs, jobs, jobs" with demonstrations, economic withdrawal, political education, and voter registration. Raby seconded this plan for the new Chicago Freedom Movement.[33]

On January 26, Martin and Coretta King and their children moved into a third-floor flat at 1550 S. Hamlin in North Lawndale, a neighborhood with eighty-two storefront churches and seventy bars,[34] nicknamed by residents "Slumdale." When Coretta first stepped into the building, she was shocked. A fresh coat of paint could not hide the smell of urine. And then there were rats. All this for $90 a month when a larger, cleaner, and safer flat could be had in a white neighborhood for $70. Dr. King said, "I can learn more about the situation by being with those who live and suffer here." He broke away from unpacking long enough to sit in his living room with six members of the Vice Lords gang, discussing turf battles and nonviolence into the wee hours. Over the next several days King walked the neighborhood, talking one-on-one with numerous residents and youths.[35]

The choice of the West Side was strategic. While the CCCO worked on the South Side, Bevel focused on the poorer West Side. With his organizers going door to door, Bevel envisioned a nonviolent army of forty thousand slum dwellers ready to participate in joint action through block clubs, tenant unions, local churches, and welfare and student groups. One victory was achieved when a group of tenant unions hosted a boisterous hearing where landlords were shouted down. A few weeks later one major slumlord yielded on a collective bargaining agreement with the East Garfield Park Union, which helped to "write a new chapter in the history of tenant-landlord relations in America." Nevertheless, Rev. Bevel was shocked at the level of lethargy, fear, and survival mentality.[36]

To celebrate the new SCLC and CCCO coalition, the Chicago Freedom Festival was held at the International Amphitheatre on March 12, 1966. Harry Belafonte, Sidney Poitier, and Chicago's own Dick Gregory and Mahalia

Jackson performed before a crowd of thirteen thousand. A handsome amount of $80,000 was raised for the campaign.[37] In his keynote address Dr. King talked about remaking the image of the Windy City from one where new-comers from the South found "their dreams deferred, dammed up, destroyed, themselves imprisoned by a new form of segregation, THE SLUM, with its crippling conditions." He voiced the hope that with the Chicago Freedom Movement, "Chicago can become a place where dreams for decent housing, quality education and economic opportunity are realizable." Al Raby intoned: "Tonight we stand on a historic threshold. We have an unparalleled opportunity to help fulfill the promise of America.... We thank you for your presence, but we offer you something more—a call to conscience and to action. Will you answer?"[38]

The movement was slow to commence, with lethargy among the black community, a lack of focus in the movement, money problems, but most of all the obstruction by a certain Mr. Daley. The mayor's approach was to triumph his own antislum achievements. After leading 70,000 marchers past half a million spectators in the annual St. Patrick's Day parade, "King Richard" announced that city workers were investigating building violations, had sprayed 29,000 apartments for rats, were maintaining Head Start kinder-gartens for thousands of ghetto children, and had visited 96,761 poor fami-lies.[39] Daley tried to suggest he was leading the War on Poverty himself.

The movement ran into all manner of delays and diversions. During the planning for a Soldier Field rally in June, Dr. King was called to Memphis to the hospital bedside of James Meredith, who had been wounded in an attack during his solo walk across Mississippi. Civil rights leaders descended on the hospital, and Dr. King felt pressured into carrying on Meredith's March against Fear. This took King out of Chicago for much of June and forced a rescheduling of the big rally with its goal of one hundred thousand souls. The movement lost critical momentum in Chicago with this unexpected event in Mississippi.[40]

Shortly before the big day, Dr. Joseph H. Jackson, a South Side pastor and the president of the 5 million–member National Baptist Convention, told a press conference he supported civil rights but disagreed with the tactics of nonviolence, demonstrations, and pressure groups, arguing that the city was making progress on race relations. He even denounced the brand-new Operation Breadbasket for using the threat of economic withdrawal in its negotiations for jobs in the milk industry. King responded quickly to his Baptist rival, addressing a group of union leaders, "Dr. Jackson's views are well known. I don't believe he speaks for Negroes in this country," and he affirmed that Jackson's comments would not dampen the success of the rally "one iota."[41]

On a bright, blistering Sunday afternoon, July 10, I carpooled with several Gresham church parishioners to Soldier Field, where we sat in a crowd estimated at thirty thousand by police, forty-five or fifty thousand by reporters and myself, and sixty thousand by the rally's leadership.[42] We listened to speaker after speaker in the 98-degree heat. All was redeemed with Dr. King's stirring speech and the velvety voice of Mahalia Jackson in song. Dr. King declared, "We are tired" of withering injustice, rat-infested slums, paying more for less, overcrowded schools, and being "lynched spiritually and economically in the north." Then he launched into one of his famous litanies, repeating the phrase "this day we must"—"declare our own emancipation," "fill up the jails of Chicago, if necessary," "purge Chicago of every politician . . . who feels that he owns the Negro vote," "withdraw our money" from banks that discriminate, and "withdraw economic support from companies who will not employ minorities in higher paying jobs."[43] I felt powerfully energized that day to increase my work with the ministers of Operation Breadbasket.

As our Gresham contingent drove home, King and Raby led about five thousand folks to City Hall, where they taped thirty-five demands on the door of Daley's citadel—à la Martin Luther nailing his ninety-five theses to the door of his parish church four centuries earlier![44] Chief among the demands were that real estate brokers support open occupancy, refuse to handle properties unless offered to black Americans, and have their licenses revoked if they discriminated; banks were charged to make mortgage loans without regard to race; an end to the detested means test for welfare recipients was called for as was enforcement of the 1964 Civil Rights Act on complaints against the Chicago Board of Education. Other demands were a two-dollar minimum wage, the revocation of public contracts with firms not practicing fair employment, and that four hundred African American and Latino American apprentices be accepted into the craft unions.[45] On Monday Dr. King returned to City Hall and presented his manifesto to an angry, red-faced mayor, who declared that Chicago already had a massive antislum program. It was a standoff.

On Tuesday, with the heat now close to 100 degrees, the West Side exploded. Some youths had opened fire hydrants, and all ages enjoyed the refreshing spray. That is, until the police moved in and shut the hydrants. The resulting anger led to gathered crowds, fights, and a few Molotov cocktails thrown at police cars. Nine people were injured, and 24 were thrown in jail. King held staff meetings the next day, seeking to calm the neighborhood, but that evening rioting broke out afresh. King and his staff were on the streets until 4 a.m. By dawn 2 people lay dead, 56 were injured, and 282 were jailed. On Thursday Governor Otto Kerner sent in 4,000 National Guardsmen. Dr. King met with Mayor Daley, who agreed to send in portable swimming pools and to affix sprinklers to fire hydrants. Back in his flat, King met with gang leaders, who poured out their grievances. Then he made his plea for nonviolence. Finally, a young man, Richard "Peanut" Tidwell, a leader of the Roman Saints, agreed and convinced his fellow members to go out with him and subdue their followers. The protest was over that evening. With relative peace restored, the *New York Times* reported that the end came not with the National Guard jeeps and guns but with King's influence on the gangs.[46]

Two weeks later, on July 30, Dr. King announced the first open-housing marches, hoping that the threat of black people walking into segregated neighborhoods would force City Hall to the table. He got more than he asked for. King was out of town for the first marches, but he learned quickly of the heightened drama with hecklers and jeering at every turn. On Friday, August 5, I and several other Breadbasket pastors left from our SC meeting and joined the marchers in the Chicago Lawn neighborhood on the Southwest Side. This middle-income area includes Marquette Park, one of Chicago's finest parks, which is surrounded by a Lithuanian American enclave well known for keeping up its cultural traditions and language.[47]

We were quickly surrounded by the local residents, who had worked themselves into a frenzy over this "invasion" of their quiet neighborhood. Fortunately, Chicago police moved in to hold back the mob. I remember walking with several hundred folks, black and white, in silence down the center of 63rd Street past some real estate offices, where we paused, knelt, and prayed for an open city, for justice and calm, while the crowd screamed, heckled, and threw stones, cans, and trash at us. This was one time I was seriously grateful for a police presence. I do not think I was alone in feeling terrified. We continued on foot, in silence or singing softly, into Marquette Park. There, seeking safety, we gathered in a huge circle surrounded by police, who held the mob back even as the residents lobbed all kinds of missiles at us over the heads of the police.

It was late afternoon, Dr. King had joined us, TV cameras were rolling. Suddenly Dr. King disappeared from view, slipping down to the sidewalk after being hit in the head by a brick or rock.[48] At about the same time, I felt a sting on my leg and discovered a one-inch by two-inch chunk of concrete at my foot and a tear in my pants. We covered our heads with our hands, crouched, and prayed. The police held their ground, the crazed crowd gradually dissipated, and we ran to our cars, some of which had been pushed into the nearby lagoon. That evening Dr. King was interviewed on TV, saying words heard 'round the world: he had never experienced violence this severe even in the South. While this episode brought shame on our city, the march exposed northern racism in all its ugliness. In the Gresham pulpit two days later, I reflected on the "crowds in our town cursing and storming and jeering a demonstration for justice, a demonstration which was utterly passive, accepting, and loving. And I have a slight reminder of Friday's event when I walk."[49] The response of my predominantly African American congregation was muted. I do not think they wanted any part of the movement at this level.

The marches continued daily against vicious opposition, but the city could no longer tolerate the exposed venom. Newspapers, politicians, even religious leaders, and some CCCO members scapegoated Dr. King, accusing him of stirring up racial tensions. Finally, both sides agreed to a summit, and the Chicago Freedom Movement (CFM) and city representatives began to hammer out an agreement. But the mayor had something else up his sleeve. On Friday, August 19, Daley secured a court injunction limiting marches to one per day of no more than five hundred people, banning marches during rush hour and after dark, and mandating that police be given twenty-four hours' notice for each demonstration. That dampened the movement's momentum though the CFM decided to comply with the new rules. However, the next day Dr. King announced a march for Sunday, August 28, on the working-class suburb of Cicero, adjacent to the city and famous for a 1951 race riot; he was moving the action beyond the city boundary and the injunction.

In the meantime, the movement followed the injunction to the letter by holding only one march a day in the city, but adding marches in the suburbs. On Sunday, August 21, King led a tense five-mile march of close to five hundred people, the injunction limit, to the East Side, near the giant steelworks. At the same hour Revs. Jim Bevel and Jesse Jackson led two hundred through suburban Evergreen Park, and an American Friends Service Committee group of three hundred marched through Chicago Heights. Not to be ignored, George Lincoln Rockwell, a neo-Nazi fanatic, was stirring a crowd back in Marquette Park. All of this, with the spectacle of a march looming in Cicero, was too much for Mayor Daley. In exchange for cancellation of the Cicero march he agreed to a summit meeting. It was high noon in the King-Daley duel.[50]

The months-long struggle for the soul of Chicago culminated in the famous Summit Agreement of August 26. Meeting at the stately Palmer House, Dr. King, Al Raby, and other CFM leaders sat with Mayor Daley and key municipal, business, and labor leaders. With the reading of the prepared document Mayor Daley sought an immediate vote and was rebuffed. When Ross Beatty, a real estate spokesperson, claimed an unfair burden on his members, several attendees assured him they would help support the realtors to do the right thing. The movement representatives called a caucus where Bevel held out against the agreement. When the summit reconvened Dr. King raised the injunction and implementation as unresolved issues. Trying to be helpful, a religious leader, Donald Zimmerman, urged that the injunction not be debated but tested in the courts. This comment stunned several civil rights activists in the room and seriously weakened the movement's position.[51] As for implementation, everyone talked conciliation, cooperation, and urgency, but without sanction. The Summit Agreement with its promises for fair housing was adopted unanimously.[52] With it the marches in the city were ended, as was any further momentum of the movement to end slums.

Dr. King hailed the Summit Agreement as "the most significant program ever conceived to make open housing a reality in the metropolitan area," and he "deferred" the Cicero march indefinitely. "But if these agreements aren't carried out, Chicago hasn't *seen* a demonstration."[53] One victory rally was muted. At another, King was interrupted with cries for "Black Power" and a SNCC flyer was distributed, which declared: "Wake up Brother! Decide for Yourself—Who Speaks for You? King says we should celebrate a 'significant victory' tonight because he got some concessions from the city. These concessions were just more empty promises from Daley, a man who has lied and lied to the black man in this city for years. Many people are calling it a sellout. . . . Wake up Brother! We got to get some Black Power."[54] The fallout continued. West Side leader Chester Robinson and CORE leader Bob Lucas both called the deal a sellout.[55] The Catholic Interracial Council's John McDermott, a participant in the summit, said, "I think we got what we could. . . . In a sense, we had reached our peak. . . . What people criticize is that many of the promises that were made to us were not kept."[56]

Over the next few months the Chicago Freedom Movement struggled with defending itself, internal confusion, and a lack of direction, leading Raby to declare, "Nothing has changed."[57] As the SNCC youth had predicted, Mayor Daley broke his promises, letting the agreement languish. With reduced SCLC staff participation and CCCO malaise, the CFM limped along, turning to voting registration and the 1967 municipal elections. A January 1967 telegram from Dr. King, Raby, and Hosea Williams, project director, urged me to announce at all services certain meetings and demonstrations to "dramatize Freedom Day" and demand local sites for voter registration.[58] Response was tepid. The city's no held firm. With the reelection of Mayor Daley in April by his widest margin ever, the CFM was essentially over. Not long after that, Al Raby quit the CCCO and went back to school. Dr. King announced that jobs were now the main priority, and the SCLC's Operation Breadbasket would carry on in Chicago.

Breadbasket Forerunners

Two programs survived the collapse of the Chicago Freedom Movement: SCLC's Operation Breadbasket and a promised open-housing effort. Per the summit, the Leadership Council for Metropolitan Open Communities was organized as a housing center to provide information on suitable homes for minorities and to monitor compliance with fair housing laws and ordinances. It was the single success birthed in the Summit Agreement. At the time of the summit, we Breadbasket pastors were busy negotiating with milk companies and beginning to investigate soft drinks.

While Dr. King brought Breadbasket to Chicago via working models in Philadelphia and Atlanta, its seeds had been planted much earlier. From the famed abolitionist Frederick Douglass, King learned that "power concedes nothing without a demand. It never did and it never will."[59] He saw this enacted with Gandhi's March to the Sea and then further interpreted by his theologian-mentor Reinhold Niebuhr, who wrote in his influential 1930 book, *Moral Man and Immoral Society*, "social injustice cannot be resolved by moral and rational suasion alone. . . . Conflict is inevitable, and in this conflict power must be challenged by power. . . . Boycotts against banks which discriminate against Negroes in granting credit, against stores which refuse to employ Negroes while serving Negro trade, and against public service corporations which practice racial discrimination, would undoubtedly be crowned with some measure of success." A few sentences later Niebuhr added almost a wish: "One waits for such a campaign with all the more reason and hope because the peculiar spiritual gifts of the Negro endow him with the capacity to conduct it successfully."[60] Dr. King quoted Niebuhr repeatedly in the movement years.

An unexpected local challenge to this systemic discrimination had arisen in 1929 and peaked the following summer when dozens of young African Americans, led by a militant black newspaper, the *Chicago Whig*, picketed white-owned stores under the slogan "Don't Spend Your Money Where You Can't Work." The Depression had hit the Black Belt doubly hard, and the timing seemed superb. The primary target was Woolworth, a department store chain; ten weeks of picketing at three stores cost the company $100,000. The giant chain hired twenty-one young black women and eventually implemented a policy of hiring 25 percent black employees in its stores, resulting in some two thousand jobs. But because of expenses, rivalries between the *Whig* and the *Defender* newspapers, a lack of community support, and a fear of militancy and backlash, the campaign fizzled out after the Woolworth fight. In the South some black ministers took up this effort, encouraging their people to avoid shopping where they were not welcome to apply for a job. For a short time several cities were involved.[61]

W. E. B. Du Bois added his voice to the support for boycotts when he wrote in *Crisis* magazine, "Wherever a careful survey of local conditions seems to justify it, colored people should organize and campaign to secure jobs in some proportion to their spending power."[62]

In 1960, inspired by the sit-ins in the Deep South, a Philadelphia pastor, Rev. Leon H. Sullivan, brought together more than four hundred African American pastors in a selective patronage program. Teams of ministers negotiated for jobs with corporations doing business in the black community. The threat of nonviolent boycotts by the people of the involved parishes led to many successes.[63] By 1963 this program, with the active engagement of seventy pastors and their congregations, opened up two thousand skilled jobs worth $2 million in annual salaries. In 1964 Sullivan established the Opportunities Industrialization Center for job training, which quickly gained the support of private industry and, later, the federal government. While his "400 Ministers" program was remarkably successful, Sullivan dropped this project of pulpit and pew power and moved into noncontroversial minority job training. By 1967 the Opportunities Industrialization Center had programs in eighty cities, and Sullivan had become a celebrity of the mainstream business community.[64]

At the height of Sullivan's selective patronage successes, he was invited by Dr. King to come to Atlanta and share his story with the SCLC board. At a luncheon on October 29, 1962, the SCLC board heard the details from Dr. Sullivan and then enthusiastically adopted the program, naming it "Operation Breadbasket." In keeping with its name, they began with the makers of bread, commencing negotiations in November.[65] From their pulpits the cooperating ministers explained the job discrimination at Colonial Bakery and urged their parishioners not to buy the company's bread. Volunteers placed signs and distributed handouts around the community urging the same. With this pressure a clergy team met with company officials and demanded they hire blacks commensurate with their business in the black community. By January 1963, Colonial Bakery agreed to upgrade eighteen black employees. Soon thereafter three other bakeries agreed to hire or promote specific numbers of black workers. When a fifth bakery refused the jobs request, some four hundred Atlanta Breadbasket pastors and allies went to their pulpits. Within two weeks and after some picketing, including Dr. King, this bakery also came to terms.

In just four months, eighty jobs worth approximately $400,000 in annual income were won. Also, the bakeries agreed to integrate their eating facilities and restrooms. Rev. Ralph Abernathy, King's close associate and the "call man" for the program, stated, "We can only consider this a beginning. The Negro is in a desperate situation as far as employment is concerned. With automation and its effect on the unskilled worker, the Negro must not continually be deprived of job opportunity and advancement."[66] Later Abernathy added, "It will be up to the priority committee as to where we shall go next. It could be the bottling industry, dairy companies or the gas company. I really don't know."[67] At a mass meeting celebrating the bakery agreements, Dr. King declared: "The Church had stood idly by while evils in terms of economic injustices were gripping society." He said he would not be satisfied until "all of God's children can make a living on the basis of merit, ability, and on the basis of humanness and not on the basis of race."[68] Atlanta's Breadbasket won four thousand jobs between the fall of 1962 and early 1966, adding $15 million of income to the black community. In 1966 the SCLC opened affiliates in eight southern cities but had only minuscule results in Florida, Georgia, and Kentucky.[69] In the fall of 1967 Atlanta's Breadbasket pastors met with Governor Lester Maddox to demand a rightful share of state jobs, and with the spontaneous oratory of Daddy King they succeeded.[70]

Sullivan-inspired projects also emerged in other cities. In New York, the targets were a dairy, a brewery, and Greyhound Bus; in Denver, a dry goods store; in Los Angeles, an auto dealer; in Jackson, Mississippi, downtown stores; and in little Cairo, Illinois, a supermarket. Some efforts were successful, but none lasted. In Chicago an interfaith, interracial clergy group called the Clergy Alliance adopted the Sullivan model and began with the milk industry in mid-1963. Unwilling to go beyond moral suasion, the group's efforts aborted within a year.[71]

Two more projects in Chicago anticipated Operation Breadbasket. In September 1964, Rev. John Porter founded a local chapter of the SCLC at Christ Methodist Church, his parish in the Englewood community. Meeting weekly, this group took on vital local issues such as gang violence, police brutality, job discrimination, and voter registration, staying active into 1967. It also produced volunteers for Breadbasket.[72] Sometime in 1965 an attempt was made to organize a Chicago Breadbasket by Rev. S. S. Morris, the pastor of Coppin African Methodist Episcopal Zion Church, and his colleagues, who brought together some fifty fellow pastors. They could find no one to direct the program, however, and believing that a full-time staffer was essential, they simply folded up their tent after a few months. The young CTS student, Jesse Jackson, attended meetings, but as a seminarian, he was seen as an interloper by the pastors. However, Jesse saw enough to catch a vision, and he convinced himself that he could pull off an effective Breadbasket program in Chicago.[73]

Conception Meetings of Breadbasket, 1965–1966

During his second year at CTS, Jesse Jackson began scouting black congregations, looking for a spiritual home compatible with his passion for justice. He found it at Fellowship Baptist Church with Rev. Clay Evans. In a matter of weeks after their initial meeting, Jesse joined the congregation and began to establish a close bond with Rev. Evans, who soon named Jesse to be assistant pastor. It was not a coincidence that Evans happened to be president of one of the major black church "conventions" in town. Prodded by Jesse, including a tour of ghetto homes, Rev. Evans's eyes were opened to the level of racial discrimination in Chicago. Pastor and student shared their concerns for justice, and "recognizing the potential power of the church" they decided to invite a small group of colleagues to join them in these conversations. Out of this emerged a group of pastors and professors that began to meet weekly to discuss the implications of the Gospel for the "causes and conditions of the slums." The African American pastors among them developed a biblical/theological framework for doing social justice and then were encouraged to find a way to participate in the emerging Chicago movement. These conversations, beginning in the fall of 1965, paralleled Dr. King's decision to come north, and the participants became the backbone of the group of ministers invited to meet with King in January and February 1966 to establish Operation Breadbasket.[74]

Jesse first met Dr. King briefly and by chance in the Atlanta airport in late December 1964, on Martin and Coretta King's return from Oslo, Norway, where King had received the Nobel Peace Prize. Jesse met him again in Selma. Just hours after hearing the news about Bloody Sunday at the Pettus Bridge in Selma on March 7, 1965, Jesse moved through the Chicago Theological Seminary corridors soliciting his fellow seminarians and the faculty members to join him in responding to Dr. King's urgent call for help. CTS's president, Dr. Howard Schomer, urged the students to stay in Chicago and stick to their books, while he himself prepared to fly to Selma on Monday. But Professor Franklin Littell sided with the students, saying, "There are times you need to get caught in the events of history." In just hours one-quarter of the student body and one-third of the faculty had left the campus, heading south in a caravan of cars. Jesse's two buddies among his classmates, David Wallace and Gary Massoni, were in the car with him. Almost from the moment of their arrival in Selma, young Jesse was up front, talking to crowds, giving directions, acting almost like a Southern Christian Leadership Conference staffer.[75]

Indeed, SCLC staffer C. T. Vivian took Jesse under his wing, and they went everywhere together. Dr. King first heard young Jesse Jackson speak at Brown Chapel at a late-night rally. King had asked representatives of student groups from around the nation to address the crowd, and the CTS contingent asked Jesse to read a declaration of support from Dr. Schomer. Since Dr. King had received his first honorary degree from CTS at the hands of Schomer, this personal connection probably added to King's impression of Jackson. Rev.

Abernathy was also quite impressed with this bright, tall, handsome, and impetuous newcomer and was among those who later recommended to Dr. King that he hire the young seminarian as a part-time SCLC staffer in Chicago. Although initially hesitant, Dr. King agreed.[76]

In the fall of 1965, Jesse Jackson made his own move to contact Dr. King regarding the Chicago campaign. He knew of the negotiations between the CCCO and King, but he also knew of the reluctance of the CCCO to involve the black churches. Jesse, however, recognized the power of these congregations, and he felt they should be a part of any revived freedom movement in Chicago. So, Jesse arranged to have Dr. King call Rev. Evans and request his help in pulling together the black clergy. Jesse was sitting in Rev. Evans's study during one of their regular sessions, and the secretary was holding all calls, as requested. Until the call from Dr. King. The secretary interrupted them from the door to announce that he was on the line. Evans quickly took the phone, and the key connection was made. "Clay was on cloud nine," Jesse remembered in our interview.[77] This church connection, along with the CCCO invitation, fueled King's determination to tackle the northern metropolis.

CHAPTER 2

THE TEAM

Our time together in Operation Breadbasket was providential....
God brought us together—preachers, lawyers, businesspeople, all kinds
of people—as a body, a group, as family.... We were a bridge between
cultures, races, denominations.—Rev. Clay Evans

Jesse Jackson's Journey to Breadbasket

The King family was settling into their Lawndale apartment; Bevel was busy organizing in the streets; the CCCO and SCLC leaders were getting acquainted quickly as they discussed goals, strategies, and timetables for the summer; and "Doc," as King was called in the inner circles, turned his attention to the churches. He signed individually all the letters of invitation to the historic meeting at Jubilee. Young Jesse was not present that day, although he was already a part-time SCLC staffer. With the reticence of black clergy to step forward, Dr. King assigned Jesse to be the coordinator for the new Breadbasket Steering Committee, saying to him, "Let's see what you can do." At an early meeting we ministers and Jesse were introduced to each other, after which we confirmed his assignment.

Jackson's journey to Breadbasket began with his birth and childhood in Greenville, South Carolina, where he grew up under Jim Crow laws. Jesse was graduated with honors from the racially segregated Sterling High School, where he served as student class president and played baseball, football, and basketball. After a year at the University of Illinois, Jesse transferred to the predominantly black Agricultural and Technical College of North Carolina (A&T) at Greensboro, where he was again elected student body president and played football, and he also joined sit-ins at a local Woolworth lunch counter. By 1963 he was leading demonstrations and sit-ins at segregated theaters and restaurants in Greensboro. In June of that year, Jesse was arrested leading a sit-in in front of the city's municipal building. With the virtual desegregation of downtown Greensboro, Jesse became a campus hero. For a time he was a field representative for CORE. During his senior year at A&T Jesse felt the call to ministry. He enrolled at Chicago Theological Seminary, arriving at the Hyde Park campus in the fall of 1964 with a handsome Rockefeller Fund scholarship in his pocket.[1]

Joining Breadbasket in 1966 as Jesse's assistant and the sc secretary was his close seminary buddy David Wallace. As our program took off, it became obvious we needed full-time staffers, and both Jesse and David simply "dropped out of cts to do the Lord's work," as David recalled.[2] They were a fantastic team, exuding total trust in each other. Before long, sclc's Operation Breadbasket began to share space at ccco's office on East 47th Street, and later we took over that office completely.

As agreed at the founding Julibee cme Church meeting, some forty pastors gathered the next Friday, February 18, at Fellowship Baptist Church. Our first meetings were led by Rev. Stroy Freeman, a strong, articulate local pastor. Within weeks, however, Jesse "presided," with Freeman filling in for Jesse when he was late or absent. Decisions were made by consensus, often after much discussion. Jesse's leadership was collegial, and we were all on a kind of honeymoon with him and with each other.[3]

At the first sc meeting, the pastors were assigned to one of four target committees covering bread, milk, soft drink, and soup companies. Within days, contacts were initiated with Silvercup Bakery, Dean Foods, Coca-Cola, and Campbell Soup. Then a funny thing happened. As though in concert, each of these companies and others requested additional time to furnish us their employment data. The president of Country Delight Dairy reacted so angrily that we had our first target handed to us. The methodology that Dr. King had laid out suddenly took on reality in a live test case.[4] In the Chicago experience King's original five steps evolved quickly into six.

The Six-Step Praxis

Step 1. Information Gathering   After initial contact with a company, a team of clergy would meet with the ceo and request a copy of its latest Equal Employment Opportunity Commission annual report, mandated by the 1964 Civil Rights Act. This form called for a breakdown of jobs in all categories by gender as well as numbers for "Negroes," "Orientals," "American Indians," and "Spanish Americans." Additionally we asked for salaries by category and, where necessary, a more recent report than the eeoc-required form. Only by insisting on firm deadlines were we able to secure the data needed for a thorough employment picture since most companies sought to conceal signs of job discrimination through delay and obfuscation.

Step 2. Committee Evaluation   Early in our negotiations, we established 20 percent as a minimum demand for African American employees. This was determined to be fair since 28 percent of the city was African American. For stores and factories in black neighborhoods, we sought somewhat higher percentages. Each company's data were reviewed in light of these expectations, and a team of four or five ministers would refine our demand, bring it to the SC, and, if approved, proceed to arrange an initial meeting with the company.

Step 3. Negotiation and Education   From the first contact with management we found ourselves teaching Social Justice 101. This continued through the negotiations, a "Don't Buy" campaign, if required, and the signing of an agreement. The use of the word *covenant* came later. The educative aspect emerged as pastors described their own experiences of discrimination, often with chilling stories. We never met without prayer for enlightenment.

Negotiations were tough but exciting, with each pastor having a specific role. My role was to hold the company executives' feet to the fire with details, the shame of specific numbers. Another pastor was always congenial and compassionate; another agreed to absolutely nothing; another told biblical stories; and Jesse would summarize the discussions with apt focus and passion. Still, we were often misled, diverted, sidetracked, lied to, delayed, and humored, even as the CEOs picked up the tabs for sumptuous breakfasts. We pushed toward specific numbers and deadlines. In a majority of cases, the negotiations evolved into an agreement. Otherwise, negotiations ended abruptly.

Step 4. Economic Withdrawal   When CEOs refused to share information or to continue discussions, the pastors went to the pulpits to announce the injustice. Our parishioners/consumers responded by joining in "Don't Buy" campaigns, nonviolent direct actions in the spirit of the movement. Details of job discrimination were presented on "Don't Buy" flyers, which were distributed at our churches, and leafleting or picketing was organized for specified locations. The early campaigns were so effective that within three to five days the targeted company would buckle under, requesting to meet immediately, which led in most cases to reconciliation and agreement.

Step 5. Agreement/Covenant   The process/praxis in our struggle for justice took us through information gathering; a teaching ministry; debate and negotiation, or stalemate and breakdown requiring direct action; and finally a return to the table for agreement in the spirit of harmony. Each written pact opened with an acknowledgment of the discrimination and the goals agreed upon to overcome this evil with specific commitments on jobs, products, and services. Then a formal signing took place with company executives joining Breadbasket ministers, Jesse Jackson, and, when available, Dr. King himself. The public setting established accountability, and press coverage helped us get the story out beyond our congregations. The early "Don't Buy" campaigns set the tone for competing companies. As word spread, we were able to complete multiple agreements in a matter of weeks.

Step 6. Monitoring   After the euphoria of an agreement, we moved on to other targets. But the need to monitor the pacts became clear when early reports usually revealed foot-dragging. Follow-Up Committees requested regular updates on the commitments made by the companies. Gradually, procedures were established for regular contact, and reporting forms were developed. Since most of us were busy pastors we did not, unfortunately, follow up on all agreements in a consistent pattern. When monitoring revealed disrespect or the betrayal of an agreement, we demanded a meeting with that company's top executives. Unless our team was satisfied with the explanations given, we moved back into direct action and repeated steps 4, 5, and 6.[5]

The Breadbasket Team

Who were these Breadbasket ministers? Of the two hundred pastors who gathered together at the birth meeting, about sixty maintained some involvement over the first months, with twenty to twenty-five attending weekly meetings. These "working clergy," as we called ourselves, were a diverse group: Missionary Baptist pastors of both small and large congregations; Methodists black and white, serving a variety of predominantly black congregations; clergy of Episcopalian, Roman Catholic, Church of God, and independent churches; and those working in smaller denominations. All were active, busy, bright, dedicated, and determined people who became, in a remarkably short time, a trusting community.

The initial core included Clay Evans, our host; Stroy Freeman; D. E. King, the godfather of Dr. King but no relation; and Claude Wyatt, Earl Simmons, Robert Weaver, Arthur Newburg, William Hogan, John Porter, Gerald Forshey, Hiram Crawford, H. B. Brady, W. L. Lambert, Willie Barrow, Washington Branch, Robert Meyners, Fleek Simmons, Thomas Ogletree, Richard Lawrence, Jessie "Ma" Houston, Larry Morkert, and myself. This group was rounded out by the staff: our leader, Jesse Jackson; his assistant, David Wallace; and, toward the end of the first year, Gary Massoni, another classmate of Jesse from CTS.[6] Reflecting on this incredible group decades later, Rev. Jackson suggested that most of these clergy were "rebels," people who refused to kowtow to Mayor Daley and his minions and who found in Dr. King and Breadbasket an avenue for genuine ministry with and for their people.[7] Of this core working group, five of the pastors and the staffers David and Gary were white. This was simply a reflection of King's commitment to integration and the "beloved community." In the early days it went seemingly unnoticed, never mentioned.

Whenever Dr. King was in town he would attend our Friday afternoon meetings in the basement of Fellowship Baptist Church. He would arrive unannounced, wave hello, and take a seat in the back, listening and observing with his attentive, dark, penetrating eyes. Occasionally he had a question or comment, but he never interrupted our deliberations. While he was eloquent and passionate before the public, in our meetings I found him quiet, soft-spoken, alone in his thoughts. But he was always gracious and frequently commended us for our efforts. Whenever possible King would attend our agreement-signing ceremonies and join Jesse in speaking to the press.

In a matter of weeks several pastors emerged as good negotiators. These people headed the teams that would meet ahead of time, discuss strategy, and establish minimum goals. Soon we moved all negotiations with company CEOs to our turf, usually at the H&H Cafe on East 51st Street, with its good soul food and private upstairs room. We were a team, and each of us had a role or roles to play. We took pride in playing our parts well.

The quarterback was Jesse Jackson. He took charge, called the meeting to order, asked one of us to give an opening prayer, and then delivered an opening statement, summarizing where we were and what Breadbasket was expecting out of the session. The scribe was David Wallace, Jesse's CTS chum. David was dedicated, competent, and steady, with a quiet humor. He took copious notes but also asked questions. He was a sharp negotiator as well. Later, Gary Massoni came aboard and provided equally strong support in all areas.

The prophet was Rev. Hiram Crawford; quoting Scripture, his spitfire words came at us as though from on high. He was responsible for focusing on Micah's question, "What does the Lord require?" The teacher would be either Rev. Stroy Freeman or Rev. Claude Wyatt. Stroy was a distinguished-looking pastor of a prominent Baptist church who commanded total attention with his strong and deliberate voice. He was the history teacher who brought out the suffering of injustice and humiliation from the days of slavery to the present sorrows and discriminations of life in the black community. He had a knack for relating the African American story to the biblical story. Claude drew immediate attention as the best-dressed preacher around, and with his soft, dispassionate voice he gave a compelling message. Claude's constancy and charm gave the team a measure of stability and security. Rev. Gerald Forshey, the tallest and most imposing fellow among us, could be prophet or teacher. In sharing stories of grievance and outrage from his parish, Jerry would connect the dots to the theological issue, bringing the conversation/ negotiation to a new level.

The wise (wo)man was Rev. Jessie "Ma" Houston, whose hunched-over physique embodied long suffering and wisdom. Ma would stare down anyone, on either side of the negotiations, who said anything inappropriate, off-color, or with any semblance of untruth or exaggeration. She was walking rectitude and occasionally voiced righteous anger at just the right moment in the discussion. Father William Hogan, whom Jesse later christened "Instant Picket" for his presence at every demonstration, played the role of bastard. A South Side Roman Catholic pastor, Bill simply disagreed with everything, found fault with every promise, and was never satisfied. Bill had the most out-of-character role, which sometimes had us close to laughing out loud in the midst of a serious debate. But he played his persona to the hilt.

Rev. Richard Lawrence, who joined us a bit later and led several "Don't Buy" campaigns, was a tenacious bulldog. He was undoubtedly the most disliked member of our team precisely because he would not budge from his knife-like questions until he had a direct answer or from his penetrating analysis of corporate sins. He was walking judgment. I was the skeptic, always questioning, challenging, referring to notes, demanding specifics. I loved this role, which in time led to my chairing several monitoring committees.

There were others: the host pastor and a Jesse confidant, Rev. Clay Evans, played both prophet and teacher roles with real command. Father Robert Weaver, an Episcopal priest, played teacher, prophet, or skeptic, depending on the need, and always brought low-key intensity, an attention to detail, and dry humor. Willie Barrow, soon to be called "Reverend," played shopper/consumer and teacher. She brought a dynamic, earthy presence that captivated her audience. She was a petite prophet, always pushing the justice angle as God's demand. Over time she became known as the "Little Warrior."

All the players brought passion and integrity to this drama, and each person was important in the final outcome. If our opponents at the table were looking for a compromiser or a softie, they never found one. It was programmed that way. Our integrated teams always stood out against the all-white, all-male, three-piece-suited executives. The camaraderie, the sisterhood and brotherhood, we felt while engaging some of Chicago's top business folks was a treasure.

Rev. Calvin Morris, a college friend of Jesse who joined the Breadbasket staff some months later, described the black clergy leaders as "larger than life, father figures, princes of the church. God spoke to them, and they spoke to us." As for our host and long-time convener, Rev. Clay Evans, Calvin described him as "grassroots, salt of the earth."[8] Looking back after forty years, Rev. Evans mused, "Our time together in Operation Breadbasket was providential; it was a miracle. The Lord tore down the walls for his purpose, to help us bring about human rights in Chicago and the nation. God brought us together—preachers, lawyers, businesspeople, all kinds of people—as a body, a group, as family. There was no Jew or Greek. We were one body in Christ. We were a bridge between cultures, races, denominations."[9]

Evans continued, "Operation Breadbasket was an arm of the church. We couldn't get the whole church behind us to do this justice work, but we were an outreach of the church and together we were able to do it." When I commented on his key leadership role, he responded, "I was just a catalyst. As president of a ministers' conference I had some influence and prominence, so I was able to do something. Providing a meeting place [Fellowship Baptist Church] was my contribution."[10] In reality, Rev. Evans's contributions went far beyond providing our meeting place. Evans took on the conservative National Baptist Convention president, Rev. Joseph H. Jackson, who despised Dr. King and the entire movement. He also stood firm against Mayor Daley, who had shut down the building addition at Fellowship Baptist because of trumped-up violations in the old sanctuary building where we met. Rev. Evans admitted, "The threat was double for me." But he never wavered. The rusted steel beams of the unfinished addition stood for years as a visual metaphor of this man of courage in his standoff with Daley's Chicago machine.

It was a privilege of a lifetime for me, a still unproven, young white pastor, to work and worship side by side with these giants of the black church in Chicago. The memories bring back the awe and respect I had for these colleagues in ministry, and Rev. Clay Evans remains one of my heroes of the Breadbasket experience.

The primary purpose of Breadbasket in the words of an early covenant (with High-Low Foods) was to develop "a creative employment and business program aimed at ending the economic indignities which lead to the spiritual destruction of Negro people."[11] The cry on the streets of Watts immediately after the riot was "All we want is jobs."[12] That four-letter word signified the difference between a life of despair and a life of dignity. A job meant putting bread on the table, caring for oneself and one's family, using one's gifts and talents, facing one's neighbors with self-respect, participating in the community, and sharing in the American dream.

David Wallace, our multitasking scribe, expressed it well in a letter to the High-Low Foods' president in the midst of tense negotiations leading up to the covenant:

> We wonder if we have adequately communicated to you, and you in turn
> to your company, the deep and destructive frustrations of generations, not

days or weeks, experienced by Negroes in a society which refuses in so many humiliating ways to confirm their very existence as persons having ultimate and proximate worth, neither because of nor in spite of color, but as children of God.

This affirmation of the essential worth of Negroes as people is at the very heart of Operation Breadbasket's request to your company, to our negotiations, to everything that we are attempting to accomplish.... We are saying that for substantial change to take place in race relations in this nation, institutions must indeed go through some changes in attitudes, employment practices, sales policies, and banking habits. We know these changes are difficult, seemingly impossible, for they require changes of habits, they cost money, they change the conditions under which our old perspectives are formed.

We know that High-Low is more than a business making profits; it is an institution affecting the lives of people in neighborhoods by its policies, practices, prices, attitudes, etc. We also know that if High-Low chose to do so, it could take Operation Breadbasket's requests and turn them from the liabilities that you seem to express into pioneering assets which could make your company the most dynamic and profitable grocery chain in the ghetto and the city.[13]

As a local pastor, I saw Breadbasket as a mission and ministry of the church. Many of my parishioners faced an arbitrary job ceiling based entirely on the color of their skin. Breadbasket allowed these same people to join together in withholding their hard-earned dollars from those companies that discriminated in employment. It was the power of pulpit and people through fact-finding, negotiations, "Don't Buy" campaigns, and covenant making that enabled us to extract a just share of jobs and services for our community. For me, Breadbasket sought justice in the gates, served the poor and unemployed, related the church to people's lives and needs, and challenged the institutions of the larger community to act fairly and do justice. This is the work of the church. Breadbasket embodied the good news of the Gospel to counter the bad news of discrimination. And the Breadbasket sc gave me a forum and a voice to participate with history-making colleagues in the black church. I have never again experienced such camaraderie.

Jesse Jackson gave an insightful explanation of Breadbasket in a celebrated *Playboy* interview in November 1969. "The essential purpose of Operation Breadbasket is to have blacks control the basic resources of their community. We want to control the banks, the trades, the building construction and the education of our children. This desire on our part is a defensive strategy evolved in order to stop whites from controlling our community and removing the profits and income that belong to black people."

When the interviewer asked about Breadbasket's role in correcting black underrepresentation in the economy, Jesse responded, "We have the power, nonviolently, just by controlling our appetites, to determine the direction of the American economy." When asked whether "today's black militancy is a quest to resurrect manhood," Jesse touched on the soul of black folks: "That's why at Operation Breadbasket meetings, which are deeply based in religion, we have a band and a Gospel choir and consciously try to capture the rhythm of our people."[14]

CHAPTER 3

EARLY CAMPAIGNS

You can't beat them. They've got that weapon [consumer dollars]
and you have to respect it. If you don't you can go broke.
—Dean Foods/Bowman Dairy official

The Dairy Dominos

Breadbasket began with bread: "give us today our daily bread." The first projects in Philadelphia and Atlanta began with bread. In Chicago, it was milk.
One of our pastors made the case: "Milk cannot be sent back to the cows
if people do not buy it for a period of a few days." From our initial contacts
with milk companies it was Country Delight Dairy's hostility and refusal to
cooperate that handed us the first target.[1]

Gary Massoni tells the story: "At a meeting on March 16, 1966, an official
of Country Delight Dairy, a subsidiary of Certified Grocers of Illinois, flatly
refused to give the Breadbasket ministers any information, saying that he did
not let union officials tell him how to run his company and he was certainly
not about to let Negro preachers tell him what to do. . . . [He] proceeded to
insult the whole black community with stereotyped statements about how
'you people are lazy,' and how Negroes prefer to be on welfare than to work."[2]
This official then turned to the white clergy present and "berated them for
working with the Negro clergymen and for concerning themselves with
men's bodies rather than their souls."[3]

Country Delight's resistance allowed us to move directly to step 4, economic withdrawal. The Steering Committee voted to launch a selective-buying campaign beginning April 8, 1966, Good Friday, following a mass rally
at Fellowship Baptist Church. That weekend, picketing and leafleting were
carried out at 10 of Certified's 108 grocery stores in the black community
(among their 787 stores in the Chicago area) urging consumers not to purchase Country Delight milk, bread, ice cream, or pastry products.

At Easter Sunday services the Breadbasket pastors alerted our people to
Country Delight's disrespect and urged our congregants to join the "Don't
Buy" campaign. At the same time the chain store attempted to "forestall

the selective buying hammer aimed at Certified," claiming it was just a bad misunderstanding, and company officials said they were willing to meet with us.[4]

While fourteen Certified stores removed Country Delight products, picketing continued. No progress was made in talks until Thursday, April 14, when an agreement was consummated, "boosting Negro jobs by 40 percent."[5] The joint statement of Certified officials and Breadbasket's coordinator, Rev. Jesse Jackson (though not ordained, Jesse assumed this title to identify with his peers), announced forty-four openings for black applicants, including fifteen truck driver jobs, and the upgrading of "some" of the one hundred current black employees. It was estimated that the new jobs, with salaries averaging $7,500 a year, would bring $300,000 into the African American community annually.

Certified agreed to ask the Chicago Urban League to help secure applicants, initiate job training, and "develop a relationship with one high school in the Negro community in order to motivate youngsters to complete their education and prepare to use their talents working in some phase of the Certified setup."[6] A week later we learned that the CUL was actively involved, and nine black Americans had already been hired.[7] Within days, a Certified official phoned us to announce fifteen additional openings. Operation Breadbasket's first victory in Chicago had come just two months after the birth meeting. In its lead article on the agreement, the *Chicago Defender* asked, "Have We Overcome?"[8] This provocative if premature question highlighted the black community's aspirations for this new program. With the Certified/Country Delight success, Breadbasket was on the way.

In evaluating our first win the SC discussed ways to communicate more quickly with pastors, mobilize picket teams more rapidly, and solicit funds to cover campaign costs. In this case the CCCO and SCLC had picked up the tab for the $1,353.73 in expenses, and they continued to do so in the next campaign.[9]

To prepare for upcoming campaigns, Operation Breadbasket held a number of rallies, including one on May 26, 1966, at New Friendship Baptist, hosted by Rev. Stroy Freeman. Music, a dialogue on our purpose, a discussion of nonviolent action, picketing and leafleting conduct, and an update on current negotiations preceded Dr. King's address to an overflow crowd. Present were several Methodist colleagues whom I had invited. Breadbasket was now gathering the supporters needed for future economic-withdrawal campaigns.[10]

The dairy dominos fell quickly. When Borden Dairy failed to respond to our request for employment figures, we telegrammed them requesting a meeting.

At a session on May 24 we learned that Borden had 23 black workers out of 435 employees, or 5.3 percent, and there were no blacks among its managers, mechanics, production workers, or salesmen/drivers. Jesse Jackson asserted that "although Borden's is very eager to sell to Negro consumers, the company's employment picture indicates a tragic disrespect for Negro people."[11]

As we deliberated on this data in the Steering Committee we felt it necessary to establish a policy regarding employment demands. With the black community at 28 percent of the city's population and undoubtedly consuming that same percentage of milk sold in the city, we set a modest 20 percent of total employment as the baseline. We also took into account the shocking fact that black unemployment was three times the city average, 8.9 percent versus 2.9 percent. In some areas it was 30 percent. Breadbasket sought only fairness and equal opportunity. Applying this new baseline to Borden Dairy led us to request sixty-four openings, which would bring Borden to 20 percent black workers.[12]

Borden informed us that it was in the midst of downsizing and could not meet this request. Rev. Jackson reminded the company that to "absorb Negro employees will be painful, but the pain is necessary to overcome the social disaster now a daily reality in the slums of Chicago." Through some tough discussions, with our usual references to biblical stories of justice, a compromise agreement was reached on June 9 for twenty jobs worth $140,000 annually, to be filled within thirty days.[13]

The *Chicago Defender*, the city's most prominent African American newspaper, gave its achievement award, the Orchid for the Day, nicely pictured, "to the ministers who have worked to make Operation Breadbasket an early success. Already they have secured over 50 well-paying jobs for Negro citizens with a belief that if Negroes share in buying—they deserve a share in building."[14] In other words, black people were to be respected as both workers and consumers. Hardly had the ink dried on the Borden-Breadbasket agreement, however, when we faced a recalcitrant Hawthorn-Mellody Dairy.[15] This company, which had withstood a selective patronage campaign just two years earlier organized by the now-defunct Clergy Alliance, may have thought it could do the same again. But Breadbasket was a new ballgame.

Hawthorn-Mellody officials argued that their black employees included several twenty-five-year veterans and nine of twenty recent hires, bringing them to 10 percent of their workforce. When they balked at doing anything further we announced a "Don't Buy" campaign. Rev. Jackson declared, "If they are unwilling to participate, they can no longer expect Negroes to purchase their products. We cannot buy goods from companies that won't hire our people." In a letter to Breadbasket pastors Jesse Jackson asked us to "urge students and teachers to send their milk back to the company until Hawthorn-Mellody is willing to give us decent jobs." Behind the scenes David Wallace worked tirelessly, coordinating the picketing with signs and leaflets.[16]

Four days of picketing forced several National Food Stores to remove the offending Hawthorn-Mellody products, which in turn led to the dairy's urgent request that we stop the picketing. It was reported to us that National's president had phoned Hawthorn-Mellody urging the company "to settle the dispute as soon as possible in order that their stores could function properly." An agreement was reached at our favorite rendezvous, the H&H Cafe, and the pact was announced on June 22. The protest garnered an agreement for fifty-five job openings within ninety days, worth $400,000 annually, and integrating "every department in its four plants here from management down to sweepers." The dairy also agreed to include some ex-convicts.[17] Jesse Jackson reminded us Breadbasket pastors that it was now our task to spread the word of these job openings. At this same time we invited Spanish-speaking pastors to join us "in this moral movement to gain jobs for Spanish-speaking people as well as for Negroes." No response was received.[18] I think we should have been more persistent in this attempt.

Another Breadbasket team reported to the SC that Wanzer Dairy needed attention. The company acknowledged having only 20 black Americans among its 454 employees. Since our goal of 20 percent would require 71 job openings, we compromised on 44 new jobs within sixty days, raising Wanzer to 15 percent. Wanzer's president said he viewed Operation Breadbasket as a "help in finding qualified employees."[19] Wanzer also offered a $2,000 college scholarship for training a black person to be a dairy engineer with the promise of a full-time job after graduation. The SC, at my request, put this package in writing and had it signed by both parties. This became routine for all future pacts. The agreement was announced on July 5. Breadbasket had gained another $330,000 in annual income.[20]

The last domino to fall was Dean Foods/Bowman Dairy just a week later. Dean's data were similar: only 27 of its 627 employees were black, including 2 among 148 driver/salesmen and 1 among 53 office workers. Again facing reality, we dropped our goal to 10 percent, or 45 new jobs, which number was flatly refused. At our next Breadbasket meeting we gave the now-familiar charge: "To the pulpits!" Picketing commenced at several stores. Jesse declared that the Dean/Bowman employment picture was "pitiful" and "a glaring insult to Negro people. We can no longer allow companies to continue taking our dollars but refuse us jobs as if we did not even exist in Chicago."[21]

Three days later Dean/Bowman backed down and agreed to forty-five new jobs. A Breadbasket team member was quoted as saying, "Bread, not bullets, is

Table 1. Employment Gains from Dairy Covenants, 1966

Company	Date Promised	No. Openings	Jobs Filled	Time Frame (as of)
Certified/Country Delight	Apr. 14	59	30	Aug. 26
Borden	June 9	20	15	Oct. 21
Hawthorn-Mellody	June 22	55	31	Aug. 19
Wanzer	July 5	44	40	Sept. 16
Dean/Bowman	July 21	45	25	Oct. 21
		223	141	

Source: PBBF.

the only ammunition against riots in Chicago."[22] Another $340,000 in annual income had been won for black families.

In thirteen weeks, five milk companies, three prodded by "Don't Buy" campaigns, had capitulated to Operation Breadbasket for a total of 223 jobs worth $1.5 million. This was a historic breakthrough in Chicago's economic scene for which Breadbasket received another Orchid award. Even though the major dailies gave limited publicity to our victories, the word was out. As we soon discovered, other food corporations wondered who was next.

Key questions emerged in these first negotiations: setting realizable employment demands, finding qualified candidates, and the need for job training and for time frames. A constant irritant was union contracts. From the outset we announced that this was a two-party negotiation. If the target company believed that a union contract was in conflict with our demands, then it would have to deal with the union(s) as best it could. We would leverage the issue with our consumer power. In reality, "doing justice" in the marketplace was often a matter of sharing the pain of job redistribution that was required in absorbing new black employees into a company, as Jesse acknowledged to the Borden executives.

We also learned that promised job openings are not jobs filled. For example, Country Delight reported that it had hired seventy-five black workers, but within a month forty-five of these had quit, been fired, or had not actually been hired, and some did not receive adequate training. A few new employees were even harassed into quitting. In reality Country Delight had filled only thirty positions. Learning this, the Steering Committee decided it was time to seek data on jobs filled versus job openings. Checking our monitoring records carefully, we discovered the statistics in table 1. So, while 223 jobs in the milk industry were promised, only 141 jobs were actually filled, and the economic gain was not $1.5 million, but $900,000. The dairies hoped we would accept their "efforts." We did, if only by our lack of persistent monitoring.

Another reality was that the quick pace of the falling dominos and the limited time of our busy pastors made it difficult to keep up with these agreements. But this in no way diminishes the far-reaching justice achieved in six months. The Breadbasket pastors, Jesse Jackson, David Wallace, and our consumers in the pews share the credit for these surprising early victories. As of July 1966, milk tasted sweeter in the black communities across the South Side of Chicago.

The Soft Drinks of Summer

> Our agreements are not contracts which we expect to enforce in a court
> of law, but covenants between the ministers and the companies which set a
> new direction in employment practices that bends toward justice.
> —Rev. Gerald Forshey

The day after the Dean/Bowman agreement, we moved on to soft drinks. Much like Country Delight, Pepsi-Cola General Bottlers made itself the first target with its uncooperative response. Pepsi's president was adamant that Pepsi was a good guy with "a long and rare history of nondiscriminatory employment procedures,"[23] but the reality was that it took repeated requests to elicit its job data.

Finally, at the end of July, we received the company's report: 370 blacks among 953 employees. While this was respectable, most blacks were employed in the lowest categories. For example, black Americans held 8 percent of managerial jobs at the top while holding 77 percent of unskilled jobs at the bottom. When we requested 58 openings, primarily in higher-paying jobs, Pepsi balked. On August 9 a "Don't Buy Pepsi" campaign was announced, and Jesse declared it was time to "go to our pulpits" and ask our folk to "cease drinking Pepsi-Cola."[24]

The next Sunday I made that request from my pulpit. On Monday, at our urging, several food stores started removing Pepsi from their shelves. When the Great Atlantic and Pacific Tea Company (A&P) ignored our request, we focused our picketing at its stores, after which it too removed Pepsi. In one week, 250 stores removed all Pepsi products. Joining our withdrawal campaign were community organizations and many area residents. After eight days of picketing, Pepsi backed down, agreeing to open thirty-two jobs, including drivers and skilled machinists, and, in a first for us, to place funds in two black-owned banks, Seaway National and Independence. Pepsi requested our help in filling the openings and asked that we inform our congregations that the boycott was over. Another $240,000 in annual income was created. My Gresham parishioners expressed pride in their pastor's involvement, but only a few indicated they had consciously not bought any Pepsi that week.

Breadbasket was on a roll. Coca-Cola had come to terms just a day earlier, on August 25. In a two-hour meeting, Coca-Cola and the Breadbasket team agreed to thirty new and upgraded jobs in addition to the nine blacks who had been hired since the negotiation began. These thirty-nine jobs gained $250,000 in annual income. Summing up the pact, Jesse announced, "Coca-Cola has made a decision to join the ministers in the revolution for human dignity and increased expectation."[25]

I was soon swept up in my first fact-finding session—with Seven-Up. Good news arrived in its initial response by mail: "Having been aware of the existence of 'Operation Breadbasket' for several months, Chicago Seven-Up Bottling Co. has conscientiously strived to upgrade the qualified Negro within the organization as well as to associate additional people. . . . The number of Negro associates has almost doubled since February (from 39 to 75)."[26] As usual, these increases had come in the lower categories, and some were seasonal jobs. Nevertheless, in the six months leading up to our negotiations the company's black employment rose from 10.6 percent to 16 percent. Clearly, news of our milk industry victories had an impact, at least on Seven-Up.

I was both excited and anxious when getting out of the car at Seven-Up's West Garfield Park headquarters on August 31. With me were Rev. Willie Barrow and Rev. W. W. Taylor, all of us on our maiden contact with a target corporation. Inside, we were introduced to Thomas Joyce, the Seven-Up distributor's top executive. After some pleasantries we entered into an uneasy discussion over the company's data. It turns out that Joyce and his staffers had given us minority numbers whereas we had asked for numbers on black Americans, and their data mixed together permanent and temporary workers. It was like extracting porcupine quills from your dog's snout. From that first negotiation session, Rev. Barrow and I developed a close bond that outlasted the Breadbasket years.

On the Sunday of Labor Day weekend, September 4, I preached to my congregation a sermon called "Joblessness in the Vineyard," indicating that work was vital to personal and national health, but black unemployment was almost 8 percent, twice the national average. I shared some employment data from Seven-Up (unnamed because of the current negotiations), which exposed "an unfair gap": 14 percent black employees while the population of Chicago was almost 30 percent black. I urged my congregants to join the ministers of Breadbasket in our fight for "jobs and rights." I recall now seeing many nodding heads whenever I mentioned Breadbasket, but the lack of real enthusiasm was a disappointment. The fact is that most of my members had jobs and did not want to disturb their new security. In retrospect, I think they had not yet moved from a survival mentality to becoming their brothers' and sisters' keepers.

Over the next weeks discussions with Seven-Up had a crusty edge. The threat of a "Don't Buy" campaign was just under the surface. The Seven-Up executives, all white men, listened, but it was unclear if they really absorbed the biblical references or had any concept of the deep economic discrimination our black pastors described from their own life experiences. For us, "doing justice" was a spiritual matter, and we closed all negotiating sessions by holding hands in a prayer circle. A few CEOs may have been converted during these Breadbasket sessions, but it was usually power not prayer that won the day.

At the SC meeting on September 16, I was reporting on Seven-Up when Dr. King, some staff, and bodyguards came in quietly and sat down in the back. He took out a pad and began making notes. I paused, and he beckoned me to continue. After the session Dr. King came forward, shook my hand, and said, "That was a mighty fine report. May I have a copy?" I handed him an extra copy on the spot. His quiet encouragement always meant so much to me.[27]

In late September, Seven-Up executives and the Breadbasket team met to confirm an agreement that opened up fifty-seven jobs, to be filled over sixty days, and included comprehensive job training. While Seven-Up offered additional openings for unskilled laborers, the test was in filling jobs in management, sales, the office, and crafts. In addition, Seven-Up agreed to hire people without high school diplomas if they could demonstrate ability. My notes indicate that we should have asked Seven-Up to place 10 percent of its moneys in black-owned banks, but this somehow slipped off the table.[28] The new openings (fifty-seven) along with jobs recently filled (twenty-eight) meant that by the year's end Seven-Up's black employment could double, bringing $600,000 in new income. As arranged, Seven-Up's Tom Joyce and I met with CUL officials to nail down the details on the applicant search.

At our next SC meeting it was decided that we would send Seven-Up a letter confirming the terms of the agreement and asking its executives to sign and return it. Rev. Gerald Forshey added, "Our agreements are not contracts which we expect to enforce in a court of law, but covenants between the ministers and the companies which set a new direction in employment practices that bends toward justice. We want a written confirmation from the company, not for legal reasons, but for the strength of the covenant."[29] This was the first use of the word *covenant* recorded in any Breadbasket document.

Table 2. Employment Gains from Soft Drink Covenants, 1966

Company	Date Promised	No. Openings	Jobs Filled	Time Frame (as of)
Pepsi-Cola	Aug. 22	32	9	Sept. 2
Coca-Cola	Aug. 25	39	4 drivers	Sept. 2
Seven-Up	Sept. 23	85	38	Dec. 4
Old Dutch Beverages	Sept. 30	letter of commendation		
Canfield	Oct. 6	12	no data	no date
		168	51	

Source: PBBF.

The word *covenant* comes from the Jewish tradition and refers to a binding consent between two parties who pledge loyalty to each other. It calls forth an inner commitment of spirit as opposed to a contract of law. The Hebrew prophet Jeremiah declared that God "will make a new covenant with the house of Israel" and will "write it on their hearts."[30] It is this spiritual aspect that distinguished a Breadbasket covenant from legal contracts, including those we helped secure later between targeted corporations and service providers.

During the Seven-Up campaign another Breadbasket team reported that Old Dutch Beverages had 16 blacks among 37 employees (43 percent). We sent a letter of commendation and closed the file. The Canfield soft drink team reported 116 blacks among 300 employees (38 percent), and while the numbers were good, most black employees were in low-paying jobs. Our request for 12 jobs in higher-paying categories was accepted, adding $90,000 in annual income.[31]

Thus, in just ten weeks, our agreements with the soft drink industry brought 131 new jobs plus 37 jobs filled during the negotiations, a total of 168. The monitoring reports revealed a more sober picture, however, though there was some significant movement with higher-level jobs (table 2).

The euphoria of the tumbling dairy dominos and the succumbing soft drink companies was, unfortunately, not matched by adequate monitoring. Carried away with quick victories, the Breadbasket pastors put our limited energy into targeting, research, and negotiations. Without consistent pressure several firms reverted to business as usual. It was a flaw that plagued us continuously.

Seven-Up exemplifies this failure. By year's end our records showed only 38 of the 85 promised jobs were actually filled. Of our soft drink pacts we can be sure of only 51 jobs, plus an unknown number for Canfield. Summing up the nine agreements in milk and soft drinks, we can claim approximately 200 filled jobs, versus the 391 promised ones. Still, this was a substantial gain of $1.3 million in annual income, and we in Breadbasket sensed we were on the cusp of an exciting new model for making justice.

In addition to poor monitoring, other problems hindered our efforts. The involvement of the Breadbasket pastors' congregations was tepid at best. We Breadbasket pastors did not take seriously enough our responsibility to publicize these job openings beyond pulpit announcements. For me, it was an energy problem. I poured myself into the Friday meetings, research, and negotiations and simply did not use this same aggressive style with my parish.

Our hope was that the Chicago Urban League would come to our aid using its skills in matching aspiring workers with specific job openings. Unfortunately, the CUL was suspicious of Breadbasket's confrontational tactics. In a Steering Committee discussion on what seemed to be CUL foot-dragging, I suggested that "Operation Breadbasket should do some missionary work with the Chicago Urban League to help it do the kind of job it should do with the people, and help it serve as our agent with the companies."[32] A committee was established to meet with the CUL about our concerns and report back.

However, at the joint meeting with the CUL, which I attended, our frustration at what seemed like the group's lukewarm support was countered by their members' explanation of the very meticulous process necessary to match individual abilities with specific job qualifications. The Urban League wanted us pastors to be more patient; Breadbasket wanted results. More bluntly, Breadbasket was the new kid on the block, and the CUL had been doing job placement for years. Our research exposed a corporation's employment picture in a new way, and it may have alienated the Urban League's methodically minded research team. Additionally, Breadbasket's more militant, public approach was possibly a threat to the CUL's support from area corporations. We continued trying to work with the Urban League, but in a matter of months our relationship just faded away. What had been reported back to the SC as a relationship with "potential benefits to both organizations" was not to be.[33]

Breaking the Chain (Stores) and Moving beyond Jobs

Even before we had finished with soft drinks, it was announced that "supermarket chains have been chosen by the ministers as the next industry to confront with the Good News that the days of the Slums are Numbered."[34] Behind the scenes Jesse Jackson pulled together a few black businessmen and began to meet with them Saturday mornings at the Chicago Theological

Seminary cafeteria. It was Jesse's vision that Breadbasket could expand its demand beyond jobs to black products and services.

Beginning with a list of six food chains,[35] we quickly chose to target the modest-sized High-Low Foods for a start. Initial contacts brought a negative response in the form of a local newspaper ad in which High-Low claimed to "hire Negroes fairly" and suggested that Breadbasket "ask our Negro employees how they feel about the treatment they receive from High-Low."[36] When High-Low officials refused to meet with us, a Breadbasket team walked into their offices on October 12, bringing our requests in person. Along with our demand for specific employment data we added, for the first time, the status of black-produced products and black banking services, based on Jesse's concurrent Saturday consultations with fledgling black entrepreneurs. High-Low promised more information later. "Later" was too late for us, so we initiated a "Don't Buy" campaign with picketing to begin November 3 at fourteen stores.[37]

In the midst of the High-Low talks, word came to us that Dr. King had appointed Jesse Jackson to be the director of Special Projects and Economic Development for the SCLC, a recognition of his fine work with Chicago's Breadbasket. In this new role Jesse was to continue guiding our job thrust but to add the development of programs nationwide to stimulate black businesses and raise funds for the SCLC.[38]

When High-Low learned of our "Don't Buy" campaign it immediately reversed position, requesting a meeting with us. At that gathering the company's top official surprised us with an offer to open sixty-six jobs for butchers, to place black products on the stores' shelves, and to deposit income from stores in black communities into our banks. Picketing was called off immediately. More negotiations followed to clarify these promises. At first, High-Low refused to display the seven requested products (Joe Louis Milk, Grove Fresh Orange Juice, Parker House Sausage, Metropolitan Sausage, Baldwin Ice Cream, Diamond Sparkle Floor Wax, and Stewart's Bleach). Then, in the midst of our Steering Committee meeting on November 18, we received a surprise phone call from High-Low's president agreeing to put out all seven black products![39] The very next day, November 19, High-Low and Breadbasket issued a joint statement using the words *covenant* and *covenantal* publicly for the first time.[40]

The opening words declared that High-Low Foods and Operation Breadbasket had entered into a "covenantal relationship . . . aimed at ending the economic indignities which lead to the spiritual destruction of Negro people." The pact promised 183 new or upgraded jobs; that seven black-produced goods would be given equal display in all stores; and that thirteen stores would transfer their banking to Seaway National Bank and/ or Independence Bank. For our part, we agreed to refer potential employees, inform our congregations of High-Low's commitment to "a substantial, far-reaching program," cooperate in follow-up, and offer pastoral support to new employees. The document concluded: "This covenant also acknowledges that men of God and good will can reason together at the table of mutual respect for the health of our city, and for the growth of our economic institutions to enhance the dignity of all God's children." Unfortunately, we failed to write in a time frame for the new jobs, an omission that was corrected in all subsequent covenants. It was announced that income for new black employees would net $1.6 million annually.[41] With news of this pact Breadbasket received another Orchid award from the *Chicago Defender*.

The breadth of the agreement was novel. Jesse Jackson stressed, "The shift to include marketing of products and banking procedures offers new scope."[42] From Atlanta, Dr. King hailed the agreement as "most significant because it shows that a large white-dominated company now understands that money spent by its Negro customers should remain in the Negro community."[43] With this covenant Operation Breadbasket began to push into new territory—black entrepreneurship and black capital development.

Support and enthusiasm were immediate. As news of this development spread, other black producers asked to be included. Within three weeks Jesse's Saturday breakfast circle at the CTS cafeteria had more than doubled, leaving students struggling to find tables to eat their breakfast. Jesse announced that cooperating businessmen would take out a full-page ad in the *Chicago Defender*. This ad, which appeared on December 1, 1966, listed 110 of us Breadbasket SC pastors along the left side with a letter from Dr. King surrounded by pictures of black products. King's message commended Breadbasket for demanding shelf space for black products, but reminded black people of the temptation to harshly judge black-produced products. "Our only hope for substantial economic growth and development will be the adoption of a spirit of mutual cooperation and concern for each other. Let us break the old pattern and respect ourselves by respecting Negro businesses."[44] Jesse's weekly meetings with the business circle coalesced quickly into support for Breadbasket and for Jesse personally.

Breadbasket held a youth convention to inspire and train high school students as picketers for "Don't Buy" campaigns and to inform them of other avenues of participation, such as supporting the Englewood shopping boycott and joining high school student unions. The event concluded with singing by youth choirs, a free dinner, and skating. For a time the young people were nicknamed "Breadbasketeers."[45]

Operation Breadbasket was increasingly asked to deal with other issues. John Porter and Richard Lawrence, two of our pastors in Englewood, urged the sc to support economic withdrawal at their local bank to help stop "urban removal." We were asked to deal with gangs, support voter registration, attend the trial of picketers from our "Don't Buy Pepsi" campaign, and more. While these were good causes, they created serious distraction from our primary focus on economic empowerment. Fortunately, a significant step to help us with the overload came with the hiring in November of Gary Massoni, a cts classmate of Jesse and David. Gary gave much-needed support in increasingly complex negotiations and in monitoring covenants.[46]

After High-Low Foods the next major target was National Tea Company. An opening meeting with National in October 1966 brought a dilatory response. In mid-November the sc informed National of our specific demands. After several tense sessions an agreement was reached. On December 9 at Fellowship Baptist in the presence of media and several Breadbasket ministers Norman Stepelton, the president of National Tea, and Jesse Jackson signed the "Covenant between Operation Breadbasket and National Tea Company and Its Subsidiary Del Farm Foods Company." The *Chicago Tribune* and even the *Chicago Defender* referred to an "agreement," unaware of our defining the pacts as "covenants."[47] Perhaps because they did not understand the significance of the word *covenant*, the news media stayed with *agreement* well into 1967.

National/Del Farm covenanted to open or upgrade 377 jobs in all categories within ninety days; provide job training; furnish us with the names of new employees; display fifteen black products in twenty stores by January 1, 1967; transfer the commercial banking accounts of twenty stores to our banks within thirty days; and make monthly deposits of federal withholding taxes, with a monthly deposit of at least $25,000 in each bank. Breadbasket pastors agreed to communicate this covenant to our congregations and the community at large and to assist in referring potential employees.[48]

Another crack in the job ceiling came when National hired a black "liaison" to help implement the covenant. National found its person in Rev. Charles Billups, a Breadbasket pastor. Interestingly, Billups was part of the sclc staff in Birmingham, where he had been beaten by police and arrested several times before coming north with Dr. King in early 1966. He had chosen to bring his family with him and stay in Chicago, perhaps to take a break from years of grueling and underpaid civil rights work. Billups became National's director of personnel, a title that sounded great but was a subordinate job disconnected from the established route of promotion. Still, it was a breakthrough.[49]

Once again Breadbasket had achieved a covenant without a withdrawal campaign. "Everything was handled peacefully, but on the other hand, we remembered how they hit Pepsi-Cola," said National Tea's vice president.[50] At Breadbasket, we were euphoric. In a large rally of Breadbasket clergy and supporters, National Tea's Norman Stepelton declared, "Operation Breadbasket is a more significant program than the late President Kennedy's 'Plans for Progress.'"[51] Frankly, all parties to the High-Low and National covenants were probably unaware of how unrealistic were the numbers, or how quickly most of these promises would unravel.

In the next weeks progress was made, and postcovenant negotiations continued. In March 1967, National agreed to contract with black scavengers (primarily small firms or even independent people who collected garbage and other refuse by truck on a regular, sometimes daily basis) to service sixteen stores as of May 1. To enable this arrangement Breadbasket helped create an alliance of black scavengers. Also in March, Jesse announced that a black contractor would build the next store for National, a Del Farm at 47th and Calumet. Weeks later, ground was broken for the first chain store built by a black contractor in Chicago and, it is believed, the first built by a black contractor in the United States. Several Breadbasket pastors, Dr. King, and Jesse Jackson were joined by National Tea's president at the ground breaking. Jesse offered a plaque to Stepelton, praising his achievements in human rights; Stepelton presented gold watches honoring their human rights work to five of our clergy. The event concluded with much backslapping from both sides.[52] Six months later this store opened with much fanfare, again with Jackson and Stepelton doing the honors. The construction work brought $250,000 into the black community.[53]

In our negotiations with both High-Low and National Tea, Breadbasket added demands that enhanced community economic development. The early covenants, eleven in all, led to 250 new jobs, increased annual income in the community by approximately $1.7 million, and gave a strong boost to black producers and service providers. In Rev. Jackson's recollection, the Breadbasket successes meant much to Dr. King. "My kinship to him [Dr. King] grew from a series of successes when he needed them." After the compromised Chicago Summit, King's leadership was increasingly challenged across the nation. Rev. Jackson believed that Breadbasket's victories helped to hold the line against those who sought to marginalize King's leadership.[54]

In addition, the summer of 1966 had witnessed the emergence of "Black Power" as shouted by Stokely Carmichael in the presence of Dr. King on the Meredith March across Mississippi. This action profoundly divided the civil rights leadership and enflamed a growing white backlash to the movement. However, it had no discernible effect on Breadbasket.

In a review of Breadbasket's early days, Rev. Ed Riddick, then the Chicago Church Federation's research director, saw an "opening wedge" to "economic independence," which "gives one a choice . . . with another voice and a more effective vote. . . . It is no exaggeration to state that Operation Breadbasket is one of the most effective mechanisms on a 'what is being done' level that the Chicago Freedom Movement possesses. It is a top priority item with wider implications than any other program."[55] Years later, Rev. Jackson reflected on our beginnings: "Breadbasket worked. The economic movement had traction. Housing was too volatile an issue and we already had the right to vote. The economic movement outlasted the open housing marches, opening up jobs for people."[56]

Newsweek picked up on the new SCLC adventure in its 1966 year-end issue. In a section entitled "Power of the Dollar" the magazine caught the essence of Breadbasket's model when it quoted a Dean Foods official: "You can't beat them. They've got that weapon [consumer dollars] and you have to respect it. If you don't, you can go broke."[57] Jesse and Breadbasket had proven wrong the early skeptics, who had claimed we were wasting our time on "Don't Buy" campaigns because the large markets could withstand our efforts. To the contrary, the dairy, soft drink, and supermarket industries came to respect the fact that Chicago's 1 million black Americans could withhold or redirect any of the $1.5 billion they spent on goods and services annually. In less than a year Breadbasket had become a player on Chicago's economic front.

CHAPTER 4

EVOLVING CAMPAIGNS

> I would rather have you picket us now because we didn't promise enough
> than to picket us a year from now because we didn't do what we promised.
> —Donald Perkins, Jewel CEO

The Jewel-Breadbasket Story

Of all our campaigns for jobs and economic empowerment, Jewel Tea
Company, the largest food chain and ninth largest company in Chicago, pro-
vides the best model and was our most successful achievement. New elements
were introduced, including job training in the covenants and the creation of
consumer (buyers) clubs in our congregations to push black products and
services. Also, in contrast to earlier agreements, the Jewel negotiations proceeded at a more deliberate pace. (It is noteworthy that the High-Low and
National agreements were disrespected and largely ignored, leading to later
withdrawal campaigns.)

During the fall of 1966 Jewel responded favorably to our request for data.
We analyzed the information and shared an outline of our demands at a
first meeting in January 1967. Jewel received our request cordially, and the
company informed us it was already making progress in recruiting black
employees.

The big snow of January 1967 shut down the city of Chicago and halted
Breadbasket's momentum. Looking out from my church onto 87th Street,
I saw buses and semitrailers scattered in every direction, like so many
Matchbox cars strewn across the room by a toss of the hand. Jesse wrote to
the ministers acknowledging that God had slowed us down and indicated
that we would be back at work shortly. "We have walked through many dark
valleys. . . . I remember the times that could have broken our spirit and broken our unity. . . . I remember those who criticized ministers and said they
wouldn't work for the betterment of their congregations, and thank the Lord
that He saw fit to use us as His instruments. . . . I thank the Lord that He has
made the Word become flesh through Operation Breadbasket, and pray that
we will continue to seek His Kingdom as servants of our Lord, Jesus Christ."

Jesse encouraged us to attend our Friday meetings and "march ahead with Dr. King with the deep faith that 'We Shall Overcome.'" It was an inspiring and rejuvenating message for me.[1]

By late February we were able to hold our first negotiating session in Jewel's home office in Melrose Park. Our initial goal was 932 jobs (bringing Jewel from 4 percent to 18 percent black employment) but to remain flexible, given the small number of Jewel stores in black neighborhoods. Our request included shelf space for black products, accounts for black scavengers, and the placing of commercial accounts in black banks.[2]

I recall that session as a kind of Sunday school class where we applied biblical stories to what God's demand for justice would require for Jewel. It was agreed that all future meetings would be held at H&H Cafe. Over the next weeks an agreement emerged with a more realistic request of 512 jobs. Our SC minutes record that Jewel's vice president, Lee Smith, "was still reluctant to talk in specific terms about the jobs requested, especially the 41 managerial jobs that would require some training."[3] At one session Smith distributed a proposed press release that seemed to "pat Jewel on the back for past programs" and "did not get down to the real issues. . . . Unless greater understanding and cooperation is expressed at the next meeting, an economic withdrawal may be in order."[4]

We wrote Jewel asking for specific answers within a week. To our surprise a telegram arrived with Jewel's acceptance of our demands. After a final session the covenant signing was set for Friday, April 28, 1967, at the new Jewel Employment Center, which was opening that very day at 2251 S. State Street. At 10:00 a.m., in a simple but stirring ceremony, Donald Perkins, the Jewel Companies' president, and Dr. Martin Luther King Jr. were the first of several leaders to sign the covenant. "Rev. Freeman, Rev. Wyatt, Rev. Evans, Rev. Jackson and Rev. Deppe joined Dr. King and the Jewel representatives at the signing table" along with other ministers and the press. Rev. Jackson declared, "The wounds and scars that characterize our inner-city will only be healed if companies like Jewel take these bold steps in creative justice to remove some of this misery and frustration. The National Guard will not be needed as an inner-city emergency unit to put out the fires of discontent that grow out of unemployment, if the major industries will absorb the fuel that feeds the fires. Jobs not fire hoses will cool down this city."[5]

Mr. Perkins stated that Jewel's goal was "to bring new Negro employees into the Jewel organization and provide them with the opportunity for advancement within every job category." Dr. King commended Jewel and encouraged other businesses to come forth with additional jobs to help the community avoid "a long, hot summer." (That was sadly prophetic since Detroit and

Newark went up in flames in July, but Chicago avoided any similar outburst.) King declared that Breadbasket's success is "the most significant development we've seen here as a result of our labors," referring to the CFM. After the statements, Rev. Jackson introduced me as the chair of the follow-up committee with Jewel.[6]

The signed covenant was crafted in the final week from a letter written and signed by Perkins and is the only Breadbasket covenant known to have originated in this way. In an interview years later, Perkins remembered that being targeted by Breadbasket came as no surprise because he had heard about the covenants signed with milk and soft drink companies and knew it was "just a matter of time before the supermarkets, including Jewel, would be approached." He remembers saying to Jesse that he did not want to over-promise. "I would rather have you picket us now because we didn't promise enough than to picket us a year from now because we didn't do what we promised."[7]

Beyond 462 new jobs, upgrading 50 black employees, and hiring 150 part-time workers, all by specified dates, the Jewel covenant promised to provide on-the-job training. Recognizing the difficulty "of disadvantaged groups to compete . . . Jewel has been assigning Negro trainees in an intensive training program to qualify them to assume management responsibilities at an earlier than normal date." By comparison with other chain store covenants, it was this training component that made the difference in Jewel's achievement of the covenant's job goals.[8] Also, training became an alternative method to matching recruits with jobs now that relations with the CUL had virtually ceased.

The covenant also called for Jewel to open shelf space for black products; form an advisory group to assist black suppliers; open accounts at black-owned banks; and utilize black building contractor, scavenger, exterminator, and janitorial services. As soon as the ink was dry the Follow-up Committee began monitoring the new covenantal relationship. Jewel submitted monthly reports, and we followed up with phone calls and quarterly meetings for clarification, counsel, and encouragement.

At the outset of our negotiations Jewel admitted that as recently as 1964 it had only 12 black employees total. Later we learned that no black employee had ever handled money at Jewel—from the local store's cash register all the way to the bank. The changes were stunning. News reports of Breadbasket's early successes with milk and soft drinks may have impacted Jewel's meteoric rise from 12 to 273 black Americans, or 4 percent of its employees, by October 1966, the baseline for the covenant (table 3). Jewel also worked with the Chicago Merit Employment Committee in sponsoring nutritional and career

Table 3. Jewel Employment Figures for Black Americans before
and after April 1967 Covenant

	Date	No. Employees	% Total Employment
Precovenant			
	1964	12	
	Oct. 1966	273	4˙
Postcovenant			
	June 1967	373	5.5
	Dec. 1967	676	10

˙Basis of the covenant.

Source: PBBF.

programs for minorities.[9] Undoubtedly this and other programs played a role in Jewel's improving signs of job fairness.

At the close of 1967, the deadline for new hires, we discovered that Jewel had actually hired 403 blacks, 87 percent of the agreed 462. This increase, bringing Jewel from 4 percent to 10 percent black employees, only happened because of an aggressive effort and a new employment center, which reported an average of 70 people entering its doors daily. No other covenant was implemented with this seriousness and result.[10]

The covenant had produced significant empowerment. The 403 jobs amounted to $2.8 million in new annual income, not including compensation or benefits for part-time jobs; there were 50 upgrades and new income for black producers and service contractors; and, finally, there was the impact this covenant undoubtedly had with other Jewel companies: Osco Drugs, Eisner Stores, Buttrey Foods, Star Markets, Brigham's Ice Cream and Sandwich Shops, and White Hen Pantries. The 403 new jobs alone would have had a value of $20.1 million in 2016. The Jewel covenant constituted an incredible success story for Operation Breadbasket, Jesse Jackson, a cadre of dedicated pastors, their congregations, and the black community itself.

Several factors contributed to this accomplishment. Jewel officials were serious and respectful and seemed to take to heart the moral suasion of our arguments. Some executives, especially Lee Smith, an active Methodist layperson, crossed the barrier from antagonist to colleague, and after the covenant signing we found ourselves working in tandem. Although not always understanding the depth of the issues—for example, the interlocking racism that tied educational discrimination in the trade schools to the lack of qualified black job applicants—Jewel officials aided us in overcoming these additional hurdles.

From the outset it was clear that Jewel saw the black community as a new market area, and it quickly seized on this expansion as a priority. The dovetailing of our goals added trust that eased communications and provided momentum. On Jewel's side, the commitment to job training led to heightened morale and helped increase the retention rate of black employees from 50 percent to 60 percent between 1967 and 1969. On Breadbasket's side, regular monitoring, aided by new consumer clubs, helped keep Jewel accountable. Our pulpit announcements provided job prospects. We engaged the Jewel leadership with counsel, an analysis of racist obstacles, and occasional chastisements. I was privileged to chair the follow-up team from the signing of the covenant in April 1967 until mid-1971.[11] Of course, these factors were backed up by the threat of a boycott. Taken together, "these elements represented a powerful methodology and a well-integrated system."[12]

All of this, along with a dogged focus, moral passion, and perseverance, aided the implementation of the Breadbasket-Jewel covenant. Dr. King came into a Steering Committee meeting one Friday as I was giving a follow-up report, and he beamed at the Jewel story. Although he did not live to see the long-term changes, he did know of our early achievement.

In the midst of this success, an African American cleric, Rev. Henry Mitchell, charged Dr. King with accomplishing nothing for the city. Rallying to King's side, the SC signed a public letter laying out Breadbasket's gains in jobs, black products displayed, and service contracts. The *Chicago Defender* editorialized, "Good work, Dr. King," adding, "Both Dr. King and the spectacular attainments of Operation Breadbasket deserve the praise of people at large. For if we are seeking a 'cool summer,' there is no better way to usher in such a climate than what Dr. King is doing to relieve anxieties, apprehension and despair. We all should be thankful for his vision of a positive approach to a stubborn social problem."[13] This isolated local criticism only strengthened Dr. King's position of leadership in Chicago's black community.

Covenants are a two-way street. Jewel's commitments were meaningless without black job applicants and consumers. So, Jesse came up with the idea of consumer clubs whose members would help move products off the shelves and into shopping carts, in essence sharing in the benefits of this new buying power. A large Breadbasket rally in April focused on consumer power, job openings, black products, the monitoring of local stores, and recruiting people for withdrawal campaigns.[14] Before long, under the able leadership of Rev. Willie Barrow, we organized twelve clubs, each with about ten members, who were charged with engaging their friends, family, and neighbors to purchase black products and services. Breadbasket businessmen were also expected to set up such clubs as part of their "attunement," a membership qualification that included a collegial attitude and the valuing of dignity and community over money and profit.[15] Club members visited North Side and suburban Jewel and National stores, comparing the quality and price of products, especially meat and produce, with the same chain's stores in the black communities. They confronted offending stores and reported any discriminatory practices back to the SC.[16]

Rev. Barrow remembers that in the beginning even club members assumed that black-produced goods were inferior to popular brands, and they often did not know a product line was black owned, unless it was Joe Louis Milk. To break this barrier the clubs held shop-ins, where members distributed lists of black products to customers at store entrances. In time, Parker House Sausage and Baldwin Ice Cream became familiar household names. Equally important, club members became a quick source of picketers for "Don't Buy" efforts.

Rev. Barrow recalled fondly the names of key participants in the consumer clubs: Rev. Addie Wyatt; Peggy Smith Martin, later a state senator; Jackie Jackson, Jesse's wife; Anna Langford, later an alderman; and Dolores Eliot. Other active women were Gurnell Sims, Evelyn Petty, Ora Saunders, Dency Chapman, May Baker, Margo Smith, Betty Magness, Hazel Thomas, and Dorothy Shaw. But it was not just women. St. Clair Booker and Richard Thomas were active in the consumer clubs before they joined the Breadbasket staff.[17]

Jackie Jackson "inspected" the stores where she shopped, including a Walgreen, a National Tea, and an A&P store. "Once a consumer club member got committed to the idea, the monitoring became easier and easier and part of your shopping. When out driving, you would see a store and just stop and check out the black products and the meats. That was your responsibility as a club member." One time at her A&P store, Jackie found Joe Louis Milk half-hidden in the back of the rack and reported it to the club captain. On her next visit, this milk was out front.[18]

The consumer clubs illustrate a broadening of Breadbasket from jobs to black entrepreneurship. Jesse Jackson's cover letter in a packet of materials for club members recognized this wider focus: "The aim of Operation Breadbasket is to create economic power and independence in the Negro community." He saw consumer power helping black people to "participate freely in the capital market. . . . If we are to send our children to school, we need money. If we are to buy houses in an open city, we need money. If we are to overcome long years of debt, we need money. If we are to become producers after years of being excluded, we need money. . . . Though money is neither a total nor an ultimate solution to our many problems—for those it will not heal, it will surely kill the pain!"[19] This letter reveals Jesse's sensitivity to the influence of our black business circle, as well as the growing pressure from the Black Muslims' successful emphasis on capitalism.

In addition to the consumer clubs, a new organization, Women of Breadbasket, focused on inspecting products, particularly meats. All too often its teams found chain stores in our neighborhoods selling "third-class meat at first-class prices" and operating in "unsanitary conditions." Women of Breadbasket brought in federal meat inspectors and even gained the support of Secretary of Agriculture Orville Freeman. In December 1967, Women of Breadbasket held a five-hour workshop, "The Meat You Eat."[20] Their advocacy and high-powered protests helped to influence the eventual passage of federal legislation, raising the standards of meat quality and meat-packing cleanliness and resulting in better protection for all people who put meat in their grocery baskets. On another occasion some months later, some 250 Breadbasket picketers circled a supermarket on Cottage Grove with signs reading "Don't Buy: Bad Meat Makes Sick Babies" and chanting "Oh, oh, oh, oh, bad meat has got to go." While the consumer clubs largely disappeared by the end of 1967, some monitoring of stores continued. Some members of Women of Breadbasket are still active in Breadbasket's successor, the Rainbow PUSH Coalition, as I write nearly fifty years later.

Jewel's own self-interest pushed implementation of the covenant. In August 1967, Jewel joined the federal Job Opportunities in the Business Sector (JOBS) program for "ghetto disadvantaged people," securing funds to cover counseling, remedial education, and prevocational training. JOBS was part of an effort by President Lyndon Johnson's administration to "restore order" following the urban uprisings.[21] Jewel also initiated a successful "coach-counseling project." Each coach was "responsible for working with a small group of new people from deprived backgrounds, helping them achieve complete assimilation into the business world."[22] Of our sixteen covenanted partners, Jewel had the best retention rate of black employees.

The value of newly hired black management is evidenced in an interoffice memo written by one such manager, Nate Armstrong, to his white colleagues. "You must realize that many of the so-called middle class Negroes with any degree of affluence, have spent their entire lives developing middle class white attitudes. These people [the new employees] are not attuned to the needs and desires of today's ghetto residents." He stressed the need for black employees to identify "with their black brothers and sisters who patronize your stores."[23] Based on their successes, Jewel officials were asked to participate in several presentations on hiring and training disadvantaged people both in the Chicago area and across the country.[24]

At the conclusion of one follow-up session with Jewel officials at the H&H Cafe, we gathered in a circle. As the convener, I asked Rev. Ma Houston to offer a closing prayer, whispering to her privately, "Keep it short, Ma, because we're way over time." She stared at me with a scowl on her long face and declared aloud for all to hear, "Rev. Deppe, of all people, you should know that you cannot put a limit on prayer. Prayer has its own time. It's God's time." Then she turned to the group and said slowly, "L e t u s p r a y," delivering an eloquent, spirit-filled prayer that seemed, at least to me, to cover most of the human concerns around the globe. My pastoral prayers have never been the same.

In late October 1968, I reported to the sc that Jewel progress had slowed. While Jewel had exceeded the covenant in three categories and in total employment by eighty-three, it fell short in butchers, drivers, engineers, and other better-paying jobs. Progress with service contracts and black products was also less than desired. The fact is we had failed to monitor Jewel closely. I indicated to my colleagues that even Jewel needed constant pressure. We were fortunate that Jewel had kept faith with the covenant as well as it had. Increased contacts with Jewel over the next few months allowed us to secure increased bank deposits and better product placement on its shelves.[25]

One Sunday early in 1969 I reflected on the Jewel covenant from the pulpit, using the image of leaven. After listing some substantial gains, I indicated that this "came about not by the Church showing the way but by piercing the structures of Jewel. . . . We are called to participate in the Church's leavening process, penetrating the world. 'The Kingdom of God is like leaven which the woman took and hid in three measures of meal until it was all leavened.'"[26]

The Gresham Methodist Church's response to the Breadbasket efforts was a mixture of pride and limited participation. Reporting to an annual church meeting in February 1969, the mission chairperson reported that the congregation was providing transportation to Breadbasket meetings, soliciting financial gifts, and making weekly announcements. Immediate goals called for the congregation "to become more involved spiritually, physically, financially" and to "realize significant changes in our community as they become by-products of Breadbasket."[27]

By April 1970, Jewel reported 997 blacks among 7,385 employees, or 14 percent (against 4 percent when we began negotiations). Journeymen butchers stood at 69, store managers at 17. In lower-paying jobs Jewel was over the covenant. Black products, on the shelves in all stores, were selling fairly well.

Table 4. Employment Gains at Jewel Food Stores, 1966–1971

Position	1966[a]		1967 Covenant No. Black Employees[b]		1971[c]		Compliance[d]
	Total Emp.	Blacks	Add'l	Total	Total Emp.	Blacks	
MARKETS							
Apprentice	595	62	57	119	530	74	-45
Wrapper					216	110	
Journeyman	854	6	31	37	993	69	+32
Ass't Mgr	228	5	5	10	249	11	+1
Manager	237	2	8	10	256	6	-4
GROCERIES							
Groc Mgr	254	3	7	10	288	17	+7
Ass't Mgr	227	5	5	10	249	16	+6
Prod Mgr	313	11	11	22	361	33	+11
Clerk	705	38	103	141	702	149	+8
Serv Mgr	239	7	5	12	256	14	+2
Ass't Serv Mgr	207	4	6	10	229	27	+17
Checkers/Pastry	864	21	139	160	989	113	-47
MANUFACTURING & WAREHOUSING							
Manufacturing	404	29	12	41	716	66	+25
Warehouse	484	68	28	96	581	141	+45
Transportation	343	4	30	34	402	17	-17
Management	41	0	2	2	53	6	+4
OFFICE							
Management	?	1			?	18	
Clerical	?	7			?	27	
Undifferentiated[e]	710				737		
Totals	6705	273 (4%)	449 add'l		7807	914 (12%)	+45

Note: All data include the latest monitoring reports in Operation Breadbasket's last year, 1971.
a   All data compiled October 8, 1966.
b   Written covenant signed April 29, 1967, without a "Don't Buy" campaign.
c   Total employment data compiled January 15, 1971; black employment data compiled June 15, 1971.
d   Total no. black employees requested in 1967 covenant minus total no. blacks actually employed 1971.
e   Jewel did not provide separate numbers for management and clerical office staff.
Source: PBBF.

While our scavengers and exterminators serviced twenty and eighteen stores, respectively, we had to keep pressure on Jewel to utilize black banks and other services. In August 1970, Jewel announced plans to hire and train 100 "disadvantaged" people over the next eighteen months. But by February 1971, Jewel's total black employees had slipped back to 12 percent (table 4). Nevertheless Jewel remained the gem of our covenants and the best model of enabling economic empowerment in the black communities of Chicago.[28]

The A&P Fight: Prologue

Just days after we signed the historic covenant with Jewel, one of our teams met with three officials from the Great Atlantic and Pacific Tea Company. At an initial meeting back in September 1966, we had learned that A&P had 830 black employees out of a total of 4,129, or 20 percent, in Chicago area stores. Requests for more data went unanswered, and another meeting four months later bore no fruit. Now, in May, the A&P officials walked in unprepared, acting as though they did not know who we were. In response, our team told them they could expect a recommendation calling for the immediate picketing of their stores. The meeting ended abruptly.[29]

Hours later an A&P official telephoned the Breadbasket office urging us not to picket. Serious negotiations resumed, leading to a covenant signed on May 26, 1967. This covenant, our biggest to date, opened 770 jobs worth about $5 million and 200 part-time summer jobs for black teenagers. The A&P covenant followed closely the template of the Jewel agreement regarding services and products as well as Breadbasket's responsibilities, but new to this agreement was assigning a staff member to work with our suppliers and utilizing the black-owned Marion Business College. The document concluded: "Operation Breadbasket and A&P intend to play a vital role in overcoming the deep social tensions that now keep the fabric of our society frayed."[30] At the press conference Rev. Jesse Jackson declared that if this supermarket chain remained honest about the agreement, "A&P will cease to be 'the Man's' store and will become our store."[31]

In late June several African American women received diplomas from Marion Business College, having received training specifically for A&P. In mid-September four black-owned janitorial services signed contracts to service forty A&P stores for three years. The 770 jobs were due by December, and implementation seemed to be on track.

High-Low Foods Re-Covenanted

Just one week after the successful Jewel and A&P covenants, our SC received a six-month report on High-Low Foods indicating that it had hired only 56 of the promised 183 people and that black products were not getting the promised shelf space. We agreed the covenant was broken, and it was back to the pulpits with "Don't Buy at High-Low."[32] On Friday, June 9, leafleting and picketing commenced at twelve High-Low stores. High-Low acted surprised but gave no indication of bending. According to a local newspaper, "At high noon there were only three cars in the huge High-Low parking lot at 111th and

Halsted, though the Jewel supermarket across the street was packed. This was the case in one after another of the fourteen stores in African American communities where Operation Breadbasket had mobilized a minimum of ten pickets each."[33] Picketers included supporters from other parts of the city and suburbs, such as members and the pastor of the Parish of the Holy Covenant (Methodist) on the North Side.[34]

In a surprise move, High-Low secured a temporary injunction on June 20, halting our picketing and deflating an effective boycott, though we were allowed to continue leafleting. Consumer club members were asked to wait for further instructions. Jesse Jackson called the judge's decision "a setback, but not a defeat," and proclaimed the demonstrations "peaceful, prayerful protests against the injustice of High-Low policy."[35] In the meantime High-Low cited the "great shortage of Negro butchers," and said it was making "every effort . . . to fill the need."[36] At the judge's urging both parties agreed to return to the table. After two weeks of talks, a new covenant was signed on July 7, 1967, which included a more realistic 126 jobs worth $800,000 in annual income; job training; shelf space for black products in all fifty-six stores; and the use of black services for the fourteen stores in black communities. It was our longest struggle at that point, but the agreement promised a new level of economic justice and respect.[37]

This covenant was never adequately monitored, however. When we reconnected with High-Low three years later, we learned that black employment had climbed from 11 percent to 21 percent but that the food chain had shrunk in total stores and jobs. As usual, higher-paying jobs fell short of the promise; lower-paying jobs were above the promise. The most disappointing figures showed only two black people among thirty-two office staff and zero blacks among ten in management. Breadbasket was so overextended at the time that we took no further action, effectively letting High-Low off the hook.

High-Low was just one of several covenants needing review. When the dairy and soft drink agreements were more than a year old, we examined Seven-Up and discovered that black employment had increased from 12 percent to 20 percent in eleven months. Jobs by category, however, had fallen short. Five office worker and four craftsmen positions were unfilled. Of five black Americans listed as "officers and managers," three were marketing representatives, including Andy Livingston, a young Chicago Bears football star, who traveled the Midwest doing demonstrations. The fourth and fifth black "officers" were a checker and an assistant checker! Concluding my report to the SC, I urged that we send a telegram to Thomas Joyce "demanding action within 48 hours on our request for four REAL managers. . . . Without a favorable response let us go to the pulpit and organize the people against this evil."[38]

Because of Breadbasket overload, my colleagues asked that I follow up by telephone, which I did. But without the threat of direct action, no improvement could be expected. Further, the targeted industries were watching, and when we failed to maintain our militant posture with one company, the others relaxed, and justice was delayed again.

Breadbasket was not immune to the social forces and attitudes of the metropolis by the lake. This came home to us in the SC quite personally when, one Friday in the fall of 1967, Dr. King arrived with a coterie of five or six people. "Doc" attended SC meetings whenever he was in town, usually without his own agenda. On this occasion he was obviously distracted, and after a few minutes he raised his hand and asked to speak. "I am among trusted colleagues here," he said, "and I want to share something personal. This past week I received more death threats here in Chicago." He indicated that he and Coretta had faced them and were prepared, but he went on, "Let me be honest. I am truly frightened for myself, but also for Coretta and the children." Doc talked about his fear and about how Jesus offers us strength for life, forgives our sins, and takes care of our deaths in his own death. He seemed to gather courage as he spoke, declaring that he would find the strength to carry on and that we all gave him strength as members of the body of Christ. He would not be deterred from his mission. It was a frightening moment as, I believe, we all trembled with him. Yet the resiliency of his faith shone through his angst-filled voice. As he talked through these fears he was also preparing us, his fellow pastors, for what lay ahead. When he was killed some months later I remembered that precious episode of confession and faith. He wavered, he was frightened, but he found renewal and refreshment to carry on.[39]

Breadbasket itself was not without threat and danger. That October, after A&P signed a pact for scavenger services through our Freedom Scavenger Association, two garbage trucks were burned and several containers were destroyed; alleys were blocked by white-owned disposal trucks; verbal threats were hurled at black workers from unmarked cars. Our scavengers were advised to "put locks on their fuel tanks, avoid parking in unlighted areas, and watch out for a two-door black Cadillac." Jesse Jackson declared, "We will not sit idly by with our locked arms, singing, and bodies bent in prayer. . . . We demand respect." In addition to these criminal acts, Jesse himself received threatening phone calls at "all hours of the night" telling him to "lay off," presumably to let go of his and Breadbasket's involvement with black scavengers. Jesse told *Jet*, "I cannot allow the threat of death to . . . separate me from my concern and involvement with the black scavengers." To help safeguard this new $30 million scavenger business, Breadbasket persuaded the Teamsters Union to make a joint investigation. Thankfully, the violence ended. Exposing the criminal activity and announcing the joint study undoubtedly helped bring an end to the terror.[40]

The Freedom Scavenger Association faced another crisis two years later, in October 1969, when the city threatened to revoke the license of the one dump available to the FSA. Rumors had it that a crime syndicate was behind this move. After two months of uncertainty, an FSA member purchased the controversy-ridden eighty-five-acre dump, secured a license, and thus thwarted an effort to force the black scavengers to locate higher-fee dumps outside the city.[41]

Certified Grocers of Illinois

> Even amid the jubilation, we must say that Certified . . . has merely
> contracted to do today what it should have done yesterday.—Jesse Jackson

Eighteen months had passed since our first "Don't Buy" campaign with Country Delight/Certified Grocers. Reports indicated that Certified had hired forty-four black Americans, as promised. However, it was time now (October 1967) to examine the Certified Grocers of Illinois. Tensions arose immediately when a scheduled meeting was canceled. Certified rejected our opening demands, claiming that it was integrated before Breadbasket arrived, 27 percent of the company's employees were black, and many Certified stores were owned by blacks. It argued that placing a black person on its board of directors would violate state and federal antitrust laws. Nor could Certified "favor" black products or black-owned banks. It would, however, discuss our demands for jobs, service suppliers, and black-manufactured products.

Jesse Jackson responded: "We cannot overlook the fact that there are some 104 white-owned Certified Stores operating in the ghetto and that these stores take $160,000 out of the ghetto each year, according to figures supplied by Certified. They make more than a marginal profit in the black communities. . . . If they want to press their legality, we shall assert our morality and simply keep Negroes out of their stores. We insist upon the banking provision." Jesse held firm on the request for a seat on the board of directors to represent the fourteen black store owners.[42]

At the SC on October 20 we decided to confront Certified. That evening, Dr. King announced a "massive boycott" against Certified stores before a capacity crowd at a Breadbasket benefit gala with Harry Belafonte and Aretha Franklin at the International Amphitheatre. King told the audience, "Negroes who fail to assist in the boycott will be turning their backs on an essential thrust toward complete freedom for black people. It's about time that we unite to make merchants show the same respect for us that they show for our dollars."[43]

As the picketing and leafleting commenced, Certified's general manager, Robert Kornik, said he felt that Dr. King was not familiar with the situation, or "I don't think he would have taken such a rash stand." As the boycott intensified, Rev. Jackson declared that Certified stores "help perpetuate the economic slavery of black people." He added that black-owned stores would not be affected. "After 30 years of cooperation with and support of Certified [by black store owners], they still have so little respect for black people they will not elect a Negro to the board of directors."[44] Here Breadbasket was pushing beyond jobs to the leadership level in Chicago's economic community.

At a Breadbasket rally during this campaign I found myself sitting next to Rosa Parks on the rostrum at New Friendship Baptist Church. Next to us were Rep. John Conyers of Detroit, Rev. Stroy Freeman, and Rev. Jesse Jackson. I remember thinking I was the token white preacher. The diminutive woman beside me seemed half my size. As the event dragged on I started a conversation with Mrs. Parks, asking about her work and life in Detroit. She gently turned our talk to me, wanting to know about my church and ministry in the black community. She was soft-spoken, perhaps even meek. After she was introduced at the podium she spoke a few words of encouragement, without even mentioning her own civil rights advocacy work in Detroit. She returned to her seat to respectful, but mild, applause. This quiet but strong Lady of the Bus had not yet become an icon in the movement. It all seemed so natural in those heady, hopeful days.

On November 8, 1967, after two and a half weeks of picketing, Certified Grocers of Illinois announced the election of Gaston Armour, a black man, to its board of directors. The 14 black members of the 725-member cooperative finally had a representative. A store owner for more than two decades, Armour admitted that his election "came as quite a surprise." Certified's action brought it one step closer to reconciliation with Breadbasket. On November 15, 90 Certified store owners met and approved a draft covenant. Kornik expressed "pleasure that the controversy has been settled."[45] Over the next weeks more Certified store owners signed the covenant. The co-op agreed to hire 32 black Americans for top management; the individual stores agreed to employment upgrades and training that included a specified number of disadvantaged people, putting sixteen black products on their shelves, and using a wide range of black-owned services, including Marion Business College.[46]

For its part, Breadbasket agreed to communicate this "far reaching program" to its congregations and community and to refer potential employees to Certified. This pact was our most extensive achievement to date. Jesse stated, "Even amid the jubilation, we must say that Certified . . . has merely contracted to do today what it should have done yesterday."[47]

Two and a half years later, in April 1970, I reestablished contact with Certified on behalf of the Follow-Up Committee only to find it uncooperative, sharing selective data and no employment figures on individually owned stores. While black-owned stores had increased from 14 to 31, Certified's total stores in black communities had dropped from 108 to 77. Certified had no accounts in black banks and did not market black products, and its warehouses showed zero gain in black employment over thirty months. In spite of this dismal and disrespectful report, we did not threaten sanctions. Only our total overload and the repeating story of so many covenant reviews can account for this lapse.[48]

What transpired with Continental Baking Company was totally unexpected. In September 1967, it reported 21 percent black employees at its five Chicago area plants. We responded with a request for 117 new jobs. By October, Continental agreed to open 92 jobs within six months, and it accepted our demands on black services and products. In exchange the company asked that we communicate "the positive steps" it was now taking "toward reconciliation with the entire Negro Community." Continental proceeded to implement its promise without a signed covenant, and within six months it had added 100 new black workers, though predictably these new hires were short in management and oversubscribed in service workers. Because of its cooperative spirit, we simply relied on Continental Baking to maintain the agreement.[49]

Empowering Black-Owned Banks

> Such funds have been collected from our taxpayers without regard to race and religion. They should be and will be used for the benefit of all of our citizens without regard to race or religion.—Adlai Stevenson III, Illinois state treasurer

At the outset of Breadbasket our SC discussed the desperate need for black people to secure credit for housing and other necessities. An ad hoc committee developed an action plan to empower locally owned financial institutions. In the late spring of 1966, Rev. H. B. Brady and Jesse Jackson met with Seaway National and Independence Bank officials to seek ways for African American individuals and community businesses to access decent loans and credit, including the possibility of a credit union among Breadbasket churches. These discussions pointed to problems beyond capitalization, "such as exclusion from distribution in chain stores." This was probably the spark for Jesse's Saturday gatherings of black businessmen in the fall.[50]

In July, tentative plans were made to meet with downtown bankers in the company of Dr. King. Our sanction, if needed, would be to ask supporters to transfer their funds out of those banks to our two black-owned banks. However, it became clear that we were not ready to engage the establishment, so the plan was shelved. Conversations with our banks led to their inclusion in the covenants with High-Low Foods and National Tea in late 1966. In December, Breadbasket pastors, joined by Dr. King, led a bank withdrawal at Chicago City Bank in Englewood, which was known to be complicit with an "urban removal" effort in that major shopping area. This event was followed by a bank-in at Independence Bank and Seaway National Bank.[51]

In January 1967, Breadbasket took another step, when our SC sent telegrams to the Illinois and Cook County treasurers and to Chicago mayor Richard J. Daley, urging them to deposit a fair share of public funds in black financial institutions. The telegram argued that African Americans, now almost 30 percent of the city, had been systematically excluded from the economy by loan refusals and nonnegotiable terms. We also wrote to pastors and business and community leaders, requesting that their organizations and individuals make deposits in black banks. "If the Negro is ever to gain a voice in the life of the city he must speak from an established economic base." So, a major new thrust was under way.[52]

Finally, in May 1967, the state treasurer, Adlai Stevenson III, announced the first-ever transfer of state funds to black financial institutions, saying, "Such funds have been collected from our taxpayers without regard to race and religion. They should be and will be used for the benefit of all of our citizens without regard to race or religion." Stevenson took a key second step: "State funds will not be deposited in banks or other institutions which discriminate on account of race or religion." He acknowledged receiving complaints of discrimination in loan policies. "We have ghetto neighborhoods in every metropolitan community in the state. The appalling needs of these communities must be met. One need is capital—capital to improve housing, to establish and expand business—and that need I can fill as state treasurer with the cooperation of our banks and other financial institutions." Stevenson said he believed that Illinois was the first state to adopt such policies.[53]

As welcome as these policies and actions were, the actual dollars deposited were minuscule. Independence and Seaway National each received $300,000. This contrasted with Continental's $8.8 million, Harris's $8.2 million, and American National's $2.1 million in government accounts. Still, Stevenson's action was valuable because it brought credibility to these small, black-owned banks and gave a challenging witness beyond Chicago and Illinois. The *Chicago Defender* editorialized that the state treasurer's announcement "will give much impetus to the drive against economic disparity.... The Stevenson plan should strengthen the financial structure of the banking institutions that are exercising equitable judgment in their services to the Negro community. They deserve to be rewarded. There can be no doubt that a man of his integrity will carry out his program precisely in a manner consistent with the outline he has given out."[54]

Stevenson's courageous actions brought a major breakthrough for justice and a clear Breadbasket victory. Adlai's father, a former Illinois governor, twice Democratic presidential candidate, and UN ambassador, who had died just two years earlier in London, would have been rightly proud of his son, as were all Stevenson fans across our state. The Jewel covenant and the state treasurer's new finance policy were the apex of the SCLC's Operation Breadbasket's first fifteen months.

Overall during 1967, Breadbasket could claim four chain store covenants that had filled 850 jobs worth $5.5 million, bringing the two-year total to 1,360 jobs worth $9 million. Gains in black service contracts brought in additional income and added another stone in the growing edifice of black economic strength. The Saturday morning entrepreneur circle, the growing numbers of volunteers in the consumer clubs and on the picket lines, and a fledgling structure—all contributed to this new empowerment. The Independence Bank president, William Franke, wrote in an annual report, "We must give credit for some of our growth to 'Operation Breadbasket' which has been instrumental in bringing many new accounts to our bank."[55]

As 1967 had begun, Jesse Jackson had stated that Breadbasket would "continue efforts to create a sense of economic power and independence among Negroes." This goal was demonstrably achieved, with empowered black neighborhood banks a major component.

The Methodist-Breadbasket Connection

During the Breadbasket years, 1966–1971, numerous churches on Chicago's South Side transitioned from all white to predominantly black congregations, as part of the influx from the great migrations. These "new" congregations, served by some white and some black clergy, joined a group of historic black churches to offer a strong base for the Breadbasket program. The five Methodist pastors active in Breadbasket brought our story to the church's annual conference, representing four hundred congregations in northern Illinois, which met in DeKalb in June 1967.[56]

Speaking to the nine hundred lay and clergy delegates, I shared the Breadbasket story. As we were entering the hot summer months, I stressed, "Upgrading of the ghetto socially, economically, educationally, politically, and culturally is all tied together. We in Breadbasket feel that economic upgrading is the base; Operation Breadbasket is the new hope, the new possibility." I closed with details of the Jewel-Breadbasket covenant and the decision of our state treasurer to transfer state funds to black-owned banks.[57]

The conference then approved $6,500 for Breadbasket in the 1968 budget, but tabled a recommendation on banking to avoid jeopardizing the free services from Harris Bank, whose owner, George Harris, was a member of the St. James Methodist Church in Kenwood. To assuage the Breadbasket supporters, the conference recommended approval of Harris Trust "and a bank of colored ownership or management as depositories for Conference funds in the treasurer's custody." There is no record of any implementation of this novel directive.[58]

At the next annual conference in June 1968, we designated the opening offering for the Poor People's Campaign, then in progress, with the proceeds to be sent to the sclc. Later, the conference approved a $10,000 grant to Breadbasket, said that available funds held by the conference "shall be deposited in banks approved by Operation Breadbasket," and authorized a committee to advise the conference on "how best to carry out the principle of economic influence as proposed by Breadbasket." It was announced that the conference had taken a first step by depositing $15,000 in each of three black banks.[59]

The requirement that conference banking needed Operation Breadbasket's "approval" did not see the light of day. The Banking Committee, chaired by the bishop, recommended a much less ambitious project to a fall session of the conference: deposit funds in black banks when possible, request all conference boards and agencies to "follow a like procedure when this is feasible," and require that Fund for Reconciliation moneys be "channeled through black banks." The delegates did not accept this backpedaling and referred the report back to the committee for further study.[60]

Finally, the conference approved money to send seven poor people and the superintendent from each of our seven districts to the Poor People's Campaign in D.C., and authorized an offering to be taken in our churches on June 16. Even though this offering only netted $2,000, the several actions taken by northern Illinois Methodism expressed a substantial commitment to the sclc's Breadbasket and the Poor People's Campaign.

In June 1969, for the third year in a row, the conference approved a subsidy for Breadbasket, this time in the amount of $9,350, earmarked as salary support for Rev. Calvin Morris, a fellow Methodist.[61] As of this writing, Calvin still reminds me of his gratitude for this financial assistance; he was living at that time on a very thin SCLC salary.

The Banking Committee, under new leadership, distributed a report offering data on the employment, assets, loans, consultative services, and fees of seven banks, including four downtown white-owned banks and two black-owned banks. Based on this analysis, the committee recommended transferring several conference accounts: checking to Seaway, credit union to Amalgamated, pension funds to Hyde Park, and Methodist Foundation funds to American National. In the words of the committee chair, Rev. Emery Percell, "The Annual Conference has a clear responsibility to use what power it has in a positive manner to strengthen the financial base of the black community. . . . To fail to use it to strengthen the black community is in fact a decision to perpetuate the financial weakness of the black community."[62]

While this report was adopted without alteration, the bishop and other conference officers blatantly ignored the conference vote calling for fund transfers to black-owned banks. Their refusal to implement this decision stands as a strong judgment against the Methodist Church leadership in northern Illinois at that time.[63] Six months later at another special session, the conference ordered that moneys earmarked for Black Methodists for Church Renewal, approximately $200,000 a year, be deposited in Seaway National Bank.[64] Later, when Rev. Lawrence, a Breadbasket pastor, questioned the lack of action on banking transfers, the bishop ruled him out of order! How we Breadbasket pastors let this slip away from us without a fight is baffling, and none of my Breadbasket colleagues or I can recall how this happened.[65]

By the next regular session of the annual conference in June 1970, the banking policy changes had been forgotten. With no shame whatever, the conference adopted a watered-down resolution asking the finance officers to find ways to use reserve funds for minority economic development, and it encouraged local churches to use black banks. On a safer issue, the conference renewed its support for Breadbasket in the amount of $10,000. In 1971, however, facing cuts across the board, the conference reduced its support to $5,000. In sum, northern Illinois Methodists contributed to the SCLC's Breadbasket approximately $41,000 over a five-year span, a not insignificant contribution at the time.[66]

Looking back, it is clear that the bishop and his inner circle were not about to transfer any funds from "our" Harris Bank, even if it meant defying the votes of nine hundred clergy and lay members of the conference. The bishop's arbitrary ruling on the question of fund transfers was not challenged. Thus, the effort to bring a major Protestant denomination aboard the Breadbasket train broke down before the shrewd manipulation of the church's leadership.

The powers and principalities of the Methodist Church held off the drive toward justice from its own progressive forces. It seems we were better at securing a measure of justice from Chicago area corporations than we were from our own church.

In spite of this, I felt then and still feel now a certain pride in the Methodist Church's involvement with Breadbasket. The chief participants were my Methodist colleagues on the Steering Committee, but also the congregations that participated in "Don't Buy" campaigns, Saturday Breadbaskets, and hunger programs and which supported our justice work with dollars and prayers.

CHAPTER 5

EXPANSION

> We are expanding our staff, both nationally and in Chicago because
> SCLC's Operation Breadbasket is a rapidly growing program that is taking
> on new responsibilities and challenges daily.—Jesse Jackson

Beyond Jobs to Economic Development

The leading edge of Breadbasket expansion was economic development, birthed at Jesse Jackson's Saturday breakfasts with black entrepreneurs. Accompanying Jesse to the CTS cafeteria was Dr. Al Pitcher, Jesse's mentor and a professor at the University of Chicago Divinity School. Al, a hard-nosed Niebuhrian ethicist, helped Jesse interpret the economic and political conditions under which black enterprises struggled. Together, they helped the youthful businessmen and businesswomen become an informed, cohesive, and confident group.

With Breadbasket's successes in opening supermarket shelves, the black entrepreneurs became enthusiastic participants. Until Breadbasket began its "constructive program," reported Dave Conway of Conway Soaps, black producers could not get their products into the chain stores. "Now the ministers of Operation Breadbasket have opened the door for us to get on the shelves of National Tea, Del Farm and High-Low stores. As we begin to compete, we urge customers to buy our products and learn for themselves that Negro businessmen manufacture first-class goods at reasonable prices." Rual S. Boles of Diamond Sparkle Floor Wax added, "Of course we praise and encourage Breadbasket. It is giving us the opportunity to become the kind of businessmen we want to be. As we grow, we can hire more people and invest more money in the development of our people. Operation Breadbasket has encouraged us to think concretely about how we participate in lifting Negroes from economic deprivation."[1]

The first major event sponsored by Breadbasket's business circle was the Negro Business Exposition and Seminar held in March 1967. Dr. King joined in the planning. The weekend event "exposed" nineteen black products and services in displays to an audience of two hundred, including black entrepreneurs, community leaders, Breadbasket pastors, and even Joe Louis, the boxing icon. Seminars were offered on issues unique to black business. S. B. Fuller of Fuller Products was a luncheon speaker, and John Johnson, the publisher of *Jet* and *Ebony*, led a merchandising seminar. Business leaders, some from companies with recent Breadbasket covenants, served as resource people.[2] A serious problem highlighted was black people's exclusion from access to capital. Jesse Jackson spoke to Breadbasket's efforts to strengthen black-owned banks and urged those present to transfer their banking accounts to the financial institutions in the African American community.

As the Saturday circle matured, Jesse sensed the potential of this fast-growing group, and he devoted increasing time to helping empower them. Bob McKersie, a professor at the University of Chicago and a Saturday attendee, created and offered courses on small business management and recruited black MBA students to assist the fledgling business leaders. In his memoir, *A Decisive Decade*, McKersie reports that two of the firms assisted, Parker House Sausage and Grove Fresh Orange Juice, both had sales of more than $1 million within ten years.[3]

At this point the Saturday movement needed some ongoing structure, and an Attunement Committee was established to screen potential members. *Attunement* meant that the participant was aligned with Breadbasket's goals of increasing jobs, strengthening black businesses, and living out "new values . . . and not focus[ing] as much on money."[4] I remember reports to the Steering Committee about arguments in the Attunement Committee over membership between those who wanted to allow only established businesses, in order to keep up an image, and those who were open to anyone who showed business viability.

By the end of 1967 business members were expected to support Breadbasket with "spiritual participation": attending Saturday seminars, using black products and services themselves, making financial contributions to SCLC's Breadbasket, joining in our "Don't Buy" campaigns, and spreading the word.[5] Over this same time came a not too subtle power shift from the Breadbasket SC to a joint two-headed animal—clergy leaders at Friday SC meetings and the business circle on Saturdays, with an alternating focus between jobs and economic development. In the early days it was all a honeymoon, and both groups were quite impressed with how well we worked together.[6]

A striking illustration of the new centrality of black businesses by December 1968 was a large poster entitled "This Black Business Supports a Beautiful BLACK CHRISTMAS." A list of dozens of black-owned businesses by category, such as food products, financial institutions, and construction, scavenger, exterminator, janitorial, and general services, surrounded the official

Breadbasket logo—a clenched fist with wheat sheaves and dollar signs—all surrounded by a Christmas wreath.[7]

In late 1968 the Attunement Committee faded away and was effectively replaced by a new Commercial Division in January 1969, when five businessmen, a business school professor, and staffer Gary Massoni met to revitalize the business sector.[8] The old spokes were replaced in this new structure by "divisions": the Ministers Division (basically the SC), the Cultural Division (band and choir), and Teachers, Labor, Health, Political Education, Data Processing, Special Projects, Fund-Raising, and Suburban Alliance Divisions.[9]

Expanding Breadbasket Nationally

Back in the spring of 1967 Dr. King had discerned the potential of Chicago Breadbasket for creating a national network and had his staff make plans for a national conference. Leading up to the event Dr. King suggested that "the new thrust in the Civil Rights Movement is, to a great degree, dependent on what can be done to help the Negro throw off the shackles of economic exploitation."[10]

Ministers were invited from across the nation to this National Breadbasket Clergy Conference in Chicago, July 10–12, 1967. The goal was to form a national Breadbasket and to address the specter of more urban riots in the summer months ahead. In Dr. King's personally signed letter of invitation, he indicated that "the buying power of the American Negro is greater than the gross national product of Canada . . . and yet we find ourselves with so little influence within the American economy that more than half of our people are struggling on an island of poverty in the midst of this ocean of material wealth. Together we can organize to help remedy this situation. . . . Your attendance is absolutely essential."[11]

Some 150 black clergy attended the event at Chicago Theological Seminary. On the second day Dr. King announced that negotiations for jobs would be "initiated promptly" in forty-two cities with black populations of more than a hundred thousand, constituting "the main thrust" of the SCLC that summer. King noted that in Cleveland an economic boycott of Sealtest milk products had just begun, "and already 19 stores in the ghetto have agreed to take Sealtest off their shelves."[12] On the last day of the conference King called for immediate negotiations with four corporations and declared that General Motors would be an early target. These lofty plans fizzled, however, when the clergy returned home just in time for summer vacations. There is no evidence of new Breadbasket chapters emerging at that time nor of any confrontations with the national corporations named by Dr. King.

Dr. King's dream of a national Breadbasket to stem the tide of despair in urban America, even had it succeeded, would have been too late for 1967. King's prescient fear became real in the riots in Newark, New Jersey, July 12–17, which left 26 dead and 725 injured with 1,500 arrests, and in Detroit, Michigan, July 23–27, which resulted in 43 dead, 1,189 injured, 7,200 arrested, and 2,000 buildings burned down.

In Chicago many of us felt a certain tension. I reflected on this crisis in an August 6 sermon. "The City of Chicago is tense, waiting, watching, praying, hoping. Will the plague hit us? . . . Like Jeremiah we can only lament what has happened." I suggested a cure with the church leading the way, lifting up Operation Breadbasket as a concrete and creative force to confront urban despair and offer hope to an entire people. I suggested that "the door is open for us to be God's instruments" and to "renew our citizenship, our humanity, our Churchmanship."[13] Fortunately, our city was spared any outbreak in the summer of 1967.

Dr. King continued to extol Chicago's program. In his report to the SCLC's Tenth Anniversary Convention in Atlanta on August 16, entitled "Where Do We Go from Here?" he declared, "The most dramatic success in Chicago has been Operation Breadbasket." King indicated that we had opened twenty-two hundred jobs worth $18 million. (My records suggest a more modest $8 million in jobs filled.) More than that, he said, "both of [the] Negro-operated banks have more than doubled their assets, and this has been done in less than a year by the work of Operation Breadbasket." King detailed our work with black-owned producers and service providers and continued, "The kinds of requests made by Breadbasket in Chicago can be made not only of chain stores, but of almost any major industry in any city in the country." King then listed Cleveland and Atlanta Breadbasket's many successes. He told his audience a "story that's not printed in the newspapers in Atlanta: as a result of Operation Breadbasket, over the last three years, we have added about $25 million of new income to the Negro community every year." Dr. King concluded his speech in a quickening cadence with a wave of eleven "Let us be dissatisfied until . . ." sentences. It was Doc's last and most penetrating address to his SCLC base.[14]

With Newark and Detroit still smoldering, Dr. King called for defusing "the ticking bombs of impatience in the big cities" with local Breadbaskets helping to "transform the rage of defiant unreachables into a creative and constructive force." King also announced that Jesse Jackson would now assume the title of national director of SCLC's Operation Breadbasket.[15]

Accompanying Jesse to Atlanta were Rev. Stroy Freeman and Cirilo McSween, both of whom were elected to the SCLC board. At our next SC meeting we congratulated Rev. Freeman and Cirilo on their election and Jesse on his new position.[16] Cirilo's commitment and gift for finance so impressed Dr. King that within a few months Cirilo was named treasurer of the SCLC in addition to his key role in Chicago Breadbasket. King liked the "concreteness" of Operation Breadbasket, seeing its potential in measurable terms. He was fascinated by the ability and willingness of Chicago Breadbasket's business leaders to raise money, reciprocating the gains they realized through our covenants. In the South, the SCLC lived by small donations, but in Chicago, the business circle raised big bucks and made substantial contributions. King realized that the movement could now be financed in a major way by newly empowered and strengthened black businesses. This was timely and crucial because liberal supporters and foundations were backing away from the civil rights movement as it shifted from integration to black empowerment, from freedom issues to the more subtle equality issues.[17]

Earlier in Chicago, Dr. King had already received a big surprise. Doc had shared with Jesse the need for a $35,000 loan to cover the SCLC payroll, and King suggested they go together to seek a loan at Independence Bank. With a nudge from Chauncey Eskridge, King's lawyer, Jesse convinced Dr. King to stop first at the home of Al Boutte, Independence Bank's vice president, to meet Al and other leading black entrepreneurs. After some pleasantries Boutte and his colleagues handed Dr. King an envelope of checks totaling $55,000. Dr. King wept. He had never seen black businessmen this socially conscious in the South, where they felt that integration efforts strengthened white businesses over them. King experienced in Chicago a kind of reciprocal thank you for the benefits black businesses were receiving from Breadbasket covenants and connections. It was certainly no shakedown, contrary to some critics.[18]

But as we came to the end of 1967, Dr. King's dream for a national network was on hold.

Saturday Breadbasket

> An unsuspecting visitor to a meeting of Breadbasket will witness powerful emotional exchanges between ministers, singers, musicians, sociologists, political figures, educators and the lay membership which often numbers eight thousand [sic] or more. — Cannonball Adderley, jazz saxophonist

The Saturday movement had evolved during 1967 from a semiprivate discussion/seminar to a public rally/workshop/celebration with a microphone, prayers, Scripture, speeches, and a small band. Breadbasket ministers began showing up along with other supporters, and it just took off. A leader emerged quickly, Cirilo McSween, the first black sales agent for New York Life Insurance Company—and a $1 million man his first year. After growing up in Panama, Cirilo studied at the University of Illinois and went on to a stellar business career, but his commitment to Breadbasket grew with us, and he became a trusted colleague to Jesse, the staff, and, later, Dr. King, becoming a member of the SCLC board and then its treasurer. In a few months the Saturday gatherings moved to a larger venue.

Saturday Breadbasket soon began to compete for attention in the Black Belt with Congressman William Dawson's Saturday Breakfast Club, broadcast live on WVON radio. A paradigm shift came when the station dropped Dawson's group in favor of Breadbasket's Saturday event. It is of note that Breadbasket's successor groups, PUSH and the Rainbow PUSH Coalition, have broadcast live over WVON for almost fifty years and continue as of this writing.[19]

Saturday Breadbasket soon came to overshadow the Friday SC meetings in sheer numbers and excitement. The saxophonist Ben Branch and his musical ensemble, the Downhomers, were hired to play weekly, bringing high-quality gospel and jazz to the Breadbasket event.[20] A core of Breadbasket pastors always sat up front to symbolize the source of Breadbasket's authority.

In Jesse's vision, Saturday Breadbasket was the church without walls, the church marching, doing justice, preaching good news to the poor, healing the brokenhearted, practicing nonviolence, addressing the "principalities and powers," and engaging people where they live, struggle, work, and play. The Bible was interpreted as a series of freedom struggles from Moses, Joshua, and Esther to Jesus, a "road map in the struggle for liberation and justice." Preaching was central because the people received their marching orders from the One who demands justice. Jesse saw Saturday Breadbasket as a synthesis between church and movement. In a way, it was a new church order, combining the best of the black church tradition with the newer theology of liberation, the church gathered for singing, inspiration, and instruction, and the church energized to engage the world in all its secularity. Some folks experienced Breadbasket as their congregation; others came as liaisons from their churches. This was the theological underpinning of the increasingly popular community forum.[21]

Richard Hatcher, the first African American mayor of Gary, Indiana, and entertainer Eartha Kitt both addressed a Saturday rally in March 1968, which drew some seven hundred folks. A *Defender* columnist, Doris Saunders, described Saturdays at Breadbasket this way: "Hottest Set in Town. . . . The 'in' place nowadays every Saturday morning is the meeting of 'Operation Breadbasket' held at the Lutheran Church . . . at 57th and Woodlawn. Rev.

Jackson runs a tight ship and folks are really talking about his ability to produce . . . where it counts . . . in the pocket book. Strangely, some of the people
who frowned when the young theologian started, have tightened up their
game and joined the parade."[22]

As attendance increased, Saturday Breadbasket moved to the larger
Parkway Ballroom on East 45th Street. The audience was areawide with the
new North Shore chapter of some hundred churches, synagogues, PTAS, and
other local groups sending carloads of people each week. On May 11, 1968,
some fifteen hundred people gathered to hear Jesse give a passionate plea for
support of the Poor People's Campaign; on May 18 singer Oscar Brown Jr. and
actor Robert Culp spoke at Saturday Breadbasket; on May 25 a poor woman
returned from Resurrection City to address two thousand Breadbasketeers;
on June 1 actor Sidney Poitier, comedian and activist Dick Gregory, and Black
P Stone Nation leader Jeff Fort spoke to the crowd. Poitier named his long-
time heroes as W. E. B. Du Bois and Paul Robeson, and then said, "I have now
come upon a new hero. Today, my hero is the Rev. Jesse Jackson." On June 29,
Rev. Arthur Brazier, president of the Woodlawn Organization, spoke to the
Breadbasket crowd in defense of his youth project, which was being challenged at that time in federal hearings. Jesse vowed Breadbasket's support. On
July 20, a record thirty-five hundred folks jammed into Parkway, bursting it
at the seams. Later in the day twenty-five hundred of the attendees went off
to picket A&P stores.[23]

In August 1968, Saturday Breadbasket moved to a still larger venue,
Tabernacle Baptist Church on South Indiana. On August 17, Julian Bond,
a member of the Georgia House of Representatives and a delegate to the
Democratic National Convention, then meeting in Chicago, introduced
Democratic presidential candidate Senator Eugene McCarthy to a crowd of
three thousand. McCarthy declared, "We cannot talk about the affluence of
the country and not expect 10 to 20 million people to say 'what about us?'
America should not have been surprised when people started rioting. Rather,
the nation should have been surprised if oppressed people didn't protest."[24]
He promised decent jobs, better education, and improved housing if he were
elected president.

The next Saturday, another Democratic presidential candidate, Senator
George McGovern, along with singer Harry Belafonte, and Rep. John Conyers
of Detroit spoke to an estimated four thousand people. McGovern said this
was the first time he had been in church on a Saturday, but he enjoyed it
more than attending Sunday services. He praised Breadbasket for "continuing
the ideals set by Dr. King."[25] Jesse Jackson criticized Mayor Daley for calling
up some five thousand National Guard troops for the Democratic National
Convention. In September, three hundred CTA workers came to Breadbasket

soliciting support for their strike; they received it when Jesse called on black citizens "to walk in dignity, rather than ride as fools."[26]

In a *Defender* column, Doris Saunders wrote of the Saturday phenomenon, "There is a new feeling of unity and togetherness in the black community, today!"[27] Leaders across the nation, especially political candidates and entertainers black and white, scheduled stops at the Breadbasket forum. With Dr. King's death, Saturday Breadbasket had become almost overnight the heart and mind of the black community, spanning its economic, political, and cultural life locally and nationally. One of Rev. Calvin Morris's fondest memories was "looking forward to Saturday [Breadbasket], when every meeting was larger than the last one. People came out of the woodwork; they came from all segments of city life and beyond."[28]

Jesse was at his charismatic peak on Saturday mornings. One of his strengths was an ability to sense the coming tidal currents and to go with the flow. With the rising black power appeal Jesse and his associate Calvin grew Afros, adopted the clenched fist, and wore dashikis, yet they always moderated their messages to the widest possible audience of blacks and progressive whites.[29] While Muslims were advocating separatism, liberals were pushing a hasty integration, and Stokely Carmichael was lifting up the African connection, Jesse and Breadbasket answered the call for black power with a program to empower the black community, enabling it to engage the mainstream economic powers on equal footing.[30]

Attending her first Saturday Breadbasket that summer was Hermene Hartman, a Loop College freshman. Her father, Herman Hartman, was the first black person to hold a Pepsi distributorship in the Chicago area and an early participant at the Saturday breakfasts with Jesse. Hermene's mother, Mildred Bowden, who frequented the hair salon across the street from the Breadbasket office on 47th Street, had been urging their daughter, a secretarial whiz who typed 125 words a minute, to offer her services at the office, but in no way to march. Her father was hesitant, concerned about his young daughter working with so many young male Breadbasket staffers. Hermene said no. When Dr. King was killed, her mother said, "See what an opportunity you missed to work with Dr. King, because you were more interested in money [being salaried]."[31] That comment and a sense of guilt led Hermene to attend a Saturday Breadbasket rally at the Parkway Ballroom. After a few weeks she discovered she had been sitting next to Jesse Jackson's grandmother Tibby and his young daughter Santita. Gathering up her courage one Saturday, Hermene went up to Rev. Jackson at the close of the service and told him she wanted to do something and she could type. Jesse introduced her to Rev. Willie Barrow, and that began Hermene's involvement.[32]

A major source of the Saturday Breadbasket spirit was the now thirteen-piece Breadbasket Orchestra and the choir, both directed by Ben Branch. The orchestra played for Breadbasket benefits and community festivities and performed at a Poor People's demonstration in Washington, D.C., and then with Mahalia Jackson before seventy thousand folks in Harlem.[33] In June 1969 the Breadbasket ensembles accompanied the Hunger Caravan across Illinois.[34] A first album was produced in 1968, and in mid-1970 the Breadbasket musicians issued a second album, *On the Case*, which contained several spirituals. On the record jacket were these words of SCLC's Rev. Ralph Abernathy:

> In the long and rich heritage of Black people, our music has been one of our greatest treasures. . . . Black people today use music in our Freedom Movement as a rallying cry, as a means of sustaining confidence, and even as a weapon to show our solidarity and determination. . . . This album . . . is a brilliant and stirring expression of music by Black people. It is the first recording by a large ensemble—21 instruments and nearly 200 voices—of this kind of music . . . music which captivates the rock and the beat, the soul of a people . . . music lovingly and superbly presented by dedicated and talented people: the SCLC Operation Breadbasket Orchestra and Choir.[35]

The Breadbasket Orchestra and Choir helped carry the Breadbasket story well beyond the Saturday morning faithful.

"The first lady of the civil rights movement," Coretta Scott King, received a five-minute standing ovation as she was introduced at Saturday Breadbasket on November 23, 1968. Coretta praised Breadbasket as "one of the finest monuments to my husband's memory. . . . When I was here last year I told my husband that it was one of the greatest spiritual experiences of my life." She indicated that Breadbasket's work for economic justice was "an inspiration for me to carry on in my way." When asked if her husband's efforts in Chicago had failed, she reminded folks, "This is what we've done." Mrs. King commended the crowd for helping foster a "society of love and brotherhood" and hailed Rev. Jackson as "one of the great young leaders of today."[36]

The public face of Operation Breadbasket had come a long way in just over two years: from a seminary cafeteria to the twenty-five-hundred-seat Capitol Theatre at 79th and Halsted. When the theater was purchased by two black brothers, it was immediately rented to Breadbasket, which moved in during June 1969.

Providing security at the Saturday rallies were the Black P Stone Nation led by Jeff Fort. They had been uneasy allies since Dr. King drew them into the movement back in 1966. Periodically, Blackstone Ranger members would show up on our Breadbasket picket lines. Now, their members patrolled the aisles of the packed theater on Saturday mornings. On Saturday afternoons Fort could be seen in the Jesse Jackson home, sitting at Jesse's feet among other eager listeners to Jesse's commentary and teaching. Jackie Jackson recalls young Fort as "brilliant, supportive, and protective of the black community. I never knew the Jeff Fort they describe today."[37] (Fort is currently in prison serving a life sentence for his gang-related crimes.)

Perhaps the most memorable image of Saturday Breadbasket is Jesse's iconic chant, "I Am Somebody," which he began to intone in the dying days of the Poor People's Campaign. In September 1969, WLS-TV did a special on Rev. Jackson entitled *I Am Somebody*, taking off on Jesse's fiery Saturday morning litany. This soul-filled call-and-response accompanied Jesse wherever he spoke across the nation. Here is one variation among many:

JESSE: I am
AUDIENCE: *I am*
JESSE: Somebody.
AUDIENCE: *Somebody.*
JESSE: I may be poor.
AUDIENCE: *I may be poor.*
JESSE: But I am
AUDIENCE: *But I am*
JESSE: Somebody.
AUDIENCE: *Somebody.*
JESSE: I may be black.
AUDIENCE: *I may be black.*
JESSE: But I am—Somebody.
AUDIENCE: *But I am Somebody.*
JESSE: I may be on welfare.
AUDIENCE: *I may be on welfare.*
JESSE: But I am—Somebody.
AUDIENCE: *But I am Somebody.*
JESSE: I may be uneducated.
AUDIENCE: *I may be uneducated.*
JESSE: But I am—Somebody.
AUDIENCE: *But I am Somebody.*
JESSE: I may be on dope.
AUDIENCE: *I may be on dope.*
JESSE: I may have lost hope.
AUDIENCE: *I may have lost hope.*
JESSE: But I am—Somebody.
AUDIENCE: *But I am somebody.*

JESSE: I am—black—beautiful—proud—I must be respected—I must be protected.

AUDIENCE: *I am—black—beautiful—proud—I must be respected—I must be protected.*

JESSE: I am—a child of God.

AUDIENCE: *I am a child of God.*

JESSE: I am—Somebody.

AUDIENCE: *I am Somebody.*[38]

Forty years later, when asked what word or phrase jumps out to him when he thinks about Operation Breadbasket, Richard Thomas, Jesse's traveling aide, replied, "I am somebody."[39]

Saturday Breadbasket became the in place to be on Saturdays, "hustling time,"[40] and the place to receive marching orders for that day's picketing. While the Friday SC still retained importance for negotiations, Saturday Breadbasket became the glue for ever-expanding programs and a gathering place for volunteers, supporters, and the eager media. However, by early 1971, weekly attendance had fallen gradually from a high of three thousand in 1968 to about fifteen hundred, and some of the newer participants were simply white suburbanites looking for movement direction or just excitement. Increasingly, a few staff, choir, and band members questioned the "circus" atmosphere, sensing a loss of focus on issues and action. A remnant of this place to be continues today in Rainbow PUSH's Saturday Morning Forum at Dr. King's Workshop on South Drexel Boulevard.

Jesse's Role Mushrooms

The expanding influence of Breadbasket in the late 1960s was, in fact, the flip side of Jesse Jackson's role in and beyond Chicago. While we in the SC focused on jobs, Jesse addressed urban removal in Garfield Park, Eartha Kitt's explosive remarks about the war in Vietnam, and the deaths of three African American students in Orangeburg, South Carolina; he also defended "naturals," the latest haircut fashion in the neighborhood. Jesse managed all this in addition to his growing schedule as the national director of Breadbasket. With high energy and passionate commitment Jesse strove to do it all. Still, in the late summer of 1967, Jesse wrote to a close college friend, a newly ordained deacon in the Methodist Church, Rev. Calvin Morris, asking him to "come to Chicago and join me in Operation Breadbasket." Morris wrote back, "Plan to do graduate work in Chicago in the Fall. Will call you then." On his arrival to begin his studies at the University of Chicago, Calvin phoned Jesse as promised, and the rest is history. Calvin postponed his studies and joined us at Breadbasket, quickly becoming Jesse's trusted associate and covering for him during Jesse's many absences on behalf of national Breadbasket.[41]

Jackson's role grew across Chicago. It was arguably "the first time Negro clergy acknowledged any real leadership beyond their own denominations and conventions. History had found a man to mold together a widely diverse group, and out of it, make a community," as I said while introducing Jesse at a community banquet. "As a result of his leadership, Operation Breadbasket today has moved out in new areas, beyond negotiations for a few jobs, to changing the hearts and opening the hands of a whole people. . . . Operation Breadbasket is Jesse Jackson. He even takes the edge off my German serious-ness. It is a joy born out of comradeship and love to introduce to you tonight the Director of Operation Breadbasket, the Rev. Jesse Jackson."[42]

Jesse's support base, originally in the SC, had moved more and more to the business spoke. While Revs. Evans, Wyatt, D. E. King, and Brady were Jesse's main protectors in terms of the black church (he was still not ordained), the business leaders showed their gratitude by providing Jesse, Jackie, and their growing family with a nice house, a car, and sustenance beyond his very mod-est SCLC salary. These entrepreneurs also bought the radio time for the live Saturday broadcasts on WVON. Their support gave Jesse total independence from the Daley machine, thus allowing him to be a free voice to deal with all things related to black Chicago and indeed black America. As Jesse said years later, there was "a kind of genius" in this development.[43] I don't think we SC pastors understood how valuable this new support base was to Jesse and to Breadbasket as a whole.

Black Expos

> Expo made room under one big tent for all these forces (economic, cultural, and political) to come together. —Rev. Jesse Jackson

One of the most exciting expansions of Breadbasket was Black Expo. Like the biblical parable of a tiny mustard seed becoming a gigantic tree reaching the heavens, the meeting of a dozen black businessmen with Rev. Jackson in the fall of 1966 led to the first Black Minorities Business and Cultural Exposition, which was attended by an estimated five hundred thousand peo-ple in October 1969!

The Expo idea surfaced unexpectedly at a staff meeting in 1969. As Hermene Hartman remembers the discussion, Jesse said that we needed something to give "exposure" to our black products and services. Someone said, "That's it. An exposition!" As they began to flesh out the idea another person voiced the worry that six weeks was too short a time. Jesse replied, "We can do it." At a later session Jesse noted, "We've got all this stuff now. What if nobody comes?" There had been little coverage of the upcoming event in the downtown newspapers, so a phone bank was set up and calls were made to all Breadbasket contacts, community groups, social clubs, businesspeople, and churches. Thousands of flyers were distributed. City permits were secured at the last minute.[44] The sc was simply informed of this new project and asked to drum up support in our congregations.

Black Expo was really an expansion of Saturday Breadbasket, and together they garnered widespread attention. The inaugural Expo took place on the weekend of October 3, 4, and 5, 1969, with massive crowds filling Chicago's old International Amphitheatre to partake of exhibits and floor shows "exposing black business and expressing black culture." At the opening event, Mayors Richard Hatcher of Gary and Carl Stokes of Cleveland joined Revs. Jackson and Evans and other Breadbasket clergy in cutting a white rope with a black ax. This was to suggest snipping the umbilical cord of a subservient economic community and opening the way to a new independent economic reality.[45]

Leading up to the Expo, Breadbasket's North Shore chapter held a rally in Highland Park attended by a salt-and-pepper audience of 350 people. This event included a potluck dinner, Rev. Ed Riddick sharing the Expo dream, and dancing with the Breadbasket Orchestra. "The air at Temple Solel was alive and electric with a kind of warmth and communication that comes, people to people, when suffering is understood because suffering has been endured," wrote Connie Seals in the *Defender*.[46]

At the Expo, the four hundred exhibitors included an array of black-owned services and black producers. Covenanted corporations, like Jewel and A&P, offered displays, as did Sears and Walgreen, with which we were in early negotiations. Cultural exhibits pictured famous African Americans but also Native Americans and Latinos. With the theme "I Am Somebody," a Breadbasket booth pictured the Black Christmas and Easter parades and the Illinois hunger caravan. One large white display board had this message:

black ball
black book
black boy
black eye
black Friday
black hand
black heart
black jack
black magic

black mail
black market
black mark
black sambo
white lies
black is **beautiful**[47]

Governor Richard Ogilvie, Treasurer Stevenson, and other politicos also attended the Expo. At Saturday Breadbasket, held at the Expo site, Jesse told eight thousand attendees how moved he was by the presence of thousands of black children who had come on field trips to experience their history and to see models of black success. Rounding out the Expo were six stage shows. Joining the Breadbasket Orchestra and Choir were such luminaries as Mahalia Jackson, Bill Cosby, Aretha Franklin, Cannonball Adderley, LeRoi Jones (later Amiri Baraka), B. B. King, Muddy Waters, the Staple Singers, and Martha and the Vandellas.

One evening during Expo, Blackstone Ranger leader Jeff Fort and his right-hand man, Leonard Sengali, interrupted a staff meeting and demanded a share of the take, saying they had provided security for Saturday Breadbasket for months and were due a share of the money pouring into Expo. They were heard out amid a quiet tension, but no response was given them on that occasion.[48]

On Sunday evening, as the throngs moved into the last stage show, hundreds of people had to be turned away at the door because of fire regulations. In the final moments the crowd sang "Happy Birthday" to Jesse, who would be twenty-eight years old on Wednesday, October 8.[49] In the words of the *Stax Fax* editors, "Black Expo 1969 was an overwhelming success and it's only the beginning of many more to come."[50] Underscoring the success, Mayor Stokes invited Jesse and Breadbasket to help organize a similar Black Expo in Cleveland. It was suggested that Breadbasket might bring this experience to other major centers with large black populations in the country.[51] As Rev. Jackson reflected more recently: "Expo made room under one big tent for all these forces (economic, cultural, and political) to come together."[52]

The second annual Black Expo, in November 1970, reached some six hundred thousand people over four days with the theme "Harambee," a Swahili word for "pulling together." Admission to the Amphitheatre event was $1.00, with a separate ticket required for the nightly entertainment. Some eight thousand folks attended each evening to hear Cannonball Adderley, Bill Cosby, Roberta Flack, Flip Wilson, B. B. King, Redd Foxx, Stevie Wonder, and the Breadbasket Orchestra and Choir.

The opening ribbon cutting was a spirited affair with Revs. Jackson and Evans; Illinois lieutenant governor Paul Simon; Mayor Hatcher of Gary, Indiana; other politicians and celebrities; and representatives from SCLC Breadbasket chapters in Georgia, New York, Texas, and New Jersey. In the afternoons thousands of schoolchildren viewed the 450 exhibits. Expo '70 added displays on the contributions of black people globally, with paintings on loan from the DuSable Museum, as well as poetry and historical writings. Jesse spoke enthusiastically: "Black Expo is our Mecca. . . . Black college students are there to portray the beauty of blackness."[53] One brochure stated that Black Expo is "black people in dialogue with themselves and the larger community."[54]

Out of Expo '70 two projects emerged: a short-lived Institute of Black American Music and a nationwide political network for future elections. While the current Breadbasket boycott of National Food Stores was shockingly ignored, voter registration booths were busy with hundreds of adults signing up in anticipation of the spring 1971 mayoral primary.[55]

Jesse reflected on Expo '70 in his *Defender* column: "Somewhere between the twilight of expectation and the noonday of realization we who are of many walks of life and a rainbow riot of colors can experience real community."[56] As Black Expo "grew like Topsy," more money came in than expected. But resentment simmered among Breadbasket business leaders who had given their hearts, souls, and cash to the Expo—and then learned that most proceeds were sent to the SCLC in Atlanta.[57]

Preparing for its third annual Black Expo in October 1971, Breadbasket secured free advertising and public relations services from some of the premier corporations in America. "All we had to do was ask," said Expo's coordinator, Richard Thomas. A glossy program included pictures, a schedule of events, and a complete list of the business and cultural booths.[58]

The anticipation leading up to the Expo was sweetly rewarded at the opening breakfast when Rev. Jackson received a surprise "soul handshake" from Mayor Richard J. Daley before five hundred business and civic leaders. In his talk, coined "Wednesday Sermon" by the *Chicago Tribune*, Jesse compared the current economic woes of the black community to the post–World War II situation in Germany and Japan when those countries rejected a welfare economy in favor of the tough work of reconstruction, aided by the Marshall Plan. "We do not want a welfare state. We have the potential. We can produce. We can feed ourselves." Jesse indicated that while blacks in Chicago spent $4.7 billion in 1970, most of their consumer dollars went out of the community. "The black community must be treated as an underdeveloped nation." Jesse called for no handouts, but instead asked simply for investment capital and a relaxation of business barriers.[59]

The *Chicago Tribune*, a conservative-leaning newspaper, declared that Jesse "showed a mature recognition of the reality that the most important problem facing the black community is economic." If Jesse "sticks to this course, and can persuade both blacks and whites that it is the right one, it should lead him a long way. It is the American course, and if given a fair chance it can work."[60]

Twenty-five thousand people jammed the Amphitheatre for the opening ceremony, where dignitaries tied together black, green, and red ribbons symbolizing African heritage with a white ribbon symbolizing the coming together of blacks and whites in business and in community. Regarding Black Expo's themes, Jesse intoned, "Not only is Black Expo a memorial to Dr. King, but it is 'Harambee,' a time for black people to come together, to come home to Mecca to work together to build a new nation."[61] The crowds then moved through the cultural, historical, and product displays; attended seminars such as "The Politics of '72" with Cleveland's Carl Stokes; took classes from the Institute of Black American Music; sat in on an athletic workshop led by Jackie Robinson and the Boston Celtics' Bill Russell; and listened to political leaders from emerging African nations.[62]

Thousands of children (sixty thousand free tickets were distributed at schools) attended two performances of the *Sesame Street* cast, featuring Big Bird, Susan, Roosevelt Franklin, and the Cookie Monster. At the last minute, the Jackson Five from Gary, Indiana, was added to the children's program, and the crowds pushed through a steel door in their passion to hear them. Michael Jackson and his siblings arrived at the stage by ambulance![63]

One evening Roy Wilkins, the executive director of the NAACP, received the first annual Dr. Martin Luther King Jr. Humanitarian Award to extended cheers and many tears from the thirteen thousand attendees. Then came the entertainers: Stevie Wonder, Cannonball Adderley, Aretha Franklin, Billy Eckstine, Albertina Walker and the Caravans, Ossie Davis and Ruby Dee, and Kim Weston singing "Lift Every Voice." Different performers took the stage on successive evenings: B. B. King, Roberta Flack, the Jackson Five, the Temptations, Odetta, Sarah Vaughan, Bill Cosby, and Chicago's own Oscar Brown Jr. among them. On Saturday three thousand people jammed Dr. King's Workshop for weekly Breadbasket. On Sunday Rep. Shirley Chisholm challenged eight hundred women to "get this country set right again," appealing for both black and white support in her presidential bid.[64]

Black Expo '71, five days in length with more than four hundred booths and an attendance pushing seven hundred thousand, was hailed as a "roaring success" by Breadbasket officials and as a wonderful cultural and community event by all who participated. A few days after it closed, Rev. Jackson announced that the Expo had netted $200,000, which would be used for

Breadbasket's Chicago programs.[65] *Defender* columnist Charlie Cherokee wrote bluntly, "Black Expo '71 was organized to help promote black business and it was itself a business and financial success. If the Rev. Ralph D. Abernathy runs short of dough at SCLC headquarters, Chicago's Operation Breadbasket is in a position to make him a loan. The Rev. Jesse L. Jackson may or may not reach the pinnacle of popular acclaim that the Rev. Martin Luther King enjoyed but he is the best American promoter since Mike Todd."[66]

On the closing day *Tribune* columnist Vernon Jarrett had raised a key question: "Now what comes after Black Expo? . . . Will more people be buying Parker House Sausage because of Black Expo? Will more big chain stores thru-out the city stock Parker House products and permit their proper display?" He gave his own answer: "First the black consumers must seek out and do business with black people. . . . Secondly, those powerful individuals and corporations that control the distribution of goods and finances will have to look at black consumers and businessmen as people—not quantities to be placated during riotous summers."[67]

Hermene Hartman participated in the first discussion about a Black Expo and then proceeded to work all three Expos. As the cultural chair of Expo '71 she helped select and contact entertainers and arrange cultural displays. Her life's career was launched, and later she served ten years on the Kennedy Center board in Washington, D.C. As of this writing, she publishes Chicago's cultural weekly magazine *N'Digo*. Hermene was a key volunteer, a stalwart staffer, and an important recipient of Breadbasket's imprint.[68]

Breadbasket's Black Expos were the model for similar expositions in Cleveland, Indianapolis, New York, and Los Angeles. Indeed, the Indiana Black Expo, first organized in 1970, "has been a pillar of the African American community for decades as a year-round multifaceted community service organization" centered in Indianapolis.[69]

Breadbasket Chapter Efforts

Dr. King had made another effort to nationalize the Chicago template at the annual SCLC staff retreat in January 1968. He appointed Calvin Morris to be the associate director for Chicago and Rev. Ed Riddick to be the national research director, freeing Jesse to work nationally. Dr. King stated that with these outstanding men "we are stepping up our aggressive campaign under the able direction of Rev. Jackson." Jesse added, "No major industry in this country can withstand the pressure of pickets effectively marching simultaneously when Breadbasket is organized nationwide in as many as 50 cities. Anyone whose margin of profit is located in the ghetto is subject to our national drive."[70]

Jesse named several target cities, began his cross-country work in Greensboro, North Carolina, and then moved on to Los Angeles, helping organize and train Breadbasket chapters. Then, as quick as he had been off, Jesse was back in Chicago. Even Doc got exasperated and charged Jesse with focusing on his own "little kingdom" in Chicago.[71]

Breadbasket made yet another attempt to spark a national effort with an orientation for ministers held in Miami, Florida, in February 1968. The plan was for ten ministers from each of fifteen major cities to organize local networks with conveners hosting weekly meetings "for study, discussion, learning, planning and executing programs."[72] Nationally, the group targeted Lorillard, a major tobacco firm that produced the well-known cigarettes Newport, True, and Old Gold. With 6,403 employees, Lorillard had production plants in Greensboro, North Carolina, and Louisville, Kentucky, and headquarters in New York City. Fourteen SCLC pastors led by Jesse Jackson met with Lorillard and demanded job data. Like our Chicago model, the meeting evolved into a Sunday school–like seminar on corporate responsibility. A second meeting, scheduled for April 8, was postponed upon the assassination of Dr. King on April 4, 1968.

When the negotiations resumed with Lorillard Tobacco Company in Washington, D.C., on May 20, Breadbasket's demands for economic justice were "quickly dismissed as an indication of naiveté or lack of business sense on the part of the ministers. The concept of compensatory justice was completely foreign to them [the company's executives]." Top Lorillard officials argued that their "union contracts were binding and that little could be done about it."[73] Realizing the enormity of the opposition from this New York–based corporation, the Breadbasket team withdrew its demands for jobs and negotiated a few less-threatening items—the use of black services and a change in some company policies—on which agreement was reached a few days later. This baptism into national negotiating was a sobering experience for the Chicago bunch.[74]

During the summer of 1968, the Breadbasket staff produced a major packet of materials to guide the development of Breadbasket chapters, called "outposts."[75] Breadbasket had, however, too few staff available to organize these chapters, and a national structure never really materialized. Some support for the three-month struggle with A&P came from Indianapolis, Cincinnati, Philadelphia, New York, and Madison, Wisconsin, but no national negotiations took place. Covenants were signed only in Chicago and Indianapolis.[76] Rev. Morris admitted, "All the newspapers gave us credit for about thirty Breadbasket chapters across the country, but most of them were SCLC chapters. About the only strong chapters Breadbasket had outside of Chicago were in New York and Cleveland."[77]

In July 1969, New York Breadbasket secured an agreement with Pepsi-Cola that promised to hire more blacks and Puerto Ricans and "increase its support of minority-operated suppliers, including financial institutions," adding $8 million of income into minority communities.[78]

In October, Rev. Jackson led a delegation to Brooklyn for the ceremonial opening of its chapter office. Jesse declared, "From the Chicago prototype of Operation Breadbasket has come the understanding that power is derived from a community of persons working collectively toward a common goal.... We not only want jobs, but we are opting for involvement in the decision-making apparatus in industry. The issue is not merely employment but empowerment."[79] The Brooklyn chapter had already negotiated successful agreements with Pepsi-Cola, Metropolitan Bottling, and May's Department Store and was in talks with Sealtest Dairy and Canada Dry. Rev. Morris remembers meeting a young Al Sharpton for the first time on that trip. Sharpton was head of the Youth Division of the Brooklyn chapter.[80]

In February 1970, the Cleveland chapter won an agreement with radio station WJMO that opened several positions for black staff. The Los Angeles chapter was rejuvenated with the help of Breadbasket supporter and advocate Bill Cosby. Accompanying Rev. Jackson on his travels were loyal companions St. Clair Booker and then Richard Thomas. Thomas remembered one occasion when he and Jesse stopped in Las Vegas on the way to LA at the request of Sammy Davis Jr., who wanted Jesse to help with a script that required a preacher's feel. With the job finished, they were leaving the hotel when Bill Cosby spotted them, calling out, "Country preacher." Cosby declared, "You look shabby, Jesse," and handed him several cards with contacts at clothing stores in LA. Cosby asked Thomas to take Jesse around to these specialty stores to build up his wardrobe, as befitted a leader of his stature. Cosby gave Thomas the cash to implement this wish. In such ways, people showed their love and care for Jesse.[81]

In October 1971, the New York chapter secured what was descibed as a "moral covenant" with Bohack Corporation, the city's largest food chain. Bohack agreed to double its black employees from 7 percent to 14 percent within six months and to invest 15 percent of its gross income in black banks and other enterprises. With the company's six thousand employees and annual sales of $300 million from 168 supermarkets in the area, this agreement had enormous potential. But specifics were absent, and discrepancies were noticeable in both employment and sales numbers. Nevertheless, Rev. William Jones of New York Breadbasket declared, "Bohack agrees to return to the black community a share proportionate to what blacks contribute in sales and profits." He added that Bohack was the twelfth New York–based corporation to covenant with the New York Breadbasket chapter.[82]

Beyond limited agreements in a few cities, however, Breadbasket's national network stalled. King's vision of taking on a General Motors or a Kellogg's went into a deep freeze after Memphis. During the Breadbasket years Jesse's heart and soul were reserved for his Chicago base. Ironically, it was only after Jesse broke with the SCLC and inaugurated Operation PUSH that a truly national effort emerged to carry on Dr. King's dream for a national Breadbasket program.

CHAPTER 6

INTERRUPTION

He was for equality, for all the people, you and me,
Full of love and good will, hate was not his way.
He was not a violent man; tell me folks if you can,
Just Why, Why was he shot down the other day?
—Nina Simone, "King of Love"

In February 1968, I was in Washington, D.C., to talk with members of Congress about the war in Vietnam in a two-day action led by Clergy and Laity Concerned (CALC). Martin Luther King Jr. was a founder of CALC. On the second day we planned to walk to Arlington National Cemetery where Dr. King would speak. I never made it. As I was stirring on the morning of February 6, the phone rang in my hotel room. It was my wife, Peg, saying she was in labor, please come home. It was the early arrival of our third child. A friend drove me to the airport, and I flew home to Chicago that morning, missing one of Dr. King's most powerful messages against the war. I never saw Dr. King again.

Memphis

We are asking you tonight, to go out and tell your neighbors not to buy
Coca-Cola in Memphis. Go by and tell them not to buy Sealtest milk.
Tell them not to buy ... Wonder Bread.—Martin Luther King Jr.,
"Mountaintop" speech

In March, racial tensions escalated dangerously in Memphis, Tennessee, during a prolonged strike by the city's black garbage workers. On Saturday, March 30, Dr. King called his SCLC staff into a special session in Atlanta to discuss the crisis in Memphis and the Poor People's Campaign. In Chicago Jesse had received a phone call late Friday evening from Rev. Ralph Abernathy telling him to take the next flight to Atlanta for the emergency session. When Jesse arrived, he remembers, everyone in the room seemed tired. Jesse took close notes of what would turn out to be a historic meeting of Dr. King with his SCLC staff colleagues.[1]

Dr. King began, "I've had a migraine headache for four days from a lot of pressure and some attacks. It is clear we are split on the campaign. We are charged without having a game plan." Andy Young interjected, "Doc, it's going to work out." King countered, "Andy, be quiet. Don't say peace, peace, when there is no peace. Let me make my case." Dr. King made his pitch for continuing the Poor People's Campaign. Jesse recalls that he and James Bevel kept asking, "Where's the hook?" The goals of securing a change in national values and an economic bill of rights were too diffuse; a concrete target was needed. Frustrated and hurt, King kept insisting that they must proceed.[2]

At this point, Jesse remembers, some staffers had fallen asleep. King continued:

> Well, I've thought about quitting. We've had a good run for twelve years now.
> I could take the presidency of Morehouse College and write some books. Then
> I thought that maybe . . . but that won't work and if I stop now I thought of
> people like Frederick Douglass and Sojourner Truth and how they persevered.
> I thought also about fasting and praying, and maybe Stokely [Carmichael],
> Rap Brown, Floyd [McKissick], Roy [Wilkins], Whitney [Young], Bayard
> [Rustin], and the others will come to my bedside at the point of death and we
> can unify our struggle. . . . We've got to turn a minus into a plus.[3]

Discussion was intense over the proposed Washington campaign:

> Bevel was mad because it was not his idea. Hosea Williams couldn't get voter
> registration off his mind. I was caught up with the "eternality of Breadbasket."
> And King persisted in demanding non-violence, saying he would write out
> a final salary check to anyone who would not hold the line. He left the room.
> The staff struggled and prayed. King came back in to find they had all united
> behind him. These disciples, like Jesus' disciples, got hung up again and again
> on their own plans and ideas. It took the spiritual and soul leadership of
> Dr. King to bring them together around his total vision, his dream, his sense
> of redemptive non-violent love.[4]

The session concluded when Doc summed up, "I think we need to fast and pray and then move on to Memphis."[5]

Jesse was reminded of Jesus in the garden of Gethsemane with the disciples asleep around him, and Jesus asking, "Let this cup pass from me. Yet, not my will but thine be done." In Jesse's memory King simply "preached himself out of depression."[6] It was strikingly similar to an experience I had had with King, under yet another death threat, preaching himself into faith at a Friday Breadbasket meeting in Chicago some months earlier.

Rev. Jackson remembers how, in one of the last staff meetings, he pushed Dr. King to broaden the fight in Memphis. Jesse urged a boycott of key consumer products in order to bring some of Memphis's economic power elites into the struggle and to challenge them to join in support of the thirteen hundred striking garbage workers. Jesse suggested, "Let us redistribute the pain. Right now it's all on the garbage workers." Dr. King mulled it over.[7]

Dr. King and his staff flew back to the boiling cauldron that was Memphis. In the early evening of April 3, Doc was resting at the motel when he received an urgent phone call from Abernathy, who was at a mass meeting for the garbage workers at Mason Temple. A rainy night had limited the crowd to about two thousand.[8] Nevertheless, Ralph told Dr. King that the people at the rally were all excited, waiting and expecting Dr. King. Ralph urged King to come over and at least make an appearance. King said, "I'll come." At the rally, Ben Hooks, Jesse Jackson, and Ralph Abernathy each took the mic to speak, using up time until Dr. King arrived. Ralph gave King a long introduction, and then King spoke his last public words.[9]

This famous sermon is remembered for its stirring mountaintop vision. All but forgotten is some of the remarkable content, including King's call for a Breadbasket-style boycott to help "redistribute the pain. . . . Now the other thing we'll have to do is this: Always anchor our external action with the power of economic withdrawal." King reminded the crowd that while many blacks are individually poor, they are collectively "richer than all the nations in the world, with the exception of nine." He continued that this was not a time for cursing and Molotov cocktails, but a time to go to the massive industries of the country and say, "We've come by here to ask you to make the first item on your agenda fair treatment, where God's children are concerned. Now, if you are not prepared to do that, we do have an agenda that we must follow. And our agenda calls for withdrawing economic support from you."[10]

King then appealed to his audience, "We are asking you tonight, to go out and tell your neighbors not to buy Coca-Cola in Memphis. Go by and tell them not to buy Sealtest milk. Tell them not to buy—what is the other bread?—Wonder Bread. And what is the other bread company, Jesse? Tell them not to buy Hart's bread. As Jesse Jackson has said, up to now, only the garbage men have been feeling the pain; now we must kind of redistribute the pain. . . . Then we can move on downtown and tell Mayor [Henry] Loeb to do what is right."

King asked the audience to help strengthen black institutions, to put their money in Tri-State Bank and in black insurance companies. "Now these are some practical things we can do. We begin the process of building a greater economic base. And at the same time, we are putting pressure where it really hurts. I ask you to follow through here. . . . Now, let me say as I move to my conclusion that we've got to give ourselves to this struggle until the end.

Nothing would be more tragic than to stop at this point, in Memphis. We've got to see it through." But there was a tragedy. Dr. King's call for a boycott to share the garbage workers' pain died with him hours later on the Lorraine Motel's balcony.

A Diary of Shattered Dreams

April 4, Thursday Our family had just finished dinner, about 6:30 p.m., when I received the shocking news by phone from Rev. Merlyn Northfelt, the aide to our Methodist bishop: "Dr. King has been shot." No sooner had I called my widowed mother to share the awful word than the doorbell rang, and parishioners began to arrive and gather in our living room, weeping quietly. My son Andrew, then just five and a half years old, remembers our living room filling up with folks crying and moaning on each other's shoulders, as he stayed in the back playroom. After a time, I put on my clerical collar and went out into the neighborhood to commiserate with my neighbors. The mood was simply sadness and grief. The West Side was already erupting in violence, but the South Side held calm. My parishioners were worried for me, their white pastor, but I felt secure with a clerical collar in my own parish. It was a long, largely sleepless night in my home and across much of the nation.[11]

My Breadbasket colleague Rev. John Porter heard the news of King's assassination while in his study at Christ Methodist Church in all-black Englewood. He was "stunned" and began to cry and pray. He walked over to his parsonage next door to share the tragic news with his wife, June. The doorbell rang, and John opened the door to David Barksdale, the twenty-three-year-old head of the Devil Disciples gang. David announced, "We suicide squad," and he and his buddies were prepared to burn down the Englewood shopping hub at 63rd and Halsted. Rev. Porter reminded David that he had played pool with Dr. King in the church basement and asked, "What would Dr. King say"? The young man quickly withdrew his threat and left. There was one small fire in Woodlawn, but the South Side mercifully avoided any major violence.[12]

My closest friend and co-worker in Breadbasket, Rev. Gerald Forshey, another white pastor serving a black congregation, reflected on those moments some days later: "The murder of Dr. King hit me hard. I was at the church [St. Luke's Methodist] when I heard of it, and I rushed home so as not to provoke any violence. All during that night, I could feel an acute sense of loss. Mixed in with my self-hatred for being white, were emotions concerning my safety, the loss of being able to talk to the younger elements in the community, the demise of Breadbasket to violent reactions, the certain deaths of numbers of black people in our cities."[13]

Rev. Calvin Morris remembered: "We were stunned. I was at a meeting at the Wabash Y[MCA] with Ed [Riddick] and Willie [Barrow] when we heard the news. We went back to the office and wept. Except for Willie. She chastened us for crying and said this was no time for that. So, we got busy and went into overdrive to deal with our grief."[14]

My wife's cousin (via a North Carolina plantation) Eleta "Cookie" Murray recalls the death of Dr. King when she was a teenager on Chicago's South Side:

> I'm 14 years old and I'm getting ready to attend a wake for a girl, age 14, who had died of pneumonia. I am not in a good mood and it's raining. Death is a complete mystery to me. Why should a child have to die? Just as I'm about to leave the house, I hear my mother give out a sob. Someone has just shot and killed Dr. King.
>
> The wake turned out to be for two people that night. Only, there was just one body in the casket. Like the rest of America, and just like on November 22, 1963, we stayed glued to the television. My mother was teary. My father was very angry and hurt. My brother and sister could not understand why someone would do something so terrible to such a good man. I, being the eldest child, knew better than to ask such a question. I was innocent about most things, but not about this.
>
> The next day at Morgan Park High School, all hell broke out. It was not pretty. Fights broke out on campus and on the street. The white kids were terrified and the black ones were just plain angry, hurt and discouraged. No one joined hands and sang "We Shall Overcome." This was Chicago—the Almighty Segregated Chicago. We're talking about 1968! Morgan Park had an integrated student body since Day 1. So what. In all honesty, the only [mixed] group of kids who were brave enough to speak to each other were those in music and sports. We were the only ones who would even attempt to dialogue. A group of us went to the principal's office and demanded that the flag be put at half-staff. This was the age of walkouts. We left school early and we didn't ask for permission.[15]

Cookie was deeply moved by Dr. King's assassination and, like many other young people, she began to attend Saturday Breadbasket. Before long she was hooked, joining Breadbasket Youth, carrying picket signs in the A&P campaign, accompanying Rev. Ma Houston to the county jail. She even became a babysitter for Jesse and Jackie's three young children, Santita, Jesse Jr., and Jonathan.[16]

April 5, Friday   I began immediately to plan for a memorial service that evening, an opportunity for the community to share grief, to comfort one another, and to declare our faith. My lay leader, Jim Barnes, was on the West Side, serving as a staff member of Newberry Center, our church's social service agency, which sat in the eye of the human hurricane. He was in the streets seeking to redirect the anger of youths in the midst of a growing riot, just as he had done in the West Side protest in 1966. He had also participated in the sit-ins in Greensboro, North Carolina, as a student at North Carolina A&T in 1960–1961. I phoned him for an update, and then asked him to please come back home long enough to sing "Precious Lord" at our service. He consented. My own grief was worked out that first day in planning, telephoning, preparing leaflets, and prayer.

The flyer we distributed across the parish was a mimeographed eight-by-eleven sheet run off over the old blue-green stencil, on which I had carved in my own hand:

Memorial Service
Tonight
8 P.M.
at
Gresham Church
in Memory of
Our Leader
MARTIN LUTHER KING

The little church, seating about 250 souls, was packed. We opened by singing the powerful words of a Welsh hymn, "Guide me, O thou great Jehovah, / Pilgrim through this barren land / I am weak, but Thou art mighty / Hold me with Thy powerful hand." After the psalter, Jim Barnes sang a heart-rending "Precious Lord." The Beatitudes were read, and we sang "Nearer, My God, to Thee." Rev. Earl Simmons, a Breadbasket colleague, gave the eulogy, which was followed by my own meditation:

> We are stunned, shocked, hurt, angry, empty, apprehensive. Our leader has been struck down. His life has been offered up on the Cross of Humanity, Decency, Justice, Brotherhood, Equality. . . . Our comfort is found in the fact that he was prepared, that he was doing the will of God as it confronted him. . . . Once again God's love has given us a son, a follower, a disciple of his way. And while shocked, we need not be surprised. For this is the way life is. This is the cost of discipleship.
>
> We are now at a loss: where do we go? . . . We need to stand united in the purposes for which Dr. King died. We dare not sit back, but rather rise up as people united, as a black community, as Americans, for justice and brotherhood, so that our children may be free and may experience the fullness of humanity.[17]

After the prayers, we held hands and sang "We Shall Overcome." Jim Barnes left immediately to get back to his crisis mediation in the volcanic rioting on the West Side.

April 6, Saturday   The regular Saturday Breadbasket service/rally had been moved to St. James Methodist Church at 46th and Ellis to accommodate the expected crowd. The church was jam-packed, with people standing along the walls. The host pastor, Rev. Phil Harley, opened with a welcome and invocation. Rev. D. E. King, the godfather of Dr. King, read the Beatitudes. Rev. Claude Wyatt prayed. Rev. Clay Evans gave a short meditation stressing King's well-known comment that it is not how long we live, but how well. He mentioned that Methuselah lived 950 years, Jesus 33 years, and Dr. King 39 years, paralleling the thirty-nine books of the Bible. Evans declared that Martin Luther King's principles would live forever.[18]

Calvin Morris introduced Jesse Jackson, concluding: "Our fallen leader has left us with disciples. We stand hopeful and grateful that the work goes on through these disciples. May our hearts be open to hear the Word from this disciple, our leader." Jesse began by expressing gratitude to be alive. He stated the reasons Dr. King had gone to Memphis, adding that Doc told a Memphis rally, "You are not garbage men, but men who pick up garbage. . . . Everyone deserves a job or income." Dr. King said that we are going to Washington, D.C., to tell the nation about this fundamental need. "For Martin this was a level of concern for all people, beyond color." Jesse noted that President Franklin D. Roosevelt had said there should be a ceiling to what anyone makes and that Dr. King said there should be a base income for everyone. Jesse reminded the crowd that Dr. King had met the previous Saturday with poor folks from across the nation in preparation for the Poor People's Campaign. This campaign would now be delayed, but it must go on.[19]

Jesse recalled King's moving "Mountaintop" speech of Wednesday evening, April 3, when, although not scheduled to speak, he had responded to the pleading of Ralph Abernathy. It was a speech the whole world would now hear. Jesse concluded by saying, "There are two types of memorials: to look sad and pitiful, or to change our behavior and act differently tomorrow."[20] It was a fitting tribute to Jesse's mentor and role model. After singing the movement hymn, we all left uplifted and comforted, many of us clergy returning to our parishes to prepare Palm Sunday sermons for the next day. Rev. Forshey remembers that "by Breadbasket service Saturday morning I was still unable to put together a sermon, but Jesse Jackson and that crowd *celebrated* the death of Dr. King. He reached deep in my life and rekindled the hope that lay dormant there. He spoke the Gospel demanding that I pick up my death as Dr. King had done with his, and when I did that, life came back to me."[21]

Later that afternoon I phoned Lee Smith, the vice president of Jewel, with whom I worked closely on Jewel-Breadbasket follow-up. I reached him at his home in suburban Barrington, and he listened as I described the conditions on the West Side. The fact was, I told him, that most of the food stores in the area had been looted and/or burned and that a food shortage was developing rapidly in the stricken area. I asked him to help get food trucked into the area. He reminded me that most Jewel Food semitruck drivers were white and would be unsafe driving in the riot areas. I agreed to drive members of my Methodist Youth Fellowship out to Oak Park, meet his trucks, and have a black youth sit next to each white driver as they went into the still-smoldering West Side. We agreed to meet at Austin and Washington Boulevards on Wednesday morning, April 10. He would provide eight semis of food; I would bring eight black teenagers.[22]

April 7, Palm Sunday In my sermon that morning I asked: "Were you there when they crucified my Lord? And when King came to Chicago? Or along his route to crucifixion?" And I concluded:

> King has raised the level of humanity, elevated the image of God in us humans toward the noblest. . . . Martin Luther King is not important in himself and he understood this. He is important as he points to what it means to be human. . . . His Gethsemane, his Jerusalem, his Golgotha are signs of human-ness, of reality. He reminds us that all is possible and he demonstrated for us a man among men. Glory hallelujah. Will we be there?[23]

April 8, Holy Monday I made preparations for traveling to Atlanta on Tuesday for Dr. King's funeral, called teenagers for the Wednesday "excur-sion" to the West Side, and led a funeral for a devoted church member. At the same hour, a memorial march, estimated at fifty thousand people, took place in Memphis, led by Coretta King and three of the King children, Revs. Ralph Abernathy and Andy Young, Rosa Parks, Bayard Rustin, Harry Belafonte, Benjamin Spock, Walter Reuther, and Jesse Jackson.

That same day the *Defender* reported Breadbasket efforts to end the rioting on the West Side. Rev. Earl Simmons, who had joined me at Gresham in the April 5 memorial service, was quoted speaking to the youth:

> Keep the peace. We of the Chicago Breadbasket will still follow our leader in non-violence. . . . Let us refrain from all attacks upon our community; let us look to God who is able to answer every individual need. Let us mourn sor-rowfully the death of Dr. Martin Luther King—that non-violence be accom-plished in his death as it was in [his] life. Remember, these are our windows you are breaking, our neighborhoods you would be destroying. The fact is we can't even have an opportunity to repair what can so easily be torn down. Stand tall, fellow citizens, hold your heads up high, the end is not yet. We still seek peace, freedom, jobs and education and a better life for poor people. Keep the peace.[24]

It had been four days since Dr. King's death, and the West Side was still in flames. Hundreds of fires were reported, twenty buildings were burned to the ground in a three-mile stretch (2000–4800 West Madison Street), and sixty businesses were destroyed from 3200 to 3800 West Roosevelt Road. Twelve people were dead, 28 people lay in Cook County Hospital in critical condition, hundreds more were injured, and 365 people had been arrested, including 47 juveniles. Mobs swarmed along Roosevelt and Madison Streets looting everything from liquor and food to appliances and furniture. Bricks from damaged buildings fell on parked cars, and fire trucks had difficulty maneuvering around debris in the streets. Damage was expected to be in the millions of dollars.[25] Chicago's experience was just one of hundreds of violent outbursts around the nation.

Shockingly, the story of Chicago's 1968 West Side uprising has never been told adequately. Daley's shoot-to-kill order (kill arsonists and maim looters) has been glossed over by historians, and the Daley Commission's recommendations on the outbreak were ignored, except for a few police instructions on how to suppress further outbreaks.[26]

April 9, Holy Tuesday   I traveled to O'Hare Airport with Jim Barnes, taking his first real break from working the streets on the West Side. When we arrived for the chartered flight to Atlanta, the plane was filled to overflowing. When a stewardess told me to get off the plane, Jim stepped between us, insisting that I, his pastor, be allowed to go, and after a quick embrace with me he promptly exited the airplane. I was humbled by Jim many times, but never more so than when he gave up his precious seat to me that day.

On the airplane to Atlanta I joined up with my Breadbasket cohorts, including Jerry Forshey and other fellow Methodists. Once there, we walked side by side all day long. First to Ebenezer Baptist Church, where Daddy King was pastor and Martin Jr. co-pastor. We stood in a massive crowd on a high mound in a vacant lot just across the street, watching people from all over the United States and the world arriving by limo. Jerry described this scene as a "carnival outside."[27]

Mrs. Coretta King and three of her children along with Harry Belafonte and several SCLC aides were the first to arrive. Foreign dignitaries walked in with politicians, celebrities, and local members of the Ebenezer congregation. The U.S. group was led by Vice President Hubert Humphrey and included the Kennedy brothers Bobby, just two months before his own assassination, and Ted; President John F. Kennedy's widow, Jacqueline; presidential candidate Richard Nixon; UN ambassador Ralph Bunche; and Supreme Court justice Thurgood Marshall. Standing in the hot sun for the more than two-hour funeral we heard only snippets of the outside broadcast, a few words, singing of hymns, and bursts of applause.

Then began the long last march with Dr. King, as some two hundred thousand mourners of all ages and colors trudged behind Dr. King's body, which was carried on a wagon drawn by two mules. Among the pallbearers was Cirilo McSween, the Chicago Breadbasket business leader and SCLC treasurer. The mules were typically stubborn, and it took Chicago's own Rev. Clay Evans, who had grown up on a southern farm, to get them moving. It was a slow procession, taking us west across downtown Atlanta, past the state capitol building, and on to Morehouse College, King's alma mater. It was a peaceful and peace-filled march. Along the way, we sang many of the movement's freedom songs and spirituals, usually a spontaneous eruption in a small group of ten or twenty but in some cases swelling to a hundred or more voices, even thousands. We chanced to see and were able to embrace people we knew from several networks: peace groups, other civil rights groups, Chicago, relatives, fellow Methodists from all over the nation. It was a community, an extended family of many hues united in Dr. King's vision for America.

It seemed as though we were marching and singing for the last time. A sense of finality was palpable to me. In residential areas the locals waved at us, some offering water and sandwiches. The procession lasted almost three hours. At the tree-covered campus we heard a moving eulogy by Dr. Benjamin Mays, the president of Morehouse, which he delivered on the lawn to the surrounding thousands. His most penetrating comment was, "We all hope the assassin will be apprehended, but make no mistake, the American people are responsible." The assassin, Mays suggested, sensed that many people wanted King dead. "We too are guilty. . . . It is time for American people to repent and make democracy equally applicable to all Americans."[28] We also heard fragments of remarks by Rosa Parks and Revs. Joe Lowery and Andrew Young. Mahalia Jackson sang "Precious Lord" to the unmistakable sounds of wailing and crying among the crowd. Finally, Dr. King's casket was moved to a hearse for temporary burial in a nearby cemetery. It was late afternoon as we returned exhausted to the airport for our flight home.[29]

April 10, Holy Wednesday   I was up early. After the Saturday phone call with Lee Smith of Jewel, I had proceeded to get parental permission to have eight teenagers from our church assist Jewel in delivering food to the still-burning West Side. So, early Wednesday morning I sardined eight strapping teenagers into my old Chevy for the trip out to Austin and Washington Boulevards at the border between Chicago and Oak Park. In minutes our youths had climbed up into the cabs of the huge trucks. What a sight it was, these young black faces peering wide-eyed out the passenger windows and waving their hands, as their Jewel semitrucks pulled away, heading east and out of sight into a heartbroken and devastated community.

Several thousand loaves of bread and hundreds of cases of mixed foods were delivered to local churches, community centers, and the local YMCA. Later that day the semis returned empty, and the youths piled back into my car with wild stories to tell all the way back to Gresham. Jewel came through in the crisis because the company knew and trusted Breadbasket to assist in this humanitarian effort. We had reached beyond a covenant of words on paper to tablets written on the heart.[30]

Lee Smith sent me a detailed delivery report with an accompanying note: "Although we all regret the actions that brought about destruction of life and property in our community, I must say that we are proud of the part that Jewel people played in coming to the aid of those in need. I have received a number of letters from representatives of the respective agencies to whom we responded, stating their heartfelt appreciation and thanks. . . . I was particularly pleased to be able to respond to your needs."[31]

April 14, Easter Sunday   My homily on this special Sunday focused on the miracle of resurrection, beginning with the fact that the disciples of Jesus did not flee but returned, regrouped, and moved out to offer up their own lives. I concluded:

> The question comes now to you and me. Is this Resurrection experience
> to take place for Peter and James and John and Bartholomew, . . . and for
> Andy and Ralph and James and Hosea and Jesse only! Certainly not. The
> Resurrection happening must become a reality for each of us. . . . What kind of
> disciples will we be—Gethsemane types or Pentecost types? Old or new, scared
> and pitiful, or bold and courageous. Easter is a choice. The prophet says we
> may choose life or death. Therefore choose life![32]

The very next Sunday our Gresham congregation held its annual meeting "in memoriam" of a beloved church member, just deceased, and Dr. King. A young adult member, Rory Falconer, gave the Breadbasket report and concluded by saying, "I would like it to be known that Gresham Methodist Church supports Operation Breadbasket" by encouraging our members to "use and encourage others to use Negro products and services." He named several and asked our members to make a contribution of at least "10 cents per person each week, as a symbolic, regular support for a program of which we can be proud."[33]

Music was a great comfort in those sad days. It also carries and cradles our memories. Dr. King had invited the Breadbasket Orchestra to come to

Memphis and play at the garbage workers' rallies. King's "last request" was made when he leaned over the balcony at the motel to ask Ben Branch, who was standing below, to "play 'Precious Lord' real sweet" at the evening rally. On the album jacket of the recording made just days later, Jesse noted, "Until the making of this album, the orchestra was never able to fulfill Dr. King's request." In addition to "Precious Lord," the recording includes "If I Could Help Somebody," "Let Us Break Bread Together," "We Shall Overcome," "Motherless Child," and "Battle Hymn of the Republic."[34]

Looking back years later Rev. Calvin Morris recalls how shaken we all were. Jesse's actions at the time brought acrimony, which has lasted "forever." The SCLC staff was covenanted to silence until Coretta got to Memphis, but Jesse broke the covenant and spoke to the press in Memphis and back in Chicago. He wore the green turtleneck sweater with blood on it for days. The effect on Jesse was deep. He felt linked to this twentieth-century prophet and saw himself as the heir apparent. The effect on Operation Breadbasket was also immense. "We had an avalanche of people coming to us, out of guilt, anger, upset—people who admitted they had been lukewarm and now wanted to do something. We were swamped, inundated, and we had no apparatus in place to relate to these folks. People fell through the cracks. . . . King's death changed all of us."[35]

Regrouping and Reassessing

A reflective mood was present when the SC reconvened following King's death and the ensuing upheaval. The altered situation called for serious contemplation and reassessment. Jesse's remarks to the SC on April 26 were notable. While most of the Methodists, including Rev. Forshey and me, were in Dallas, Texas, attending the general conference of our newly formed United Methodist Church, David Wallace recorded Jesse's words:

> The meeting tomorrow [Saturday Breadbasket] will be held at the Salaam Restaurant, the restaurant owned by Muslims. The ministers and the people of Breadbasket are concerned about the unity of black people, and are interested in building bridges where others have attempted to divide us. In the meeting we will show that membership in Breadbasket is based upon a creative change in behavior. . . . In reassessing our job one thing that we cannot falter or compromise on is the conflict between black and white. This matter is a sickness of America that we are attempting to heal, and we cannot accept a black-white division. Our foundation must be deeper and more permanent. . . .
> *Negotiations for jobs must be accelerated, for black people need jobs.*
> *Breadbasket can never be identified only as developing black businesses. This*

means that the ministers must be prepared to move out in small groups for split-level negotiations, that is. For jobs on one level, and for business gains on the other. Rev. Wyatt is going to set up the jobs division in the office to work with people looking for jobs.[36]

The sentences that David emphasized suggested that Jesse wanted to restore balance between entrepreneurship and jobs, clearly good news to the Breadbasket ministers. With the aid of Gary Massoni's list of criteria for targets, the sc then developed a list of forty-five area businesses. Employment data were requested by letter, spreading a wide but thin net and hoping for a lucky catch. We were back to our bread-and-butter work.[37]

Two days later, Rev. Ralph Abernathy, King's successor at the SCLC, came to Chicago, preaching at Sunday morning, afternoon, and evening services, all of which were meant to convey a smooth transition of authority. Many Breadbasket ministers were present to welcome Abernathy at the 3 p.m. service at Mt. Pisgah Baptist Church. Jesse's public role had changed overnight with the death of his mentor. He was thrust, and thrust himself, into the position of heir apparent, speaking with increased confidence, if not audacity, on behalf of black people wherever he appeared.[38]

In the midst of the West Side rioting after Dr. King's death and responding to community entreaties, some of the city's youth gangs made a peace pact. The Blackstone Rangers helped to keep the South Side calm; the Disciples and Vice Lords established distribution centers for food and clothes donated from city and suburbs. However, these efforts did not end the gang problems, including teen shootings. The entertainer Oscar Brown Jr. addressed Saturday Breadbasket with a plea for adults to help stop the renewed gang warfare. "To those of you who say you believe in the Redeemer, I ask, what do you redeem if not your own youth? The kids who are out on the streets killing one another are our own youth." He asserted that the Rangers "are fighting for attention. They even have to write their name on your wall before you pay any attention to them." Brown praised Breadbasket and Jesse Jackson for efforts to show another way.[39]

At the national level, the last legacy of Dr. King was the Civil Rights Act of 1968, known as the Fair Housing Act. While this legislation had been close to passage, it was still being held hostage in the House Rules Committee, but within one week of King's death it passed both houses of Congress and was signed into law by President Lyndon Johnson. This landmark act has been called "King's last victory."[40] For us in Chicago, it was also a belated victory of the Chicago Freedom Movement's struggle for open housing to end slums and was a deferred twist to the compromised summit so often blamed on Dr. King.

Poor People's Campaign

> I can see nothing more basic in the life of an individual than to have a job or an income. . . . If people do not have jobs or income, they're deprived of life; they're deprived of liberty; and they're deprived of the pursuit of happiness.—Martin Luther King Jr., "Why We Must Go to Washington"

On December 4, 1967, Dr. King had announced what came to be his final campaign. It was, in reality, an extension of Operation Breadbasket's success and vision from the private to the public sphere. The SCLC would "lead waves of the nation's poor and disinherited to Washington, D.C. next spring to demand redress of their grievances by the United States government and to secure at least jobs or income for all."[41] Against the advice of his associates, King had secured the reluctant support of the SCLC board to take on this new and, he admitted, "risky" venture. Not to do so, given the anger demonstrated in the ghettos in the previous two summers, would be "moral irresponsibility. . . . We intend to channelize the smoldering rage and frustration [tape interrupted] in our new Washington movement. We also look for participation by representatives of the millions of non-Negro poor: Indians, Mexican-Americans, Puerto Ricans, Appalachian whites, and others. And we shall welcome assistance from all Americans of good will."[42]

King called for bringing the poor to the nation's capital from ten cities and five rural areas. These people would be trained in the discipline of nonviolence and the purpose of securing employment. An intermediate goal would be to create "massive dislocation without destroying life or property." King hoped this effort to highlight the economic crisis as he saw it would receive "sympathetic understanding across our nation." Such support would in turn add to the pressure for the elected government to take action. He dismissed a possible backlash.[43] King was willing to move in a broad stroke against endemic poverty in a land of plenty. This was a step beyond freedom and equality in public accommodations and voting, and beyond our opening foray in the battle for economic justice through Breadbasket. It was a dramatic challenge to the economic system of democratic capitalism.

In February 1968 in Chicago, Rev. Jackson issued a call for "persons of poverty" to sign up. The SCLC's local coordinator, Bill Hollins, told supporters that Dr. King wished to "harness . . . non-violent tactics" to "establish a new relationship between government, the impoverished, the rich and the poor." He contrasted the huge war budget, which required $500,000 to kill each Vietcong soldier, against the $53 allocated to keep a single poor person alive in America, concluding, "There is an emergency at home that must be met immediately."[44] A flyer circulated in the suburbs challenging "non-poor" folks to travel to Washington, D.C., to assist with direct action and lobbying "so that poverty will no longer be a secret; it will be a visible fact."[45] At a March press conference, Jesse listed the demands to be presented to lawmakers on their return from the Easter recess: a guaranteed annual income, jobs for the unemployed, a minimum wage, adequate housing for the poor, and repeal of a House bill severely limiting welfare payments. Jesse indicated that Chicago would support these efforts and bus to D.C. five hundred poor people and additional non-poor supporters.

While the assassination of Dr. King was a devastating wound to the Poor People's Campaign (PPC), the SCLC decided to carry out King's wish, with only a short postponement.[46] The first caravans of poor people set off for Washington, D.C., on May 2, 1968. Departing from some fifteen cities and six rural counties the buses picked up additional people along the way, arriving in the nation's capital on May 11. The caravan from Mississippi stopped in Selma, where Rev. Abernathy preached to a large crowd. He appeared tired and unfocused and kept referring to Dr. King. His uncertain performance was a disappointment to many listeners that day. At the same time a subtle disinformation campaign led by FBI chief J. Edgar Hoover was sabotaging the SCLC's recruitment efforts, especially across the South. Rumors were spread that people participating in the PPC would be cut off from welfare benefits, and this effort held recruitment way down in many cities. This was just a part of the FBI's COINTELPRO, which was perpetrating a siege mentality about the hordes of black folks expected to descend on D.C.[47] By early May the capital was in a state of "near hysteria."[48]

The first Chicago contingent of four hundred people left for Washington, D.C., in fourteen buses on May 8. They hoped to pick up an additional thousand en route, arriving in D.C. on May 16. A send-off rally of about two thousand folks gathered at Liberty Baptist Church to hear speeches from Jesse, Calvin Morris, and C. T. Vivian of the Urban Training Center. Morris said, "We are going to Washington because we must change the values of this society. There is no reason for people to be poor in this nation today. . . . we will rise up and say to President Johnson and the Congress that they must feed the hungry." Vivian added, "We are going to Washington not to get charity" but rather to "make this nation really do what we have been asking, what we have already earned through 300 years of our labor." Rev. Barrow announced that eighteen hundred sandwiches had been put aboard the buses for the travelers.[49] The second Chicago group of about five hundred people left on May 15.

The week after that, I wrote to my Gresham church parishioners: "Business as usual" is no longer possible; we "cannot hang his [King's] picture in our homes unless we get busy with the unfinished task to which he gave his life." I urged the members to write to Mayor Daley on their views of his shoot-to-kill order and to join our Gresham busload for Poor People's Campaign events in D.C. in June, among ten "concrete suggestions." The response was less than I hoped for.[50]

In the capital, demonstrators from around the country erected a camp called Resurrection City on a sixteen-acre site near the Lincoln Monument. By May 20, some two thousand pilgrims were housed in hastily erected plywood huts, and another three to four thousand were housed in local churches. Problems emerged quickly. The SCLC leaders were consistently late to press conferences, and rough-talking marshals acted like thugs in blocking the media from entering the "city" or interviewing the protesters. It often took the intervention of Andrew Young to calm down the marshals and wave the press in. This problem was never solved, contributing to negative reporting and the gradual alienation of the press corps.[51]

Petty theft and fistfights began in the camp almost from day one and only increased. This created a growing sense of insecurity and caused many people to depart. Even though the staff sent two hundred gang members home at one point, this issue persisted. Squabbles ensued between different ethnic groups, particularly between the SCLC staff and Mexican American leaders, whom Dr. King had recruited to be full partners. These manifold distractions did not go unnoticed in the capital's black community, where Rev. Bevel campaigned vigorously to tepid response. The SCLC staff seemed helpless and in over their heads. The absence of Dr. King was obvious and devastating.[52]

The weather was another continuing problem. The press played up the fact that the PPC staffers (Ralph Abernathy, Andrew Young, James Bevel, Wyatt Walker, and Bayard Rustin) stayed in a motel, modest as it was, while the masses were out in the rain and mud. In spite of these difficulties the gathered poor and their supporters demonstrated at several government buildings for some days, promoting a legislative "economic bill of rights" with the goal of an investment of $30 billion.[53]

In late May, Rev. Abernathy named Rev. Jesse Jackson to be the "mayor" of Resurrection City. This was a highly visible position and exacerbated tensions among the SCLC staff. But Jesse took this new role in stride. According to Ethel Payne, writing in the *Defender*, Jesse emerged "as a new hero in the Poor People's Campaign. . . . When he strides into a tense situation as occurred during arrests of 18 demonstrators outside the House Office Building last week he raises a clenched fist and shouts 'Soul Power' and the crowd goes wild. Jackson is proving a skillful negotiator and arbiter in calming down tempers, and the police have come to respect him."[54]

Political reaction was varied. Senators Russell Long, Howard Baker, and Robert Byrd indicated they would not respond to "threats" by poor people. Byrd claimed that federal spending for the poor had reached an astonishing

$138 billion since 1960. But New York governor Nelson Rockefeller was more sympathetic, looking on the demonstration "as a new imaginative way of creating a lobby, to bring attention to congressmen [that] they have a problem, they want help."[55]

An estimated forty thousand people from across America were expected to take part in Solidarity Day on June 19, carrying "the battle of the poor to the doors of our nation."[56] Joining me in the Chicago contingent of about two thousand people was my mother, Florence Deppe, a widow who lived in suburban Glen Ellyn; her pastor; three teenagers from my Gresham parish; and three other Methodist pastors. We were in a caravan of fifteen buses, including two buses full of Blackstone Rangers. (Dr. King himself had urged that they be included.) After an emotional Breadbasket-style send-off of prayers, speeches, and songs, we finally rolled out of Chicago at 7:45 p.m. bound for Resurrection City and the next morning's events.

Our first major stop was for an early breakfast at the mammoth Breezewood Plaza along the Pennsylvania Turnpike. It felt like we were taking over the cafeteria with our sheer numbers. The gang members from Chicago swept through the lines, taking whatever they wished and simply walking past the cash registers. Their swagger, loud voices, and intimidation were so intense that the restaurant staff simply let go, and everything was suddenly free. It was a startling experience for a straitlaced white cleric like me. Then it was back to the buses and on to Washington, D.C.

Solidarity Day began with a march to the Lincoln Memorial. A crowd of fifty thousand, made up of tired, muddied residents of the tent city; weary travelers just off buses; and others arriving by foot, rail, car, and air, was juxtaposed with an elaborately staged program. Presided over by Dr. Benjamin Mays and Rev. Wyatt Walker, the rally displayed a panorama of civil rights history. Speakers included the SCLC leadership of Lowery, Abernathy, Young, and company; Coretta Scott King; the NAACP's Roy Wilkins; the Urban League's Whitney Young; an African American U.S. senator from Massachusetts, Ed Brooke; the United Auto Workers' Walter Reuther; Johnnie Tillmon of the Welfare Rights Organization; and representatives of Hispanic and Native American groups. Interspersed with the speakers were singers Mahalia Jackson and Aretha Franklin and religious leaders offering prayers.

Coretta gave a moving speech highlighted by an indictment of violence— the violence of poverty, of a starving child, of neglected schoolchildren, of ghetto housing, of ignored medical needs—the contempt for equality, and even the "lack of will power to help humanity." Then she turned to the violence in Vietnam and closed with a call to nonviolence in the spirit of her fallen husband. The crowd gave Coretta a thunderous standing ovation as she left the podium in tears. Mrs. King was followed by Rev. Abernathy, who stirred the audience further, summarizing some meager gains and offering another list, the umpteenth revised list, of PPC demands, including ending hunger, bad housing, and unemployment—a pie-in-the-sky dream with no specifics. His oratory ended with applause, a poor people's litany was read, and the crowd sang "We Shall Overcome." Though many of us stood up, exhilarated by the emotions of the moment, we did not realize that this event would bring down the curtain on the drama, effectively ending the campaign.[57]

The last instruction given to us, while people were dispersing in every direction, was to walk over to the Department of Agriculture and demand "protein power." Our numbers thinned as we marched. We learned that legislation was in the works to distribute surplus food to the poor and that Secretary of Agriculture Orville Freeman was offering a broadened food stamp program. This was but a pittance compared to King's goal for a $30 billion commitment to an economic bill of rights. For me, this late afternoon demonstration was a final goodbye to the vision.

The sight of shanties in ankle-high mud across the once beautiful mall was depressing. With the nation having turned against this witness, as evidenced by our dropping numbers and the negative, almost nasty media coverage, the effort was on its last legs. It was time to admit defeat and go home.[58] The Poor People's Campaign is reflected in a poem written by J. Edward Haycraft, a black veteran of the movement and a participant at Resurrection City:

To me comes a voice thru the air . . .
A voice that is timid . . . Yet bold . . .
It thrills me . . . It chills me . . . 'Tis full of despair . . .
This voice from the depth of a soul . . .
'Tis crying, "Help me . . . help me . . . Oh help me I pray . . .
Help me to rise from the mire . . .
Help me . . . Help me . . . Oh help me today
To fulfill my heart's desire . . ."
Now it is singing its praise to God . . .
The one whose love it knoweth . . .
Who knows when it's happy . . . And cares when it's sad . . .
'Tis only the voice of a poet.[59]

A flyer distributed on the day of the rally announced a seminar beginning the next day: "POVERTY WORKSHOPS for the NON-POOR" at the Poor People's University tent. "IF YOU CARE—BE THERE." It turned out to be the last event of the campaign. On June 24, since Resurrection City did not have a permit extension, the tent city was closed down by police as of 9:45 a.m. and the main power pole wires were clipped at 11:10 a.m. There were a few more night meetings with flashes of oratory, a few more demonstrations and arrests, but it was over. In a few weeks all SCLC staff were gone.[60]

Under Dr. King's guidance, this effort was to have been the most massive, widespread campaign of civil disobedience yet undertaken. With his assassination the shattered hopes of many had shifted to Senator Bobby Kennedy, a presidential candidate, but he too was assassinated, on June 6. Devoid of charismatic leadership, undermined by the COINTELPRO program, troubled by thievery, gang outbursts, and undisciplined marshals within the camp, receiving increasingly bad press, without concrete legislative proposals, unable to win over any segment of middle America, abandoned by the president and the Congress, and with terrible rainfall day after day, which made people sick and made a swamp of the campsite, the whole effort floundered. There was to be no resurrection.

However, for Rev. Jesse Jackson something did emerge. He recalls standing on a truck preparing to address a remnant of the crowd. "The White House had turned its back on us, almost hoping we would fail and go away. And so had the Congress. . . . People began to look to me for something, for some leadership, for some direction, for some hope, and I had nothing to give them, no money, no bus fare, no train fare." As he looked into the faces of the crowd, now largely women and children, he felt paralyzed. "I remembered Howard Thurman's book *Jesus and the Disinherited* where he said 'the irreducible essence is you are still somebody.' So I started to say, 'I am somebody. I may be poor, I may be unskilled, I may be alone, I may be lost, I may be . . . whatever, but I am somebody. God does not reject me. I am black, I am beautiful, I am proud, I am somebody. I am God's child.'" So was born, in Jesse's mind, the chant "I Am Somebody," which became his signature mantra.[61]

Just a few days after the closure of Resurrection City, Calvin Morris was ordained an elder in the United Methodist Church at his home conference meeting in Philadelphia. Not to be outdone by his pal, Jesse scheduled his own ordination for two weeks later. Jammed into a pew at Fellowship Baptist Church on Sunday evening, June 30, I participated in an emotional service in which Jesse finally became Rev. Jesse Jackson officially. Along with the overflow congregation, I heard renowned preacher C. L. Franklin of Detroit deliver a sermon on Ezekiel's vision, "Can These Bones Live?" In place of any notes he held a huge towel and repeatedly wiped perspiration off his brow as he preached, pacing back and forth across the chancel. One could almost hear the rattling of the bones as they came together in the preacher's impassioned story. Aretha Franklin seems to have inherited from her father her intense and passionate singing voice.

Jesse seemed deeply humbled by the spiritual nature of this ceremony. It did not prevent him, however, from saying, with some humor and pride, "I have already received my anointment. I'm just going over to Fellowship to get my appointment." While this brought a laugh, theologically he had it backward: he already had his appointments as the associate pastor at Fellowship and as the national director of the SCLC's Operation Breadbasket. He was now receiving his anointment in the church to preach the word of God in season and out and to administer the sacraments. Following the ordination a splendid reception was held. Shortly thereafter, Rev. Evans named Jesse to be the co-pastor of Fellowship Baptist Church, a kind of "ceremonial position to help his stature when he traveled about the nation."[62]

Rev. Willie Barrow never was ordained officially. As she relates it, whenever a date was set by her pastor, Rev. Claude Wyatt, she was out of town or too busy with Breadbasket business. In her mind, "God calls you to preach." Ordination simply "allows you to marry and bury."[63] Willie's later honorary doctorates, eight in number, including one from Harvard Divinity School, thoroughly authenticated her gifts and graces for ministry and her life as the unofficial Rev. Willie Barrow.

In my view, Dr. King's death was in many ways the end for the civil rights movement. That was the mood I experienced while singing freedom songs as we walked across Atlanta in mourning. The white backlash that emerged out of the urban riots was already in full swing, and the outpouring over King was only momentary in a nation shouting "Enough!" Operation Breadbasket became instantly a part of King's legacy; the end of his oversight led to Jesse's complete ascendancy. And Jesse's urgency and instinct increasingly drove the Breadbasket engine. Change was evident in the growing popularity of Saturday Breadbasket with its average attendance of thirty-five hundred people and the guest appearances of celebrities, politicos, and national black leaders. But in spite of Jesse's verbal promise to redress the imbalance in our work, the SC struggled, with little staff support, to maintain any momentum in the nitty-gritty work for jobs and justice.

CHAPTER 7

BREAKING THE CHAINS

> Because the A&P situation has continued so long, people will think
> SCLC is not a winner if we fail. We must win this battle and must win it big.
> A&P needs a good whipping. —Rev. Andrew Young

In March 1968, just weeks before Dr. King's assassination, a Breadbasket team monitoring A&P's covenant of May 1967 discovered major problems. As soon as we had recovered sufficiently from the tragedy of King's death, our team resumed efforts, despite much obfuscation from the company, to secure its data. What emerged was a clear picture of failure. A&P had filled only 83 of 770 promised jobs; the products of black-owned companies were not kept in stock or displayed adequately; and A&P had reduced scavenger services, lowered deposits in black banks, and made no use of black construction contractors. Except for an increase in retail store managers, the story was one of reversals. The company had promised seventy-five meat journeymen but instead lost six; had promised forty-four truck drivers but lost three; had promised eight warehouse supervisors but gained only one. Out of fifty-two secretaries not one was black, although ten had been promised.[1]

Beyond all this we needed to review the covenant because it was outdated; we had progressed in the last year and expanded our demands, particularly in economic development. So, A&P faced a double challenge.

A&P executives explained that their business was down everywhere and that they could not afford to hire. In this situation we offered A&P a compromise: 40 jobs a month for six months, or 240 new jobs, a steep drop from the original 770 jobs. When A&P responded that it could not make this commitment, the Steering Committee declared it was time to go back to the pulpits.[2]

At Saturday Breadbasket on July 6, 1968, Jesse announced that a "Don't Buy" campaign would begin immediately because A&P had reneged on its covenant. The *Defender* soon printed pictures of picketers, black and white, marching with signs at two stores, and the accompanying article said that five hundred people walked the picket line at five stores the first day. The leaflets we distributed detailed the disrespect of A&P and concluded: "Don't shop at A&P until you hear A&P has signed a new agreement with Operation Breadbasket."[3]

Two Saturdays later an estimated twenty-five hundred people went off to picket at twenty-four A&P stores, including stores in suburban Maywood and Wilmette. About twenty Blackstone Ranger members, who were among the team serving as security that morning, joined the crowds dispersing to the picket lines. At one store Rev. Morris was arrested for questioning a police officer about the arrest of a young black person for underage purchase of wine. Calvin had asked if the person selling the wine should not also be arrested. The officer became belligerent, arrested Calvin, and charged him with being "disorderly" and resisting arrest, a felony. In court later, our lawyer convinced the judge that Calvin's action was a simple misdemeanor. Calvin remembers Jesse being "amused" at his arrest, while Calvin was in fact "frightened." The only outcome of this nonsensical arrest was to generate more publicity for us, increasing the numbers of picketers over the next weeks.[4]

A more troubling incident occurred the next weekend at a North Side A&P when a hundred black youths bolted from the picket line and entered the store to protest the prices. This was, in my opinion, an overreaction from our more militant Black P Stone contingent. When the store security guard brandished a pistol in an effort to hold back the young people, they became enraged. Two youths picked up a cash register and ran to the street, dropping it as the police gave chase. More scuffling ensued, leaving behind a looted store, twenty-five people arrested, and twenty injured.

Picketing continued throughout July with some 230 people on the lines at five South Side stores on July 31. A&P sought to counter the boycott with a statement claiming that "A&P is an equal opportunity employer, and is proud of the good relationships it has enjoyed with the non-white community—including customers, our fellow workers, and our suppliers. The fact that more than a third of our employees in Chicago are non-white should serve as sufficient evidence of our sincerity."[5]

Our A&P campaign had vigorous staff support out of the 47th Street office. Since her parents had told her not to march, Hermene Hartman would arrive at the Breadbasket office in the midafternoon after high school was out and pour herself into typing, phoning, and note taking for staff and committee meetings. She received calls from the picket lines and functioned as a dispatcher. Using a wall chart Hermene "made sure that the teams always had enough people" and that "signs and flyers were delivered fresh and intact." She noted unique incidents and informed Rev. Jackson about any unusual situations because "he moved around a lot." Hermene also recalls that one day Jesse asked her to contact President Lyndon Johnson. She phoned the White House repeatedly until, days later, she had LBJ on the line. The president asked, "Is this Rev. Joseph Jackson?" Before Jesse took the phone, Hermene corrected him, "No, this is Rev. Jesse Jackson of SCLC Operation Breadbasket in Chicago." Ironically, the president had taken the call thinking he had the National Baptist Convention's president on the line.[6]

We had other supporters too. In August both singer Harry Belafonte and Senator George McGovern addressed Breadbasket rallies, voicing support for the A&P campaign. Belafonte promised to return to Chicago and walk the picket line. In early September the Black Power Conference meeting in Philadelphia endorsed Breadbasket's campaign against A&P.[7] Clearly, this group of African American advocates recognized the SCLC and Breadbasket to be true allies in securing black power.

Along with other clergy across the Chicago area, I received a signed letter from Earl Poyner, A&P's Chicago superintendent, dated August 29, 1968. Acknowledging the current picketing and the 1967 covenant, Poyner asked me to consider whether A&P merited the "public condemnation of pickets and boycotts." He laid out the company's progress with black products and services. As for jobs, he claimed that A&P had hired 697 and upgraded another 167 black employees, but he omitted the fact that most newly hired blacks did not remain with A&P. "For reasons beyond our control (other jobs, marriages, relocations, studies, etc.) the total employment in Chicago does not reflect the full impact of our new employees." His reasons were specious, however, as we discovered the high dropout number was due primarily to insufficient job training and low morale, the very items that Jewel had overcome. Poyner closed by saying, "We are proud of our record and of our good relationship over the years with the black community."[8]

Rev. Gerald Forshey responded with a letter to our Methodist bishop, noting: "Mr. Poyner's letter is a masterpiece of deceit.... He never raises the question of why, when they hired 697 employees, only 83 chose to remain with the company. We contend that something disastrous is wrong with A&P if this is the case. . . . Since it appears that Methodist ministers are now receiving these letters, I wonder if you would consider sending out a letter which will deal with A&P's deception and their attempt to split the religious community and the work of Operation Breadbasket."[9] Preempting such a letter to just Methodists, Breadbasket sent a rebuttal addressed to all pastors on the Chicago Church Federation's mailing list, with these closing words, "We hope these facts will strengthen your support of Operation Breadbasket, and that you will actively encourage others to cooperate in the consumer withdrawal from A&P."[10]

I pointed to the struggle with A&P in a Sunday sermon, telling my congregants, "A fellow preacher from [suburban] Robbins told me he needed four ears of corn so he went past a picket line into an A&P store. But he came out without the corn, deciding not to feed himself but to feed others—through jobs and justice."[11] As I recall, the Gresham people participated faithfully in the A&P boycott though only a very few actually picketed. Early on, I had decided that my time in Breadbasket meant attending weekly SC meetings and monitoring covenants. Thus, I attended only an occasional Saturday rally and carried a picket sign only a few times. This may have been an excuse, but I was a busy, involved local pastor.

Picketing continued through September at thirty-five stores. Additional forces arrived from our North Shore chapter and from other area groups, including the Organization for the Southwest Community. A&P asked to resume talks but then rejected a carefully drafted proposal from the Breadbasket side.

The SC felt it had no choice but to expand the picketing. Ten stores, four in white areas and six in black areas, would be added the next day.[12] Then, quite spontaneously, exhausted from the constant tension with A&P, the ministers present at that SC session burst out in a flood of cathartic comments on why we picket. I quickly jotted some down: "best way to let people know where you stand is to stand; to keep your weight down and to oppose discriminatory policies; picketing puts you between the one who is wronged and the one who is wrong; to hurt A&P cash registers; to educate the community and free the people; to communicate the truth about an injustice to those who suffer it and to those who have a conscience; to give black folks self-respect."[13]

As the meeting continued, Rev. Andrew Young, visiting from Atlanta, commented, "Because the A&P situation has continued so long, people will think SCLC is not a winner if we fail. We must win this battle and must win it big. A&P needs a good whipping." We left the meeting determined to intensify the boycott immediately.[14]

In early September 1968, during the A&P battle, Breadbasket was urged to support a wildcat strike by black transit workers against both their union and the Chicago Transit Authority (CTA). Rev. Jackson declared, "The ministers of Operation Breadbasket want the CTW [Concerned Transit Workers] to know that we support them in their struggle for decent working conditions, adequate union representation and for safety for customers and employees."[15] The following Saturday three hundred striking bus drivers appeared at Breadbasket, and Rev. Jackson asked the community to form car pools for a Montgomery-like boycott. The pool of 360 cars would operate during rush hours along key streets carrying signs reading "Courtesy Car, CTW–SCLC."

Less than a week later 14 bus drivers were arrested for picketing at their South Side bus barn and were found guilty of violating a court injunction handed down hours earlier. After three weeks the walkout still commanded

660 of 4,000 black drivers, costing the CTA an estimated $165,000 a day. At Saturday Breadbasket, CTW leader Waymon Benson surprised the crowd by calling off the walkout without warning, saying, "We've just retreated to pick up the casualties." He denied this was a defeat, although 50 men, himself included, had just been fired. While a swift reversal, this raised issues that would, hopefully, be addressed in the future.[16]

The A&P confrontation had drawn several newcomers, among them Richard Thomas. He joined a picket line directly from his job as superintendent at a local foundry. His wife, Hazel, had been active in Breadbasket programs while he was putting bread on the table. Now, with a request to join the struggle against A&P from his friend St. Clair Booker, another Breadbasket volunteer, Thomas took the leap and joined the witness. When Thomas's one-week vacation came up a few weeks later, he set off to picket an A&P store every morning at 8 a.m. This decision emerged, he told me, from an increasing awareness of racism in Chicago, his wife's involvement, and Dr. King's death, which he described as "monumental." "Dr. King was everything," a "special person in my life." With his job secure at the foundry Thomas felt ready to join the movement. Before long, Rev. Jackson challenged him to leave his job and join Breadbasket as the manager of a small store at 50th and State, in the "projects," where black products were sold exclusively. He was unable to resist Jesse's persuasive powers, and that was just the beginning. By early 1969 Thomas had become a confidant to Jesse and his primary travel aide.[17]

Throughout all these campaigns our go-to person was Cirilo McSween. Behind the scenes of so many Breadbasket successes, Cirilo was a trusted advisor, tireless worker, fabulous fundraiser, and steady anchor. He once said that he modeled his life after Dr. King's, and he was a model of dignity, determination, and fair play in the economic leadership circles of Chicago. His self-esteem was evident in the way he walked, the command of his speech, and the elegance of his dress, always wearing a suit with a wide, bright tie and a straw hat in season.

Rev. Gary Massoni wrote this testimony after Cirilo's death on November 4, 2008, the very day Barack Obama of Chicago was elected president of the United States:

> Cirilo and I spent many hours together over early morning breakfasts, or just
> meeting in his office, or before and after various meetings—discussing the
> directions of Breadbasket, and how to make its program and its members
> more consistent with Dr. King's goal of "redeeming the soul of America." He
> had a great capacity to listen to ideas, absorb them, challenge them, modify
> them and then reach conclusions and recommendations that would work.

He used not only his money and his position, but more importantly his mind and his values and his commitments to make justice possible. This is what makes Cirilo great to me.[18]

Jesse put it succinctly at the funeral service when he whispered to me, "He was a big piece of Breadbasket." Cirilo was an unsung hero and a major player in the Breadbasket narrative.

After fourteen weeks of sustained picketing, A&P finally responded with a counterproposal, which Rev. Lawrence read aloud at our sc meeting on October 4, 1968. Amazement hardly describes our emotion as we recognized what amounted to A&P's capitulation. The brutal fact was that our picketing had severely damaged A&P's standing in the community. It would have been "easier for A&P to go out of business than to improve its policies," Rev. Lawrence commented. We approved the A&P proposal, called off all picketing, and commended our negotiating team for their hard work.[19]

At Saturday Breadbasket the next day some four thousand people watched as Rev. Jackson, Earl Poyner, and others signed a new covenant. Shouts of "Soul Power" rose from Jesse and the crowd. Jesse recalled that this moment was "six months to the day" after Dr. King's assassination. (He was off by one day.) "I am grateful to Dr. King today. . . . he always said that if you just don't hate, you can separate sin from the sinner . . . and fight through hard times, not giving up. We have won today because the leader is alive. . . . victory with A&P was accomplished without anyone getting shot, beaten or killed." Mr. Poyner of A&P read aloud the three-page covenant and declared, "This is a wonderful day. It is one of the finest days I think I'll ever enjoy." He called the accord "a personal victory for me" by which he meant "the picketing is over."[20]

A Breadbasket volunteer couple wrote to my mother, Florence Deppe, a fellow picketer: "The covenant was signed on Saturday, as you know—and I'm just sorry that everyone who worked hard on the picket line couldn't be there at the Breadbasket meeting to be recognized when Rev. Jackson asked for all the pickets from the suburbs to stand and be applauded. Thank you so much for your help on the picket line. We feel that this new A&P Covenant is a good one—if it is carried out the way it should be."[21]

For the sc the new covenant brought both relief and exhilaration. We had entered the campaign exhausted after Dr. King's death, the riots, and the Poor People's Campaign. Now, after a bitter three-month struggle, we Breadbasket clergy could catch up on our local pastoral duties.

A&P had offered "a three pronged attack upon the problems created by discrimination and segregation inflicted upon black Americans."[22] In employment A&P agreed to recall 300 black employees, employ 268 more blacks within a year, conduct sensitivity courses for all employees in cooperation with Breadbasket, hire two black executives for recruitment and employee training, open an employment center, and make monthly reports to Breadbasket.

In economic development A&P agreed to continue all service contracts in consultation with Breadbasket, ensure black building contractors an open bidding process, advertise with black-owned agencies, market the products of black producers and suppliers in all 160 stores, maintain substantial balances in Seaway and Independence Banks, hire a black executive as a liaison with black businesses, and establish an A&P advisory group to counsel black business owners.

Finally, A&P agreed to establish a Businessmen's Advisory Council to advise black entrepreneurs in all areas of their business operation. Details were spelled out in the language of the covenant.

Breadbasket agreed to inform the black community of A&P's new policies and job openings. Together we agreed to demonstrate that "cooperative efforts between the black community and the private sector will beneficially influence the economic and social welfare of the entire Chicago metropolitan area."[23]

The following Sunday we Breadbasket pastors distributed to our congregations a flyer that read: "A&P SIGNS PACT! We won because you helped. By respecting our picketing campaign you helped SCLC Operation Breadbasket achieve [a list of the 268 jobs and other items of the covenant]. The ministers, staff and workers of SCLC Operation Breadbasket thank you for your support. Join our program for economic development every Saturday at 8:00 a.m.— 4130 S. Indiana."[24] The toughest and longest Breadbasket campaign was over.

The following Friday, Poyner held a covenant orientation with sixty A&P store managers at a North Side site in the presence of several Breadbasket pastors. Later, Jesse told the press that with the precedent of this covenant, Breadbasket would expand negotiations with other chains in Chicago and with A&P in other cities. For his part Poyner pointed out, "It is my responsibility to uphold the new agreement and to see that A&P builds lines of cooperation with black people." The next morning, Rev. Abernathy addressed Breadbasket and congratulated us on the covenant with A&P. He announced that "nationwide economic withdrawals" would become "a major thrust" of SCLC's programs.[25] That turned out to be a hollow promise.

On November 10, 1968, I addressed the A&P breakthrough in a sermon, pointing out that Jesus mentions money numerous times and that our own use of money reflects our loyalties. I referred to the recent boycott as a prime example of the proper use of our "talents," which in this case meant withholding our dollars until a measure of justice had been achieved. "We can store it up, we can waste it, or we can use our talents, our salaries, our energies, our all, as faithful stewards. The choice is ours."[26] There were several "Amens" to the A&P announcement.

While the A&P covenant was the only major pact signed during 1968, the agreement broke ground by expanding into new areas. Also, the Construction Division facilitated several joint ventures with contracts netting $3–4 million in jobs and development. These things helped compensate for, and hide, the lack of additional covenants.

In mid-November 1968, Rev. Jackson was in the hospital when the CTA announced a fare hike. Jesse was suffering another outbreak of sickle cell trait, a disorder that causes the nervous system to function at a full level even during rest and sleep. Jesse's doctor, Andrew Thomas, insisted he reduce his work, delegate more responsibilities, get better sleep, and establish an exercise regimen.[27] In spite of his doctor's orders, Jesse carried on from his hospital bed.

Rev. Jerry Forshey and I were visiting him at St. Joseph's Hospital as he held a bedside press conference, attacking the CTA's fare hike from thirty cents to forty cents. Jesse assailed the CTA board for having no black members and called the decision "taxation without representation." He criticized Mayor Daley for supporting an increase levied by "white people who are affluent while the impoverished black and Puerto Rican community will have to bear the burden."[28] Then, out of the blue, Jesse suggested forming an independent bus company, subsidized by the government. Jerry and I remember being aghast at the unreality of buying a bus, let alone creating a separate bus company. Nonetheless, Jesse pursued his vision by writing to President-elect Richard Nixon, urging the administration "to take black capitalism seriously by taking the black community's needs for capitalization of essential programs seriously."[29] To my knowledge, Jesse received no response to this scheme.

Breadbasket began an intensive follow-up with A&P soon after the ink was dry on the covenant. We were relieved to learn in February 1969 that laid-off workers had been rehired, 103 of the promised 268 new workers had been hired, including 2 of 3 black executives, contracts were being signed with black services, and deposits had been made in black banks.[30] One serious failing was A&P's proposed seminar. Rev. Forshey found the plans inadequate and naïve, and he requested that A&P secure an outside organization to prepare the racism-awareness materials; A&P agreed reluctantly. Apparently the grueling boycott had little effect on A&P's understanding of systemic discrimination.[31] My records show a gap here for about a year.

In a belated follow-up meeting at A&P's general offices on February 18, 1970, A&P officials admitted their South Side stores had still not fully recovered from the boycott. They urged us to reassure the black community that A&P was serious about keeping the covenant. Indeed, their written reports indicated that black employment and black services were on target and that black products were on shelves in all 176 Chicago stores. To their complaint that sales were disappointing in the stores in black areas, we suggested consumer education and more creative marketing. A&P trumpeted the fact that it had more money on deposit in black banks than did Jewel. That was fine with us. The frosting on the cake of these gains was a new A&P store built with black contractors, and a black butcher appointed as the meat department supervisor for 14 stores. Inexplicably, A&P danced around our request for a job breakdown in the bakery, hid management figures, and continued to mix full-time and part-time workers.[32]

In June 1970 an article appeared in the *Chicago Defender* praising A&P as "one of the most venerable of American institutions." The unidentified writer affirmed that A&P had begun "a new phase of cooperating with black workers and black business people" with "expanded employment opportunities" and with its initiative in stocking black products. Clearly, A&P was still struggling with the boycott fallout and sought this avenue to reclaim its credibility in the community. The truth is that any A&P initiative came only after the punishing "Don't Buy" campaign. If "the seventies" held a "great deal of promise for the company," as the writer claimed, it was because of the A&P–Breadbasket battle, the resulting covenant, and A&P's new social awareness. This claim was yet to be tested.[33]

By August 1970 A&P reported that since the 1968 covenant it had closed six stores in the black community, and now had only thirty-seven stores with more than 50 percent black customers. Black products were on the shelves in these stores, but only a few such products were in all metro stores. Black scavenger, exterminator, and janitorial services were being provided in most of the thirty-seven stores. We learned further that A&P's new black executives in employment and services were struggling to educate their colleagues about the covenant goals. It was clear that we needed to keep pressure on A&P simply to maintain the gains.

In the fall of 1970 A&P initiated a consumer education program in the Cabrini-Green housing projects. Some twenty-five women participated in the opening nine-week class. The response was so positive that A&P planned to expand the program in other area stores. Evidence of Breadbasket's impact was a joint ad in the *Defender* entitled "Best Food Buys," highlighting a dozen food items each for National Tea, Del Farm, A&P, High-Low Foods, and Jewel.[34]

Completely separate from Chicago Breadbasket's new covenantal relationship and follow-up with A&P, our Brooklyn chapter initiated a national SCLC Breadbasket boycott over grievances against New York area stores. Without consulting our Steering Committee, Rev. Jackson announced a nationwide boycott "against the mighty Atlantic and Pacific (A&P) Chain." It soon had the support of ten Breadbasket chapters and a number of national figures, including Ralph Abernathy, Roy Wilkins, Shirley Chisholm, James Farmer, Ossie Davis, Bella Abzug, and Charles Kenyatta. I doubt Jesse ever realized the embarrassing bind this created for the SC as we struggled to maintain our rapport with A&P in Chicago while ignoring the national boycott. In New York, twenty-one ministers were arrested for sitting-in at the midtown office of the A&P president, William Kane. He vowed that he would not "sit down to negotiate with ministers, insisting instead, that they confer with some of his regional underlings," a tactic used unsuccessfully by Chicago's A&P three years earlier. The national A&P fight continued, but the complications for Chicago Breadbasket were ironic and sad.[35]

The A&P–Breadbasket story must be seen against the backdrop of A&P's colossal decline nationally. Founded in 1859 in New York and coming to Chicago immediately after the 1871 Chicago fire, A&P had 200 stores at the turn of the century. It added meat markets in 1919 and by the 1930s had grown to 15,000 stores. In the 1940s the company transitioned to larger stores and finally to supermarkets, reducing total stores to 4,252 by 1959, its hundredth anniversary. A&P was then the top food chain in the country with over $5 billion in sales. As people moved to the suburbs and competition increased, A&P retrogressed, revealing a clear lack of vision, creativity, and competence to adjust to the new competition and a changing urban environment. Seemingly unaware of this trend or its causes, A&P leaders proceeded in 1965 to build the largest food-manufacturing and -processing facility in the world at Horseheads, New York. Yet the company's decline continued, with only 1,500 stores in the 1970s and fewer than 1,000 stores in 1982, when it returned to profitability as a much leaner food chain.

A&P's precipitous retreat in the 1960s coincided with the demand for economic justice delivered by Operation Breadbasket. Whether out of insensitivity, racism, incompetent management, or a combination of these factors, A&P stumbled. The May 1967 covenant with Breadbasket had called for 770 jobs. Yet, in fourteen months A&P had filled only 83 and had failed on all other promises. A&P's explanation was not altogether without merit when it admitted that business was down locally and nationally. But when Breadbasket offered compromises, A&P refused, leading to the fourteen-week boycott. The October 1968 covenant opened a new chapter as A&P made a serious effort to keep its promises, and progress was made.[36] However, the black community never fully trusted A&P again. Truth be told, the company paid a dear price for the 1968 boycott.

Construction Job Gains

> For so long black people were locked out of many unions, particularly the building trades. We were not heard in our cries for justice because we had no power to be heard.—Revs. Arthur Brazier and Jesse Jackson

One of the most effective units of Breadbasket going back to mid-1967 was the Construction Division, under the leadership of Dr. Alvin Pitcher. Al was a participant in the original cadre of professors and preachers in Breadbasket, later a member of Jesse's inner circle, and then the volunteer coordinator of this vital sector.[37] He put together the panel that reviewed membership attunement, drafted contracts, and offered counsel to contractors.[38] Al attended sc meetings periodically to help us set covenant demands on the use of black contractors.

To help achieve these larger contracts the division created new joint ventures with electrical, plumbing, heating, and air-conditioning companies. For example, early in 1969 Revs. Jesse Jackson and Arthur Brazier of the Woodlawn Organization announced a joint $400,000 contract to four black electrical contractors for work in the Woodlawn Gardens. "For so long black people were locked out of many unions, particularly the building trades. We were not heard in our cries for justice because we had no power to be heard."[39]

By December 1969 Pitcher reported construction contracts worth more than $12 million, almost double the previous year. This included new construction and the renovation of stores in compliance with Breadbasket covenants. Al was able to report, "With a little luck and some systematic work we predict that our contractors should be operating at the rate of $100,000,000 a year within three or four years. The attempt to collapse twenty-five years of development into five requires special attention. . . . What we need are the compensatory opportunities and a staff to discover and develop the talent." Al pleaded for additional staff without success. I think Jesse felt that Al, with his amazing energy, genius, and dedication, could do it all by himself.[40]

During 1970 twelve Breadbasket contractors won a $1.2 million deal to build twelve low-income residential buildings in Lake Park. Officials of Chicago's "big three" construction firms signed a letter of intent with Breadbasket promising to "maximize the development of Black contractors" in construction at Chicago State and Kennedy-King Colleges. Two black contractors won those two jobs, worth $4 million. Additionally, the Construction Division bid on work at Hyde Park High School, the new Sears Tower, the CNA building, Crane High School, a Standard Oil gas station at 63rd and Drexel, a Chicago fire station at California and Roosevelt, and the University of Chicago.[41]

The sanction of direct action was ever present and was employed when necessary. In August 1971 some twenty Breadbasket volunteers, including Alderman William Cousins and Jackie Jackson, picketed a public library construction site in Chatham. Within minutes all twelve workers left with their bulldozer. A Breadbasket spokesperson commented: "It's a library which will be used by black people in a black area and it's on Dr. King Drive. Here we have 25.4 percent of the black construction workers in this city unemployed. If we can't work outside our community, we're going to insist we get it inside." State senator Charlie Chew asserted, "Blacks are going to build the library by agreement, and there will be no more work done at the site until this is straightened out. We want the contract renegotiated so there will be a guarantee of black contractors." Martin Construction Company won the renegotiated contract and built the library. This was thought to be the first public library in the United States built by a black contractor with federal and state dollars.[42]

An overview of Breadbasket's development gains was prepared in mid-1970 and revealed that Joe Louis Milk's sales increased 400 percent from 1966 to 1970 with a new $90,000 contract to supply milk for the Chicago Hunger Feeding Program. In that same time, Rual's Floor Wax's distribution had expanded to thirteen states. Scavengers, exterminators, and janitorial services each held eighty-three service contracts through the network. But the most impressive gains were in construction. Collectively, black contractor agreements brought in a stunning $18 million for the year 1970. These contracts produced jobs for apprentices, skilled and semiskilled workers, managers, and architects as well as the general contractors. It is safe to say that several million dollars were added to black businesses and black households through the labors of this effective, tight-knit Breadbasket cell. Pitcher's earlier vision of a major expansion of the black construction industry was coming to fruition.[43]

Coalitional Empowerment Campaigns

Early in 1969, a new Coalition of United Community Action (CUCA) emerged under the leadership of Rev. C. T. Vivian. A former SCLC staffer and now the head of Chicago's Urban Training Center, Vivian pulled together six South and West Side groups: Taylor Residents United, the Garfield Organization, the Woodlawn Organization, Concerned Shoppers of Ickes, Dearborn and Hilliard (Homes), and the Lawndale People's Planning and Action Conference. With his history he prevailed upon Jesse to bring Breadbasket aboard. That decision never came to the sc.[44]

Red Rooster

The CUCA chose to begin with a relatively easy target, a small white-owned chain of seven food stores called Red Rooster. These stores, all in black communities, were already in serious trouble with the city, four of them facing license revocations. Breadbasket had received customer complaints of bad meat, unsanitary conditions, rotten fruit, and high prices for months, but we were nursing our wounds from the long A&P battle. While Red Rooster lay dormant on our to-do list, it was a ready-made campaign for the new coalition.[45]

Jesse asked our sc to develop the coalition's demands, which we did, using our customary model for jobs and services.[46] When the CUCA received no response to these demands, picketing began at all seven stores on March 1. Some eight hundred people left Saturday Breadbasket for the picket lines under the theme "Pulling Feathers," forcing an early closing of all Red Rooster stores that day. When the chain then threatened to fire three hundred employees, Rev. Jackson responded, "Red Rooster is using an old trick of the slave masters by trying to create a fight between the house slaves, or their employees, and the field slaves, or the six organizations picketing their stores . . . . We shall fight Red Rooster's exploitation in our community until we get justice and respect for black customers and black employees."[47]

During the first week of picketing Red Rooster accused Rev. Jackson of slander and threatened a lawsuit. "Jackson is nothing but an opportunist and a liar . . . and he doesn't care one bit about the black community." Additional groups jumped on the bandwagon, partly in response to the attack on Jesse. Six quickly mushroomed to forty, including the Chicago Tenants Union, Black Student Federation, Concerned Parents, KOCO, Afro-American Patrolmen's League, Concerned Black Catholics, Calvary Presbyterian Church, and major street gangs the Conservative Vice Lords, Black P Stones, and Cobras.[48] The coalition hoped that gang participation would lead to new careers for these young men if they gained steady jobs coming out of any agreement.

At one point some Breadbasket women on the picket line received threats from Red Rooster employees on a counterpicket line. Rev. Barrow remembers that some Black P Stone members in the picket line came to the rescue, interspersing themselves among the women.[49]

After a week of picketing, Red Rooster's owner, Bernie Hahn, offered to meet. (The word *Hahn* is German for rooster, and the family probably chose

"Red Rooster" to honor their German ancestry.) Picketing was halted, but Mr. Hahn's sudden hospitalization led to cancellation of the talks, more acrimony, and resumed picketing. Without warning, Red Rooster's black vice president, Richard Kay, announced plans to lay off 150 black employees and predicted violent confrontations if the picketing continued. Mr. Kay sent Red Rooster employees to the sidewalks as counterpickets; they carried signs saying "Jesse Jackson Is Wrong" and "Jesse Jackson Is Not for the Black Community." Fortunately no violence occurred.[50]

Out of the blue Richard Kay showed up at the next Saturday Breadbasket. Before thirty-five hundred Breadbasket faithful, Mr. Kay reversed course completely and announced Red Rooster's acceptance of the coalition's demands, saying, "I am speaking as a black brother to black brothers and sisters. We are united on all 18 demands." He retracted his statements against Jesse, blaming his outburst on pressures generated by the campaign. Later, Kay admitted that this struggle caused Hahn to change his mind. Rev. Vivian termed the agreement a major achievement, praised the community for maintaining unity in the boycott, and added, "The Red Rooster fight is over. And the whole black community has won. Now there is no longer the South, West or Northside, but just one side—the black side."[51]

This victory was a first of its type for Breadbasket. While we SC ministers helped prepare the demands and Breadbasket people provided the bulk of the picketers, we were simply members of a community coalition. There was no reference to a covenant or monitoring, and our SC never discussed the implications of this change in our modus operandi.

In the Red Rooster boycott Breadbasket and Rev. Jackson had faced threats and possible violence for the first time. In addition, opposition emerged in the voice of a West Side militant, Russ Meek, who intoned: "I agree that the Rooster should not crow in the black community, but I don't feel there is real sincerity in Jackson's attempt to block the chain. There are plenty of black stores in the ghetto who sell bad meat. The same is true of National Tea and some of the others, but Breadbasket has not touched them." On the contrary, Women of Breadbasket monitored meats in several stores under covenant and made periodic complaints. Meek also attacked our businessmen: "They're at Breadbasket every Saturday, but the rest of the time is spent on shortchanging black people." No evidence was given for this wild claim. Still, these incidents served as a warning that Breadbasket could expect roadblocks along the way to "making justice in the city gates."[52]

Six months later Red Rooster went bankrupt. The company's behavior in the fight cost it dearly, and it struggled in vain to regain business. On news of the bankruptcy, looting was attempted at two closed stores, and police arrested seven people. The *Defender* reported, "All that hell-raising about those Red Rooster stores seems to have helped pave the way for bankruptcy. An ex-employee said the blacks made the whites see red." Red Rooster was then purchased for $11 million by three black businessmen and renamed Horn of Plenty–Finer Foods. One of the new owners exclaimed, "This is a 'soul' ownership, and we don't have any connections with the former owner, Bernie Hahn or anybody white. We will change the company policy and offer our customers only first class merchandise."[53] These changes voided the coalition–Red Rooster agreement.

Building Trades Struggle

The CUCA, now sixty members strong, resumed its public witness on July 22, 1969, with a protest against job discrimination in the building trades.[54] This represented a gigantic leap in targeting, from a tiny food chain to a major industry with deep ties to the city of Chicago and its mayor. Picketing began at First National Bank while a smaller group moved to the Building Trades Union Council offices nearby and sat-in. Copies of their demands were dropped to reporters outside the office through an open transom, the key demand being ten thousand on-the-job minority trainee openings. When police arrived, the group began to leave peacefully only to be arrested for trespassing. All seventeen were members of the Black P Stone Nation. Over the next days, the demonstrations effectively closed down twenty-four construction sites in black communities. Then, protest leaders were arrested, negotiations were begun, and a court injunction was approved to prohibit mass picketing. Rev. Jackson was among the leaders named in the injunction.[55]

A previous struggle over discrimination in the building trades had commenced in Philadelphia in the spring of 1963 with major demonstrations led by the NAACP and CORE. These protests had "national resonance" and led to President John F. Kennedy's executive order calling for "affirmative action" in government-contracted construction. Subsequently, Presidents Lyndon B. Johnson and Richard M. Nixon issued slightly stronger executive orders in 1965 and 1969, respectively.[56] Whether connected or not, the Chicago struggle coincided with a wave of protests across several cities, led again by Philadelphia.

Following the court order in Chicago, construction work resumed with small forces at most sites. Everyone waited for the other shoe to drop. After Saturday Breadbasket on August 16, 1969, some nine hundred people joined a motorcade to the Loop and then staged demonstrations at the Civic Center and at building trade and union offices. The SCLC's national convention adjourned in mid-session in Charleston, South Carolina, on August 21 and reconvened in Chicago, bringing national support and attention to the construction fight. Rev. Abernathy addressed twenty-four hundred delegates to the Illinois AFL-CIO convention, challenging them to be the first to open the construction industry to minorities. When the group adopted a bland statement of support, coalition members interrupted the proceedings, calling on supporters to walk out. The meeting was immediately adjourned, averting a walkout.[57]

For days, negotiations between contractors, union officials, and the CUCA were scheduled and canceled; proposals were submitted and rejected. On Labor Day, coalition supporters held impromptu rallies among picnickers at several Chicago parks. Rumors spread that AFL-CIO officials had instructed local unions "not to settle the dispute for fear that blacks would be in control of the building training program." On September 8, more than five hundred people, including Revs. Jackson and Vivian, defied the injunction by entering a University of Illinois–Chicago construction site, where they were confronted by two hundred helmeted police officers. The coalition leaders were allowed in for fifteen minutes, shouting took place as they walked out, rocks were thrown, and police quickly arrested Jesse and three others. From the police squadrol, Jesse declared, "We came here to get jobs for our people and we said we wouldn't let nothing like jail cells or death turn us around, and we intend to stay here until our demands are met."[58]

Rev. Jackson and his colleagues refused $250 bonds. Jesse spent the next three days in the jail hospital being treated for bronchial pneumonia. From his jail bed Jesse penned an open letter: "We are seeking meaningful participation in the American economy . . . not just a minimum wage but a livable wage. . . . It is significant that a period of despair and hopelessness, characterized by the slogan 'burn, baby, burn,' has been transformed into a period of hope with new possibilities characterized by the slogan, 'build, baby, build, earn while you learn.'"[59] This appeal was inspired, no doubt, by Dr. King's 1963 "Letter from a Birmingham Jail."

Community ministers, labor leaders, city aldermen, and state legislators called for Jesse's release while Calvin Morris requested Mayor Daley's intercession. The regional office of the Department of Housing and Urban Development called a hearing to investigate whether federally funded projects with contracts over $100,000 were in compliance with President Nixon's executive order 11246.[60] The Building Association announced that an employment recruiting center would open on the South Side within a week. Some 250 mothers and kids picketed the University of Illinois's Circle Campus site without arrests while construction workers watched the marchers. Jesse was released on a recognizance bond. The mayor urged all parties to reduce their negotiating teams. Coalition leaders appeared in court on contempt charges for defying the injunction. Concurrently, building trade demonstrations were taking place in Albany, New York City, Seattle, and Oklahoma City, pushing for implementation of Nixon's new Philadelphia Plan based on his recent executive order.[61]

About four thousand people gathered for a Black Monday at the Picasso in front of the Civic Center. Then they marched to the trade council/union offices where Rev. Jackson informed the crowd that 42 percent of Chicagoans (a stretch) were black, but barely 3 percent of its construction workers were black.[62] More closed meetings of the warring parties were held in the mayor's office, and the coalition called a moratorium on demonstrations to encourage progress at the table. HUD's hearing turned out to be a fiasco as coalition speakers, including Jesse Jackson, had to be ushered in by armed marshals through the boos and taunts of thousands of whites lined up in front of the building. Inside, the testimony reflected the ongoing tug-of-war.[63]

When the *Defender* headlined its October 4 edition "Jobs Plan Accord Reached," hopes were raised, but a marathon meeting in Mayor Daley's office produced only a draft agreement. Rumors spread that union cards were being given out at the new recruitment center and that two hundred black workers had been hired and referred to job sites on a trial basis. It was all untrue. Some people intuited that the contractors and unions hoped to stall long enough for the cold weather to bring an end to both construction work and picketing. A tentative Chicago Plan was signed on November 6, but coalition members immediately discovered critical omissions, and the building trade officials denied they had agreed to enroll four thousand blacks in special training. To keep the CUCA "vital and viable," the coalition held a major benefit at the Auditorium Theatre with Dick Gregory, Oscar Brown Jr., and Mahalia Jackson among the entertainers. As the year ended the conflict was over five months old and counting.[64]

An agreement was finally reached on January 12, 1970, in Mayor Daley's office. The warring parties initialed the Chicago Plan for Equal Opportunity, which offered four thousand jobs and training positions in four categories. While the coalition relinquished any more specific numbers on recruits and any control of the training, Rev. Vivian indicated the pact was a "good step forward." Another CUCA leader added, "We will know the impact of the plan when we can see in five years a representation across the crafts that will be in proportion to the black population in Chicago."[65] Since the coalition was to be represented on all committees, he felt the pact could be monitored adequately. For all its involvement, Breadbasket was not even mentioned in reports of the settlement. Unfortunately, the coalition had clearly worn out its participants on this hard-fought effort and as a result was unable to either monitor the agreement or initiate further campaigns. It simply fell away. Its leaders turned their efforts to creating the Black Strategy Center, which also folded in months.[66] Yet, when the Nixon administration's Philadelphia Plan was upheld in federal court in early 1970, affirmative action in government building contracts became the law across the land.[67]

To be truthful, coalitions were not Jesse Jackson's or Breadbasket's style. For us in the SC, working with the CUCA was at arm's length and uncomfortable at best. We never picked up on Dr. King's vision of collaboration, which he had demonstrated with the Poor People's Campaign. We focused narrowly on what we could do. Jesse's persona, especially after King's death, was so elevated, both publicly and in his own mind, that he found it increasingly more difficult to reach out and work in coalitions. For example, we never joined the national Welfare Rights Organization's campaign against Sears, seeking a financial credit system for people, primarily women, living on welfare. Except for some good chemistry between Jesse and Fred Hampton, the charismatic young leader of the Black Panthers in Chicago, Breadbasket saw the Panthers as militant West Siders and they saw us as mainstream South Siders.[68] While we supported the UFW grape campaign sporadically, it was never collegial. Even with the CUCA and his colleague C. T. Vivian, Jesse felt uneasy not being front and center, a preacher in full command. Earlier, our efforts to work with the CUL had run aground. One can only imagine what might have been had Breadbasket and Jesse Jackson welcomed a broader coalition laboring on behalf of economic justice for all people.

CHAPTER 8

THE HUNGER CAMPAIGN

Hunger is a hurtin' thing.—Large sign above the stage at anti-hunger
meetings across Illinois

Illinois Campaign to End Hunger

In keeping with Dr. King's vision, Ralph Abernathy introduced phase 2 of
the Poor People's Campaign at an Easter banquet in Chicago in April 1969,
with the goal of ending poverty and hunger across the land. The next day
Revs. Abernathy and Jackson journeyed to Montgomery, Alabama, to kick
off the drive with demonstrations. Arriving home, Jesse called on Chicago
and other northern cities to join in the SCLC's drive "for economic justice,
respect and an economic base for all poor people. We are going to shake this
nation up, a nation that refuses to give people a job or income which they
deserve and need, yet will pay farmers $30,000 and $50,000 a year not to
farm, while families of seven and twelve are forced to live on $177 a month."
Chicago Breadbasket would target Illinois, specifically the state legislature in
Springfield.[1] Our SC accepted this new directive with enthusiasm, even though
our role was not "steering"; rather it was to offer support and to encourage
our parishioners to participate.

This was a new ball game for Chicago's Breadbasket, which had focused
on economic empowerment using pulpits and parishioners. Breadbasket
had relied on the power of a financial sanction, the boycott, to force private
employers to come to terms with our demands for fairness in employment,
products, and services. The fight combating hunger and poverty was aimed
at the public sector, by creating an informed citizenry that would join us as
allies in a demand for fairness from government at all levels. To relinquish
the sanction of economic withdrawal for the much less secure moral suasion
was no easy transition. Enormous energy would go into this very different
campaign.

Hearing that the federal government had no plans to combat hunger, Jesse
declared, "We, the ministers of SCLC's Operation Breadbasket announce that
hunger is much too serious a problem to be postponed as a national priority.

Hunger is the most critical issue of this nation and of this state. Therefore, we cannot take the President's lead on this matter, for it would divide us into those who can eat and those who must starve or go hungry." Jesse indicated that fifty thousand families in Cook County and twelve thousand in wealthy DuPage County faced hunger.[2]

The Illinois anti-hunger drive began in late April with a walking tour of the once affluent, now depressed Kenwood neighborhood, led by Revs. Jesse Jackson and Curtis Burrell, the head of the Kenwood Oakland Community Organization. Followed by a stream of reporters and photographers, they interviewed residents door to door, exposing serious needs. The first of a series of statewide hunger hearings was held at a small Kenwood church. The next day members of Breadbasket and the CUCA met with several of Illinois's eighteen black legislators to hammer out proposals to deal with the issue.[3]

A week later in Springfield, Rev. Jackson and sixty followers met with these legislators to craft a bill, taken from Jesse's position paper on "human subsidy."[4] Jesse recognized that legislators were easily led to vote for subsidies for businesses wanting protection. He envisioned transferring this concept to people, offering an alternative to the degrading system of welfare handouts.[5] The recommended legislation proposed declaring hunger a disaster; pronouncing slums illegal; replacing "welfare" with a decent "subsidy" (minimum wage) for all people; removing the means test to end abusive and embarrassing disclosures of personal finances; abolishing the food stamp system; and establishing emergency job training.[6] State senator Richard Newhouse stated that a "subsidy of human beings makes sense as we subsidize commercial institutions and land. Subsidy must cease to be only the aid of the affluent, but aid to all citizens, especially those in need. Illinois has the opportunity to become the first state to establish human subsidy."[7] This bill zeroed in on hunger and wisely let go of other SCLC goals.

Back in Chicago, Jesse announced plans for mass rallies in Springfield to support the new subsidy bill. The timing was fortuitous since the legislature was about to debate cutting back the welfare program. Referring to the Illinois House speaker, Ralph Smith, Rev. Morris commented, "While he is making that proposal, we'll all be demonstrating for our bill that would upgrade and not downgrade the economy of the poor."[8] Jesse urged teachers, students, churches, and businesses to join this effort by going to Springfield.

The opening rally at Union Baptist Church in the capital offered a rousing start. Several black legislators spoke and joined in singing freedom songs led by the Breadbasket Orchestra and Choir. Jesse declared, "If no action is taken on our bill we're going to hit those highways next week marching to Springfield." The crowd sang out, "Ain't gonna let nobody turn me around," adding, "ain't gonna let Governor Ogilvie turn me around" and "ain't gonna let Mayor Daley turn me around."[9]

The next day, with four thousand folks demonstrating outside, Speaker Smith withdrew his controversial bill slicing the welfare budget by $125 million and allowed it to be replaced by the human subsidy bill offered by Representative Harold Washington and colleagues. The crowd outside moved to a rally at the Armory where, in a surprise appearance, Jackie Robinson, a baseball icon and Hall of Famer, told the crowd that Rev. Jackson was "the next Martin Luther King, Jr. If [only] some of us had the same courage as Jesse."[10]

Back inside the Capitol, the Senate suspended the rules to hear Rev. Jackson, who received a standing ovation. Jesse asserted that as a Christian minister he was concerned with "the elimination of hunger. . . . Hunger knows no color line. And in our state there are many more white persons who go to bed hungry at night than there are blacks." The problem in Illinois is not money, but priorities, he said. "The federal government pays into Illinois $97 million annually to farmers for not growing food and only sends in $6 million for relief of the needy. Now it's time to reverse the process." Then Jesse moved to the heart: "The biggest problem for you to face is the need to change your attitudes. You look upon help given the farmers as a 'subsidy' and yet you call aid to the poor and disadvantaged 'relief.' The people need subsidy not stigmatization." Jesse's remarks were warmly received, and debate resumed on the human subsidy bill though no action was taken that day.[11]

At the next Saturday Breadbasket, with action stalled on the subsidy bill, Jesse announced plans for a statewide caravan against hunger. Senator George McGovern declared that he had come to Chicago to support "the young civil rights leader" and to "underscore the importance of ending hunger in this rich country. We have a twin burden on our back and it's the Vietnam war and hunger. . . . the U.S. has got to stop killing Asians and start feeding its millions of poor. . . . it should choose a federal budget of life and not one of death." Summing up the excitement of the week's events in Springfield, Representative Corneal Davis told the crowd that Jesse had accomplished in three hours what black legislators had been attempting for eighteen years. He called Ralph Smith's withdrawal of the welfare bill an "unheard of thing. . . . Never in all my 27 years in the legislature have I seen a Speaker of the House back down on his own bill."[12]

Two days later Jesse was in Washington, D.C., addressing a group of black entrepreneurs. He said that it's not enough to be on "the man's payroll at a high salary because this won't buy individual freedom" and decried the "trend of using blacks as fronts to perpetuate white economic colonialism." With some foresight Jesse predicted that within a decade 25 percent of the workforce could be producing 75 percent of the goods, causing an ever-larger pool of unskilled, unemployed people.[13]

A planned meeting in Springfield between Governor Richard Ogilvie, labor leaders, and Rev. Jackson was aborted when Ogilvie refused to include Jesse in the session. Apparently, the governor did not want to appear to be buckling to the campaign. Also, Ogilvie sought support for a new state income tax while Jesse insisted that his support was contingent upon earmarked funds for hunger. Looking at this impasse Jesse declared that the governor could not meet with the alliance because it "was politically dangerous for him. It's a new political ball game now." Later, in a strategy session of allies, Jesse announced that the campaign would continue "until the hunger for food of every child in the state, black or white, is satisfied."[14]

At the next Saturday Breadbasket, Adlai Stevenson III indicated that, contrary to rumors, the state was solvent and had $300 million set aside with $100 million available immediately:

> There is something wrong, very wrong with our priorities when we keep more than $7 million in an agricultural pension fund, another $1.8 million to pay for county fairs, another $1 million to take care of race horses in Illinois and another $90 million sitting year in and year out in funds earmarked for roads but not being used for roads or anything else. Then we have only about $286,000 for school lunches and $312.24 for milk for school children. . . . We ought to and we could put an end to hunger in this state. . . . You keep the pressure up to end hunger. Stay on the case, Jesse.[15]

With a totally different take from Stevenson, Mayor Daley refused even to meet with the campaign leaders, sending his deputies. At the meeting Jesse requested that the mayor help persuade Governor Ogilvie to support the human subsidy bill and a breakfast/lunch program for all schoolchildren. Jesse also called for a state income tax of 6–8 percent on corporations and earmarking moneys for hunger and education. While unrealistic, these goals were meant to alert the mayor and his deputies to the gravity of the situation. Jesse urged better communication between the mayor and the black community. Still, the Breadbasket–coalition team could get no word on a definite meeting with Daley. Over the coming days Rev. Morris and Willie Barrow led meticulous organizing for a downstate caravan to build support for the human subsidy bill.[16]

The downstate motorcade began on June 12 in Rockford with local leaders taking Breadbasket people through some poverty areas. One visitor described the scenes as "unbelievable and inhumane." That evening, in a high school under a huge sign, "Hunger Is a Hurtin' Thing," more than eight hundred people, mostly local residents, politicians, and journalists, listened to personal stories of poverty from both black and white people. A twenty-three-year-old pregnant woman told of pleading unsuccessfully with city officials to help her find a place to live. A mother of five told of surviving on a welfare check of $228 a month. "If it weren't for my family and friends giving us something, we'd starve." A mother of seven with a blind husband related how they would eat one chicken over an entire week. "We just can't live. We need more money."[17] Breadbasket's musicians gave a soothing touch to an emotional session. Then it was back to Chicago for Saturday Breadbasket.

At the morning rally Senator Charles Percy reversed his public position and came out in support of the campaign. "It's unthinkable to allow hunger to exist in America when we are approaching a trillion dollar economy. Many in Congress say we can't afford to alleviate the hunger problem now, but I say they can do it and have got to do it now." He told of his own mother being on welfare in the Great Depression and promised to urge Congress to "pay not a penny to farmers over a $20,000 limit" and to utilize the saved funds for food programs. Percy commended Breadbasket and Jesse, saying, "You are helping to fulfill the dream of the late Dr. Martin Luther King, Jr. and today as a result of your work, none can say that hunger and malnutrition don't exist."[18]

A week later the caravan arrived in East St. Louis. Walking through blighted areas Rev. Jackson and his followers were shocked by "the maze of broken down shacks, outhouses, junk piles and train trestles," the "wide ravines of polluted water, discarded lumber, and refuse" in "this bleak housing area," as described by Faith Christmas, a *Defender* staff writer who accompanied the tour. Rev. Riddick exclaimed, "This is East of Eden, south of freedom, and a slum city beyond the Gateway Arch." A mother of three told Jesse her welfare check of $125 went for food stamps, rent for a three-room house barely standing, and basic necessities. "I just try to make out with what I get, but sometimes I don't have anything to feed my kids." A disabled World War II veteran opened his two-room shack to the touring group and said his $105 monthly pension check meant he often went hungry. Other mind-boggling stories were shared that evening at the hunger hearing at Pilgrim CME Church.[19]

After a two-day tour of depressed Cairo, Illinois, the caravan pulled into Springfield. Several thousand people, black and white, rallied outside the Capitol as Jesse taped a copy of the human subsidy bill to the building's doors. At almost the same time inside, the House of Representatives adopted the bill, sending it to the Senate. Later, Jesse addressed six thousand cheering supporters: "We are here to challenge the governor and the state legislature to feed its poor."[20]

Breadbasket office volunteer Hermene Hartman cut classes at Loop College to join the rally in Springfield. At one point Hermene noticed National Guard troops standing on rooftops, holding rifles aimed at the crowd. She remembers becoming quite frightened and letting out a cry. "Jesse grabbed my hand and stopped the line and made us get on our knees and pray. I was scared to death. He gave me a real lesson in leadership. And that was that you don't lead with fear, from the front of the line. It was also a real lesson in nonviolent practice." When they resumed the march, Jesse asked her, "Are you still scared?" Hermene replied, "No."[21]

Back in East St. Louis, Jesse testified to Senator McGovern's Committee on Nutrition and Human Needs. He urged that federal subsidies given to Illinois farmers not to grow food should be used, instead, to feed the hungry, and surplus crops should be distributed to the needy. Jesse noted that Illinois botched its chance for $6 million for school lunches because of a failure to match the federal grant, leaving Cook County with meals for only a small portion of its poverty-level children. Jesse called for the elimination of the means test and praised the Black Panther Party for initiating the "most creative and revolutionary food program where thousands of hungry children are fed. The only prerequisite for the Panthers program is that the child be hungry, and no one needs to be examined and his stomach x-rayed to find out if he's really hungry." Jesse again challenged Illinois's governor to support the subsidy bill. Senators McGovern and Percy commended him for "arousing and alerting America to the hunger crisis." Percy promised to share Jesse's statement with his colleagues in Congress, and McGovern hoped Congress would authorize a billion dollars for food stamps.[22]

After two weeks crisscrossing the state, the Breadbasket troops returned to Chicago. While the band of brothers and sisters was weary, we were all pleased with the positive responses from the hearings, conversations, crowds, town mayors, and newspaper coverage in and beyond Illinois. Most encouraging was passage of the human subsidy bill in the Illinois House. Dr. King would have been proud of Chicago Breadbasket's trailblazing drive to keep alive his dream of the Poor People's Campaign.

Touched by the extent of the hunger problem, Edith Lovejoy Pierce, a well-regarded poet from Evanston, penned "Hidden Hunger":

I chew the hidden hunger, taste the curse
That all our dislocating days disperse
Like grit in sugar and like sand in sauce.
The hungry all about, I dine alone.
I gnaw the unrelenting chicken bone
Which is as ragged and as hard as pain.
A bowl of flowers is a center lure—
A pot in which despair has dropped its spoor:
The waxen-petaled faces of the poor.[23]

Ratcheting up pressure on the Senate to pass the subsidy bill, Rev. Jackson announced statewide demonstrations, saying that we would "go to schools in poverty areas where we know children are hungry and can't learn abstract numbers on an empty stomach. A school will have the choice of watching us picket and protest, or feeding the children. Police and jail will not stop us." With representatives from fifteen Illinois cities at his side, Jesse promised that Breadbasket would start a free breakfast program in churches. He challenged the governor not to "play politics with hunger."[24]

In August, Rev. Jackson attacked President Nixon's recently announced welfare reform because of its "contempt for the poor." Jesse rejected Nixon's premise that welfare recipients do not desire to work and called for a Marshall-like Plan to counter the "vicious triangle that locks people in poverty: houses, jobs, and schools. . . . We do not need in this nation a redistribution of welfare stations; we need a redistribution of wealth."[25]

In Springfield, facing stiff opposition, Breadbasket ally Representative Robert Mann offered a watered-down bill subsidizing school lunches at a price tag of $5.4 million. Even with the support of all eighteen black legislators, the compromise was a devastating setback for the human subsidy bill that had passed the House. The substitute bill was adopted and signed into law by Governor Richard Ogilvie on August 19. Jesse put the best face possible on this limited victory. "In a time when the nation, including the President is cutting back on the needs of hungry people, Governor Ogilvie has taken a humane and farsighted step for the hungry children of this state." From Atlanta, Rev. Abernathy declared, "Illinois has taken a step toward significant achievement. Perhaps the Governor is learning that it is not the presence of the military, but the absence of hunger that can make Illinois a great state. I hope President Nixon takes notice of such moral leadership exerted in Illinois."[26]

Rev. Jackson made it clear that the new program fell short of the mark, saying, "Many hungry people are preschool age and adults not covered by this bill. We still look to Governor Ogilvie to take additional steps to feed the hungry of this state, 60 percent of whom are white." Jesse urged that hunger in Illinois be declared a disaster and that the federal government work with the state to raise the subsidy level for all people and to develop job training for the poor and hungry.[27]

The anti-hunger campaign took Breadbasket beyond the power of the pulpit, which had served so well in negotiating covenants. Poor people were a powerless and unstable constituency. In this new environment Breadbasket relied on moral suasion buttressed by personal testimonies in public hearings. In addition, the war in Vietnam exposed the grim truth that guns and butter, including bread for the poor, were more than the American people would tolerate. Viewed in this light, the victory of free school lunches was a remarkable, if partial, achievement.

Inaugurating Free Breakfasts

Just as Governor Ogilvie was signing the bill authorizing school lunches, Operation Breadbasket initiated free breakfasts at two South Side churches, picking up on the Black Panthers' West Side program, which was feeding a thousand children a week by their count. As of October, two thousand people were being fed weekly at the Breadbasket sites, and three additional churches were added. Rev. Morris declared at Saturday Breadbasket, "It is not enough that our efforts during the summer helped get a free lunch program and forced the withdrawal of a bill that would cut welfare payments by $125 million. Hunger is still prevalent across the state and we must continue our fight to eliminate this injustice. . . . We have to go back on the road to seek free breakfast programs for every needy child in the state."[28]

"Back on the road" included downstate Cairo. Rev. Barrow announced Operation Lift for Cairo, declaring, "Black people are guaranteed to starve in Cairo, Illinois, now that they have been cut off from food and medical services." She asked for donations of children's clothing, food, and medical supplies to help alleviate the suffering, which was due in part to a seven-month boycott of downtown businesses. The contact person for donations was Alice Tregay, a Breadbasket regular. In the earlier A&P "Don't Buy" campaign, Tregay was the lone female picket captain, and she made it almost a family affair by bringing several family members along to picket a South Side A&P store. She soon became a valued Breadbasket staff person coordinating political education classes.[29]

One Saturday Breadbasket climaxed with three great saxophonists—Cannonball Adderley, Gene "Jug" Ammons, and Breadbasket's Ben Branch—along with Cannonball's quintet and the Breadbasket Orchestra offering a "soul mass" of sound. Their playing of "Red Top" was a stirring highlight of what Jesse called a "Black expression of our thing."[30]

Breadbasket's campaign forced the hunger issue onto the national agenda. While Senator Percy managed to secure a vote continuing the Senate Committee on Nutrition and Human Needs, he admitted at Saturday Breadbasket in early November that more was needed to alert the nation to "the catastrophe" facing hungry folks across America.[31] A very reluctant White House held a food conference in December with speakers blaming Congress for America's hunger. Rev. Jackson, a panelist, charged that there was something wrong with a nation that sends three men to the moon who bring back two boxes of rocks at the cost of $25 billion, but will not spend $5 billion to feed hungry people on planet earth.[32] Jesse criticized the conference as stacked and unrepresentative of the poor. Fannie Lou Hamer of Mississippi refused to attend "another conference" and instead brought poor people into the halls of the Capitol. An American Friends Service Committee report documented that federal food programs were reaching less than half of those in need. While the White House and Congress took quite a rap, the conference helped expose the shameful reality of hunger across the land.[33]

This spotlight on hunger led Chicago's WTTW-TV to preempt regular programming on two evenings to present *Hunger: A National Disgrace*, with excerpts from the White House event, which was followed by a local response, *Town Meeting: Who's Hungry in Chicago?* Other cities followed suit, and several segments were sent to the food conference staff who were preparing a summary for Congress. This was the peak of Breadbasket's impact on hunger in the United States.[34]

Entering 1970, Breadbasket began its seventh month of offering free meals to children and needy people at five churches weekly. The North Shore chapter supported this program with donations of money and three carloads of food per week. Volunteers came from across the city; social clubs contributed food and cash; and workshops were held on how to "make hunger illegal." WTTW-TV ran a week-long program, *To Feed the Hungry*, with camera shots into Uptown and West Side ghetto apartments, contradicting the mayor's claim that "there is no need for anyone being hungry in Chicago."[35]

Breadbasket Links Anti-Hunger Campaign to Health Crisis

While City Hall blocked any hunger initiative, Cook County Hospital announced that overcrowding would now limit admissions to emergency cases only. Jesse suddenly saw hunger and health as issues that could be joined, and in no time he came up with an eight-point Hunger and Health Manifesto challenging the city and state "to eliminate the twin evils of hunger and poor health care." At Saturday Breadbasket volunteers held up placards declaring, "Full Stomachs Mean Healthy Minds."[36]

In his *Defender* column Jesse illustrated the hunger/health crisis by highlighting one neighborhood, Kenwood-Oakland, where "more than 45 of every 1,000 babies die before the second week of their lives. Seventeen of every 1,000 families are stricken by tuberculosis. This beleaguered slum is yet a hunger and health hazard, where 56,000 people live with only four doctors in the total neighborhood." Jesse wrote that Cook County Hospital was now characterized as a "dumping ground" for black patients, who made up 85 percent of its patient load. "We call for an end to the total hunger and health crisis as a necessary step toward rebuilding a new and more human city."[37]

The manifesto called upon the city council to "declare hunger illegal," offer breakfast for two hundred thousand needy children, and join with the county board to establish comprehensive medical care through neighborhood clinics. The manifesto urged Illinois to adopt an adequate minimum wage and apply for federal funds to meet hunger needs across the state, and it challenged Congress to pass human subsidy legislation. Jesse summed up, "Our choice is not between feeding the hungry or not feeding them. It is a choice between life and death for this city, this state and this nation."[38]

At a Saturday Breadbasket Jesse called on the city and the state to adopt "our manifesto" or come up "with one of their own." To jump-start the action, Jesse announced an investigative tour of Cook County Hospital and visits with city aldermen. He also presented the manifesto on channel 11, prodding black politicians publicly: "There is no reason why all the black aldermen and state legislators can't agree on this one issue of hunger, even if they haven't agreed on one single thing before. On this, there just shouldn't be any debate."[39]

Struggle at City Hall

The mayor ignored Breadbasket's manifesto for several days. Finally, Rev. Jackson was allowed to present the plan at the city council, where he called for an emergency $35 million to feed impoverished families.[40] At the public hearing on this request, four hundred Breadbasket supporters lined the gallery as several poor people, black and white, testified. The next day, testimony was abruptly limited to Dr. Deton Brooks, the black director of the city's Human Resources Department. As Jesse led fifty prepared witnesses and supporters out of the hearing, he assailed the city council: "Many hungry people came here today to testify and had to listen to three hours of reasons why they are hungry. ... We're not here to sit all day while you play games with the poor." Jesse promised to bring poor people back every day until action was taken, and if they were locked out, "they will sit outside the doors and eat crackers."[41]

On the third day, the city's finance committee adopted a watered-down ordinance containing not one single dollar. Rev. Morris called the resolution "totally unresponsive" and charged the city with "repressive action" against two hundred mothers and children who were blocked by uniformed police as they attempted to enter the council gallery. Breadbasket had hit another brick wall.[42] The Campaign to End Hunger was stalled; it seemed like the city was allowing the public's anger to rant and rave itself into exhaustion. Two weeks later, the city council adopted a paltry $500,000 emergency food program to commence in two weeks at fourteen outposts with no means test.[43] While this six-week clash took an enormous toll on overall Breadbasket energies, the sc stayed out of the fray and worked on covenant follow-ups. The limited resources of full-time pastors did not allow us to participate, beyond support and encouragement from our pulpits, in this and several other Breadbasket programs.

During the tango with City Hall, the health care component of the manifesto disappeared. With Jesse, when something didn't fly well, you simply parked the loaded airplane in the back hangar. So, the health issue went down, as voter registration went down, and the hunger fight, while lasting a little longer, also went down, with only a modest emergency food program to show for the bruising battle with the entrenched powers.

Rev. Abernathy took up the hunger issue with the Los Angeles Breadbasket chapter, telling its members that the United States must realign its priorities. "If America does not declare hunger and poverty illegal, then we will give the nation an opportunity to feed us in its jailhouse." He said that the SCLC was giving about $100,000 each to the Breadbasket chapters in major cities to feed the poor, secure better education, and negotiate with food chains for jobs and services.[44] Since Abernathy's rhetoric showed no connection with our struggle in Chicago, and no financial assistance ever arrived, it appeared that Ralph and Jesse were not in serious communication. When Jesse Jackson made the cover of *Time* magazine, Charlie Cherokee, a columnist in the *Defender*, wrote that Abernathy "is reported to have uttered several syllables in an unknown tongue."[45]

Campaign Limps On

In April, several hungry people shared their stories at a "Hunger in Wards" hearing in a South Side church. Rev. Barrow slammed public officials for not listening to this "chronic condition" from their own constituents. Senator McGovern convened a hearing at the People's Church on the North Side to prod Senate action where, before an audience of six hundred people, Dr. Deton Brooks, the city's human resources director, admitted that more money was needed to eliminate hunger. Jesse assailed the mayor: "It is cruel that Dr. Brooks should be stuck with the burden and trapped here trying to explain the city's programs, inadequate as they are. The Mayor should be here instead, testifying for himself instead of serving wine, tea and roses for his 16-year celebration as mayor."[46]

On April 30, after two days of the new city food program, thirty-five hundred people had been fed in eight centers. Rev. Barrow protested the meager

$500,000 appropriation and the limited hours, 10 a.m. to 3 p.m., excluding all school-age children. "We shall meet, feed, protest, picket, march or whatever is necessary to end hunger in Chicago." Brooks defended the city, charging Rev. Barrow and others with political rather than humanitarian motivations.[47] During this battle of words, Breadbasket maintained its free breakfast ministry. Social groups, schools, congregations, and temples collected food; Simeon High School in Chicago and Barrington Consolidated High School in the suburbs held food drives. Apart from our feeding program, Breadbasket's anti-hunger campaign slipped off the radar, and staff turned to other things.

In early September 1970, Rev. Barrow announced at Saturday Breadbasket that the archdiocese was now feeding ten thousand children in thirty-eight parochial schools, but she reminded the crowd that "hunger is a hurtin' thing" for six hundred thousand people in Chicago alone. Rev. Morris recalled that just a year earlier Mayor Daley had claimed there was no hunger in Chicago, and religious leaders had remained silent. Now, when the archdiocese had finally begun a feeding program, John Cardinal Cody invited no one from Breadbasket or the Black Panthers, who had modeled the program, to the opening ceremony. Calvin noted, "Before Mayor Daley, Deton Brooks, Cardinal Cody, Senator Percy or Senator Smith moved on the hunger issue, we were already working to eliminate hunger and to declare it illegal and were feeding people.... The unsung heroes are those who saw the moral issue and decided to fight to end hunger in America."[48]

Ironically, less than a month later Breadbasket abruptly terminated its feeding program. Our volunteers were exhausted. While some of the need was covered by the new feeding program in the Roman Catholic schools and by the city's new emergency feeding program at eight centers, Breadbasket's withdrawal was a major disappointment to the community.

In a symbolic closing gesture, Breadbasket distributed 1,168 bags of food to an overflow group of hungry folks gathered at Christ the King Lutheran Church. In a poignant description, Sheryl Butler, a *Defender* staff reporter, wrote that she saw

> a chain of humanity, linked hand in hand, the old, the young, the shabbily dressed, the neatly attired men, women and children. Swaying from side to side, they sang with all their hearts ["Down by the Riverside"]. Some had tears in their eyes, others with their eyes closed, had a look that transcended what was occurring. In a corner, an old man wept shamelessly. What was occurring was unbelievable.... Not in Chicago. But the proof was here in the church. These people came because they were hungry.... Operation Breadbasket, which had been helping to feed the hungry for more than a year and a half, was closing down its food storefront and its director, the Rev. Jesse L. Jackson had come to distribute the last of the food to those who needed it.[49]

After eighteen months, exhaustion and program proliferation had simply overwhelmed the Breadbasket family, and the Illinois Campaign to End Hunger with its hearings, caravans, protests, and free lunches had effectively ended. A fundamental shift from using consumer power to chanting with pride on Saturday mornings, from negotiating backed by economic sanction to heartrending pleas in anti-hunger hearings, had brought meager returns. The demise of this Breadbasket campaign notwithstanding, these limited successes foreshadowed long-term changes to the landscape: breakfast and lunch programs would become staples of both public and parochial schools throughout Illinois and across the country.

The welfare crisis erupted again in the fall of 1971. It would be one of Breadbasket's last campaigns. Governor Ogilvie ordered $52 million chopped off the welfare budget. This appeared to be a callous attempt to solve the state's deficit on the backs of the poor. Immediate complaints came from hospitals, which depended on state aid for up to 40 percent of their budgets. Provident Hospital's director declared that this raised the issue of "whether Chicago's black community will allow itself to become a wilderness without adequate hospital and medical care."[50]

Speaking for an emergency welfare coalition, Breadbasket's Ed Riddick announced that the group would seek an immediate meeting with the governor. He indicated that five hundred thousand "black and poor people" were served by three threatened hospitals. "Ogilvie's fund freeze will lead to catastrophic levels [of untreated medical cases], and will subordinate Chicago's health system to one of hopelessness."[51] At Saturday Breadbasket Senator Percy announced efforts to seek emergency federal help to compensate for the loss of state funding. After the rally, eight hundred people marched on Englewood Hospital to show support. Even Cook County's board president and public aid director appealed to the governor to take "a more humane look at priorities."[52]

While Breadbasket volunteers began preparing emergency relief packages of food and clothing, a temporary injunction blocking the welfare cutback was ordered by the circuit court. At the same time that Jesse led five thousand folks in a robust rally in the state capital, in Chicago Rev. Riddick, Cirilo McSween, and other coalition leaders met in a closed session with Ogilvie. When the governor pleaded for more time, McSween shot back, "The welfare cuts must be restored."[53] A few days later the circuit court judge ordered the $21 million cutback restored. Though the funds were delayed, recipients received their November payments in full, ending the crisis.[54] This coalitional effort to hold the line on welfare payments was Breadbasket's last foray in ending hunger.

Operation Breadbasket
Consumer Guide packet,
May 1967.

Operation Breadbasket logo.

Flyer for July 10, 1966, event distributed on Chicago's South Side and used as insert in the Gresham Methodist Church's Sunday bulletin.

Program for Breadbasket worship rally, May 26, 1966.

Front-page
coverage of
Freedom Rally
at Soldier Field,
July 1966. *Chicago
Defender.*

VOL. XI — NO. 87   MONDAY, JULY 11, 1966   Price 10 cents

Hot Afternoon Of Non-Violence

Thousands Join Dr. King's Rally At Soldier Field

A Digest Of SCLC Demands-- See Page 4

What SCLC Leader Said -- See Page 3

Dr. King's 'Freedom' Congregation

Some 30,000 gathered in Soldier Field Sunday to witness Dr. Martin Luther King, Jr. and other civil rights leaders ignite the main thrust of the Chicago freedom movement. The day culminated in a mass march to the loop with Dr. King attaching civil rights demands to the main door of City Hall. (Defender Photo by Bob Black)

Dr. Martin Luther
King Jr. and
Rev. Jesse Jackson
with Breadbasket
Steering Committee
members, ca.
October 1967.
Left to right:
Revs. Stroy
Freeman, John
Thurston (*seated*),
H. B. Brady, and
Clay Evans.

334 Auburn Ave., N.E.
Atlanta, Georgia 30303
Telephone 522-1420

Southern Christian Leadership Conference

Martin Luther King Jr., *President*   Ralph Abernathy, *Treasurer*   Andrew J. Young, *Executive Director*

July 21, 1967

Rev. Martin Deppe
8712 S. Emerald
Chicago, Illinois

Dear Rev. Deppe:

I would like to begin by thanking you for the marvelous contribution that you made at the Conference on Operation Breadbasket in Chicago. Ralph Abernathy will be communicating with you relative to some of the details of the conference within the next thirty days. Also, under separate cover you will receive a summary of the conference.

As you know the tenth Anniversary Convention of the Southern Christian Leadership Convention is August 14th-17th in Atlanta, Georgia. I want to take this opportunity to personally invite you to the convention. It is my feeling that we will be grappling with some of the real issues confronting our nation. There will be a session on Business and Economic Development which will further explore many of our points of discussion in the Chicago Conference.

This is the tenth Anniversary of the Southern Christian Leadership Conference and I would certainly want you to be a part of this convention. The convention will be formally opened at 8:00 p.m. on Monday, August 14th with Sidney Poitier addressing the Anniversary Banquet. I would hope that you could spend at least three of the four days with us.

For additional information, contact Miss Carole Hoover, who is the coordinator of this year's convention.

Sincerely,

Martin Luther King, Jr.

gss
Enclosures 2

Gresham
Methodist Church
87th Street and
Emerald Avenue,
Chicago, where
the author was
pastor 1964–1970.
Photo by Margaret
Deppe.

Author greeting
parishioners after
worship at Gresham
Methodist Church,
ca. 1965. Photo by
Margaret Deppe.

Two-page ad distributed on Chicago's
South Side, December 1966.

Brochure for Operation Breadbasket Seminar for Negro Businesses, March 1967.

To Save Souls through the Breadbasket

Coverage of "Don't Buy" campaign success, June 1967. *Chicago Citizen.*

CITIZEN NEWSPAPERS
HIGH-LOW BOYCOTT IS SUCCESS

Signing the Breadbasket-Jewel covenant, April 28, 1967. *Left to right*: Donald Perkins (president of Jewel), Rev. Stroy Freeman, Rev. Clay Evans, Dr. Martin Luther King, Rev. Jesse Jackson, Rev. John Thurston. The author recalls standing on Perkins's right at this photo shoot. *Chicago Defender*.

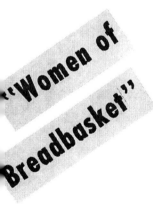

Women of Breadbasket with Coretta Scott King, October 1967. *Standing, left to right*: Mable Brown, Jacqueline Jackson, Rose Rhem, Rev. Willie Barrow, Rev. Addie Wyatt, Phyllis Jenkins. *Sitting, left to right*: Mary Whitfield, Coretta Scott King, and Mrs. Charles Bayer.

Coverage of Breadbasket benefit concert, October 1967.

Alice Tregay's daughter, also named Alice, carrying picket sign in "Don't Buy at A&P" campaign, July 1968. Courtesy Alice L. Tregay.

"A&P Signs Pact" flyer, October 1968.

Campaign to End Hunger flyer, summer 1969.

Food distribution in Uptown, Chicago, April 1970. *Left to right*: Senators Charles Percy and George McGovern, Rev. Jesse Jackson.

Coverage of the Campaign to End Hunger, ca. March 1970. Rev. Jessie "Ma" Houston attending a poor person; Rev. Calvin Morris speaking at Saturday Breadbasket; a child looking at a campaign sign.

HUNGER

S.C.L.C. OPERATION BREADBASKET

Sen. George McGovern (D-S.D.) speaks at Saturday's Operation Breadbasket meeting. (Sun-Times Photo by Pete Peters)

McGovern spells out his plan of 'human security' to end poverty

By Larry Weintraub

Sen. George McGovern (D-S.D.) spelled out a four-point "human security" plan here Saturday that he said he would present to Congress as an alternative to "our degrading and ineffective welfare programs."

McGovern said his proposal, which could cost the nation as much as $35 billion annually, also is intended as an alternative to President Nixon's family assistance program, now pending in Congress.

McGovern told some 5,000 persons at a meeting of Operation Breadbasket his plan is "a program of dignity," not based on an embarassing means test or artificial poverty lines.

He outlined the program at the regular Saturday Breadbasket meeting in the Capitol Theater, 7927 S. Halsted.

Guaranteed jobs

It would provide for a $50 to $65 allowance a month for every child in the country, guaranteed jobs for all able-bodied citizens, increased Social Security benefits for the elderly and disabled and a federally administered public assistance program for those not covered by the other portions of the plan.

McGovern attacked the Nixon administration's spending priorities at the Breadbasket meeting, which was billed as a convention against hunger.

The senator said if Americans want this to be "a nation of law and order," and he said he believes they do, "we must make up our minds that hunger is the worst crime of all, and it must be illegal from here on out."

Under the McGovern program, the children's allowance would be paid regardless of a family's income. He noted that there already is such an allowance in the form of the $600-per-child federal income tax exemption, but it tends to benefit wealthy and middle-class families most.

If the provision is adopted, the senator said, it would cancel tax exemptions, but still would cost an estimated $10 billion the first year it was paid.

Responding to allegations that the allowance would amount to a "baby bonus" and raise the birth rate because families wanted higher payments, McGovern cited studies in other countries which offer such payments.

"There are many reasons people have children," he said, "but collecting $50 a month is not one of them."

The senator said he has worked with officials of Breadbasket and other organizations that work with the poor in developing the program and plans to continue doing so before introducing it in Congress. However, he expects to offer the bill no later than March 1, McGovern said.

The Rev. Jesse L. Jackson, national leader of Operation Breadbasket, the economic arm of the Southern Christian Leadership Conference, cautiously endorsed the McGovern plan.

The Rev. Mr. Jackson said that, historically, social progress has been made in this country when the rich have been shown how they could gain from it.

McGovern's plan helps the poor but has an appeal to the rich, the Rev. Mr. Jackson said.

"Strategically, it's the best plan in the country today. And we hope to keep working with the senator on it. Eventually, every one in the country will have to have a job or an income."

Senator George McGovern speaking at Saturday Breadbasket, February 1970. Courtesy *Sun-Times Media*.

"Don't Buy Bad Meat" campaign, October 1969. Rev. Calvin Morris is carrying sign at far right.

Flyer for the second Black Expo, November 11–15, 1970.

Telegram

LLT387 (01)SHCA365
XCT2712 LK PDB CHICAGO ILL 21 434P ST
REV MARTIN DEPPE GRESHAM UNITED METHODIST CHURCH
8700 SOUTH EMERALD AVE CHGO
WE SUBSCRIBE WHOLEHEARTDLY TO YOUR OBJECTIVE OF ENDING ECONOMIC
REPRESSION ANYWHERE IN THIS COUNTRY, IN OUR RELATIONS WITH THE
PUBLIC AND OUR EMPLOYEES WE HAVE ALWAYS WORKED TOWARD THIS GOAL,
WE HAVE HAD A LONG STANDING POLICY OF STOCKING BLACK PRODUCTS
AND WE ARE LISTED AMONG SOME OF THE FIRST CUSTOMERS OF VARIOUS

LONG ESTABLISHED BLACK COMPANIES, OUR POLICY OF HIRING BLACK EMPLOYEES
IS WELL KNOWN AND WE ARE AMONG THE TOP FIRMS PROVIDING A MANAGMENT
OPORTUNITIES FOR THEM. WE ARE AND HAVE BEEN AT ALL TIMES WILLING
TO MEET WITH YOUR REPRESENTATIVES AND DISCUSS THE MEANS OUR
COMPANY CAN CONTRIBUTE TOWARD THE
SOLUTION OF OUR SOCIAL AND ECONOMIC PROBLEMS AND WE WOULD RESPECTFULLY
LIKE TO INDICATE TO YOUR MINISTERIAL GROUP THAT NO EXTERIOR PRESSURES
ARE NEEDED TO ASSURE OUR HONEST COOPERATION
    C R WALGREEEN DRUG STORES
(526).

Telegram from C. R. Walgreen Drug Stores to author, May 21, 1970.

DO NOT SHOP AT

NATIONAL FOODS

UNTIL THEY SIGN A NEW COVENANT WITH OPERATION BREADBASKET

because National Foods signed a Covenant in 1966 and broke it.

- National Foods did not hire 117 employees costing us an estimated $4,000,000 in salaries
- National Foods did not transfer accounts from 20 stores to Seaway and Independence Banks . . .
- National Foods did not require black liquor salesmen for 20 stores in the black community
- National Foods did not even report 238 supervisory jobs because 221 of them are filled by whites. This "oversight" cost us over $4,000,000 in salaries
- National Foods did not report its employment in Kare Drugs, O'Bee Foods, So-Fresh and National Labs robbing us of 50 jobs and $160,000 in salaries
- National Food Stores profoundly disrespects the black community, Operation Breadbasket and minority workers everywhere. This fight is joined by the U.F.W.O.C. and we support their demand that National Foods buy only Union lettuce.

SOUTHERN CHRISTIAN LEADERSHIP CONFERENCE

OPERATION BREADBASKET
7941 So. Halsted Street   Chicago, Illinois 60621
Phone: 651-6000
"YOUR MINISTERS FIGHT FOR JOBS AND RIGHTS"

"Do Not Shop at National Foods" flyer, December 1970.

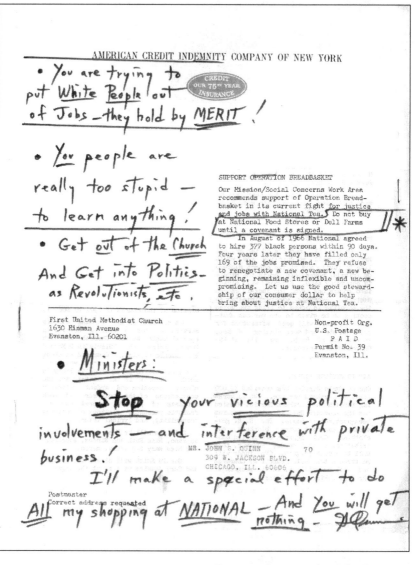

AMERICAN CREDIT INDEMNITY COMPANY OF NEW YORK

- You are trying to put White People out of Jobs — they hold by MERIT!

- You people are really too stupid — to learn anything!

- Get out of the Church And Get into Politics as Revolutionists, etc.

SUPPORT OPERATION BREADBASKET

Our Mission/Social Concerns Work Area recommends support of Operation Breadbasket in its current fight for justice and jobs with National Tea. Do not buy at National Food Stores or Doll Farms until a covenant is signed.

In August of 1966 National agreed to hire 377 black persons within 90 days. Four years later they have filled only 169 of the jobs promised. They refuse to renegotiate a new covenant, a new beginning, remaining inflexible and uncompromising. Let us use the good stewardship of our consumer dollar to help bring about justice at National Tea.

First United Methodist Church
1630 Hinman Avenue
Evanston, Ill. 60201

Non-profit Org.
U.S. Postage
P A I D
Permit No. 39
Evanston, Ill.

- Ministers:

Stop your vicious political involvements — and interference with private business!

MR. JOHN S. QUINN   70
309 N. JACKSON BLVD.
CHICAGO, ILL. 60606

I'll make a special effort to do

Postmaster
Correct address requested

All my shopping at NATIONAL — And You will get nothing — JQuinn

Response from member John Quinn
to "Ministers" at First United Methodist
Church, ca. November 1970.

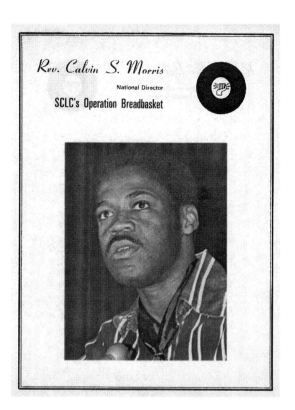

Rev. Calvin S. Morris, associate director, SCLC's Operation Breadbasket, October 1969.

Rev. Willie Barrow, director, Women's Division and Special Projects, October 1969.

Breadbasket reunion, ca. 2005. *Left to right*: Rev. Gary Massoni, Richard Thomas, Rev. Jesse Jackson, St. Claire Booker, Rev. David Wallace. Courtesy Gary Massoni.

Rev. Calvin Morris's seventieth birthday party, March 2011. *Left to right*: Rev. Morris, Rev. Willie Barrow, Rev. Martin Deppe. Courtesy Calvin Morris.

CHAPTER 9

PROLIFERATION

Operation Breadbasket's effectiveness began to suffer as a result of the proliferation of programs, the accumulation of so many auxiliaries, and the disintegration of the various program threads.—Rev. Gary Massoni

While the bread and butter of Operation Breadbasket was investigating and negotiating for jobs and services and promoting economic development, we found ourselves constantly tempted into other issues. Part of this was the world's agenda, such as hunger, poor schools, inadequate housing, and gang violence, demanding attention and response. But on other matters Jesse simply grabbed the headline and carved out his own agenda, often with good intuition but without reflection or consultation. Several worthwhile ideas never got off the ground as a result. Jesse's handsome figure and easy one-liners made for great TV clips, and he loved the attention.

Breadbasket programming also expanded, much of it germinating in the fertile and sometimes frenetic vision of our leader. Jesse came up with an idea a minute and he wanted everything implemented right away, whether or not it was practical or even possible. By mid-1970 our modus operandi involved multiple layers of divisions, spokes, and auxiliaries totaling forty to forty-five units. Other groups had formed, morphed, or disappeared along the way. With staff energy directed at new projects, our Steering Committee was shorthanded in monitoring covenants and selecting targets. Indeed, we frequently met without Jesse or other staff members present.

Black Holidays

At a November 1968 Saturday Breadbasket, Rev. Jackson shared his vision for a Black Christmas, voicing the hope that this event would encourage black pride, support black businesses, and enable our people to give of themselves. Rev. Morris explained that in place of a "fat, white power image," Santa would be a "strong black image. . . . It's time our kids realized that all good doesn't come from the white man."[1]

Sensing some unease, Jesse emphasized at a press conference that Black Christmas was not a white boycott, but an affirmation of black people, which was underscored by the presence of sixty black business owners or representatives standing with him. Jesse hoped that Black Christmas would also serve as a spiritual uplift, encouraging people to "adopt" a welfare family or "sign out" a prisoner on Christmas. He urged mainstream firms to use black products in their Christmas basket donations.[2] The following Saturday some twenty-five hundred people walked behind Revs. Jackson and Willie Barrow from Tabernacle Baptist to the black-owned 51st and State shopping mall for the opening of two stores filled with Breadbasket displays and products. One of the biggest Christmas items that year was black dolls, and their sales skyrocketed.[3]

At the Black Christmas Parade on a sunny but chilly December 7, an estimated thirty thousand people lined the parade route to watch fifty floats representing black businesses, several school bands, and a black Santa. Jesse rode in a horse-drawn wagon, recalling the Poor People's Campaign. Earlier, Jesse had introduced a welfare family of seven as "our celebrities" and encouraged the capacity crowd to give of themselves at Christmas. Jesse shared incidents from his own childhood and said, "I'm not crying because I'm hurt; I'm crying because I'm happy today."[4] At the mall, Jesse received attention for physical exhaustion, and then proceeded to address a small cheering crowd, which had been entertained by celebrities and the Breadbasket Orchestra and Choir. On Christmas Day, black Santa joined Ma Houston and other Breadbasket ministers at Cook County Jail, bringing baked goods, personal items, and good cheer to the inmates.[5] As of this writing Jesse still visits the county jail every year on Christmas Day.

In mid-March 1969, Rev. Jackson announced a Black Easter celebration to capture "the rhythm of our people." It would coincide with the first anniversary of Dr. King's assassination. "We cannot depend on white America to give legitimacy and validity to our celebrations of holidays. Easter, which means spring, is defined in a black context for the renewal of the black community." Jesse emphasized renewing relationships with black brothers and sisters. "Black Easter is SCLC Operation Breadbasket's way of expressing new life through our black consciousness and our black cooperation."[6]

Black Easter events began on April 4, Good Friday, when a group of black business folk laid a wreath at 35th and King Drive. Several Breadbasket supporters attended this opening event.[7] Three performances of the traditional black Passion play, in its fortieth anniversary year, were given before capacity crowds. The King memorial service was held at Saturday Breadbasket and broadcast over WVON radio. On Easter Sunday some 150,000 people lined King Drive to witness the Resurrection Parade, a two-hour pageant of floats and bands saluting black heroes from Harriet Tubman to Malcolm X. Dr. Daniel Hale Williams, the first surgeon to perform open heart surgery, was portrayed by a twelve-year-old boy wearing a white cap and gown; six other youngsters in green intern costumes walked beside him as his patient was wheeled along in front of them.[8]

At a closing banquet, the SCLC's Rev. Abernathy announced phase 2 of the Poor People's Campaign, to commence the next day in Montgomery, Alabama. The target was poverty, and the SCLC would demand of Alabama free food stamps for the poor and of the federal government a commitment to ending unemployment. Abernathy praised Rev. Jackson as a "loyal staff member" and challenged the audience to continue working with Jesse and Operation Breadbasket in the struggle for human dignity.[9]

Feeling the need as a Breadbasket minister to deal with these black consciousness events, I posed some questions to my congregants on Palm Sunday: "Where will you and I be on Good Friday? Would we be sitting inside our own churches, or demonstrating outside our downtown Cokesbury Book Store with Project Equality? Would we attend Saturday's Peace March or Sunday's Black Easter Parade? An interesting week-end of causes. You choose your own cause! But not before you ask, what would Christ have me do?"[10]

If the SC had adopted these black holidays, I would have participated. However, I believed then, as now, that Christmas and Easter stand on their own. While the messages of the incarnation, crucifixion, and resurrection need to be contextualized and brought down to earth, attaching race or color directly to them struck me as an overreach. Pushing black products only added to the growing commercialization of these holy days. In retrospect these many years later, I feel that the black emphasis on these holidays was appropriate, however. Certainly the parade of black heroes illustrating new life and resurrection was a positive experience for many. That these events did not become institutionalized and died away in a few years seems to illustrate their one-time value.

On Saturday, December 6, 1969, the second Black Christmas Parade stepped off from 39th and State. About a hundred floats representing black enterprises and school bands passed an estimated 175,000 people lining the parade route to the mall at 47th and King Drive. There, a ribbon cutting opened the new Black Trade Center with its exhibit of black products and services. To a cheering crowd Rev. Morris declared, "The Black Christmas Parade is for all of us—to show what we have done and are striving to do; it is our parade and our day." He concluded by wishing all "a happy, happy Black Christmas, and a cool Yule."[11]

Available free at the center was a new *Black Book Directory*. To distinguish it from the familiar *Yellow Pages*, its cover and pages were orange. In addition to listings and ads for black businesses and services, the directory contained several small boxed biographical pieces on people like Harriet Tubman,

Langston Hughes, Jackie Robinson, and Sojourner Truth. This novel directory was also spiced with many morsels tucked in the pages:

> It's a smile to us, to be of service to you.
>
> You are "Taking Care of Business" when you use the mellow pages.
>
> Businessmen! The Black Book Directory is your thang!!
>
> The Black Book Directory is like a snow-ball rolling down the side of a hill; it
> keeps growing as it goes. Where it's going to stop Nobody Knows!
>
> "Anxious to please" is the slogan of "all" the Beautiful People in the Black Book
> Directory. Give us a try the next time you buy.[12]

The first copy of the *Black Book Directory* had been presented to Rev.
Jackson at Saturday Breadbasket by the publisher, Donald Walker, who
announced that three hundred thousand copies would be available for Black
Christmas events.[13] Leafing through the classy booklet years later I am struck
with the wealth of community and business information gathered together
for the first time. It was a remarkable resource, revealing the beginning pene-
tration of the city's economy by black entrepreneurs.

Also on December 6, 1969, Rev. Jackson made his debut with the *Chicago
Defender*. In his new column, "On the Case," he wrote, "Black Christmas is
a return to the meaning of the first Christmas. We are challenged to give of
ourselves," as the wise men gave of themselves. Jesse challenged his readers
to visit brothers and sisters in hospital or jail. "If you must give gifts, give
something that will help the whole black community. We have products and
services, all black-owned, that need to be supported. . . . So instead of giving
your son a toy gun, why not give him a savings account at a black bank."[14]

After two seasons on friendly South Side streets, the third Black Christmas
moved downtown in 1970. To the theme "Buy Black, Give Black, and Save
Black" was added "Bacon for Christmas"—supporting Warren Bacon for
president of the Chicago School Board.[15] On a frigid Saturday, December 5,
some five thousand people braved the elements, walking down State Street
chanting, "We want Bacon for Christmas," and effectively tying up traffic.
Leading the parade was black Santa with his Soul Power bag of goodies. Jesse
intoned, "If the Mayor persists in 'burning our Bacon' then we shall make
the cost of 'Bacon' approximately $1 million per pound or translated, $175
million, which is the amount Loop merchants will lose in a meaningful boycott." People along the parade route were encouraged not to shop downtown,
although they were already downtown shopping when the parade passed by.[16]

Using a familiar ploy, Mayor Daley deferred the election for school board
president. In the *Defender* the country preacher reminded his readers, "Justice

deferred or delayed is justice denied. . . . The children of the city of Chicago are being denied and deprived much more than is Warren Bacon." Jesse noted that blacks were 54.8 percent of the school population while they were only 5 percent of school principals; he concluded, "Since we got no Bacon, the merchants downtown get none of our bread. . . . Stop! Don't shop downtown!"[17] But the downtown boycott fizzled in the winter cold.

As Christmas approached, Roberta Flack headlined a "Black Christmas Special" with two shows at Breadbasket's newly purchased Capitol Theatre. On Christmas, WCIV-TV did a show entitled *Soul Train Christmas*. In his *Defender* column Jesse wished "A Blessed Black Christmas to All of You."[18] The experiment with black holidays ended without fanfare.

Dr. King's Birthday: Annual Events

At Saturday Breadbasket on January 11, 1969, Rev. Jackson declared January 15 a holiday and urged black people to stay home to observe Dr. King's birthday. He reported that President Nixon had ignored a telegram from Rev. Abernathy urging him to make King's birthday a national holiday. Jesse asserted, "If America's government does not respect King, his people will." On January 15 some 150,000 students stayed home, and many black stores closed. The memorial service at Fellowship Baptist overflowed to the sidewalks on what would have been Dr. King's fortieth birthday. Fr. George Clements called for the Catholic Church to declare Dr. King a saint. Jesse gave an emotional speech, and Dr. D. E. King gave the eulogy. Many drivers kept their headlights turned on all day as an additional tribute.[19]

The following January, Mayor Richard J. Daley, King's fierce opponent just a few years earlier, declared January 15, 1970, to be Martin Luther King Jr. Memorial Day in Chicago, urging all citizens "to mark the occasion with suitable observances which honor a leader of a great cause and a man of peace." At Holy Angels Church, Fr. Clements led a mass attended by more than a thousand schoolchildren and parents, focusing on King's love for "young and gifted black children." At Fellowship Baptist, Rev. Jackson outlined a ten-point program for 1970 before a packed congregation. At both services, attendees were encouraged to carry out King's dream by volunteering to assist with anti-hunger feeding programs and by signing petitions promoting weekend voter registration in Chicago neighborhoods. Hundreds signed these appeals. The mood of the day was "spirited and spontaneous."[20]

On Friday, January 15, 1971, the Capitol Theatre was packed for the celebration honoring Dr. King's forty-second birthday when the ceremony commenced outside. With traffic blocked on Halsted Street, Rev. Jackson unveiled a new marquee sign replacing "Capitol Theatre" with "Dr. King's Workshop." Jesse reminded those gathered of Dr. King's extraordinary concern for the poor and oppressed, saying that he sought to "destroy evil and in its place develop a program of rebuilding, and this is exactly what we're going to do in his workshop." Rev. Wallace asked the crowd to sign petitions making January 15 a legal holiday, adding, "SCLC Operation Breadbasket is Dr. King's legacy in Chicago, because he started it here in 1966." The effort to make this birthday a national holiday would bear fruit years later, but only after several long legislative battles, when it was signed into law by President Ronald Reagan on November 2, 1983.[21]

An effort to capitalize on the third anniversary of Dr. King's assassination was a flop. Despite enormous planning and publicizing by a broad-based committee and the endorsement of the mayor, a minuscule eight hundred people marched from the Civic Plaza to a coliseum rally on Saturday, April 3, 1971, where signs and speeches against the Vietnam War "far outnumbered those honoring Dr. King." Earlier in the day, Rev. Jackson and other protest leaders had met with Mayor Daley and presented their concerns for enforcement "of one housing market, one school system and one standard of justice under the law for all citizens."[22] Jesse's effort to start a spring offensive with a King memorial march was hardly recognizable.

The Jail Ministry

The Steering Committee was also challenged from within to maintain a few additional pastoral projects. Whenever Rev. Ma Houston walked into one of our meetings, her jail ministry slipped seamlessly into the agenda. Ma was a grandmother, a button-wearing activist, a self-appointed reverend, and a walking miracle of new health in a once broken body. Ma captured our hearts in describing conditions at the Cook County Jail where she volunteered as a chaplain with special access to all inmates. While Ma participated in negotiations and picketed in "Don't Buy" campaigns, she hounded each of us to bring toothpaste and toothbrushes for her weekly distribution at the jail. In March 1968 she convinced us to accompany her on a tour of the county jail. Rev. Calvin Morris wrote up his experience later that same day.

> Seventeen Breadbasket ministers went to the County Jail this afternoon to acquaint ourselves with the drastic conditions described week by week by Rev. "Ma" Houston. Unable to tour the cell blocks because of disturbances within them, the ministers had to wait amidst the stench of corruption pervading the atmosphere and the flow of unfiltered rumors and fears of riots and tear gas. . . . Mr. Moore [the warden], worn out by over 24 sleepless hours and harassed

from every angle, expressed his dismay of being placed in an impossible position of having too little food budget to feed the inmates, too few guards to insure the safety of the inmates, and no professional staff to rehabilitate the inmates. . . . Mr. Moore wearily pleaded for the ministers to communicate the terrible conditions . . . to our congregations. . . . We bowed together in real "hard times" to pray with and for the warden, his staff, and the prisoners engulfed by the flames of hatred and violence.[23]

The following Sunday I sermonized on our visit, describing

a food budget allowing 5 cents per prisoner per breakfast. What food there is, is terrible, not eatable. Some inmates actually die from malnutrition because they are strong-armed out of their portion and there are not enough guards to see that each person eats, each gets his share. The warden said he cannot rehabilitate men who are forced to live by the jungle just to exist. . . . Bread: the first matter of priority in the jail is adequate bread. . . . We need to put pressure on the County Board to increase the budget for decent food and for reliable staff. In the office I saw tear gas powder stacked in boxes everywhere. Homemade weapons—the end of spoons filed to a point and bundles of table legs and clubs, etc. The answer is not more beatings and suppression. Bread. Give us, give them this day our daily bread.[24]

Ma Houston had just beamed when her Breadbasket colleagues accompanied her to the jail. "Ma was the driving force" of the prison ministry, but "she was always critical. We didn't give her the support she felt she deserved."[25] While we Breadbasket pastors mostly used our limited time and energy on jobs, Ma's persistence kept the county jail on our agenda. Her heartfelt stories broke through my own stubborn focus on covenants at many SC sessions. Some pastors continued to assist her in the jail ministry throughout our time together.

Black Panther Fred Hampton Assassinated

Chicago's Black Panther Party, in spite of militant rhetoric and posters of gun-wielding angry young black men, was actually engaged in carrying out simple survival programs, including free health care at neighborhood clinics and feeding a thousand children a week at West Side sites. Breadbasket literally copied the Panther program on the South Side beginning in August 1969, with free meals for children and the elderly at two, then five, churches. But the public had been systematically frightened of the Panthers by the political establishment and the press.

At 5 a.m. on Thursday, December 4, 1969, Fred Hampton, a youthful and charismatic Black Panther leader, was shot to death in his bed on Chicago's

West Side. The initial newspaper account stated that "seven alleged members of the Black Panther party . . . staged a wild gun battle with police" lasting twenty minutes. At the end of this barrage Fred Hampton, twenty-one, and a Panther leader from Peoria, Mark Clark, twenty-two, lay dead, and five other Panther members were hospitalized, all with one or more bullet wounds. Of twelve policemen who took part in the raid under state's attorney Edward Hanrahan, two were slightly injured, one from flying glass.[26]

The initial police reports were filled with lies. Given the attacks on Panther leaders across the nation in the previous eighteen months, many Chicagoans were instantly suspicious. The Chicago police were apparently so incompetent that they failed to seal the crime scene immediately. When word got out that the house was open, people flocked there to see for themselves. That same morning I went to the downtown office of my bishop, Thomas Pryor, and pleaded with him to accompany me to the site. To my surprise he indicated that this was my role as chair of the Methodist Conference's Board of Christian Social Concerns. My wife, Peg, and I then drove directly to the West Monroe two-flat, and found ourselves in a line of people at the front door.

Instantly shocking was to note the dozens of bullet holes in the front door with clean holes on the outside and splintered openings on the inside. Every single bullet went in! Rather than a "gun battle," this was a terrorist attack by police on the people asleep inside. Entering the bedroom we saw blood everywhere, with Fred's blood-soaked sheets and blankets still on the bed. By the time the Chicago police closed the house, hundreds of people had seen the truth for themselves.

The terror continued when, just twenty-four hours later, Chicago police raided the apartment of another Panther leader, Bobby Rush, later our long-serving First District congressman. Rush was not at home, but the police found an unregistered gun and issued an arrest warrant. Learning of the raid, Rush's lawyer Jeff Haas went to Jesse Jackson for support. Jesse suggested that Bobby come to Saturday Breadbasket and be arrested in the safety of the Breadbasket crowd.[27]

It was an electric moment when Bobby walked into the overflowing Capitol Theatre on Saturday morning, flanked by Renault Robinson of the Afro-American Patrolmen's League and District Commanders Robert Harness and George Sims. Jesse told the cheering crowd, "Bobby will not be whipped or taken advantage of." Commander Harness assured everyone that Rush would receive "fair" treatment. Bobby told the awestruck gathering, "I came here because, black people, our survival is at stake. . . . If I had been there, they'd have killed me too."[28]

Rev. Jackson announced his support for an investigation of the killings, initiated by local community organizations, and said he was "personally grieved" over Hampton's death because "he was a personal friend of mine." I had met Fred Hampton twice at Saturday Breadbasket meetings, one of which he had addressed. I found him brilliant, intense, never wasting a moment, always conferring heatedly with someone in the corridors. I never saw him with a weapon.

In my sermon the next morning, December 7, I had an instant illustration of the Scripture reading handed to me out of the week's tragic event. "Today we have John Baptists—crackpots and wild men—calling for change and repentance. They might not sound religious but they have come to prepare the way .... Among these was Fred Hampton. He did not have a wild personal appearance, but he had a message that frightened the system. His life will not be in vain if people are awakened to the dangers threatening our civil liberties, if people will admit the horrendous situation and needs, and if people will repent and change." I mentioned that Sam Tate, a church member who was sitting in our midst, had told me he worked side by side with Fred Hampton in the post office for a whole year and found him to be a "fine fellow, brilliant, full of potential." I asked that we all "pray that Fred Hampton's life and death will serve in some small way to bring repentance and change."[29]

Some five thousand people walked past Fred Hampton's coffin at the visitation, and hundreds packed a local Baptist church for the funeral. Dr. Benjamin Spock was among the mourners. Revs. Abernathy and Jackson gave eulogies. Jesse talked about a "crucifixion." But instead of underscoring Fred's own vision of multiracial activism through survival, health, and good nourishment, Jesse called on the mourners to buy black products and services and to register voters. It revealed a disconnect between them, reflecting Hampton's own critique of some months earlier: "Operation Breadbasket ... programs are to benefit businessmen. It's not geared toward the masses."[30] In his remarks Bobby Rush said, "Hampton had the power to make people see that the power structure has genocide in their minds. But Hampton wasn't killed because the enemy was so strong, but because we were so weak." The service closed with "We Shall Overcome."[31]

Fred's pallbearers reflected the fledging "rainbow coalition" of youth groups and gangs brought together by the Chicago Panthers to protest police brutality: Jose "Cha-Cha" Jimenez of the Young Lords, Jeff Fort of the Black P Stone Nation, Obed Lopez of the Latin American Defense Organization, and the Panthers' Bobby Rush. Others in this loose multiracial alliance were JOIN of Uptown, the Young Patriots, and Rising Up Angry. But Fred's vision really died with him. Rush went into hiding, and Jimenez went underground for several months. The only remnant, finally, was the name, which Jesse appropriated when he formed the National Rainbow Coalition in 1984 during his first run for the Democratic nomination for president.[32]

Calls for an investigation mushroomed. The Chicago Conference on Religion and Race urged a blue ribbon commission;[33] Roy Wilkins of the NAACP and Arthur Goldberg, a retired Supreme Court justice, demanded an inquiry "into the incidents in Chicago, Los Angeles, Detroit, New York and elsewhere in which Black Panthers have become the object of attention by law enforcement agencies."[34] Spotlighting Chicago's murders, an ad hoc hearing by five black congressmen, led by Representative Adam Clayton Powell of New York, convened in Chicago two weeks later. In his testimony, Rev. Jackson said that the Hampton and Clark deaths were "part of a process of systematic elimination," pinpointing the black community's "condition of powerlessness" as the root of the problem.[35]

The establishment was clearly taken by surprise, believing that Chicago mirrored the nation in disdain for the gun-toting Black Panthers. Mayor Daley remained silent. Ed Hanrahan, the state's attorney and Daley's heir apparent, saw his own career effectively shut down. As Rev. Jackson remembered it decades later, "Their [Hampton's and Clark's] blood had transformative power."[36] It should be noted that the Chicago assassinations ended overt attacks on Panther leaders across the nation. Perhaps the shame of it all was even too much for the ruling principalities and powers.

In his next *Defender* column Jesse used the Hampton tragedy to shine a spotlight on the city's police, noting that the department was overwhelmingly white in a city that was more than 30 percent black. Jesse dropped this bombshell: "If black policemen are not assigned in the white community in the same measure as white policemen now occupy the black community, then, we call for the total withdrawal of all white policemen from the black community."[37] His threat ignited a feverish debate across Chicago. The Hampton assassination had stung Breadbasket, the establishment, and the nation. As of this writing, the problem of predominantly white police forces in largely black urban and suburban areas remains, sadly, unsolved.

School Reform

When the SCLC came to Chicago and joined the CCCO, the focus on Willis wagons and segregated education was shifted to the wider issue of ending the slums. Education reform lay dormant for months. Sometime in 1968 a group of public school teachers attending Breadbasket came together as an Education (then Teachers) Division and began holding weekly community forums.

Quite independently, several black high school student groups organized a stunning walkout of thirty-three thousand students on a Monday in October

1968. Demands included their participation in policy and curriculum development, rehabbing older buildings, courses in Afro-American history, and more black teachers as success images. Within a few days Breadbasket's teachers (some three hundred), who were then promoting teacher training in African American heritage,[38] announced their unanimous support of the students. The following Monday, despite threats of disciplinary action, an estimated twenty thousand students and seven hundred teachers walked out. More than four hundred teachers crowded into Fellowship Baptist that morning to hear students, community leaders, and educators lay out the need for more qualified black teachers and a more streamlined certification process.[39] On the third Monday almost sixteen thousand students walked out. Then dawn turned to dusk for the students. A group of parents met with student leaders, urging them to "take it slow." Without parental encouragement and without further community or Breadbasket support, the valiant student effort faded away.[40]

In the spring of 1969 the Chicago Teachers Union decided to strike on behalf of more state aid. Breadbasket's teachers surprised everyone by refusing to participate unless black schools received a fair share. The Teachers Division submitted a list of reforms to be included in any union negotiations, but it was rebuffed twice over a nine-month period by an intransigent white power structure in both school board and union. Nevertheless, its concerns ended up on the table in future negotiations, and in time these reforms became reality.[41]

Some fallout from earlier struggles for equal education arrived with the long-delayed trial and conviction of Dick Gregory. He had been arrested for crossing the line in a 1965 demonstration against the infamous Willis wagons. Right after Easter 1969, Gregory entered Cook County Jail to begin serving a five-month sentence. At Breadbasket, hundreds of petitions were signed urging Governor Ogilvie to commute his sentence. On Sunday, four hundred Breadbasket protesters gathered at the jail. While everyone sang freedom songs and marched back and forth, Gregory appeared at the gate and was allowed to address the crowd. After forty-five days Gregory was given clemency and released. Addressing Breadbasket two days later he drew "sustained laughter" when he exclaimed, "I was sentenced to jail because I was accused of biting and kicking some cops while they were trying to throw me in front of a train."[42] Gregory was both a comedian and a social activist. Over the next few years he would address Saturday Breadbasket with both insight and humor. I think it can be said that his passion and perseverance enabled the fledgling movement in Chicago to hang on until we were joined by Dr. King and his SCLC forces. Dick Gregory was one lonely prophet.[43]

In the summer of 1970, ten white principals were removed from black neighborhood schools where parental pressure had mounted for some local control. This group included Michael Fabing, the principal at Ryder Elementary, which my sons attended. In my contacts with Fabing I had found him generally competent but detached, not living in the neighborhood, not sensitive to the culture of his students nor to the vast changes going on around him. My wife, Peg, had been involved in the community group seeking his transfer, and we both rejoiced that our neighborhood request, with pressure from Breadbasket teachers, was accepted at the highest level.

Breadbasket's efforts also helped midwife the creation by Deputy Superintendent Manfred Byrd of district and local school committees with co-responsibility for selecting principals. This change came out of a list of reforms promoted by Breadbasket's Teachers Division. The battle for high-quality and equal education would continue for years. Decades later these local committees became the model for local school councils.

Violence in the Neighborhoods

The summer of 1970 saw an eruption of violence in two black communities. As if anticipating this problem, Breadbasket had just formed Black Men Moving (BMM) to raise black men's presence in the neighborhoods. In July, two white police officers were killed by snipers in the near-north Cabrini housing projects. Four black youths were arrested. Rev. Jackson urged restraint, "Many police are super trigger-happy and looking for revenge right now. Certainly, I want the killing stopped, but I don't want any more innocent black people hurt." One slain officer's mother called for calm after being consoled by Cabrini residents at the visitation. "My hurt is so deep, but their hurt must be deeper. I don't want any more misery for any more families."[44]

Holding court at the funeral, Jesse declared the Cabrini homes "a disaster area—spiritually and physically." He introduced a six-point plan that included training the unemployed (25–35 percent of male residents) and a civilian night patrol. He telegrammed President Nixon requesting that Cabrini be declared a disaster area "due to the potentially dangerous conditions." The White House announced the next day that Rev. Jackson's request was under study.[45]

A week later BMM joined the Northside People's Coalition in marching from Cabrini through the Gold Coast and on to the Civic Center to support Jackson's call for a "disaster area" designation. At the rally Jesse announced, "We asked Mayor Daley to meet with eight of us and since he has refused to do so, we brought 8000 today." Later BMM and the People's Coalition established a night patrol. The president's response was to send George Romney, the HUD secretary, to tour Cabrini with Rev. Jackson. Romney voiced support for a local condominium proposal, submitted by two hundred Cabrini residents, and for recreational facilities. He also named two regional officials of HUD as a liaison team between residents and HUD. Here was, at least, some short-term support from D.C.[46]

Jesse was not immune to criticism. In a *Defender* column entitled "'Silent' Blacks Doing Slow Burn," one reader stated: "Jackson doesn't seem to realize that these kids are a tremendous threat—he yaps about riot action and tension because a white victim is felled—well, these gangs have the black citizens suffering the same tension. They've been talking about the cause of gang violence long enough, it's time to end it; making racial progress isn't worth a damn, if we don't have peace and unity in the black neighborhoods."[47]

Meanwhile, across town, there was a face-off between the Kenwood Oakland Community Organization and the Black P Stone Nation. Rev. Curtis Burrell, the KOCO chair and the pastor of the local Mennonite church, fired several disruptive staffers who happened to be members of the Stones. They were vigorously opposing KOCO policies and operations.[48] In retaliation, Burrell's home was firebombed, the KOCO offices were attacked, and graffiti proclaiming "Stones Run It" appeared overnight. Burrell responded by gathering a few dozen folks to march in a Walk against Fear with him, while across the street a larger crowd of about two hundred youths walked with signs saying, "Destroying People Is His Game / Burrell Is His Name." The standoff continued for five weeks, and then Burrell appealed for help. Jesse responded by sending BMM.[49] While this conflict was a question of personalities and turf, it suddenly became a problem for Breadbasket when Jesse interceded on the side of Rev. Burrell.

In late July, Rev. Burrell was ambushed as he entered his church and was nearly killed. Witnessing this assassination attempt, BMM's Rev. John Barber stated, "We now see it as a fight for control of territory between black men and black teenage would-be gangsters. The question which must be resolved is whether the Stones will run the KOCO area, or whether honest, legitimate, black leadership will take over. . . . Black Men Moving will now move to mete out justice, and we're praying for the Main 21 [the Stones leadership], and all boys who think they can disobey their fathers."[50]

Two days later, after an early morning fire gutted his church, Rev. Burrell and Jesse Jackson stood together amid the smell of charred wood. Jesse called the fire a "tragic example of the evil forces in our community," adding as he hoisted his small sons, Jonathan (four) and Jesse Jr. (five) to his shoulders, that he too had received threats. "This [crisis] is too serious to let slide by and if I live, I am going to help rebuild this church." Jesse also assailed "outside forces of evil that include the land gentries, the paid blacks, the Mafia and elected politicians."[51] The Stones denied any involvement. The next Sunday an outdoor "service of reconciliation and reconstruction" was attended by about three hundred people, who heard Jesse preach an emotionally charged sermon on "the valley of dry bones" with music provided by Ben Branch on the saxophone.[52]

When Rev. Barber stated on television that "we are going to deal with the gangs and tell them that 'you don't run it; black men run it,'"[53] Jeff Fort, the Stones leader, countered that BMM was "a vigilante group out to kill black leaders such as me."[54] This was a smokescreen since most of the BMM members were fathers or veterans who had marched in Cabrini and with Rev. Burrell in his Walk against Fear. Dr. Charles Hurst, the president of Malcolm X College, cautioned, "Above all, recognition of the real enemy, the common enemy, must be kept in the forefront at all times. And the real enemies are not poor, black and powerless. Neither do they live in the black community."[55]

Leonard Sengali, a spokesman for the Black P Stone Nation and a former staffer at KOCO, acknowledged the conflict. "Contrary to what a lot of people are saying, the Stones don't want to run KOCO. I know that there are a lot of things wrong and that some weren't doing their job, but all we're asking is that when KOCO is rebuilt, let it be done so as to represent the whole community."[56] With this opening, a private meeting was arranged between the combatants, Revs. Burrell and Barber, and Fort and Sengali. No resolution was ever announced, however, and the issue appeared to dissipate in an uneasy truce, leaving the community without direction. No one was ever charged for the church burning or the other acts of violence during the skirmish.

Before moving on to other things, Rev. Jackson joined Duke McNeil, the president of the Woodlawn Organization, in lashing out at all levels of government and the media for their "silence and ineffectiveness in dealing with the present black on black crime crisis." They called for more black police officers to bring the 16 percent black officers closer to the 30 percent black population. They challenged all politicians to investigate, legislate, arrest, and prosecute those responsible for black-on-black crime. Beyond this rhetorical charge, the black leadership in Chicago was sadly silent, and the discussion of black-on-black violence simply disappeared with a whimper.[57] This situation has hardly improved in almost fifty years, as I write these words.

Politics

Unlike Dr. King, Jesse waded into electoral waters. In 1968 he endorsed Richard Ogilvie, a Republican, for governor of Illinois and Hubert Humphrey, a Democrat, for president of the United States, in part to counter Rev. Joseph Jackson's endorsement of Richard Nixon. The so-called pope of conservative black churches, Joseph Jackson even had his church mailing address changed from King Drive to the side street, 31st Street. Jesse sought to defuse a black boycott of the election, arguing that the world could not afford to be put "in the hands of Nixon and Wallace."[58]

The following year Breadbasket established a school for political organizing with co-deans Alice Tregay and Leon Davis, fifteen instructors, and a range of classes on ten successive Wednesday evenings. The several hundred adult and youth graduates became a support base for Breadbasket's move into electoral politics. Graduates included Illinois state representative Peggy Smith Martin, Chicago alderman Ed Smith, and others who helped elect Chicago's first black mayor, Harold Washington, just a few years later.[59]

In the fall of 1969 Rev. Jackson made a surprise appearance at the Cook County Democratic slate-making committee. Allowed to speak, Jesse argued for the endorsement of an additional black congressional candidate. When the committee reslated a white incumbent in the predominantly black district, an alderman predicted problems "in the heart of Operation Breadbasket territory," where "Breadbasket can influence and Rev. Jackson can, like the Pied Piper of Hameln, lead some 3000 of the 17th ward's voters to hell, if necessary on behalf of black ascendancy." The reality was different, and the incumbent won.[60]

The next move in Breadbasket's efforts to influence electoral politics came in January 1970. When the Election Board rejected a request for neighborhood registration Breadbasket organized a voter registration drive, and Rev. Jackson led a caravan of five hundred cars to the Loop, clogging streets right up to City Hall. At stake were thousands of unregistered black voters who, if organized, could reasonably elect twenty of fifty aldermanic seats, way beyond the current eleven. But the Election Board controlled the keys to registration and thus the election. Mayor Daley stonewalled, waiting for the opposition to wear down, go back to work, and accept their place.[61]

Breadbasket volunteers canvassed door to door, collecting three thousand change-of-address cards and the names of five thousand unregistered people. Rev. Morris declared that these cards would be submitted to the Election Board and that Breadbasket would continue to fight for voter registration in the neighborhoods. He also urged any unregistered voters to take advantage of the one legal day left to register in their own precinct, February 16.[62]

Breadbasket volunteers assisted in the election of Mayor Kenneth Gibson in Newark, New Jersey, as they had earlier with Richard Hatcher in Gary and Carl Stokes in Cleveland. In mid-1970 Stokes announced that the city would hold a Black Exposition, saying, "Chicago started it but Cleveland would not be far behind."[63]

This shift in Breadbasket's focus was finalized at a staff retreat in August 1970. Gary Massoni tells the story: "Rev. Jackson announced that Breadbasket's primary thrust would be political action, with economic concerns—including negotiations for jobs, the hunger campaign, and business development—as the secondary thrust. In terms of priorities, resources, and the assignment of staff, Breadbasket was moving directly and primarily into political activity."[64] While the staff questioned the viability of this effort, with just seven months remaining until the mayoral election, Jesse solidified staff support for what would be his own run for mayor.[65]

Leading up to the election in the fall of 1970, Breadbasket volunteers encouraged "voting black," and Jesse endorsed Democrat Adlai Stevenson for the U.S. Senate and Republican Bernard Carey for Cook County sheriff. With their victories, Jesse claimed the black vote was a gift to them. Then, in a big surprise, Jesse declared that it was time for a black person to consider running against Mayor Daley in the next primary. He dropped hints about his own interest. When Jesse's lawyers discovered that party candidates needed only a small fraction of the signatures that independents needed (four thousand as opposed to fifty-eight thousand), they filed suit in federal court charging discrimination. Jesse's political ambitions were now the talk of the town. On a parallel track, Breadbasket coordinated a People's Convention, which convened on December 19 at Dr. King's Workshop. Some fifteen hundred delegates of every hue nominated seventeen "independent" aldermanic candidates. Most attendees declared it a good beginning.[66]

Entering 1971, Breadbasket commenced "a 45-day blitz to bring political change to this city. We will be marching, door knocking, speaking and holding rallies" to elect our aldermanic candidates, wrote Rev. Jackson in his first *Defender* column of the year. Here was the focus, energy, and seriousness of Breadbasket for the new year. Goodbye, National Tea. A second People's Convention approved a reform platform calling for open meetings, a review of subsidized housing, more health centers, and televised city council meetings. Strangely, the platform omitted any mention of long-sought school reform.[67]

Rev. Jackson's lawsuit challenging the discriminatory signature numbers for independents was dismissed in late January. His lawyers appealed the decision to the Supreme Court. Defying the election statutes, Jesse filed just seven thousand signatures as an independent candidate for mayor, far short of the fifty-eight thousand required, yet almost twice as many as Mayor Daley secured. To a Breadbasket crowd Jesse declared: "No more pieces, no more tokens, no buy-offs. We're running for this. We're going into politics because politics is power.... We want to run our own lives, to plan our own future and to reap the rewards of our efforts." Since blacks now constituted more than 30 percent of the city's populace, Jesse envisioned a coalition with other minorities that could win the mayor's office. The crowd responded to Jesse's speech with a standing ovation.[68] The rhetoric, however, had sporadic and limited local organizing to back it up.

The following week Rev. Ralph Abernathy announced Rev. Jackson's leave of absence from SCLC's Breadbasket and voiced support for Jesse's candidacy. "We find ourselves in a no-man's land, with the Republican Party treating us with benign neglect and the Democratic Party taking us for granted." On the eve of the primary, however, the Supreme Court denied the Jackson appeal, abruptly ending Jesse's mayoral bid. On top of this setback the aldermanic election in February was an unmitigated disaster. Aside from popular incumbents Leon Despres and William Cousins, only Anna Langford, the first black woman alderman, won election from the Breadbasket slate. Winning just three of seventeen seats was a stunning reminder of how entrenched the Daley machine continued to be. While Breadbasket could point to significant gains in economic empowerment and cultural pride, in politics it was all Daley.[69]

With almost 70 percent of the vote Mayor Daley coasted to victory. Even blacks voted overwhelmingly for Daley over Republican Dick Friedman. In analyzing the vote, Jesse wrote, "The feeling of defeat and crucifixion that descended upon the black and poor communities throughout Chicago following the city election on Tuesday, April 6, is a real fear, not just a feeling of the imagination.... The present state of Chicago is a city with order, but not justice.... Therefore, our role in SCLC Operation Breadbasket has not changed regardless of the outcome of the election. We are still called, even more than ever, to be the conscience of the city."[70] Asked to say something about Jesse and Breadbasket during a South Side performance a few days later, Dick Gregory brought down the house by saying, "I ain't talking about no ministers during Holy Week. But really, if I was a minister on Good Friday, I'd lay down in the middle of the street and have them arrest me and throw me in a cell ... then when they came to open the cell doors on Sunday, I'd be gone.... now wouldn't that blow some minds?"[71]

A few weeks later Rev. Jackson made his last foray into the political arena under the Breadbasket umbrella. He met with the Congressional Black

Caucus to test out his vision for a third party. While the idea received some sympathy, an all-black ticket was considered hopelessly unrealistic. However, Jesse's statement that a number of blacks were qualified to be president struck a positive chord. Back in Chicago Jesse held another confab with black leaders. No clear word emerged, but in the end Shirley Chisholm of New York made her historic (first black and first woman) run for president the following year.[72] And it would not be too many years before Rev. Jackson himself made respectable runs for the Democratic nomination for president of the United States. On the surface, Breadbasket's and Jesse's foray against Daley's machine had been a debacle. Nevertheless, Breadbasket's political organizing and educating planted seeds that would bloom another day.

United Farm Workers

In preparing for the Poor People's Campaign, Dr. King had finally reached out to Cesar Chavez, just then recuperating from a hunger strike. King telegrammed Chavez his plan, amid a jammed schedule, to visit migrant labor camps from California to Appalachia. Any possible coalition between the SCLC and the UFW then died in Memphis.[73]

In November 1968 Jesse announced Breadbasket's support of the UFW grape boycott, joining a "campaign against the indecency of 'Stoop' labor," which he indicated was a scandalous injustice for thousands of Mexican and Filipino Americans. Jesse reported that more than 85 percent of farm workers received wages substantially below the minimum wage, but that their hours "extend from dawn to dusk and involve arduous, back-breaking toil day in and day out with no relief. They have no sick benefits or insurance."[74]

Jesse continued, "Moreover, whole families work in the fields. Children begin work at the age of eight. These are the sweated acreages of exploitation. They comprise some 70 ranches with over 180,000 tons of grapes, grown on them each year. Housing conditions are absolutely deplorable with many migrant workers living in adobe hovels or, in some instances, converted boxcars." Jackson ended on a crescendo: "The greed and insensitivity of grape growers, processors and retail grocers has been primarily responsible for perpetuation of this waged slavery. For they have extracted profits but left the abject poverty of a harvest of shame. They have built surpluses for themselves and left suffering and starvation for their workers. We will not eat the grapes of wrath ... and we urge all Americans to join us. We greet Cesar Chavez and his fellow workers—Viva La Huelga [Long Live the Strike] until we again see harvests of abundance."[75]

The reality is that Jesse and Breadbasket never really took action on these fine words. Calvin Morris said, "There was an identification . . . with what

Mexicans were going through."[76] But without Jesse's leadership, any issue just withered away. For example, the SC did not even discuss taking this matter to the pulpits. What might have been a significant coalitional effort, bringing together Hispanic and black economic concerns, simply died with the rhetoric. The UFW leader in Chicago, Eliseo Medina, was a young, charismatic disciple of Cesar Chavez and organized a successful boycott of grapes, particularly among white liberals in the suburbs. I was so moved in my conversations with him that I participated in the UFW boycott completely independently of my Breadbasket involvement. It seemed to me that Jesse's charm sometimes blinded him to real empathy, feeding a kind of condescension that contributed to his inability to be a coalition builder.[77]

In August 1969 Rev. Jackson again announced support of the UFW grape boycott and called for leafleting at Jewel stores. His plea was persuasive, and after the Saturday Breadbasket rally two hundred people went off to picket at three nearby Jewel stores.[78] But Jesse had not consulted with Eliseo, who would have told him that Jewel had already pulled grapes from its stores in the neighborhood. When this news came back, Breadbasket staff redirected the volunteers to Jewel stores in the suburbs. Ironically, at this same time, I was in regular contact with Jewel on covenant follow-up. All I could do was tell my Jewel contacts that the grape issue was a separate matter. I did not tell them how sad I felt about this disconnect between two movement groups.

I continued to personally boycott grapes. Months later, my three-year-old daughter, Beth, was at a church potluck and asked me, "Daddy, what are these?" as she pointed to a bunch of green grapes. The net effect of Breadbasket's effort on the grape boycott was at best minimal. But it made an impact in our household.

Contract Buyers League

In March 1970, leaders of the struggling CBL, a group of black homeowners who were demanding the renegotiation of exploitative home mortgage contracts, asked to meet with Rev. Jackson. He agreed to talk with them from his bed at home, where he was contending with a bronchial virus. Sixteen families had just now been evicted in the two-year battle. Since December 1968 dozens of league members had placed their mortgage payments in escrow to protest the situation and to demand reconsideration. Whenever evictions were attempted by Cook County Sheriff squads, ousted owners had fought back with the help of neighbors, who would move their furniture from the curb back into the house as soon as the sheriff's crew left.

That resistance ended suddenly on March 30, 1970. Four families on the 9500 block of South Emerald Avenue were firmly evicted by the sheriff with the additional help of about 150 Chicago policemen sealing off the block from supporters. These were the first successful evictions since the strike began. I remember hearing the commotion from my Gresham church just down the block, walking down to the site, and offering our church gymnasium to store their belongings, which were being roughly tossed out onto the parkway. By compacting the loads we were able to squeeze in two households of belongings, which remained with us for about a month. In this small way our Gresham parish offered solidarity to these courageous homeowners.[79]

The *Defender* wrote a strong editorial, "Stop Evictions," and the Urban League joined in support. The CBL's visit to Jesse brought them his support and the podium at Saturday Breadbasket for several weeks. On April 4, 1970, the second anniversary of Dr. King's assassination, the evicted homeowners were introduced and honored. As Jesse wrote in his *Defender* column, "We shall honor Dr. King by pledging our full support to helping CBL members live in the face of tyranny. . . . Dr. King would be far more gratified by the flags flying at half-mast for the evicted CBL families than for [the memorial day] for him."[80]

Rev. Jackson joined the CUL's Bill Berry, Methodist bishop Thomas Pryor, and other community leaders in urging Mayor Daley to intercede. After days of negotiation the mayor proudly announced a tentative agreement to end evictions, with owners paying their mortgages in full, pending the outcome of a federal court case. However, CBL members felt that without a commitment on the renegotiation of contracts, they had to continue to withhold mortgage payments. So, evictions continued, and the issue dragged on.[81]

Months later Breadbasket jumped back into the fray, supporting the contract buyers and challenging the federal government to support their new lawsuit. When four CBL members were arrested in September, Women of Breadbasket protested at Cook County Jail.[82] A day later the four were released with the judge's admonition to move, seek a mortgage, reach a settlement, or request extended time. Later that day Rev. Jackson met with CBL leaders and Mayor Daley to no avail. During the next week a vacant CBL home was burned down and a real estate office involved in selling repossessed homes was bombed.[83] Inexplicably, Jesse and Breadbasket soon disappeared from the ongoing story.

The Contract Buyers League fought heroically against the real estate companies, the builders, and the owners of contracts, who were supported by the courts and the sheriff's forces. It was a tragic and painful six-year struggle, ending finally with minimal improvement but much sorrow and exhaustion in mid-1975. Only a small number of the original forty-eight hundred families received a renegotiated contract or a settlement.

Finally, thirty-five years later, the CBL story was told. A Chicago native, Beryl Satter, wrote a marvelous account of this incredible story of grit and sacrifice in the face of blatant greed and racism, which would be echoed years later in the subprime loan scandal.[84]

Every public alert of social injustice seemed to end up on Breadbasket's table. In 1969 Breadbasket joined in the struggle of St. Dorothy's Roman Catholic parish to have Cardinal Cody appoint their popular black priest, Fr. George Clements, as pastor. At that time only one black priest served as a pastor among 450 parishes in the archdiocese. Breadbasket pastors signed petitions, and Rev. Jackson preached at a "unity mass" attended by four thousand people. Six months later Clements was named pastor of historic Holy Angels Church in Bronzeville, where he began a distinguished ministry.

In May 1970 Breadbasket held a Chicago rally and march against police repression, as part of a nationwide SCLC effort stemming from the police assassination of Fred Hampton. It turned out to be a crowd-pleasing one-time affair with no real follow-up.[85] In D.C., Jesse met with "peace bloc" senators and pledged Breadbasket support in their efforts to end the war in Vietnam.[86] Breadbasket even supported the beleaguered government of Guinea, West Africa.[87]

In a startling development in late 1970, a former army intelligence officer revealed that the U.S. Army had been spying on hundreds of Illinois civilians, including Rev. Jesse Jackson. The officer revealed that Jesse was targeted because of his role as the leader of Operation Breadbasket and "because he's the most powerful black spokesman in Chicago." Jesse commented: "These acts of spying on black and white citizens are the manifestations of a guilty nation that is running from itself." Another official indicated that Jesse was under surveillance because the "military thought Jackson was the ideal man to contact, to help quell a civil disorder if one occurred." The whole episode brought a chill not only across the black community but across the country. Referring to Adlai Stevenson and Jesse Jackson, among others, Alderman Sammy Rayner and Representative Abner Mikva said they were "happy to be in the company of such great men," but were displeased at being the targets of spying.[88]

In April 1971 Breadbasket brought two busloads of folks from Chicago to a major antiwar rally in Washington, D.C., where Jesse joined Coretta Scott King and Ralph Abernathy among the speakers before a crowd estimated at three hundred thousand.[89]

In July 1971 the U.S. Postal Service announced plans to move thousands of jobs to the Chicago suburbs. In a tour of the city's main post office, Rev.

Jackson broke the news to employees. He expressed "extreme anxiety" that nine thousand blacks would be laid off over the next three years. In August Jesse traveled to New York to inspect postal facilities and discovered the same pattern of shifting jobs to the suburbs. Home again, he declared that the imminent loss of nine thousand jobs in Chicago would hit many families, raise black unemployment (already 9 percent), impact welfare rolls, increase hunger, and have a ripple effect in the community. He announced the formation of both Chicago and national Save the Jobs groups. Joining Breadbasket's efforts, the NAACP, the Congressional Black Caucus, and the National Alliance of Postal and Federal Employees announced hearings in five cities to prepare federal legislation to counter discrimination in the postal service.[90]

Also during 1971 Rev. Jackson became the spiritual advisor to the revolutionary activist Angela Davis, visiting her at Marin County Jail in California. Davis's mother spoke at Breadbasket in June, describing the deplorable prison conditions and pleading for Angela's release on bail after seven months of solitary confinement on murder conspiracy charges. Jesse and Breadbasket added voices to the "Free Angela on Bail Now!" movement.[91]

Perhaps the most audacious move for Breadbasket was Jesse's request in a meeting with UN secretary general U Thant for NGO status for the SCLC's Operation Breadbasket. This designation would give Breadbasket an unofficial delegate to the UN and that delegate would be none other than Rev. Jackson. Jesse planned to use this role to secure access for the Congressional Black Caucus so that it might make its case of "black America as a nation within a nation" before the General Assembly. U Thant agreed to support Jesse's request and also accepted his invitation to address Saturday Breadbasket in Chicago, which did not happen only because Breadbasket folded just weeks later. Some of us could only smile at Jesse's audacity and his brilliant grasp of the levers of power.[92]

In sum: over the course of six years, 1966–1971, the SCLC's Operation Breadbasket experienced phenomenal growth and expanded influence. But a major cost of this proliferation of programs and activities was an exhausted staff and volunteers. None of us could keep up with the Olympic-like pace of the leader. However, Jesse's occasional bouts with sickle cell anemia and mononucleosis reminded at least some of us that our leader was of mortal flesh. Somehow, we in the SC managed to carry on—investigating, negotiating, and monitoring through all the distractions and hoopla of Breadbasket's newfound fame.

CHAPTER 10

INTERNAL ISSUES

> Charismatic grounds [authority] rest[s] on devotion to the specific and
> exceptional sanctity, heroism or exemplary character of an individual
> person, and of the normative patterns or order revealed or ordained by
> him.—Max Weber, *The Theory of Social and Economic Organization*

From Collegiality to Charisma

The Breadbasket team led by quarterback Jesse Jackson had smooth sailing
for its first several months. The camaraderie and trust between us deepened
with the early victories. Thus, I was surprised to learn of "internal tensions"
at the SC in January 1967. Without warning, Jesse admonished those present,
about fifteen of us, that "in a movement such as Operation Breadbasket it
is important to utilize all the talent we have" and "remember we are equals,
even though some are Negro and some are white, some are male and some
are female, some are pastors of churches and some are ministers without
churches."[1] I do not recall this matter being mentioned again.

During our first year the SC was constantly learning, shaping, and experi-
menting—and having fun at it. Decisions were made by consensus, and votes
were taken only to gauge where we were headed. The trust level enabled us
to work through most issues to an agreed position, and the lone voice or
two would yield. But as any movement becomes an organization, the modus
operandi shifts toward more permanent processes. Goals, methods, and
shortcuts evolved between negotiations. With fluctuating SC attendance it
took time to build consensus. But the pivotal factor that moved us away from
consensus was Jesse himself. As his leadership role grew in public, he moved
almost imperceptibly toward a charismatic leadership style in which both
voting and consensus become simply suggestions to the leader, who makes
all key decisions.[2]

Jesse was aided in this shift by the development of the businessmen's breakfast late in 1966, which grew into the public Saturday Breadbasket meetings.
By mid-1967 Jesse had discovered a new base in the business group and a
new spotlight in the Saturday morning rallies. The SC and the business cadre

together gave Jesse a new level of support and loyalty, which emboldened his drive toward the charismatic approach.

The speed with which Breadbasket grew, the expansion of programming and groups, initially called "spokes" and later "divisions," only complicated the running of the fledging organization. When action was needed it was easier for one person to make the decision. And when you have a brilliant, articulate, fast-learning, tall, handsome, and confident young man, who had grown up in the black Baptist Church tradition, where all authority in a local church centers in the pastor, you have all the pieces necessary for charismatic leadership. As Jesse's confidence grew and his public persona clicked, he gradually adopted this mantle of Baptist-style leadership. Jesse would test his constant flood of new ideas with a few close advisors and then approach the SC for confirmation.

In reality we had three subgroups within the SC. One was the clergy contingent of Jesse's circle of advisors, a kind of kitchen cabinet. A second group was primarily Baptist pastors who enjoyed sitting on the dais with Jesse at Saturday rallies. Behind their backs they were called the "ceremonial clergy." The third group was the working-stiff clergy who attended Friday meetings regularly and took assignments for investigations, negotiations, and follow-up. There was some overlap, and a few people were active in all three groups.[3] I was happy to be a part of the working clergy, but less happy about the breakdown of unity and trust that had bound us together in the opening months. Several of us grew uneasy with this transformation from collegial work to charismatic authority.

This shift mirrored the SCLC structure, where staff ran the show. Still, Breadbasket was more constituency-based, and the pastors were unwilling to give up the collegial style that had worked well in the early months.[4] These undercurrents developed over the course of 1967. As Breadbasket expanded, new staff were hired, including Gary Massoni, who, like his CTS colleague Dave Wallace, was white. This created a dilemma for Breadbasket's public image at the very time that black power had emerged as a new self-understanding in the community. This was solved when Jesse hired a long-time friend, Rev. Calvin Morris, as his top associate.

Personally, I never felt excluded as a white man and learned only much later that Rev. Willie Barrow had vouched for me throughout our time together in Breadbasket.[5] That undoubtedly stemmed from our early bonding when we teamed together to meet with Seven-Up Bottling executives. At the same time, it is true that when we were working, all were equal, but when we were in a public situation, our black members, whether staff or ministers, were out front. And this included picture taking at covenant signings.[6]

Dr. King was so impressed with our Breadbasket staff that in January 1968 he appointed Rev. Morris to be the associate director and Rev. Ed Riddick to be the national research director of SCLC's Breadbasket. King stated that with the addition of these outstanding men "we are stepping up our aggressive campaign under the able direction of Rev. Jackson to establish economic security and control within the Negro community." Jesse added, "We are expanding our staff, both nationally and in Chicago because SCLC's Operation Breadbasket is a rapidly growing program that is taking on new responsibilities and challenges daily."[7]

We now had the SC, the business group, the staff, the inner circle, and Jesse. The relationships among these groups remained fluid, but essentially each group's power was in its ability to influence the decision maker, Jesse. Even when Rev. Morris was given authority to act in Jesse's absence, his decisions might be countermanded by Jesse on his return. Rev. Morris recalls what happened to a short-lived program called Operation Green Power. "It was one of the many ideas and concepts that constantly came from the fertile mind of Rev. Jesse Jackson Sr. Like many of those ideas, there was little serious thought or preparation to assure that the idea might be implemented.... It was a great idea but its promise was not fulfilled and carried forth." In Jesse's absence, Rev. Morris recalls, the staff tried to jump-start the project. On Jesse's return Operation Green Power was ignored and simply disappeared.[8]

Rebellion Snuffed Out

In early 1968 the authority question broke into the open when a contingent of SC pastors attending a national Breadbasket workshop in Miami took time to discuss the home front. During their conversations they discerned several needs for Breadbasket structure and authority. Back in Chicago, Rev. D. E. King, made specific recommendations to the SC on March 1:

- We will continue to hold two weekly meetings: the SC on Fridays at 1 p.m. at Fellowship Baptist Church with Revs. Freeman and Wyatt presiding, and a rally on Saturdays at 8 a.m. at CTS, presided over by Rev. Jesse Jackson.
- The role of Breadbasket staff will be guided by the clergy of Chicago's Breadbasket.
- Breadbasket will participate in coalitions or alliances on recommendation of the SC.
- A new Educational Division is to be set up and directed by Rev. John Porter, and other divisions are to be added as the needs arise.[9]

The SC readily approved these directives and named Rev. Clay Evans the overall convener of Operation Breadbasket in Chicago. In his report to the SC as the national director of Operation Breadbasket, Jesse made no reference to the decisions just made in his presence.[10]

When the Steering Committee met the following week, day turned to night. Instead of Freeman or Wyatt presiding, Evans took charge. After the opening Scripture and prayer, he called on Morris to join him. To my amazement, they announced a wholly new structure, dismantling the decisions of the previous Friday. Replacing SC authority was an Executive Committee appointed by the national director of Breadbasket (Jesse), made up of four SC ministers, four staffers, and one businessman. The kitchen cabinet of earlier days was essentially elevated to officialdom. The SC would now make suggestions to this executive cadre. Our role was reduced to the "responsibility for Research, Negotiations, and Follow-up of Covenants." The rationale given was that "the Executive Committee is a safeguard for policy since the SC is an open meeting to all ministers." There was no hint of tension over the participation of us "whiteys," as we were sometimes affectionately called. But, as the role of non-executive staffers was curtailed, tensions developed in the staff paralleling the split in the SC. In Calvin Morris's recollection "the Executive Committee was a 'cover' for Jesse, deflecting stuff from Atlanta."[11]

Rev. Jackson defended this reversal to the SC in words summarized in Wallace's minutes: "Breadbasket's new structure is important because this is a tremendously involved organization and the stakes are getting higher as we continue to raise profound and sensitive issues. An open meeting, the Steering Committee alone is too dangerous for several reasons including ignorance, corruption, or jealousy. This body of ministers is doing what others are only talking about around the nation."[12]

This was a shocking development. I do not recall anyone challenging Jesse's charge of "ignorance, corruption, or jealousy." On the contrary, I believe we trusted that he knew some things we did not know, and clearly, infiltration was a common practice of Chicago's machine. But we working clergy shared a solid trust in each other, and without evidence Jesse's claim seemed ludicrous. In our open meetings no opposition was voiced to this inside coup. March 8, 1968, was, in my view, the low day of Operation Breadbasket until the tragic event in Memphis, Tennessee, a few weeks later.

Jobs versus Entrepreneurship

Dr. King's vision for Chicago Breadbasket, enunciated at our birth meeting, was to deliver jobs. Our slogan was "Your Ministers Fight for Jobs and Rights." By demanding jobs commensurate with the population, and backing up that demand with consumer power, we had filled 1,360 new and upgraded jobs worth $9 million in just two years. Speaking to Saturday Breadbasket in March 1967, Dr. King called Jesse "a great dreamer and a great implementer of dreams" for winning jobs and "building the economic base through Negro businesses."[13]

But King was uneasy with a simplistic drive for jobs and economic development. In that same speech, Doc said that "a white man who preached black capital accumulation to poor people reminded him of somebody 'telling you to lift yourself up by your bootstraps' while he was standing on your foot." King remained critical of corporate power, stating that "American industry and business, as part of the broader power structure, is in a large part responsible for the economic malady which grips and crushes down people in the ghetto." At Breadbasket in July 1967, King questioned the capitalist economy, declaring, "the earth is the Lord's and the fullness thereof." He addressed us ministers, saying that our primary concern should be the "least of these." As we negotiated for jobs, we should pressure the CEOs to "set aside profit for the greater good" and to support a "restructuring of our whole society."[14] King was simply reminding the SC pastors what had been his vision from day one. It was clearly not black capitalism that was the goal, but a new social/economic ordering, and King saw Breadbasket leading the way on the corporate/enterprise side.[15]

Dr. King restated this purpose, in terms of the government role, in a January 15, 1968, speech, "Why We Must Go to Washington": "I can see nothing more basic in the life of an individual than to have a job or an income.... If people do not have jobs or income, they're deprived of life; they're deprived of liberty; and they're deprived of the pursuit of happiness."[16]

When Breadbasket added black products and services into our covenants the dynamics changed. Along with the internal power shifts came an energy swing from jobs toward entrepreneurship and economic development. In the SC, however, we working pastors held fast to a focus on jobs. Enabling black men and women the opportunity to work and support their families allowed us to be in solidarity with our parishioners at the center of their lives and livelihoods, their dignity and personhood. It was an awesome goal and a compelling challenge.[17] But the economic development side continued to mushroom. As the young black entrepreneurs offered a higher level of personal allegiance to Jesse and financial support to Breadbasket, he gradually shifted his primary attention from the SC. By August 1968, our *Directory of Black Businesses* listed 155 enterprises in eleven categories, including food products, cosmetics, financial institutions, construction companies, and scavenger services.[18]

The turn to entrepreneurship exposed a conflict with Dr. King's increasingly radical vision of America, his dream of transcending both authoritarian communism and money-driven capitalism. The Executive Committee, as announced to us on March 8, signaled a shift of primary attention from jobs to development, from a ministry with people on the street to the advocacy of black business. The fact that we secured only one covenant during 1968 and dropped negotiations with Walgreen and Hammond Organ illustrates how much we had slipped from our base. Nonetheless, the addition of black businessmen into the hub of Chicago Breadbasket and the concomitant attention to economic development for the benefit of the community was an important expansion. The 1969 Campaign to End Hunger was another expansion on the public/governmental side of the quest for economic justice. However, the question remains whether we successfully avoided compromising King's far-reaching vision after Memphis.

So, while the Saturday rallies were gatherings of inspiration, information, community building, and commissioning, the Friday meetings remained the heartbeat of the clergy who carried on the work of fighting for jobs and rights. If some of us got discouraged over these changes, we nevertheless found renewed strength in our camaraderie, our achievements, and our hopes for a more just and equitable social system for our City of the Big Shoulders.

With the assassination of Dr. King, the entire Breadbasket operation was altered. Jesse revealed a change of heart in his address to the SC on April 26, saying, "Negotiations for jobs must be accelerated, for black people need jobs."[19] Whether it was Jesse's earlier tussle with the SC, or Dr. King's passion for jobs as expressed in his final speech in Memphis, something caused Jesse to yield and accept the need for balance between entrepreneurship and jobs. While this was joyous news to the SC, the announced shift of priorities never materialized, at least not as I observed. Tensions simply continued both in the SC and among the staff over Jesse's forceful leadership and uncertainty about our organizational structure, modus operandi, and accountability.[20]

At the same time Jesse saw the forces of black power and the black Muslims coalescing ahead of him. Shrewdly, Jesse issued a memo to the staff and ministers in September 1968, recognizing that in this "more conservative political climate, building economic viability in the black community shifts our focus from economic security to economic independence. As this occurs we need to understand that BLACK COOPERATION IS THE MOST EFFECTIVE EXPRESSION OF RESPONSIBLE AND MEANINGFUL BLACK POWER THAT IS POSSIBLE FOR BLACK PEOPLE AND BLACK ORGANIZATIONS."[21] This was Jesse's way of acknowledging the shift in mood, particularly of black power advocates like CORE's Floyd McKissick, but drawing a distinction between black empowerment as a carbon copy of mainstream capitalism, and black independence, leaving the door open to King's vision of a third way.[22]

The debate over jobs versus entrepreneurship resurfaced the next year. In his campaign for president, Richard Nixon pledged to assist "black capitalism," a phrase cooked up by his people. Whether intentional or not, it had a negative, divisive ring in black America. Speaking to a Breadbasket crowd, Rev. Abernathy rejected Nixon's proposed program of black capitalism in favor of the SCLC's "black socialism" with its focus on securing jobs and control for black people in black communities. Abernathy saw Nixon's program as making a few people rich while the majority stayed poor.[23]

Rev. Jackson called Nixon's proposals a "catch-all for dealing with the economic ills of the black community in America," which would only "widen the gap between impoverished blacks and [the] black brother who is beginning to acquire a more substantial income and to assume some of the styles of life common to the middle class. . . . Since it obscures the real issue, 'Black Capitalism' breeds confusion. The issue is not to add a few additional entrepreneurs. . . . At stake is the demand for the total economic development of the black community. . . . The term 'Black Capitalism' describes less a goal than a gimmick."[24]

Over the next weeks black capitalism was opposed both by CORE and the AFL-CIO Council, which called it a "dangerous, divisive delusion." Instead, the council offered to help enable black people to move "into the nation's mainstream."[25] Speaking to Chicago's Community Renewal Society, Rev. Morris indicated that it was ironic for whites to suggest that blacks were talking separation, when whites had so effectively isolated and separated black people. Calvin asserted that blacks must begin where they are, use black power to develop their own communities, and then create "a real coalition of blacks and whites to sit down on an equal basis to develop strategies for necessary changes in America."[26] Rev. Morris's vision went beyond any narrow definition of black capitalism.

Tension had also developed with the black Muslims and their black economic enterprises. Soon after Dr. King's assassination Rev. Jackson arranged for a Saturday Breadbasket to meet at the Salaam Restaurant as an outreach to the South Side Muslim community. As Jesse told the SC, "The ministers and the people of Breadbasket are concerned about the unity of black people, and are interested in building bridges where others have attempted to divide us."[27]

Little came of that contact. Some months later, Chicago attorney Chauncey Eskridge, the counsel for both the SCLC and the Muslims, facilitated a meeting between Elijah Muhammad and the Breadbasket leadership. Remembering this meeting, Rev. Morris "found Elijah a diminutive figure, soft-spoken, not terribly articulate. Nothing came of this meeting." Presumably, black Chicago was big enough for both the Muslim and Breadbasket brands of black power economic development. While the Muslims expressed little interest in follow-ing Breadbasket's move toward politics, their newspapers carried reports of some Breadbasket initiatives and campaigns.[28]

The question for those of us in Breadbasket was neither black capitalism nor black socialism. Our task was to seek job fairness, strengthen black busi-nesses, and thus uplift the entire community. We recognized that African Americans lived in two worlds: the black community and the larger society, in this case metropolitan Chicago. Abernathy's call for black socialism fell as flat as black capitalism. Sadly, Dr. King's deeper social vision beyond capital-ism and communism died with him in Memphis.

Jesse's new understanding of balancing jobs and economic independence seemed to vanish when he launched into his priorities for 1969 at the first Saturday Breadbasket of the new year: a holiday to honor Dr. King's birth-day, Black Easter, a bank-in, financial help for Provident Hospital, renam-ing Washington Park and public schools for black heroes, establishing black apparel shops, and prodding the Catholic archdiocese to name black pas-tors.[29] Breadbasket's original goal, our meat-and-potatoes work of seeking jobs, was absent from Jesse's list as was his newer focus on black economic independence. We sc pastors were definitely on our own as 1969 began.

South Side versus West Side

Although the SCLC began its major organizing on the streets of the West Side, Breadbasket began and remained ensconced on the South Side. The sc meet-ings, Saturday Breadbasket, rallies, picketing, workshops, and negotiating sessions were all held on the South Side. In March 1969, aware of the black community's cleavage, which involved class differences and jealousies as well as geographical separation, the sc decided to hold an open meeting at New Friendship Baptist on the West Side.

I recall the nervous tension as we introduced ourselves to our West Side colleagues. At that meeting Rev. Forshey reported on A&P, and I reviewed Jewel's numbers. Seeking to gain some local interest and involvement from our new colleagues, another pastor reported that a West Side Sears store had just one black person among fifty-seven managers, among several other ineq-uities. On my recommendation the sc decided to make decisions on targets such as Walgreen and Sears at the next meeting. A curve ball was then thrown into the meeting by Rev. Earl Simmons, one of the most faithful members. He blurted out: "What is the Steering Committee steering?" exposing to our West Side guests that any decisions on targets would not be made by us. They could guess who would decide. Silence reigned, and then we moved on.[30]

Our coming to the West Side was poorly received by the leading black pastors in the area, who retained their suspicions of our more "bourgeois" South Side organization.[31] Sadly, we gave in, and the following Friday we were back in our comfort zone at Fellowship Baptist on South Princeton. So, while all Breadbasket covenants had metropolitan-wide implications, most programs were aimed at the South Side. That riots broke out on the West Side at the news of Dr. King's assassination while the South Side maintained an uneasy calm only deepened this division. Our failure to include the West Side in the Breadbasket family led to the charge that we were "middle class" and purposely avoided the "lower-class" West Side. Had we solved this problem Breadbasket would have significantly increased its effectiveness in Chicago.

The West-South divide broke open anew in the Illinois End Hunger campaign when Jesse announced that Breadbasket would begin to offer free breakfasts. This concept, initiated by Black Panther leader Huey Newton in San Francisco, had become the signature program of the Black Panthers on Chicago's West Side. Already suspect to the young Panthers as catering to middle-class bourgeois blacks, Breadbasket seemed to be usurping their program. The resulting bad blood extended to other community and coalitional efforts. On one occasion Rev. Morris rose to speak at a West Side community meeting only to have all the Black Panthers present stand up and walk out en masse as he began.[32]

This split was totally unnecessary. Independently of my work with Breadbasket, I had been working with a small group of young Panthers who had requested space at my Gresham church and who met there regularly for months. They were unarmed, gentle, courteous, and simply attempting to organize the local residents around hunger and other survival issues. They were the furthest thing from the demonized image of crazy, gun-toting revolutionaries portrayed in the local and national press. At this writing I cannot recall why I did not share my work with the Panther youths with other members of the SC. Clearly, Breadbasket made a big mistake in not seeing the young Panthers as allies in our justice work.[33]

Steering Committee and Staff Struggles

The Executive Committee became a source of friction over the course of 1968 and eventually gave way to an even smaller group. When Jesse was out of town, Calvin Morris gathered Cirilo McSween, Willie Barrow, and another staffer or two for decision making. Even this cabinet could not reduce the staff tensions or resolve all problems. There were also personality conflicts, issues of style and expectation, and some black-white tensions during this black power period. The program areas seemed to be abandoned as well.[34]

Rev. Jackson made a now rare appearance at the sc in September 1969, thanking us for support in his recent arrest. He explained that "it would not be possible or necessary that he attend every weekly meeting." It appeared that Jesse had become bored with the mundane work of targeting, investigating, covenanting, and following up, so he left that in our hands. He described the upcoming Black Expo and urged us to come, to encourage attendance, and to invite our church choirs to join the mass choir at the Gospel Festival.[35]

In our Friday meetings much time was spent on announcements and on ways we ministers and congregations could support Breadbasket's ever-proliferating programs. Rev. Wyatt recommended that we pastors lead devotions and altar calls at Saturday Breadbasket, Rev. Henry Hardy suggested that we needed midweek worship with preaching, and Rev. Evans asked that we work "on Wonder bread and the bread of life together."[36] But the involvement of the sc in the cultural side of black pride and power was simply beyond the time available for busy pastors. The working clergy simply ignored most of these requests.

This was a critical period for the sc. With reduced authority, a lack of staff, and the many diversions, it is understandable that we produced no new Breadbasket covenants over several months. While the sc remained a vital group with bright, committed, theologically attuned pastors of a wide ecumenical rainbow, Jesse's absence and his dominating style alienated several colleagues. Being marginalized and without a role appropriate to their talents, some of these pastors abandoned ship. In this atmosphere the sc floundered, attendance withered, and only a passionate commitment to the cause kept the rest of us going.[37]

As Breadbasket entered its fifth year, all sc clergy received a letter from our convener. Addressing each of us as a "Co-Laborer in Christ," Rev. Clay Evans urged us to attend sc meetings. "I am sure you are aware of the importance of our staying at the helm of the ship. As we launch forth in our new thrust for 1970, we need you with the Minister's point of view for the spiritual and moral projection of our destiny."[38] While we were clearly not at the helm of the ship, the letter did increase attendance that first week. At that meeting Brother Evans urged: "Ministers must regain interest in the meetings, because Ministers were and still are the backbone of the movement."[39]

Unfortunately, this was not where Jesse's head was. His "new thrust for 1970" called for increasing the number of black-owned radio and TV stations, improving transportation, strengthening black finance institutions, increasing the number of black aldermen and committeemen, ditto the number of black architects, improving black schools, making "Black Health Is Black Wealth" a motto for better health care, and making hunger illegal. This was a laundry list from heaven, but no one could dream dreams better than Jesse.[40]

Attendance at the sc meeting was down again the next week. After prayer, Rev. Evans asked for a count of those who had attended the remembrances of Dr. King the previous day. He stressed the need for us to participate in the feeding program and the upcoming voter registration drive and to attend Saturday Breadbasket and sit on the stage to "add moral support to both the speakers and the people attending. Ministers must realize the part they have played and will continue to play in the life and continued growth of the movement." Volunteers were requested to drive Ma Houston to the county jail. As the chair of follow-up I announced several upcoming appointments with our covenanted companies.[41]

Rev. Evans's renewed leadership, Rev. Lawrence's release from jail after a civil rights arrest, the arrival of some new pastors, and Gary Massoni's return as staff support brought us new resolve and energy. Massoni wrote me a detailed memo listing the contact people for all the companies with which we were in covenant or conversation and added, "I am glad that the Steering Committee is beginning to move ahead again."[42] We resumed negotiations with Walgreen and launched a major investigation of Sears. Dr. Al Pitcher, the Construction Spoke leader, popped in one Friday and dove into a lecture on choosing targets, urging us to consider larger enterprises like Standard Oil, Walgreen (Al did not know we were already negotiating with that drugstore chain), the Chicago White Sox, General Motors, Sears, Polk Brothers, Greyhound, and McDonald's.[43] Even with Al's passion and prompting and his closeness to Jesse, we were never sure that any recommendations we made on targets or deadlines would see the light of day with Jesse.

A long-awaited sc retreat was planned for Friday, April 10, 1970, at the Colonial House.[44] The morning agenda would have included a review of our history, sc responsibilities and relationships, negotiating and follow-up procedures, and a discussion of the need for unity and improved morale. After lunch the ministers were to meet with staff, set future goals, and go forth after a prayer by Ma Houston. The agenda, a list of forty-three Breadbasket ministers and nine staffers, and a summary of eight recent follow-up reports were prepared on my typewriter with copies for everyone. But this retreat never happened, vetoed undoubtedly by Jesse Jackson.[45]

As a response to this roadblock, a group of sixteen Breadbasket ministers, led by Rev. Lawrence, met with Jesse on April 20. I absented myself because of my disappointment and disagreement. Rev. Lawrence raised four needs: some form of council "to tie together the various programs of Breadbasket and to work out priorities"; a staff person assigned full time to negotiations; "clarity" on the relationship between Operation Breadbasket and the new Breadbasket Commercial Association; and an avenue for ministers "to share in the planning of national negotiations and the coordination of various local activities." According to Massoni's account of this meeting, "Rev. Jackson responded only in general terms to three of the points, but he did assign a staff person to work on negotiations without interruptions from other programs. This was the first time since 1967 that any staff member had been assigned to work exclusively with the negotiations which were supposed to be the core of Breadbasket's operation."[46]

With some relief we resumed our labors, grateful for staff assistance. At the same time, we felt uncertain about recommendations we might make on targets, campaigns, or covenants and the level of support we could expect from the Breadbasket network if we began another "Don't Buy" effort.

The Breadbasket staff was also struggling with low morale, and they convinced Jesse of the need for a discussion of internal issues. At a week-long staff retreat in late May 1970, tensions came out into the open as staff members confronted Jesse on questions of role and authority. As a result of this interchange they agreed on a new "strategy board," which was launched in June only to fall apart by August. While some small progress was made, key issues went unresolved, resulting in a lack of coordination and lagging programs through the summer of 1970. There was a rumor that Rev. Morris was resigning. With Jesse back as the lone decision maker, programmatic and structural matters languished. The staff expended much energy going in circles. Even Jesse declared, "All motion is not progress."[47]

Our SC frustrations notwithstanding, Breadbasket was blessed with an awesome staff. By our fourth year it included Calvin Morris, Ed Riddick, Willie Barrow, St. Clair Booker, Lucille Conway, Cirilo McSween, Richard Thomas, Dave Wallace, Gary Massoni, Roberta Jackson, Jo Ella Stevenson, Paul Walker, Al Pitcher, and at various times, Hermene Hartman, Leon Davis, and Alice Tregay. It was an able, if underpaid, team, all working diligently 24/7 with remarkable loyalty to Breadbasket and to Rev. Jackson. In Jesse's absence, Calvin chaired the weekly staff meetings. Since it was impossible to keep pace with Jesse and his demand that everyone produce 187 percent as he did, Jesse's confidant Richard Thomas took on the role of "staff defender" at times, interpreting the needs and limits of human beings to Jackson.[48]

One staffer who seemed to be everywhere was Rev. Willie Barrow, the "Little Warrior." From our beginning together investigating Seven-Up, Rev. Barrow went on to organize Breadbasket youths, consumer clubs, and Women of Breadbasket. Willie coordinated special projects and led teams monitoring covenants and inspecting stores for bad meat. She arranged picket lines, headed the emergency food drive for Cairo, coordinated busloads of people and thousands of sandwiches for the Poor People's trek to D.C., and oversaw the free breakfast program. Willie perceived her role primarily as "building relationships" out of the churches, businesses, and community groups. Her strength was "people. I love people. My spirit goes out to others." Years later Willie was finally recognized for her deep commitment, superb organizing skills, and great spirit: "I didn't have any trouble fighting."[49]

Black power never became an overt issue in Breadbasket generally or in the SC specifically. However, after Dr. King's death, the vision of a fully interracial movement had clearly lost its primary champion, and we had to rely on other key individuals to insist on respecting and trusting the white people on the SC. Calvin Morris, Willie Barrow, Ma Houston, and Clay Evans never allowed any comment or act of "reverse discrimination" toward us. I only occasionally felt slighted on subtle things in more public settings, like opening prayers. To the end I felt trusted in my labors and commended for my participation.

The Jesse-Noah Dance

At the beginning of 1970 Rev. Jackson appointed Noah Robinson, who had just graduated from the famed Wharton School, to be the director of Breadbasket's Commercial Division. Jesse declared, "Noah's joining our staff represents a significant victory for the Black Community at large. Too often our best heads have been lured away. . . . The coming of Noah 'back home' we hope will signal a reversal of a trend that has long plagued our people." In his statement Jesse did not mention that Noah was his half brother. Strangely, the appointment was not even mentioned at our SC meeting the next day.[50]

Noah spent his first months building rapport with our business cadre, signing up new businesses, establishing fees for division membership, and creating new procedures. It was hoped that with his sharp intellect and no-nonsense style he would assist us in strengthening both discipline and relationships in the division. He attended SC meetings periodically and participated in covenant reviews. His intellect was impressive, but some of us SC pastors sensed an attitude. Little did we know that this was the hint of a storm on the horizon.

Soon, Noah was creating confusion among us. In a memo to Dr. Al Pitcher, the coordinator of the Construction Division, Noah wrote, "I don't want, nor do I need any *yes* men. But after the discussion and *I* have decided upon a course of action, you are to do everything in your power to get it done. Understand? *Do* it, *don't debate* it!" In another memo: "Pitcher, I have *asked* you to work on this several times. In reality though, I was *telling* you to do so. . . . your responsibility is to carry out the directives of your superiors."[51] In response, Al wrote to Noah:

> For four and one-half years I have worked for the Freedom Movement in Chicago—half time for six months of each year and time and one-half for the other six months for nothing—in many cases carrying expenses for parts of the operation myself. To insinuate that I am concerned about money for myself or that the size of the salary has anything to do with myself is absurd. To have motives and loyalties questioned every time one turns around is to destroy one's capacity to act. If you and Jesse and Calvin want strong men around you, another way has to be discovered to deal with them.[52]

In March 1970 Noah established a separate Breadbasket Commercial Association (BCA) with its own office on South State Street, effectively dissolving the Commercial Division. Its board of directors was a carbon copy of Breadbasket's business leaders, many of them participants going back to the early Saturday breakfasts with Jesse. Rev. Morris urged Jesse to oppose this move and keep the BCA and Noah within Breadbasket, but Jesse was "blind to the warning." The Breadbasket businessmen were now confronted with a challenge to their loyalty: Jesse or Noah. It was not a happy scene. In a handwritten memo to Dr. Pitcher, Noah put it succinctly: "What is the Breadbasket Commercial Association, Inc? The BCA is the mother organization of the commercial division of Operation Breadbasket." It was simply a takeover.[53] Noah was building his own little empire. He announced the addition of the Freedom Scavenger Association, when in fact it had been a part of Breadbasket since Jesse organized the scavengers in 1966. Still, Noah secured several new black businesses that joined in for the first time.

The Jesse-Noah dance had begun in their childhood back in Greenville, South Carolina. Noah Robinson Jr. was raised as a privileged son of a relatively well-to-do black businessman. Jesse, his half brother, was raised next door as the secret son. Although older, Jesse always felt insecure in the presence of his siblings, and he longed for recognition and acceptance equal to that given his brothers, whom he would observe by peering into the windows of their house. Now, with his remarkable achievement in Chicago, Jesse the underprivileged brother had hired the privileged brother—straight out of the Wharton School. Since Jesse and Calvin had no training in economics, Jesse felt that his brother could provide this missing piece. Noah had stated publicly that he wanted to make money and become a millionaire in his thirties, while "Jesse was into speech making and civil rights."[54] Given the family system and his jealousy and insecurity, Jesse found it difficult to deal with his brash and brilliant brother.

In July 1970, with no warning, Noah Robinson wrote a vitriolic and accusatory letter to the president of Jewel Food Stores, complaining about the treatment of Rual Boles, a black producer of industrial wax. Noah claimed that "Rual has been denied full access to the Jewel market," an action that "smacks with overtones of disrespect for a respected community figure." Noah demanded "immediate clarification" to "prevent further undermining of the covenantal relationship . . . between Operation Breadbasket and the Jewel Companies."[55] Noah copied Mr. Boles, Jesse, the sc, and top Jewel officials. When this letter was read aloud at our Friday meeting, it was noted that "this issue has already been settled to Rual's satisfaction."[56] In spite of this, Noah wrote next to Jewel's Nate Armstrong, accusing him of failing

> to keep your word. What you must clearly understand is that Breadbasket is sick of white companies using niggers as buffers, and sick of niggers playing the roles as major obstacles to Black economic progress. . . .
>   You ought to view yourself as an infiltrator of Jewel rather than an assimilated integrator. Your real power is us . . . your people. . . . Nate, the Basket ain't bullshitting anymore. Either stand with your people or be driven out with the alien invaders. There isn't any middle ground.[57]

The coup de grace came in a third Robinson letter to Jewel, responding to Nate's written appeal to Jesse. Noah pontificated that before Breadbasket or even before Dr. King, there was a Noah Robinson who had two sons, himself and Jesse, "a moving saga. . . . I view Nate's letter as a power play in its most uninhibited form, one that challenges his [Nate's] seniority of association with Operation Breadbasket versus my organizational and very personal relationship *to* Jesse, the prize or point at stake being Jesse's assessment of who rates more value to him." Noah was incensed that Nate refused to recognize his leadership of the BCA, and suggested that if Jesse even replied to Nate, Noah would immediately resign or "reassess what, if any relationship there is that remains between Jesse and myself." He concluded, "I bear no malice toward Nate. He is obviously not well, and needs help. I am disregarding his personal attacks upon me in the form of allegations and accusation, for he knows not what he does."[58]

This was sheer transference concerning who was not well and who knew "not what he does." Interestingly, the sc did not receive a copy of this third diatribe. Jesse tolerated this extreme behavior because of an inability to confront his brother, both for their own relationship and for the good of Operation Breadbasket. A glimpse of the Jesse-Noah rift was revealed at one sc meeting when Noah defended the BCA by saying, "We're the moral mafia," to which Jesse responded, "Noah, you've got to be careful; this can look like extortion."[59]

Just a few weeks later, without notifying ground control, Noah Robinson spread Breadbasket's wings to Detroit. Noah set up a BCA office there, established a few local contacts, and got in touch with A&P's Detroit division. After some initial communication, A&P became unavailable for meetings and, according to a memo from Noah, "Their rationale was that the covenantal thing was only a Chicago phenomenon, applicable and enforceable only in Chicago."[60]

Noah decided to fight, telegramming A&P Detroit that "A&P's ass was grass and that we were an anxious lawn mower." This arrogance was a far cry from King's dream of plain confrontation, corporate power versus consumer power, driven by the pulpit of moral America. But Noah was a smooth talker, and he persuaded thirty-one BCA supporters from Chicago to join him in Detroit over the Labor Day weekend to picket selected A&P stores. Noah claimed in a memo that the A&P clientele simply dried up before the "onslaught." "The neophyte picket line troops were like sharks tasting blood—as soon as one store went down, rather than retire, they went after a new one. Stores were announcing over the parking lot P.A. systems that milk and bread and related items were being reduced to half price. The effect was devastating. . . . Like a snowball rolling down a hill, we were picking up momentum. The day was ours—we could do no wrong!"[61]

But back in Chicago the Breadbasket leadership realized it had a wild stallion on the loose. Rev. Jackson and the SC saw the Detroit events for what they were—a gang-like extortion. It was not a local campaign based among residents, A&P customers, and local churches. It was an attempted takeover from outside. Noah and his allies were instructed to return to Chicago, which they did, thankfully, ending an embarrassing moment for Operation Breadbasket.

Jesse then called Noah to his home for what appeared to be a severe dressing down, lasting three hours. Noah's memo to BCA staff two days later recognized that in Jesse's view the "BCA appears to be bucking Operation Breadbasket and operating as a separate entity" and had "become an emotional liability to SCLC in general and Jesse in particular." Noah indicated that Jesse reaffirmed the BCA as a division of Breadbasket accountable to Breadbasket and insisted that BCA participants be Breadbasket members, attend membership meetings, pay dues, and participate in special events like Black Expo. Noah concluded, "Gentlemen, the absence of communication has been rectified. It is but my duty to report." But Jesse took no action to enforce his demands, and Noah and the BCA continued on their independent course.[62]

After an extended intermission, the Jesse-Noah dance broke into open maneuvering in December 1970. Word leaked out that Jesse had called a private meeting with members of the old Commercial Division, now leaders of the BCA, hoping to bring them back under Breadbasket's and Jesse's authority.

Two BCA staffers wrote to Noah complaining that Jesse's move would threaten the BCA's autonomy, and one of them resigned. To avoid public embarrassment, Jesse quietly canceled his meeting, and both he and Noah denied a power struggle. Again, Noah was able to escape a review of his operation, and the tension was temporarily reduced.[63] However, Noah's attempt to intimidate Jewel and the disastrous operation in Detroit were unresolved issues. It could not have been a very merry Christmas for the Jackson and Robinson families.

Noah Robinson remained in the doghouse. His abrasive style was an irritant to both Jesse and Rev. Abernathy. In July 1971 Abernathy asked Noah to change the BCA's name and make a clean separation with the SCLC. When Noah refused, arguing that a name change would create more "confusion," the SCLC's Chauncey Eskridge threatened a lawsuit. The impasse ended at the SCLC convention in August with the SCLC board backing down. Abernathy offered the hope that the SCLC and the BCA "would continue to work cooperatively and in unison toward the common goal of alleviating the social, political and economic ills that beset the poor and oppressed of the nation." The real hope was that SCLC's Breadbasket and the BCA would actually cooperate and coordinate their economic justice efforts. As the *Defender* aptly headlined the story, "A-Tisket-a-Tasket, It's Noah's Basket."[64] The fiery story of Noah Robinson, Jesse's half brother, continued after Breadbasket, leading eventually to his life imprisonment for racketeering and murder-for-hire charges in conjunction with the El Rukn (former Black P Stone Nation) street gang.[65]

Steering Committee Diminished

In September 1970, after Jesse left a Friday meeting early, we clergy shared our recurring frustrations. We crystallized our concerns in a telegram to Jesse with three demands: the appointment of a staff person to replace Gary Massoni, who had just left to complete his studies at CTS; the appointment of a Chicago director to fill a serious void; and authorization for a retreat for staff, the SC, and division representatives, as originally scheduled for April. Our SC minutes noted: "Until these requests can be satisfied we cannot continue our activities as the Steering Committee of Op. Breadbasket."[66]

Jesse responded by assigning us a new staffer, Rev. C. Hiram Melson, changing the name "Steering Committee" to "Ministers Division," shifting meetings to Wednesdays, changing the minutes to a newsletter, and agreeing to a retreat. In October, Jesse led a clergy "workshop," not a retreat, and introduced Rev. Melson. Although Rev. Lawrence led a discussion on "prospective actions" and I gave the follow-up report, our SC had been essentially reined in and put under the supervision of Jesse's new aide. The agenda sheet noted: "The Ministers Division is and has been the most important agent in making meaningful negotiation. Thus, each one who has played an effective role in the past is extended gratitude from the National Director in hopes you will continue in our vigorous program of economic justice. . . . The organization [Operation Breadbasket] pleads for men like yourselves to buttress its every endeavor."[67] If this statement was meant to reconcile the working clergy with these newly imposed changes, it fell far short.

At the first meeting of this Ministers Division, Rev. Melson handed out a sheet describing our structure and operation, with ten "dictates," each beginning "There will be." Among the disturbing changes was that to "clarify" our relationship with Noah and the BCA, all contacts for service and product contracts would be made by the Breadbasket Commercial Association, and its recommendations would "carry the weight of the minister's Negotiating Committee." This dictate reduced the SC to a rubber stamp for the BCA and Noah Robinson on what had been major components of our negotiation and covenant making. In spite of feeling taken over, we clergy continued our work under the new constraints.[68]

In the midst of one upsetting session, I had submitted a written report on the condition of our fifteen covenants. It stated that most of the companies "had clearly broken their covenant with Operation Breadbasket, on the basis of employment figures alone" and suggested that, except for A&P and Walgreen, "all former agreements are well out-of-date, so that re-negotiation is in order sometime in the future." On the positive side, 69 percent of promised jobs had been filled. The report concluded: "For that we ought to praise the Lord, and work the harder."[69] Since we continued to call ourselves the SC and insisted on continuing to meet on Fridays, we regained some of our former stature, at least symbolically. But our earlier collegiality and conviviality with Jesse were now history.

In sum, Breadbasket's internal power struggles sapped energy, exposed disunity, and weakened our focus on the common enemy: economic injustice and discrimination in the total society. It also revealed how very human were the committed colleagues of Operation Breadbasket.[70]

The Jesse-Ralph Dance

Another internal struggle that broke into the news periodically and was a portent of things to come was between Jesse Jackson and Ralph Abernathy. Tensions between the SCLC president and Breadbasket's national director began in the moments after King's assassination in April 1968. The SCLC staff agreed not to talk to the press individually. But Jesse flew immediately back to his base in Chicago and addressed the press, pointing to his bloody shirt and claiming to be the last person to speak to Doc. Ralph had been at King's side on the motel balcony, and he knew otherwise. For many months afterward, Ralph and Jesse barely tolerated each other, yet they managed to maintain a public face of cooperation and unity.

Although Ralph and Jesse joined together in launching phase 2 of the Poor People's Campaign in the spring of 1969, rumors of dissension kept cropping up, as evidenced by a front-page *Defender* article entitled "Rev. Jackson vs. Rev. Abernathy." Jesse's mushrooming popularity, the national coverage of Saturday Breadbasket, and word of a physical altercation with Hosea Williams, Jesse's nemesis on the SCLC staff, only fed the feud. Jesse's standing ovation before the Illinois legislature in Springfield at the same time that Ralph was addressing Congress in D.C. reportedly upset the SCLC leader. Robert Lucas, a KOCO leader, declared, "It's not a secret. Everyone seems to be aware of it except the people at Operation Breadbasket and SCLC."[71] In Chicago Breadbasket we simply ignored the rumors and went about our work.

Jesse Jackson's appearance on the cover of *Time* magazine in April 1970, while a remarkable achievement for a twenty-nine-year-old black American, was too much for Ralph Abernathy, whose response, it was reported, amounted to uttering several syllables in an unknown language.[72] Two weeks later Jesse attended the SCLC board meeting in Birmingham, while still ailing from a ten-day bout of bronchitis. At the meeting, rumors of dissension were strongly denied by the SCLC chair, Rev. Joseph Lowery, who called these stories a "figment of the white press who want to choose our black leaders." To placate Jesse and stanch the rumors, the board recommended that Rev. Jackson be elected vice president at-large at the SCLC's summer convention. Jesse accepted the offer.[73]

The following Saturday Ralph joined Jesse at Saturday Breadbasket in Chicago, where he told a large crowd, anxious over that day's *Defender* headline—"Jesse Losing Breadbasket?"—that Jesse would not lose Breadbasket. "Rev. Jackson's job title will remain unchanged. He will continue as the national director of Operation Breadbasket." The *Defender*'s Monday headline read, "Jesse to Keep Breadbasket."[74]

In early 1971 the national Urban League's distinguished leader, Whitney Young, drowned in a freak accident off a beach near Lagos, Ghana, while attending the African-American Dialogues Conference. Rev. Jackson, also in attendance, delivered the eulogy at a memorial in Lagos. Speculation began almost immediately that Jesse, already on a ten-week leave of absence for his Chicago mayoral campaign, might abandon the SCLC and Breadbasket to take the helm of the Urban League. Gossip was fanned, but Jesse ended the uncertainty with a clear denial. The whole issue simply enhanced Jesse's national stature.

After his leave, Jesse was welcomed back at the SCLC board meeting in Detroit. When the news media reported that the organization had voted to centralize all SCLC departments in Atlanta, including Breadbasket, rumors rolled that Jesse was maneuvering to replace Ralph as the SCLC president. Ralph denied it. Rev. Lowery added, "Jesse asked us to restore him in his position and we were glad to do so. Jesse has a great future in SCLC and in the nation and I don't want to see the organization get bogged down with positionitis."[75] Lowery insisted that the Chicago Breadbasket office would continue to function. Jesse charged that the rumors of his leaving Chicago were "character assassination."[76]

Back in Chicago, Cirilo McSween exclaimed, "Someone's trying to create division in the ranks of SCLC. Such publicity only hurts the organization." Some five hundred local pastors petitioned Rev. Abernathy to keep Jesse and his staff in Chicago. Thousands more petitions were signed and sent to the SCLC. Bobby Rush, a Black Panther leader, telegrammed Abernathy pleading the case. Whether orchestrated or not, Jesse found himself on a pedestal of support upon his return to Breadbasket.[77] Meanwhile the Jesse-Ralph dance took a hiatus for several months, but it did not go away and carried within it the seeds of renewed confrontation.

DECLINE AND TRANSFORMATION

I think it is most unfortunate that SCLC should be put in a position of losing a person of the enormous skills and dedication of Jesse Jackson. . . . It was silly of Ralph. He should have known better.—Rev. Walter Fauntroy

The SC led a major review of all covenants during 1970; it had been more than two years since most agreements had been seriously monitored. In a sit-down session with Seven-Up's Tom Joyce we learned that the company's black employment had risen from 12 percent to 33 percent (table 5). Joyce indicated that Seven-Up was looking for opportunities to increase black employment "because we've seen the results." We encouraged him to begin using black banks and other black services and suppliers, which were not included in the original 1966 covenant. The Pepsi-Cola review exposed more modest gains. Continental Baking reported black employment had climbed from 21 percent to 28 percent in less than three years, eliciting a letter of satisfaction, one of the few we ever wrote. Dean Foods' response was a letter of high-sounding words, sans data. High-Low Foods reported that black employment had climbed from 11 percent to 21 percent in three-plus years but that its business was in serious decline. Similarly, Certified Grocers showed an increase from ten to thirty-one black-owned stores, but with a reduction of stores in black communities. Sadly, due to our limited energy, the SC made little effort to upgrade these older covenants or even to maintain pressure on the reviewed companies, except for National Tea and long-time target Walgreen.[1]

Walgreen: A Last, Partial Victory

When Breadbasket first investigated Walgreen in March 1968, we were encouraged by the discovery that it had 36 percent African Americans among 2,500 employees. After Dr. King's death in April we communicated a modest request of 107 higher-income jobs aimed at cracking the ceiling. Walgreen replied that it needed time and had some "legal hang-ups." Three months later Walgreen announced that it would hire an additional sixty black people in the next thirty days and open an employment/training center on

Table 5. Employment Gains at Seven-Up Bottling Company,
Chicago, 1966–1971

Position	August 26, 1966		September 9, 1966*	January 31, 1971	
	Total	Black Emps.	No. Blacks Requested	Total	Black Emps.
Manager	37	1	6	48	5
Professional	3	0	1	3	0
Sales	101	15	5	96	16
Office	39	2	6	25	10
Craftsman	27	0	5	17	4
Operative	104	19	0	110	43
Laborer	107	14	0	97	53
Service	0	0	5	0	0
Total	418	51	28	396	131
Percent		12.2			33

Note: The higher-paying jobs were hardest to secure.

*Unwritten agreement reached September 13, 1966, without a "Don't Buy" campaign

Source: PBBF.

the South Side in the next few months, which it did.[2] Still, Walgreen continued to obfuscate and stall through the summer. In October the SC voted to send a strong telegram, but no telegram was actually sent. This fiasco of unfinished business with Walgreen resulted from total overload—the Poor People's Campaign, the A&P battle, and the diversion of church politics for us Methodists. Walgreen was off the hook.[3]

More than a year passed before we resumed efforts to secure data from this drugstore chain. In the spring of 1970, Walgreen stonewalled again with a telegram to me trumpeting the company's good works, subscribing "wholeheartedly" to our objectives, and claiming a "long standing policy of stocking black products" and hiring black employees. Company officials agreed to meet with us but indicated they needed no "exterior pressures" to assure their cooperation.[4] Our response was a "final" request for data to be produced in person on June 3 at 2:00 p.m. at the Gresham church. When the Walgreen representatives failed to appear, the SC voted for an immediate withdrawal campaign, and it was to the pulpits.[5]

Breadbasket picketers distributed thousands of "Don't Shop at Walgreen Drug Stores" leaflets during picketing of several stores on June 6 and 13, urging support "until Walgreen respects the community." Our North Shore chapter coordinated picketing in the suburbs. During this Walgreen battle I preached my last sermons at the Gresham church before my transfer to the First United Methodist Church of Evanston, a suburb just north of the city. In one sermon I reflected on Breadbasket: "There are signs of hope. . . . In the Walgreen fight we are attempting to open up a major company to improve working conditions and minority opportunities. Breadbasket is a sign of renewing the economic life of our city, a sign that jobs ought to be for all people equally. Breadbasket points to the Kingdom, with economic gates open to North, South, East and West. How can we not participate in Breadbasket if we live in Christian hope!"[6]

In one week the Walgreen boycott brought forth the long-delayed data. Picketing planned for June 20 was suspended as Walgreen met with our team to carve out a covenant. Playing it both ways, Walgreen counterattacked, planting an article in the *Defender* extolling the "success story" of a retired black pharmacist whom they quoted saying, "Walgreens is an ideal company to work for. It offers so much opportunity to a young man if he's ambitious." Anonymously written, this propaganda piece slipped through the cracks of an outstanding black newspaper.[7]

At Saturday Breadbasket on June 27, 1970, Charles R. Walgreen Jr. and four company officials signed the Breadbasket-Walgreen covenant, along with Revs. Jackson and Morris and eight SC pastors. The document mirrored our covenant with A&P. Walgreen agreed to hire 385 black employees within eighteen months, conduct "sensitivity seminars," hire executive staff for recruitment and training, and submit regular reports to Breadbasket. Walgreen also agreed to provide shelf space for black-produced goods, sign several service contracts, and hire staff to be responsible for marketing, covenant monitoring, and advising black business clients. Breadbasket agreed to advise our constituencies about this covenant and maintain an ongoing relationship of counseling and monitoring. Mr. Walgreen told the audience he was "happy to cooperate with Operation Breadbasket." Rev. Lawrence announced that the new jobs would increase annual income in the community by $2 million.[8] With this pact Breadbasket expanded our model for other corporations to emulate in rectifying systemic discrimination.

Now part of the economic landscape in Chicago, Breadbasket covenants were reproduced for use and study in businesses and in universities across the nation. While economic impact is hard to quantify, it is clear that during these years of urban unrest and riots, boosting black employment became a nationwide priority, and Breadbasket offered a unique model.[9]

Almost before the ink was dry we had to prompt Walgreen to share copies of the covenant with all of its employees, as agreed. In late August Walgreen reported hiring only twenty-five black people in the first two months, below the needed average, and as of September it had barely made a beginning with service contracts and products.[10] At a follow-up session we reminded Walgreen that the sensitivity seminars were to be planned "in conjunction with Breadbasket" and that the twenty-seven black products needed to be in all stores posthaste. We discussed the roles of the new black executives, James Rucker and Oscar Smith, in their presence. It was a lively, informative meeting with several issues resolved and promises made.[11]

Under-the-table notes passed at these sessions reveal the collegiality and concern for detail among the Breadbasket team. Rev. Lawrence received this note: "Ask if Oscar Smith has access to top management. For example, has he met with C. R. Walgreen Jr. yet?" And this one: "Dick, we are 98 positions short on page 12 alone." I was slipped this scribbled request: "Deppe, I think we should hammer them on: Our concern is with employment categories and classification, not the additional numbers of blacks employed. What are the black employees doing . . . once hired?" Another note read: "Walgreen *profits* up last qt. (11 percent). Walgreen is expanding—so why not Black staff? Tell them to hold their conversation to what's on paper." Finally: "I am really disturbed. If they only know 'off-hand' in terms of specifics, how the hell do we know if totals are correct?"[12] A little levity helped to keep us overly serious clerics somewhat sane.

By late October 1970, Walgreen had secured scavenger and exterminator contracts for 30 stores and placed seven black products in all 128 area stores. Other products, including Joe Louis Milk and Parker House Sausage, were available in less than a dozen stores. Five more stores were banking at Independence and three at Seaway. As requested, Walgreen sent us a list of job openings, which we distributed. By January 1971, Walgreen seemed to be on schedule to reach the eighteen-month goal of 385 new black employees. All good so far.[13]

Then Walgreen began to slip back. With three months to go, it had filled less than half of the 385 jobs. Progress was mixed with black contracts and products, though we were encouraged by product purchases amounting to about $50,000 per quarter. During June, Walgreen began a "Back Black" ad campaign promoting black products in thirty stores. "We hope to build a stronger Black consciousness among black shoppers," said Walgreen's black development director. "We've done several market studies and we feel that it's not that blacks don't want to buy black products, but simply that they aren't aware of which products are Black manufactured."[14] A new symbol helped folks to identify black products. By October 1971, Walgreen announced that "Back Black" had helped increase the movement of black products by about 10 percent.[15]

To what extent these gains in black products and services fed back to Breadbasket is not clear. The Attunement Committee had long since been replaced by the Commercial Division, which since January 1970, was under the aggressive leadership of Noah Robinson. The business circle's loyalty was split between Noah and Jesse, which undermined the old attunement attitude of supporting Breadbasket and the black community.

Nevertheless, Walgreen fell short of the covenant goals. This was all the more glaring in the light of Walgreen's announcement that 1971 sales rose 9.9 percent and earnings were $10.6 million, up 12.7 percent over 1970. Given this success, Walgreen's failure to better implement the covenant was a disappointing conclusion to an agreement that had commenced with such great promise on both sides.[16]

After six exciting, fast-moving, and exhausting years the SCLC's Operation Breadbasket was running out of gas. The decline was evident in our final confrontation with National Tea.

National Tea: The Last Campaign

> "Well, Rev. Lawrence, are you ready to go to jail for the cause of economic justice?" What could I say? . . . I am never ready to go to jail, and I am afraid of what goes on in there, but I assumed Jesse would be going with us, so I boldly announced that I was ready.—Rev. Richard Lawrence

A long-overdue review of National Tea commenced in early 1970. While the number of retail stores had dropped 18 percent over three years, black employment had increased 24 percent, from 660 to 929, including a substantial increase in drivers, from 4 to 41. At the same time, National had fallen short in store managers and reported only 11 blacks among 238 people in management. After more foot-dragging by National we met with their officials in July with a proposed update to the covenant. Based on recent successes we included specific numbers for jobs and for black-owned products and services. National requested more time.

When we reconvened in August, National reported adding eleven store accounts to black-owned banks; new scavenger, exterminator, and janitorial contracts for thirty-two stores; and a willingness to negotiate bids for black car dealers and black advertising and construction services. The company requested a hold on our demand of 390 jobs until after a sales meeting in September, admitting that this number of jobs could not be filled within ninety days, and it waffled on hiring thirty black executives. We acknowledged significant movement, but pressed National for action. Negotiations stalled.

It had not dawned on us that National's problems with the revised covenant mirrored its failure to cope with the changing times and with increased competition in the Chicago market.[17]

Several weeks of ping-pong communications occurred until our teams met in November, when again National claimed it was doing the best it could "in all good conscience." One more fruitless session followed, and then we announced a direct action campaign. Immediately, letters went out to our churches and an order was placed for fifty thousand copies of a "Do Not Shop at National Foods" leaflet proclaiming that National "profoundly disrespects the black community, Operation Breadbasket and minority workers everywhere." It showed our Breadbasket symbol of a fist grasping wheat and dollar signs with the familiar "Your Ministers Fight for Jobs and Rights." Using a list of thirty stores having a majority of black customers, five starred as "pressure-sensitive" stores, Breadbasket volunteers began weekly picketing on November 28 and continued through the end of 1970.[18]

In June 1970, after serving the Gresham church for six years, I was transferred to suburban Evanston's First United Methodist Church, but I commuted back for weekly sc meetings. In late November, at my suggestion, the Evanston congregation's social concerns group placed a blurb in *Soundings*, the church newsletter, urging members not to shop at National stores. In the mail I received a copy of *Soundings* with a note scrawled in red ink across the cover: "MINISTERS: You are trying to put White People out of Jobs they hold by MERIT! ... Get out of the CHURCH and Get into POLITICS as Revolutionists. ... STOP your VICIOUS political involvements and interference with private business! I'll make a special effort to do ALL my shopping at NATIONAL and You will get nothing." It was signed by a local church member.[19]

National Tea held out, and Breadbasket's picketing limped along. In the words of Massoni, Breadbasket did not take "decisive action against National in support of the negotiating ministers. With attention focused primarily on political activity, Breadbasket mustered only shabby support for the boycott."[20] Then, out of the blue, without consulting or informing the sc, Jesse announced a nationwide boycott of A&P! This he did while standing with some Breadbasket ministers in Brooklyn, New York. Along with a lack of support of our National Tea boycott in Chicago, Jesse's lone ranger action only deepened the frustration and disillusionment of the sc pastors, myself included.[21]

At some point in the fall Breadbasket launched RESIST, inviting people to join other "resisters," like Dr. King, Malcolm X, Jesus of Nazareth, Moses, and Gandhi. Jesse wrote, "Not everyone can march or picket or demonstrate. But many of us can mail $5 or more to OPERATION BREADBASKET RESIST and receive from us an official RESIST card." A brochure gave news of the National Tea boycott and upcoming Black Christmas events. This ambitious idea never got off the ground.[22]

Some of us recognized a looming defeat, but without clear direction from Rev. Jackson, we muddled along while most of Breadbasket's energy went into the second Black Expo and preparing for Jesse's run for mayor. Action continued into the new year with thirteen stores picketed on a Saturday early in January, but without enough leaflets or signs. Our offer to extend the deadline for jobs was rejected, and the deadlock continued. Word came down that the SC was not fully supporting the effort, but this was a deeper problem involving the whole ship.

A Breadbasket newsletter dated January 30, 1971, suggested that we end the "hassle" with National. With cold weather and not enough leaflets or volunteers, the "Don't Buy at National" campaign quietly ended without a whimper or public acknowledgment. Three months later a letter from National informed us that it had closed all manufacturing and bakery operations, resulting in the loss of 229 jobs, 52 held by black employees, and very soon it would close twenty-five stores. While this correspondence revealed serious retrenching, our minutes state that the company's message contained "nothing new." Clearly, if we had faced the reality of National's deteriorating situation, we might have been more flexible and salvaged a reasonable agreement.[23]

In June, for reasons unknown to the SC negotiating team, Rev. Jackson relaunched the campaign against National Tea. In his *Defender* column Jesse charged National with abandoning the black community while continuing to make a profit overall, $9 million in 1970. Jesse claimed, "WE HOLD THE MARGIN OF PROFIT. . . . We can control that margin and that is what we will proceed to demonstrate tomorrow. National Tea must cut us in or cut it out. . . . So come with your walking shoes prepared to do business." Picketing resumed at multiple stores on June 12 and continued on several Saturdays with as many as forty people on some lines. Jesse commented, "Last week your little walk cost National about $21,000 in its inner city stores. . . . Stay out of National until National decides it will respect the black community and stay in a good relationship with Us!" Whether because it was summer, vacation time, or because of weariness, the Breadbasket forces did not succeed in forcing National back to the table.[24] In the midst of all this, another anonymous death threat against Rev. Jackson was received at the Breadbasket office. Calvin Morris and Jesse's secretary, Lucille Coleman, simply "buried" it, rather than add to his burdens.[25]

During July, an internal National Tea memo came into the possession of the SC, which suggested to all employees that stores were being closed because 40 percent of black customers already used National stores outside the black community. That was a suspect figure. We felt that the reduced black clientele, due in part to our earlier boycott, was simply National's excuse to abandon the inner city and build larger stores in white areas. The fact is that Breadbasket had no power to stop National from leaving.[26] Going on the offensive, National Tea proudly announced through the local newspapers sixty new college and high school scholarships, ignoring Breadbasket and appealing directly to the community, the old familiar divide-and-conquer strategy. As National stonewalled, Breadbasket escalated the picketing.[27]

At this point the SC wrote to National Tea to expect our negotiating team at its headquarters on July 9. As Rev. Richard Lawrence, the chair of our team, remembered, "They were ready—not for a meeting but for a confrontation." In the lobby the pastors were approached by a uniformed security officer who declared that the group was "trespassing on private property" and that "we must leave or the Chicago police would be called and we would be arrested. We thanked him, reiterated our desire for a meeting with the President of National Food Stores and reaffirmed our intention to stay right where we were until we got one. Rev. Jackson did all the talking." Rev. Lawrence's account continued: "When Jesse was finished, he turned to me and asked, 'Well, Rev. Lawrence, are you ready to go to jail for the cause of economic justice?' What could I say? . . . I am never ready to go to jail, and I am afraid of what goes on in there, but I assumed Jesse would be going with us, so I boldly announced that I was ready. . . . Jesse told us he could not be arrested because he was needed 'to take the message of what went on here today to the flock' so we had prayer, and the Chicago police arrived." Jesse left just before his three designated pastors, who refused to leave, were arrested, charged with criminal trespass and taken to jail.[28] I wonder yet if Jesse would have included me in the designated group, had I been present.

After spending the night in jail the three men attended court early Saturday, pleaded not guilty, and were bailed out in time to attend the end of Saturday Breadbasket, where they were welcomed as heroes. Jesse wrote a few days later, "We salute those ministers, Revs. Lawrence, Forshey, and [Frank] Watkins, who took our case to the jailhouse and therefore spread our witness for justice. The picketing of National Tea continues this week . . . with some new stores."[29]

A few weeks later, Rev. Lawrence came to Breadbasket prepared with lots of signs, hoping to secure several volunteers to join him on the picket line. It was agreed that Jesse would give the effort a major plug. Unknown to Lawrence, however, a new crisis had arisen, and Jesse announced that on the meeting's adjournment he would lead a march to Provident Hospital. As head of the National team, Rev. Lawrence felt let down, knowing that most supporters would follow their leader. "When Jesse asked for some folks to 'stay and follow my [Lawrence's] directions to the National Food Store targets we would be picketing,' there was a hollow ring to the announcement." Just enough people joined Lawrence to effectively picket two stores.[30] These constant distractions weakened our efforts with National Tea.

Quite independently, the National Consumers Union, a North Shore group with members in four states, began investigating chain store pricing. At a National Tea shareholders meeting, NCU members were brushed off and their resolution regarding Chicago's operations was defeated.[31] A few weeks later the union's leadership contacted National to ask about the Breadbasket arrests, and they were rebuffed. With that, the NCU joined the Breadbasket campaign. Jesse called this "a new ballgame." Operation Breadbasket and the NCU "will together picket stores thru-out the city, for no longer is this a black issue, but a black and white consumers' issue which National executives have continually failed to deal with." On July 24 NCU supporters joined Rev. Jackson and a Breadbasket contingent in picketing a National Food store in suburban Wilmette. Breadbasket observers now estimated that National's business in the community was down by 35–40 percent. In August, Seventh Ward Independent Democrats joined in picketing and carpooling shoppers to other chain stores in the East Side area. National Tea remained unmoved.[32]

After eight weeks some community members began to fear that the boycott would take away jobs. A letter to the *Defender* by "three black sisters" affirmed the boycott in a dramatic defense and dared the editors to publish it, which they did.[33] Then, in late September the picketers disappeared. No announcement. No fanfare. No waves. As Rev. Lawrence recalled it, some National meatcutters went to Rev. Jackson and warned him that the continuing boycott was causing National to cut staff. They urged him to stop the boycott in order to save their jobs. The Amalgamated Meat Cutters' Charlie Hayes contacted Jesse directly with the same message. While Charlie was dedicated to Dr. King's vision and to Breadbasket, his primary loyalty was to his union colleagues. Jesse gave in. The message got out quickly to "cool it, let it go." After months of struggle, including winter boycotting, and now another fourteen weeks through the hot summer, the fight was over.[34]

Who won? Perhaps a few meatcutters for a limited time. Clearly not National: while the company managed to cut its losses, its relationship to black Chicago was destroyed. Certainly not Breadbasket: we lost fifty-three meatcutter jobs and many other jobs, service contracts, and product shelf space. We used up enormous energy, and our image as a mover and shaker for justice was seriously damaged. It might have been otherwise. In the fall of

1970 we had negotiated from a too-rigid position, not recognizing National Tea's precarious state. Both sides drew lines in the sand, which turned into Maginot Lines. A possible new day for National Tea in Chicago was history. Both sides suffered, but by far the biggest losers were black people—those who lost jobs, businesspeople who lost service and product contracts, and residents who lost neighborhood stores within walking distance from their homes. This turned out to be the single major defeat in Breadbasket history.

Rev. Jackson, on the other hand, told me that he does not see our struggle with National as a defeat. He believes that National withstood our campaign to avoid another fanfare of covenant signing in front of four thousand cheering Breadbasket supporters. Jesse avers that National went about implementing many of our changes on its own.[35] Due to the rupture with National Tea, Breadbasket received no further monitoring reports, so it is impossible to verify Jesse's claim. I know that, at the time, the SC considered the ending of the Breadbasket-National struggle to be a capitulation on our part.

The Empty Breadbasket

The SC pastors plodded on, denying the events swirling around us if only to keep our eyes on the prize. But an inescapable sign flashed before us in July 1971, when Rev. Calvin Morris announced he was leaving to resume his studies in graduate school. Calvin had given his all for four years, and dealing with Jesse day in and day out had increased the psychological toll on him. It was a tough loss for the entire Breadbasket family: Jesse lost a trusted confidant; Saturday Breadbasket gave up Calvin's inspired leadership in word and song from the podium; the staff would miss Calvin's steady voice and mediating manner; and we SC ministers lost an important ally. Calvin's departure was a significant loss to Chicago's black community and to the entire city.[36]

In his official resignation Calvin noted, "The past four years must rank as the most meaningful and deeply revealing years of my life" and have "afforded me the opportunity to be involved at a direct level with numerous significant and historic events."[37] In a statement honoring Rev. Morris, Fr. George Clements declared that while for him Dr. King was the spirit of Breadbasket, Jesse the soul, Willie the heart, Ma Houston the mother, and Ed Riddick the mind, Calvin was "the hands and feet of Breadbasket....I respect Calvin because he works, he gets things done, he produces, he takes care of business."[38]

Rev. Jackson wrote a tribute to "my dearest friend outside my own family . . . my closest confidant in the family of man . . . my most loyal Associate." Rev. Morris came to Chicago "to pursue his doctorate in history....he turned his efforts instead, toward making history." Jesse saw "an inner light from the man whose favorite hymn was 'If I Can Help Somebody.'"[39] In a last press conference Rev. Morris expressed the need to "get some distance" to "objectively analyze and evaluate what has happened, why, what [effect] these occurrences will have on the future. I certainly know that Chicago needs a Breadbasket that remains strong, as I certainly believe it will. But whether it will continue its historical trend of economics is debatable."[40] Looking back almost forty years later, Calvin described those years as exhilarating and hopeful. "Breadbasket was traumatic; no experience was more gripping. We were engaged in issues of the time. We were part of a cadre, the cloud of witnesses making history, helping to make America what it really should be."[41]

With Calvin's departure hardly behind us, Jesse announced sweeping changes. He named Thomas N. Todd, a Northwestern University law professor, to be the president of a new Chicago chapter of the SCLC and assistant to the national director, saying, "Tom brings an unusually keen mind and persuasive and strong voice to Operation Breadbasket. . . . hearing him in court is like hearing an Advocate with thunder in his voice." Simultaneously Jesse named a new thirty-five-member board for the chapter. Jesse claimed "full concurrence" from Rev. Abernathy, but it was clearly a unilateral change, making Chicago's operation effectively autonomous and independent. Rev. Morris's accountability had been to the SCLC through Jesse. Todd's accountability would be to Jesse and the Chicago board, a fundamental shift in the lines of authority.[42]

In late November 1971, while Jesse was engaged in a public school crisis, news broke that the SCLC was investigating Chicago Breadbasket. In an interview with Rev. Abernathy, the *Chicago Tribune*'s Angela Parker revealed that the SCLC had just learned that Black Expo was secretly incorporated on September 14. Abernathy told Parker that "a department cannot make legal moves of this kind without the approval of the national president and the board of directors."[43] For months Ralph and Jesse had waltzed around their differences, but this account brought the conflict into the open.

Abernathy admitted he had avoided any public confrontation with Jesse because the "freedom movement was at stake and that's all the white power structure would need—to see internal strife within the most vibrant civil rights organization in the country." He considered "the liberation of the black and the poor people much more important than dissipating energies and resources seeking to deal with organizational structure, with Rev. Jackson or anyone else. . . . SCLC has never had a tight structure." Abernathy said that the recent move making Chicago Breadbasket a chapter with its own board of directors added considerable autonomy to the operation.[44]

Behind the authority issue lurked money. Since the first Black Expo in 1969, three-quarters of the income had remained with Chicago Breadbasket and one-quarter had been sent to the SCLC in Atlanta. Accordingly, $60,000 was sent to Atlanta from the first Expo and $11,000 from the second Expo. With the incorporation of Black Expo in September 1971, no money was sent to Atlanta. Since the salaries of Breadbasket staff continued to come from Atlanta, it looked like a rip-off to the SCLC board.

From the perspective of the Chicago Breadbasket leaders around Jesse, it was unfair to raise significant dollars in Chicago and send them to what they considered a floundering post–Dr. King national organization.[45] In addition, Jesse's supporters had purchased a nice house for him in South Shore, and they wanted their leader to live at a level not so removed from their own. This was no different from the attitude of many local churches who want their pastor to live on a respectable level, if not a pedestal, as a matter of some pride.[46]

The response from Rev. Jackson to the explosive *Tribune* article was silence—for a day. Rumors that Jesse had been dismissed were vigorously denied by Rev. Lowery. Jesse announced that he had no plans to quit, was disturbed about the public airing of the controversy, and would continue his efforts on the school crisis: "My first priority is to keep our students in school."[47] Then, several local groups, including the Chicago Welfare Rights Organization, the Woodlawn Organization, and Women Mobilized for Change, sent telegrams to Rev. Abernathy urging him to retain Jesse. These telegrams were addressed to Abernathy at the Marriott Hotel in Chicago, where he and the SCLC board were meeting.[48]

At that meeting the SCLC board suspended Jesse for sixty days with pay because of "repeated violation[s] of organizational policies." In his announcement, Lowery made clear there was no indication of financial irregularities. The next morning at Breadbasket, Jesse told the cheering crowd that he was glad his integrity was unquestioned and added, "I respect Dr. Abernathy, his job and his right to hire, fire or discipline persons by any rational means. I can't name five black men today who have done more to make the poor visible in the last five years." Then Jesse charged that the white media sought to divide black leadership: "This same media that took a trip to Atlanta can't make it from the Chicago Tribune Towers to Dr. King's Workshop to report our positive thrust. Our problem is economic and our goal is economic. Don't lose sight of the goals and start reacting to the wrong issue.... If my judgment has gotten me in trouble, so be it. My title is gone, but my responsibilities linger on and I will continue to stay in the struggle because the movement must go on."[49]

In response to Jesse's suspension and to questions about Expo income, Al Johnson, a leading Chicago auto dealer and Black Expo's treasurer, argued that it was not Jesse but black businesspeople who had incorporated Expo as a not-for-profit entity. They did so to provide legal protection against "personal and individual liability." While admitting that the original idea for Expo was Jesse's, Al claimed the Expos were sponsored by the business members in cooperation with Operation Breadbasket. He reported that almost $85,000 was sent to the national SCLC in 1969 and $12,500 in 1970. Johnson added that Expo '71 had a projected net income of $176,000 and that "his group will again concur with any financial arrangement Operation Breadbasket wishes to make in channeling a percentage of the 1971 funds to Atlanta-based headquarters."[50]

At this point all hell broke loose. On Friday, December 10, Jesse telegrammed Rev. Lowery with his resignation, effective the seventeenth. Jesse wrote, "60 days is too long for Operation Breadbasket to go without leadership."[51] Also resigning by telegram was almost the entire SCLC Chicago board of thirty-five and the twenty-five staff members. The next day at Saturday Breadbasket, Jesse came in to a standing ovation and had to leave the hall, momentarily overcome. Later he declared to the crowd that he was leaving in "love and peace and with no hatred nor malice for anyone. . . . I love Dr. Abernathy and the parent organization and I am glad that we have the same goals, although choosing different roads. . . . I offer no apologies and no regrets for the work I've done." His speech was followed by much applause and weeping.[52]

To think that mere dollars was the issue that led to separation is simplistic. There was rivalry and jealousy intertwined with love and respect between two determined personalities in the movement. Ralph was steadfast and hurt; Jesse was ready to move on, to grow, to expand "his" Breadbasket to a truly national level. This was never going to be possible within the constraints of a southern-oriented civil rights organization based in Atlanta. Like the birthing of Breadbasket in February 1966, this was a new beginning, a catharsis, a breakaway, a dawning.

On Sunday, Jesse met secretly in New York with key supporters from around the nation, including Mayors Carl Stokes and Richard Hatcher, entertainers Aretha Franklin and Roberta Flack, prominent black lawyers and businessmen, and his own associates Thomas Todd and Al Johnson. This group sketched out plans for a new organization to be headed by Rev. Jackson. On Monday, December 13, Rev. Abernathy expressed regret over Jesse's departure, offered help in his new efforts, and commended him by saying, "I think Rev. Jackson is a very fine person and has certainly made valuable contributions to the struggle for economic justice for the black and poor people." Then he added, "But if he professes to love me and SCLC so much, why would he encourage the staff and board to resign?" Rev. Abernathy was quick to claim that Chicago SCLC would continue with an expansion of its operations, returning to the "main focus of jobs and income in the economic department."[53]

On Tuesday a *Defender* editorial asserted that "the clash of personalities was an inevitable tragedy" and concluded that "without Jackson, Operation Breadbasket will be lifeless, empty and the SCLC itself may lose its shaky footing in the field of social action."[54] The former Breadbasket band leader, Ben Branch, declared, "I think Rev. Jackson was working toward [his resignation]. Whatever happens I hope the situation will turn out that the black community will have a solid organization. I'm remaining with SCLC." Rev. Walter Fauntroy, a congressman for Washington, D.C., a former aide to Dr. King, and a close friend of both Ralph and Jesse, expressed his distress, saying, "I think it is most unfortunate that SCLC should be put in a position of losing a person of the enormous skills and dedication of Jesse Jackson." Some days later, sitting in his office, Rev. Fauntroy muttered over and over again, "It was silly of Ralph. He should have known better."[55]

On Wednesday, December 15, the SCLC executive board telegrammed Jesse that it was refusing his resignation. Rev. Joseph Lowery said, "In the spirit of our founder, Dr. Martin Luther King, we hold our arms open to Mr. Jackson as our brother to remain and of course to work within the rules and policies of the organization." He talked of Jesse's impatience and expressed the hope that together they could work things out. On Thursday Jesse indicated he would reconsider his resignation but "only under certain conditions."[56] But everyone knew, including Jesse, Ralph, and Joe, that it was too late for any serious rapprochement.

On Saturday, December 18, Jesse's new organization was launched before three thousand folks jammed inside and out on the sidewalks of the Met Theatre on South King Drive. The name, Operation PUSH (People United to Save—soon changed to Serve—Humanity), was unveiled by Thomas Todd, who said that Operation PUSH is "an organization that belongs to, of and organized by the people." Jesse declared that a charter would be drawn up immediately and he would soon be traveling nationwide to set up chapters. The structure would parallel that of Operation Breadbasket with additional departments as needed. To a cheering crowd Jesse declared that we would not only "picket, boycott, march and vote, but if necessary will engage in civil disobedience" to implement our programs for the poor and oppressed. "Pain, not color, sex or economic class is the common denominator of PUSH."[57] Present at the rally were several of Jesse's national supporters and new PUSH board members.[58]

That same day Jesse sought to explain the break in his *Defender* column:

> When it becomes necessary for two parties to part, there should be an amicable separation.... This was for me and my staff a very grave decision. Since 1966, I have been privileged to work on the staff of the Southern Christian

Leadership Conference and to have the benefit of counsel and advice from the late prophetic giant, Dr. Martin Luther King, Jr. and from Dr. Abernathy. I do not regret or forget those years. I revere and remember them with a great depth of meaning.... During this crisis, I have suffered, but as I have told my people time and time again, "to live is to suffer, and to survive is to find meaning in the suffering, if you choose to live at all." Again, we see this not as a split, but as a new birth. A spreading out, more accurately.... If one asks how I am leaving, I leave in peace. I love Dr. Abernathy, and I love the parent organization. Our roads now separate, but our goals remain the same.[59]

In reflecting on the separation years later, Rev. Jackson told an interviewer, "We had a crisis we could not resolve, so we dissolved. We just went our separate ways. But it never became acrimonious as with Malcolm and Muhammad, because we were talking. I never attacked SCLC and I kept relationships with other staff members. In time the overt tensions began to fade away. Some years later Dr. Abernathy's Atlanta congregation moved to a new building and I gave the second sermon delivered in his church!"[60]

Operation PUSH

Operation PUSH was officially established on December 25, 1971. Calling it "a baby born on Christmas Day," Jesse outlined an ambitious twelve-point program before an overflow crowd of twenty-five hundred people, many of them undoubtedly having switched allegiance from Breadbasket at the Capitol Theatre to Operation PUSH at the Met Theatre:

1. PUSH for comprehensive economic gains for black and brown people with initiatives made to the International Monetary Fund and the World Bank;
2. PUSH for revival of the labor movement;
3. PUSH for humane alternatives to the welfare system;
4-6. PUSH for a Bill of Rights for children, the aging, and veterans;
7. PUSH for full political participation for all;
8. PUSH to elect persons at all levels of political office committed to humane economic and social programs;
9. PUSH for humane conditions in prisons and sound rehabilitation programs;
10. PUSH for adequate health care for all people based on need;
11. PUSH for quality education regardless of race, religion or creed; and
12. PUSH for economic and social relationships with nations of Africa in order to build African–Afro-American unity.[61]

Rev. Jackson's sermon was centered in the biblical story of Christ's birth and drew parallels between conditions then and now. He said that PUSH was "rooted in the tradition of the church and is the church in action." Jesse announced a membership drive, and yearly pledges were taken ranging from $3 to $1,000.[62] The full story of Operation PUSH goes beyond the scope of this book. Still, it can be stated unequivocally that PUSH became a worthy successor to Dr. King's vision for economic justice through the SCLC's Operation Breadbasket.

Rev. Jackson's resignation from the SCLC was hardly a surprise to anyone, certainly not to most of us in the SC. Jesse's thirst for national leadership, Breadbasket's political defeats by the Chicago machine, the National Tea debacle, Rev. Morris's departure, and the Ralph-Jesse jealousy—all these things raised the temperature over the boiling point. Even Jesse's charismatic leadership style could not contain the decision of his own business supporters to incorporate Black Expo as a separate entity without informing the SCLC. When this was discovered by SCLC leaders, it was all over. While Jesse's suspension was a clumsy move, it hardly mattered. The bridge was crossed, and Jesse's move to set up his own organization was simply the next step. Interestingly, he never looked to a clergy base, but rather moved ahead with his connections among black stars in entertainment, business, sports, government, and academics, along with a few trusted clergy colleagues. The Operation PUSH board of directors looked like a "Who's Who in Black America."

What remained of Breadbasket in Chicago was a building, Dr. King's Workshop, and a few clergy who tried to reorganize from scratch. Even with the appointment of C. T. Vivian as the director, the renewed SCLC Chicago chapter never got off the ground. Essentially, the people chose Jesse. I personally did not make this transition. My fundamental loyalty was to the SCLC and Dr. King, and already I had been participating for the previous eighteen months from my new parish assignment in Evanston. My Breadbasket work was concluded. Operation PUSH made one effort to secure my files, but I was still too burned to give them up. Those files would later become the basic resource for this book.

In the words of a *Defender* editorial, Chicago had "an empty Breadbasket."[63] PUSH, on the other hand, was just beginning a long run. It achieved several nationwide economic covenants, and eventually led to Rainbow PUSH and Rev. Jackson's campaigns for the Democratic Party's nomination for president of the United States in 1984 and 1988.

AFTERWORD

We all felt a part of Breadbasket. We wouldn't be where we are today without Operation Breadbasket.... Young people today do not realize the sacrifices made in the 1960s.—Walter Grady, Seaway National Bank president, 1980–2014

Between 1966 and 1971 Breadbasket filled at least 2,250 positions, in all classifications from unskilled to management, shattering the job ceiling. This does not include upgraded jobs, jobs added by black producers as these fledgling companies expanded, or jobs gained through service contracts, including electrical workers in construction contracts, scavenger truck drivers, janitors, bank tellers, exterminators, and lawyers. Neither does it include some noncovenanted companies with which we negotiated. With some evidence, I have estimated that an equal number of jobs were opened via services and products. Thus it appears that some 4,500 new jobs were filled, most of them ongoing (table 6).

Taking these 4,500 jobs and using $6,500 as an average salary (based on the salary structures in our covenant negotiations), I estimate a total annual salary increase of $29.2 million in 1968 dollars. This sum would translate to $199 million in 2016. While not a great gain in the overall Chicago economy, it was substantial and profoundly important for the people and families affected. Symbolically this economic result was illustrative of what could be achieved when African Americans, led by their moral leaders, acted together with nonviolent yet coercive force.

A review of the progress in the distribution of black products and the use of black-owned services over these six years can be summarized in both actual and estimated figures. A fair approximation of the annual sales of black products is just over $5 million (table 7). Again, while a relatively small figure for the Chicago market, this constituted a gargantuan gain for the small black businesses, allowing them to hire additional workers, expand production, add new products, and increase their visibility in the Chicago economic scene.

A larger gain was made in black-owned services (table 8). Again, I have used both hard figures and estimates. With eighty-three new contracts each, scavengers and exterminators gained together about $1.6 million. Janitorial services

Table 6. Employment Gains from All Breadbasket Covenants

Industry/Company	Year of Covenant	Increase to 1971	No. Jobs Filled	Total Annual Salaries ($)
NEW JOBS				
Milk companies (5)	1966	incomplete data	141	916,500
Pepsi-Cola	1966	0	0	0
Seven-Up	1966	51 to 131	80	520,000
Coca-Cola	1966	incomplete data	15*	97,500
Canfield	1966	incomplete data	6*	39,000
High-Low	1966	240 to 284	44	286,000
Continental Baking[†]	1966	274 to 418	144	936,000
National Tea	1966	660 to 929	269	1,748,500
Jewel	1967	273 to 918	645	4,192,500
Certified	1967	incomplete data	16*	104,000
A&P	1968	977 to 1339	362	2,353,000
Walgreen	1970	1158 to 1346	188	1,222,000
Sears[†]	1971	(5% increase)*	340*	2,210,000
Subtotals			2250	$14,625,000
Jobs gained by upgrade			750*	4,875,000
Jobs gained by black producers			750*	4,875,000
Jobs gained by black services			766	4,980,000*
Total jobs gained	(1966–1971)		4516	29,355,000*[‡]

Note: Employment gains were permanent as of the end of 1971. All data include the latest monitoring reports in Operation Breadbasket's last year, 1971.

*Estimate based on extrapolation of limited data.

[†]Verbal agreement, no signed covenant.

[‡]In 2016 dollars, $199,000,000.

Source: PBBF.

Table 7. Gains in Sales of Black-Owned Products, 1966–1971

Company	Covenant Year	No. Stores	No. Products	Annual Purchases
High-Low	1966	25	12	$250,000*
National	1966	33	25	1,000,000
A&P	1966	37	25	1,000,000*
Certified	1966	77	20*	400,000*
Jewel	1967	20	25	750,000*
Walgreen	1970	28	13	600,000
Other stores				1,000,000*
Total gain				$5,000,000*

Note: All data include the latest monitoring reports in Operation Breadbasket's last year, 1971.

*Estimate based on extrapolation of limited data.

Source: PBBF.

Table 8. Gains in Use of Black-Owned Services, 1966–1971

Company	Service	No. Stores	No. Contractors	Annual Contract
HIGH-LOW	scavenger	8		$14,400
	exterminator	11		860
	janitorial	?		?
	advertising		7 newspapers	25,000˙
NATIONAL	scavenger	19	10	33,240
	exterminator	24	3	1,872
	janitorial	27	3	950,400
	advertising		12 newspapers & radio	148,870
A&P	scavenger	26	9	46,800
	exterminator	34		2,650
	janitorial	10		355,560˙
	advertising		12 newspapers & radio	129,000˙
JEWEL	scavenger	20	8	36,000
	exterminator	18		1,400
	janitorial	20˙		711,100˙
	advertising		12 newspapers˙	100,000˙
WALGREEN	scavenger	28		50,400
	exterminator	28		2,200
	janitorial	?		?
	advertising		9 newspapers & radio	150,000˙
Subtotal		2,760,000*	(from primary covenant contracts)	
Construction contracts		16,000,000*		
Other services		3,000,000*		
Total gains		21,760,000		

Note: All data include the latest monitoring reports in Operation Breadbasket's last year, 1971.
*Estimate based on extrapolation of limited data.
Source: PBBF.

brought in just over $2 million and advertisers $553,000. Construction contracts had reached $16 million as of 1970. Other black services, such as real estate companies, car dealers, lawyers, and media added conservatively $3 million annually. Combining the annual dollar increases in jobs, black products, and black service contracts, by 1971 the black community of Chicago was gaining $57.5 million annually from Operation Breadbasket's justice work. These dollars translate into $391.8 million in the 2016 economy.

Breadbasket's impact on black financial institutions was also pivotal in the life of the community. While deposits add strength to banks and to their ability to make loans in the community, these deposits do not constitute a dollar value similar to an annual salary, a product sale, or a service

Table 9. Gains in Deposits in Black Banks, 1966–1971
(based on $0 at inception)

	Date Reported	Seaway	Independence	Highland	Savings and Loans[a]	Subtotal
National Tea[b]	Apr. 1971	340,000	132,000	—	—	$472,000
Jewel[b]	June 1971	125,000	125,000	—	—	250,000
A&P[b]	Sept. 1970	125,000	245,000	—	—	520,000
Walgreen	Oct. 1971	80,000	93,000	31,000	30,000	234,000
State of Illinois	May 1967	300,000	300,000	—	45,000	645,000
Subtotals		1,120,000	895,000	31,000	75,000	2,121,000
BANK ACCOUNTS						
Black businesses						2,500,000
Churches and individuals						400,000
Total						5,021,000

Note: All data include the latest monitoring reports in Operation Breadbasket's last year, 1971. No data had
been received from High-Low as of May 1971. All figures are actual except those for Jewel and A&P and the bank accounts,
which are estimates based on extrapolation of limited data.
a Hyde Park Savings and Loan, Illinois Federal Savings and Loan, and Service Federal Savings and Loan.
b No data because covenant did not include requests for Highland Bank or S&L deposits.
Source: PBBF: Breadbasket.

contract. At Seaway National Bank by 1971, deposits made in direct response
to Breadbasket covenants and requests to the state of Illinois amounted to a
minimum of $1.12 million (table 9). At Independence Bank, these deposits
came to $895,000, with smaller sums deposited at Highland Bank and the
three black-owned savings and loan institutions. The total deposits (average monthly balance) amounted to $2 million. This figure, however, does
not include substantial deposits made by black-owned businesses, churches,
and individuals (for which no data were kept). Thus, the total deposits may
well have reached $5 million in annual assets, a significant sum available to
black banks for making loans in the community and investments in the larger
economy.

The banking story is seen best with the gains made by Seaway National
Bank, which opened its doors on January 2, 1965, with $1 million. At the end
of its first year Seaway National's assets had grown to $5 million. Annual
increases over the Operation Breadbasket years were phenomenal and speak
for themselves. At the close of 1966 assets had climbed to $7.5 million; by the
close of 1971 assets stood at $35.6 million.

When the long-serving CEO of Seaway, Walter Grady, began with the
bank in 1972 he found that many board members had been enthusiastically

involved in Breadbasket activities. Grady recalled, "George Jones talked about Breadbasket all the time. He was my guy. We all felt a part of Breadbasket. We wouldn't be where we are today without Operation Breadbasket." Seaway Bank's president and CEO, 1980–2014, Grady spoke wistfully of those days, saying he wished we still had a movement like Breadbasket. "Young people today do not realize the sacrifices made in the 1960s." Just as it did at the beginning, Seaway continues to focus on Chicago's black community. On May 18, 2007, the bank opened a new facility at 11116 South Michigan, signifying its "genuine commitment to the revitalization of the Roseland community." As of that year, Seaway's annual assets had grown to $350 million. Grady's personal goal for Seaway was $1 billion in assets.[1]

The Seaway Bank story symbolizes the tremendous influence of Breadbasket on black business empowerment. From inclusion in covenant agreements to advocacy at Saturday Breadbasket, from exhibits at Black Expos to promotion at Black Christmas festivities, from consumer clubs to the *Black Book Directory*, black businesses were given a tremendous boost. The total impact in dollars, in economic growth, and in pride and confidence was immense.

A fascinating, if difficult to measure, influence was the alarm bell that went off among Chicago's top business executives as they read about covenant signings and boycotts. From our negotiations we discovered a community of business leaders where word of mouth often led CEOs in similar industries to jump aboard the justice train in hopes of preempting any confrontation when Breadbasket came calling. This is unquantifiable, but it was undoubtedly a significant factor in Breadbasket's six-year imprint.

Paralleling the Breadbasket story of economic empowerment in Chicago was the emerging story of affirmative action, spurred by building trade demonstrations from below and from executive actions in the White House. Presidents Kennedy, Johnson, and Nixon all issued executive orders prohibiting discrimination in federal contracts in construction and thus opened the door to affirmative action in many other areas of civic life.

A final Breadbasket influence was national, both through fledgling chapters where some limited economic agreements were reached and through the spillover effect from publicity in a given urban area. While not measurable, these influences were useful to the coming thrust of Operation PUSH against corporate giants. Breadbasket's economic justice work was its foundation and centerpiece through which it brought improvement to the lives of thousands of black people in Chicago and economic strength, independence, and buoyancy to the black business community. This achievement was the bread and butter of the SCLC's Operation Breadbasket, its lasting legacy to the civil rights movement.

A *Time* magazine special issue, "Black America 1970," highlighted Operation Breadbasket's achievements in its cover story. *Time* suggested that Breadbasket symbolized a new localism, offering a model for grassroots empowerment and a shift from the days of Dr. King's national leadership, and argued that Jesse Jackson was now "one leader among many." The article summarized Breadbasket's achievements in jobs, products, and service gains while recognizing the reality of its minimal accomplishment in "eliminating racism in the Chicago area." *Time* quoted Jesse: "We didn't change the hearts of the executives. We simply changed the behavior of the corporation. You don't strive for love between institutions; you strive for love between individuals and justice between institutions. And sometimes justice has its own way of creating, if not love, at least respect." *Time*'s articles and its analyses of the residual racial inequities in black family income, employment, union membership, and business ownership revealed to a national audience the seminal importance of the SCLC's Operation Breadbasket.[2]

OPERATION BREADBASKET CHRONOLOGY

(Nationwide civil rights milestones are italicized)

1954	
May	*Supreme Court rules against segregated schools in Brown v. Board of Education of Topeka, Kansas*

1955	
Dec	*Rosa Parks refuses to give up her seat, sparking Montgomery bus boycott; Dr. King emerges as leader of Montgomery Improvement Association*

1957	
Jan	*Southern Christian Leadership Conference established by Dr. King and colleagues*

1960	
Feb	*Lunch counter sit-ins begin in Greensboro, North Carolina, and Nashville, Tennessee*

1961	
May	*First Freedom Riders leave from Washington, D.C., heading for New Orleans*

1962	
Jan	School sit-ins begin in Chicago, followed by picketing of mobile Willis wagons and periodic school boycotts (through 1965)
Apr	Coordinating Council of Community Organizations is formed
Sep	Operation Breadbasket is inaugurated by SCLC in Atlanta

1963

Apr	*Birmingham campaign and Dr. King's "Letter from Birmingham Jail"*
Jun	First of three efforts to establish a Breadbasket-like program in Chicago
Jun	*Medgar Evers assassinated in Jackson, Mississippi*
Aug	*March on Washington, D.C., and Dr. King's "I Have a Dream" speech (August 28)*
Nov	*President John F. Kennedy assassinated in Dallas, Texas (November 22)*

1964

Jun	Dr. King speaks at Soldier Field rally
Jul	*Civil Rights Act signed by President Lyndon Johnson (July 2)*
Sep	SCLC chapter founded by Rev. John Porter at Christ Methodist Church, Chicago

1965

Mar	*Bloody Sunday at Pettus Bridge in Selma, Alabama (March 7)*
Jul	Dr. King visits Chicago, addresses rallies, evaluates city as possible campaign
Jul	Daily marches against Superintendent Benjamin Willis, many led by Dick Gregory
Aug	*Voting Rights Act signed by President Lyndon Johnson (August 6)*
Aug	*Watts neighborhood of Los Angeles goes up in flames (August 11–17)*
Aug	West Side of Chicago erupts in three-day disturbance
Sep	Jesse Jackson pulls together weekly seminars of black clergy and theologians in what becomes conception meetings of Operation Breadbasket
Sep	Chicago Freedom Movement commences with united forces of CCCO and SCLC; SCLC staffers arrive and begin organizing on the West Side

1966

Jan	Dr. King and Al Raby of CCCO announce CFM's "war on slums"
Jan	Dr. King and family move into West Side apartment
Feb	Birth meeting of Operation Breadbasket (February 11) at Jubilee CME Church
Feb	First Operation Breadbasket Steering Committee meeting at Fellowship Baptist Church
Apr	First of five agreements with Chicago area dairies after three short "Don't Buy" campaigns
Jul	Chicago Freedom Movement rally at Soldier Field
Jul	West Side riot breaks out
Jul	Dr. King announces first open-housing marches

Aug	Summit Agreement between the CFM and Mayor Daley's forces, effectively ending the Chicago Freedom Movement
Aug	Leadership Council for Metropolitan Open Communities established
Aug–Oct	Five agreements with soft drink companies, after a short "Don't Drink Pepsi" campaign
Oct	Jesse Jackson inaugurates Saturday morning breakfast with black entrepreneurs
Oct	*Black Panthers founded by Huey Newton and Bobby Seale in Oakland, California*
Nov	First public use of the word "covenant"; signed with High-Low Foods
Dec	Covenant signed between Breadbasket and National Tea

1967

Jan	Breadbasket asks state of Illinois, Cook County, and city of Chicago to transfer funds to black-owned banks
Feb	Attunement Committee established for guiding Breadbasket's black entrepreneurs
Mar	Negro Business Exposition and Seminar sponsored by the black business circle
Apr	Covenant signed between Breadbasket and Jewel Tea Company
May	Consumer clubs established to help move products off shelves and to monitor covenants
May	Illinois treasurer Adlai Stevenson III transfers first funds to black-owned banks
May	Ground breaking of first chain store built by black contractors in Chicago, a Del Farm supermarket of National Tea Company
May	Covenant signed between Breadbasket and A&P
June	"Don't Buy at High-Low" campaign leads to signing of new covenant
Jul	National Breadbasket Clergy Conference at CTS
Jul	*Newark riot (July 12–17); Detroit riot (July 23–27)*
Aug	Cleveland Breadbasket wins agreement with Sealtest
Aug	SCLC's tenth anniversary convention; Jesse Jackson named national director of Operation Breadbasket; Cirilo McSween and Stroy Freeman named to SCLC board
Sep	Saturday Breadbasket begins live broadcasts on radio station WVON
Oct	Agreement with Continental Baking Company
Oct	SCLC benefit concert at International Amphitheatre
Oct–Nov	Boycott leads to covenant signing with Certified Grocers of Illinois
Dec	*Dr. King announces Poor People's Campaign*

1968

Jan	Dr. King appoints Rev. Calvin Morris to be associate director and Rev. Ed Riddick to be national research director of Operation Breadbasket
Jan	Women of Breadbasket begin major inspections of meat
Mar	Poor People's Campaign announced in Chicago by Jesse Jackson
Mar	Breadbasket Steering Committee placed under Executive Committee
Apr	Dr. King's last speech urges Breadbasket model in Memphis
Apr	*Dr. King's assassination in Memphis (April 4)*
Apr	*Riots across the United States, including Chicago's West Side*
Apr	*Civil Rights Act of 1968, prohibiting discrimination in housing, signed by President Lyndon Johnson (April 11)*
May	*Poor People's Campaign's first contingents arrive in Washington, D.C. (May 11)*
May	Saturday Breadbasket moves to Parkway Ballroom
Jun	*Assassination of Senator Robert F. Kennedy in Los Angeles (June 5)*
Jun	*Resurrection City camp closed down (June 24)*
Jul	"Don't Shop at A&P" campaign begins three-month fight
Oct	Covenant between Breadbasket and A&P signed
Nov	Breadbasket announces support for United Farm Workers grape boycott
Dec	Black Christmas parade inaugurated (first of three annual celebrations)

1969

Jan	Martin Luther King Jr. birthday celebration (first of three annual events)
Mar	Agreement between Coalition of United Community Action and Red Rooster after "Don't Buy" campaign
Apr	Black Easter celebration
Apr	Illinois Campaign to End Hunger commences
Jun	Saturday Breadbasket moves to Capitol Theatre on South Halsted
Jun	Commercial Division secures $10 million in contracts
Jul	CUCA begins picketing construction sites
Aug	Breadbasket announces free breakfast programs in area churches
Oct	Black Minorities Business and Cultural Exposition (Black Expo)
Oct	SCLC Breadbasket inaugurates Brooklyn, New York, chapter
Nov	American Airlines agrees on 1970 black employment goals, but without a covenant
Dec	*Black Book Directory* inaugurated
Dec	*Fred Hampton and Mark Clark, Black Panther leaders, assassinated in Chicago (December 4)*

1970

Jan	Settlement reached between CUCA, building trades, and construction owners
Jan	Breadbasket establishes voter registration drive
Mar	Breadbasket Commercial Association replaces Commercial Division
Apr	Jesse Jackson appears on cover of *Time's* special "Black America 1970" edition
Apr	Continental Baking reports compliance with our 1967 agreement
Apr	Breadbasket announces support for Contract Buyers League
Jun	"Don't Shop at Walgreen Drug Stores" campaign commences, leading to covenant
Jul	Breadbasket creates Black Men Moving to help resolve gang violence
Jul	Noah Robinson leads campaign against A&P in Detroit
Nov	Boycott of National Tea stores begins
Nov	Black Expo
Dec	Breadbasket hosts People's Convention

1971

Jan	Capitol Theatre renamed Dr. King's Workshop during celebration of Dr. King's birthday
Feb	Jesse Jackson takes leave of absence for Chicago mayoral campaign
Apr	Mayor Richard J. Daley coasts to reelection
Apr	*Supreme Court upholds busing as legitimate means for achieving integrated schools (April 20)*
May	Jesse Jackson leads supporters at Springfield rally for welfare reform
Jun	Jesse Jackson issues call for a black president of the United States
Jun	Boycott resumes against National Tea Company
Jul	Three Breadbasket pastors arrested in National Tea's Chicago headquarters
Sep	Struggle with National Tea ends as Breadbasket quietly drops the boycott
Sep	Black Expo
Oct	Breadbasket leads successful effort to restore Illinois welfare cuts
Oct	New York Breadbasket secures its twelfth covenant with Bohack Corporation
Dec	Rev. Jesse Jackson suspended, then resigns as national director of SCLC's Operation Breadbasket
Dec	Operation PUSH inaugurated by Rev. Jesse Jackson in Chicago

OPERATION BREADBASKET ORGANIZATIONAL CHARTS

Operation Breadbasket Organizational Chart, 1967

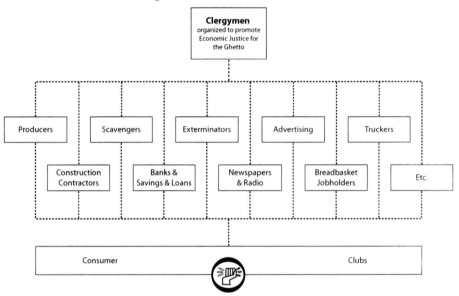

Operation Breadbasket
Organizational Chart based on March 8, 1968, Announcement

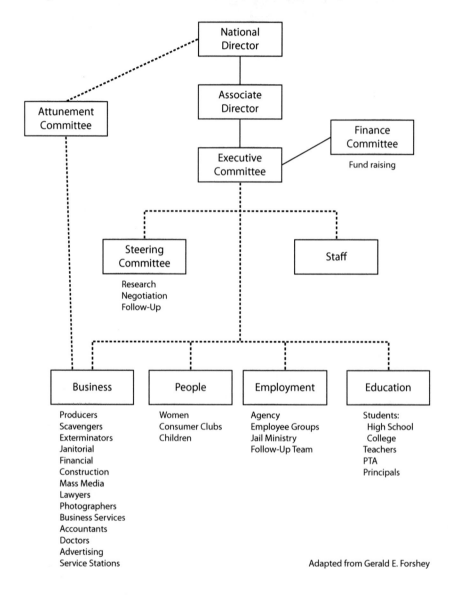

Adapted from Gerald E. Forshey

OPERATION BREADBASKET STEERING COMMITTEE

This information is gleaned from sc Minutes and PBBF.

Core Staff

Rev. Martin Luther King Jr., February 1966–April 1968, founder, advisor
Rev. Willie Barrow, ca. January 1967–December 1971
Ms. Lucille Coleman, ca. January 1967–December 1971
Rev. Jesse Jackson, February 1966–December 1971
Rev. Gary Massoni, November 1966–August 1970
Rev. Calvin Morris, October 1967–August 1971
Rev. George "Ed" Riddick, January 1968–December 1971
Rev. David Wallace, February 1966–December 1971

Core Clergy

Rev. Otis Anderson
Rev. Willie Barrow
Rev. Charles Billups
Rev. H. B. Brady
Rev. Washington Branch
Rev. Raymond Brewster
Fr. George Clements
Rev. Hiram Crawford
Rev. Thomas Cross
Rev. Martin Deppe
Rev. Clay Evans
Rev. Isaac Fincher
Rev. Gerald Forshey
Rev. Stroy Freeman
Rev. William Hagerty
Rev. Shelvin Hall
Rev. C. Abner Hammond
Rev. Henry Hardy
Fr. William Hogan
Rev. Jessie "Ma" Houston

Core Clergy *(continued)*

Rev. D. E. King
Rev. William Lambert
Rev. Richard Lawrence
Rev. Robert Meyners
Rev. Larry Morkert
Rev. Frank Morris
Rev. Arthur Newburg
Rev. Thomas Ogletree
Dr. Alvin Pitcher
Rev. John Porter
Rev. Earl Simmons Jr.
Rev. Fleek Simmons
Rev. John L. Thurston
Fr. David Walker
Rev. Douglas Walters
Rev. Frank Watkins
Fr. Robert Weaver
Rev. Henry Wheaton
Rev. Claude Wyatt

BREADBASKET BUSINESS DIVISION

This information is gleaned from sc Minutes and PBBF.

Core Participants

Rual S. Boles, Diamond Sparkle Floor Wax
Alvin Boutte, Independence Bank of Chicago
Ernest Bush, Capital Construction Company
Argie B. Collins, Mumbo Barbeque Sauce
Dave Conway, Conway Soap Products
S. B. Fuller, Fuller Products Company
Darryl Grisham, Parker House Sausage
Herman Hartman, Pepsi-Cola distributor
Celious Henderson, Marion Business College
Al Johnson, Al Johnson Oldsmobile
George Johnson, Johnson Products Company (Ultra-Sheen)
John H. Johnson, Johnson Publishing Company (*Ebony* and *Jet*)
George Jones, Joe Louis Milk Company
Cirilo McSween, New York Life Insurance Company
Willard Payne Sr., Metropolitan Sausage Manufacturing Company
Charles Petty, Petty's Exterminating Company
Joseph Robichaux, Baldwin Ice Cream
Cecil Troy, Grove Fresh Orange Juice

Advisors

Dr. Alvin Pitcher, Divinity School, University of Chicago
Dr. Robert McKersie, Graduate School of Business, University of Chicago

COVENANT BETWEEN SCLC OPERATION BREADBASKET AND THE CHICAGO UNIT, GREAT A&P TEA COMPANY

October 5, 1968

The Chicago Unit of the A&P Tea Company has been closely associated with the central city for almost a century. When others began following the movement of people to the suburbs, we made a decision and built new stores in the inner-city.

This decision carried with it the intent to continue to provide in all of its stores the best of food products, the lowest possible prices, and good service by well trained personnel.

Today there is wide spread recognition that conditions which affect the black American who inhabits the central city require the sincere attention of the business community.

Since A&P has and wants to continue to serve the central city it wants to become more involved in helping to solve the problems which exist for these Americans. We therefore pledge to undertake renewed efforts designed to begin closing the gap between the promise and the performance of American democracy.

We propose a three pronged attack upon the problems created by discrimination and segregation inflicted upon black Americans. It is our objective to develop creative and sustained programs in employment and economic development. In addition, we propose the establishment of a business advisory council.

While we must limit our proposals to those things which seem possible at this time, we do pledge ourselves to periodic evaluation of our progress and sincere efforts to keep pace with changes that may make it possible to do more.

At this time we specifically propose the following:

Employment

1. Upon removal of anti A&P activities we will immediately begin the recall of black employees who are now on layoff.
2. Concurrent with the recall of laid off employees we will systematically seek new black employees and upgrade our present black employees currently employed.

This example of a covenant is presented here verbatim; capitalization, spelling, and language are all per the original.

3. Within one year of the adoption of this proposal we will employ 268 more black Americans than the 1,060 we had on our staff as of February 24, 1968. We pledge to have a total of 1,328 black employees on our payroll by October 1, 1969. The categories and numbers of new positions we will make available are listed below.

Implementation

In order to implement and achieve this aggressive goal we will:

1. Inform in writing all unit employees of this proposal and enlist their support in making the effort successful. Copy to Operation Breadbasket of letter to Unit employees.
2. Conduct for all executives and managerial personnel a series of "sensitivity seminars" prepared in cooperation with Operation Breadbasket. These seminars will be designed to make management more aware of the effects of prejudice and assist them to develop action toward implementing this strengthened policy.
3. Place on the unit staff a black person to serve as liaison in employment between the company, the black community and Operation Breadbasket. This person will be mutually acceptable to Operation Breadbasket and A&P.
   A. This person will have the responsibility for developing an effective recruitment program and will monitor turnover, counsel new employees and conduct exit interviews. He will also inform the unit personnel director of any grievances he becomes aware of.
   B. He will direct the completion of reports on progress toward established goals, prepare reports for monthly meetings with Operation Breadbasket.
   C. Hold monthly meetings with representatives of Operation Breadbasket in order that an on-going and frequent evaluation can be established. Make available to Operation Breadbasket a monthly report on progress toward the numerical goals, and advise Operation Breadbasket of current job openings.
4. Open an employment center on the South Side which will be convenient to individuals who dwell in that area, and support our recruitment efforts with whatever means are required.
5. Make available to Operation Breadbasket a quarterly report on progress by job and department classification.
6. A black person will be assigned the responsibility for employee development and training.
   A. This individual will be responsible for the acceleration of present on the job training efforts and the development of cooperative training programs with schools, agencies and other black controlled training facilities. He will also investigate other means of assuring that the company training for unskilled but employable candidates for positions will be available.
   B. Sensitivity training, referred to in No. 2, will be extended to all employees, both black and white.

Economic Development

A&P recognizes the importance of the economic development of the black community. Several meaningful relationships have already been established. We will analyze
the existing and potential relationships and create new ways to foster progress in this
area.

We propose these immediate actions, and will review details on a regular basis:

1. We will provide Operation Breadbasket with an organizational list indicating the
   Executive-Managerial positions and their areas of responsibility.
2. We will continue to contract the services of black-owned companies such as
   scavenger, exterminating and janitorial services on a three to five year basis with
   options to renew the contracts on a bid basis, in consultation with Operation
   Breadbasket.
3. We will continue to ensure that black building contractors and sub-contractors
   have an opportunity to bid on and get contracts for new construction, remodeling
   and refurbishing work. This will be on a metropolitan basis but will especially
   apply to work in the black community.
4. We will continue to use a black public relations agency.
5. We will continue to advertise in the black media on a basis that is equitable to our
   total advertising expenditures.
6. We will intensify our efforts to market products of Negro producers and suppliers
   in metropolitan stores.
7. We will continue to do business with black-owned banks. Substantial balances will
   be maintained in both banks.
8. We will include in the "sensitivity seminars" which will be conducted for all management level personnel, a specific section on ways that A&P can assist in the
   business development of the black community.

Implementation

We will place on our staff a black person as liaison with black businessmen. He will
have the responsibility of facilitate the concentration of company resources in this
area. He will have direct access to the executive level of the unit. In addition he will
develop creative programs for marketing and promoting the products of black businessmen. The elements of such a program include:

A. Education of buyers about the program and the policy behind the program for
   assisting the development of black businesses.
B. Continuing education of all store managers and store personnel about the policy
   and program.
C. Placement of black businessmen's products in the regular goods order book where
   demand is such and the item can be carried in stock.
D. Survey of all stores to determine where each product is currently stocked.

E. Systematic way to ensure that these products are not out of stock before they are re-ordered.

F. Ensure that store managers are aware of all products supplied by black businessmen so that they can be more sensitive to their promotion.

G. Direct the installation of "new item centers" to feature these products on a regular basis.

H. Project regular promotions for these products with appropriate advertising. Basket and floor displays will be used where sales potential justifies.

I. See that the Chicago Unit creatively participates in the advertising efforts of black businessmen, making the talent and resources of this unit available.

J. See that adequate shelf space will be given new products and those being promoted.

Businessmen's Advisory Service

In addition to the above we propose to establish a "Businessmen's Advisory Council." In order for black businessmen to meet the test of free and open competition without chronic self-doubt, self-denial and even self-hate, they must be exposed to the competence which comes from experience.

We will provide company personnel to counsel black businessmen in the areas of management, financing, distribution, marketing production methods, auditing and accounting. The liaison person will arrange this service in consultation with Operation Breadbasket upon request of the businessman or suggest that it be used when the need is obvious.

The ministers of Operation Breadbasket agree to support and assist A&P in this cooperative endeavor by a sincere effort to advise the black community of A&P's policies and efforts.

They will communicate to their membership and to the community at large this effort to attack the problems of economic deprivation, unequal employment and lack of inclusion that has affected both individuals and institutions in the black community.

Representatives of Operation Breadbasket and the Chicago Unit of A&P will establish an on-going relationship which will demonstrate to all people the fact that cooperative efforts between the black community and the private sector will beneficially influence the economic and social welfare of the entire Chicago metropolitan area.

Additional Employees Pledged by Classification

Retail Stores	156	
Managers		12
Head Cashiers		10
Meat Dept. Heads		14
Meat Journeymen		20
Meat Apprentices		15
Wrappers		5
Grocery Clerks		80

Grocery Warehouse	16	
Supervisors		3
General Office		1
Selectors		10
Equipment Operators		1
Others		1
Meat Warehouse	22	
Supervisor		2
General Office		3
Maint. Mechanics		1
Selectors		6
Production Operators		10
Produce Warehouse	23	
Supervisors		1
Buyers-Inspectors		2
General Office		4
Laborers		11
Merch. Handlers		3
Equipment Operators		2
Office	35	
Officials		2
Auditors		2
Professionals		1
Gen. Office		15
Secys.-Stenographers		5
Machine Operators		10
Garage	16	
Supervisors		1
Drivers		12
Mechanics		1
Dispatchers		2
Grand Total	268	

Southern Christian Leadership Conference's
Operation Breadbasket
366 East 47th Street, Chicago, Ill.

Great A&P Tea Company
Chicago Unit
2622 North Pulaski Road, Chicago, Ill.

ACKNOWLEDGMENTS

A few months after the demise of Operation Breadbasket I received a phone call from Rev. Ed Riddick, then on staff with Operation PUSH. Ed asked if I would please give my Breadbasket files to PUSH. He noted particularly my "covenant follow-up" files. I told Ed the files belonged to SCLC, and I could not release them. He accepted my decision graciously. Over time I softened and planned to give the files to PUSH but never got around to it.

I carted these old Breadbasket files from parsonage to parsonage before I finally opened and leafed through them in the summer of 2006. Curiosity led me to explore the relevant civil rights literature at nearby Sulzer Regional Library, where I was shocked at the absence of any real account of the Breadbasket story.

This book was waiting to be born in that box of files. Sharing my initial surprise with trusted colleagues, including several Breadbasket pastors, I was met with unqualified support to do something. Before long I felt a new calling to fill this gap in the civil rights story, and this book came alive over the next several months.

I am most grateful to the many family and friends who have supported and encouraged me through this project. The late Dr. Gerald "Jerry" Forshey, my close friend and colleague in Breadbasket, offered files, anecdotes, and advice. Dr. Calvin Morris shared scrapbooks, several interviews, phone calls, and constant support and wisdom throughout the entire gestation. Rev. Gary Massoni helped in many ways beyond interviews, offering memos, anecdotes, references, and encouragement. I was fortunate to have in my files a weathered carbon copy of Gary's CTS dissertation, "Perspectives on Operation Breadbasket," the only Breadbasket account I know of, which was invaluable to me throughout the creation of my narrative. Dr. Joel Stillerman, a long-time family friend, has given invaluable guidance and unstinting support throughout. Several members of the New Gresham United Methodist Church have prodded and supported me along the way. In some ways this book is for that congregation, which offered me the most significant and discerning years of my pastoral ministry.

Among those who gave of their time and insight in extended interviews during 2008 and 2009 were Rev. Clay Evans, Dr. Calvin Morris, Rev. Richard Lawrence, Rev. Willie Barrow, Dr. Gerald Forshey, Rev. John Porter, Rev. Gary Massoni, Ms. Hermene Hartman, Ms. Alice Tregay, Mr. Richard Thomas, Rev. David Wallace, Rev. Robert Weaver, Rev. John Baggett, Mr. Russell Ewert, Ms. Eleta "Cookie" Murray,

Mr. Walter Grady, Mrs. Jacqueline "Jackie" Jackson, and, of course, Rev. Jesse Jackson Sr. Some of these people also sent e-mails, shared files and pictures, and phoned me with anecdotes. Words cannot capture the centrality of these people to the Breadbasket narrative or my appreciation of the support they have given me in telling the story. Others who gave encouragement but were no longer able to answer questions about their involvement include the late Rev. Claude Wyatt, Rev. Addie Wyatt, and Cirilo McSween.

The librarians at Chicago's Sulzer Regional Library and Harold Washington Library were most helpful and always gracious. Without knowing it, Dr. Al Pitcher was vital to this book with his voluminous notes, minutes, memos, and contracts in the W. Alvin Pitcher Papers in the Special Collections of the Regenstein Library at the University of Chicago. The librarians there gave me courteous assistance whenever I requested help. I am indebted to the *Chicago Defender* and its archived collection of complete newspapers for the period 1966–1971, without which I could not have corroborated many stories and facts.

Especially important were my readers. Cathy Deppe, my sister; Andrew Deppe, my son; and Lynne Marek, my friend and editor, read the entire manuscript at different stages and gave invaluable advice; Andrew and Lynne helped select the illustrations. Revs. Calvin Morris and Gary Massoni, Dr. Joel Stillerman, and Frederick Deppe, my son, read portions and provided critical advice. I owe special gratitude to Dr. James R. Ralph Jr., a civil rights historian, who offered corrections and constructive comments on the entire manuscript and then graciously wrote the fine foreword to this book.

My technical limitations were more than compensated by expert assistance from two cousins: first, the late Stephen Andrews and then, Michael Collins, to whom I am deeply indebted. While the lengthy publishing saga has been arduous, the struggle came to an end with my very first contact with Walter Biggins, an editor at the University of Georgia Press. Every communication with Walter, and then with his colleagues, has been met with interest and respect, and our rapport has only grown. These editors, especially John Joerschke and Merryl Sloane, have responded quickly to every e-mail and to every question, no matter how trivial. I am profoundly grateful to have been led to this press, to Walter, and to his team of editors.

What can I say about my wife, Peg, who shared the six jam-packed years of Breadbasket not once, but twice! She has been beyond tolerant for the many hours this project has taken me away from her and from our family, not unlike the similar experience with a busy pastor during the Breadbasket years. Peg has been a gift, an anchor, a challenge. Thanks be to God for all those who have been a part of the incredible story of SCLC's Operation Breadbasket.

NOTES

Foreword

1. Hall, "The Long Civil Rights Movement," 1234–35; Joseph, "Introduction: Toward a Historiography of the Black Power Movement," in his *The Black Power Movement*, 3–4.

2. Massoni, "Perspectives on Operation Breadbasket."

3. Marshall Frady praises the achievements of Operation Breadbasket, but he offers only brief coverage of its programs. Frady, *Jesse*, 257.

4. Meier and Rudwick, "The Origins of Nonviolent Direct Action in Afro-American Protest: A Note on Historical Discontinuities," in their *Along the Color Line*, 316–32.

5. Morris, *Origins of the Civil Rights Movement*, 48–63, 211–12, 269–74. For a broader perspective on the use of consumer power by African Americans, see Cohen, *A Consumers' Republic*.

6. Sullivan, *Build, Brother, Build*; Countryman, *Up South*, 100–119.

7. For a sweeping account of the importance of economic inclusion in the postwar era, see MacLean, *Freedom Is Not Enough*.

8. Deppe's account runs counter to the contention that Jackson's and Operation Breadbasket's orientation was not embraced by King as he turned more toward a social democratic agenda in the last years of his life. See Garrow, *Bearing the Cross*, 584–86; Jackson, *From Civil Rights to Human Rights*, 303–7.

9. In his history of the black power movement, Peniel E. Joseph describes Jackson as a transitional figure. Joseph, *Waiting 'til the Midnight Hour*, 277–83.

10. For an overview of the northern struggle, see Sugrue, *Sweet Land of Liberty*.

11. The most thorough account of the Chicago civil rights movement is Anderson and Pickering, *Confronting the Color Line*. Anderson and Pickering were involved in the Chicago movement, and while they acknowledge Breadbasket's significance, they do not view it as carrying on the earlier fight or as a successor to the CCCO.

12. See Massoni's analysis of Breadbasket as a coordinating center in "Perspectives on Operation Breadbasket," 281–83. One could also extend Morris's concept of a local movement center to apply to Operation Breadbasket. See Morris, *Origins of the Civil Rights Movement*, 40, 284–85.

13. For an assessment of interpretations of the Chicago Freedom Movement, see my 2006 essay, "Interpreting the Chicago Freedom Movement: The Last Fifty Years," in Finley et al., *The Chicago Freedom Movement*, 83–99.

14. See, for instance, Finley et al., *The Chicago Freedom Movement*.

15. Theoharis and Woodard, *Freedom North*.

16. See Cohen, *A Consumers' Republic*, 370–73, for an effort to place Operation Breadbasket within the wider history of black consumer protest.

17. Erik S. Gellman, "'The Stone Wall Behind': Chicago's Coalition for United Community Action and Labor's Overseers, 1968–1973," in Goldberg and Griffey, *Black Power at Work*, 112–33.

18. For a complementary memoir-history, see McKersie, *A Decisive Decade*. For an assessment of the mobilization of white Protestants into the civil rights movement, see Findlay, *Church People in the Struggle*.

Preface

1. "Mississippi Journal," 1964, unpublished paper by author, 2, PBBF.
2. Martin Luther King, *Strength to Love*, 127–34.
3. Ralph, *Northern Protest*, 33.

Introduction

1. Branch, *At Canaan's Edge*, 587.
2. Sugrue, *Sweet Land of Liberty*, 417.
3. Black, *Bridges of Memory*, 360.
4. Fairclough, *To Redeem the Soul of America*, 285, 287, 349–50.
5. Peake, *Keeping the Dream Alive*, 3, 8, 218–19, 287–89.
6. Ralph, *Northern Protest*, 228–29.
7. Theoharis and Woodard, *Freedom North*, 204.
8. Anderson and Pickering, *Confronting the Color Line*, 217–19, 333.
9. Travis, *An Autobiography of Black Politics*, 356, 370–71, 404–5.
10. Garrow, *Bearing the Cross*, 569, 585.
11. Martin Luther King, *Where Do We Go from Here?* is the text of his annual report delivered at the Tenth Annual Convention of the Southern Christian Leadership Conference, Atlanta, Georgia, August 16, 1967.
12. Washington, *Testament of Hope*, 283.
13. McKersie, *A Decisive Decade*, 153–73.
14. Chappell, *Waking from the Dream*, 31–38, 124–47.
15. Coretta Scott King, *My Life with Martin Luther King, Jr.*, 289–90.
16. These Breadbasket statistics were gleaned almost entirely from monitoring reports submitted by companies in covenant with Operation Breadbasket.
17. This question was reported at a Steering Committee meeting. See also McKersie, *A Decisive Decade*, 157.
18. Reynolds, *Jesse Jackson*, esp. 105–53.
19. Clay Evans interview, August 22, 2008.
20. *Chicago Daily Defender* (now the *Chicago Defender*), October 10, 1967.
21. Jackie Jackson interview, March 13, 2009.
22. *Jet*, November 9, 1967.

Chapter 1. Beginnings

1. This report on the February 11 birth meeting of Operation Breadbasket is based on my personal recollections, notes, and sermon excerpts.
2. My estimate at the time was three hundred. In a letter I received four days later

from Rev. Andrew Young on SCLC letterhead, Andy indicated that six hundred ministers attended and voted unanimously for the Breadbasket project. PBBF.

3. Rev. Martin Luther King Sr. had his own national standing in the black church, so his presence in Chicago served to increase enthusiasm for this new project among his fellow pastors.

4. Edmund J. Rooney, "New Pressure Campaign Goal—Negro Jobs," *Chicago Daily News*, February 12, 1966, as quoted in Massoni, "Perspectives on Operation Breadbasket," 6–7.

5. Clay Evans interview, August 22, 2008.

6. A truly four-star account of the color line in Chicago's housing is found in the classic work by Drake and Cayton, *Black Metropolis*. Also valuable is Abu-Lughod, *Race, Space, and Riots*, 43–72; and Hirsch, *Making the Second Ghetto*.

7. City of Chicago, *Chicago's Black Population*, Harold Washington Library, Government Publications, Chicago; Chicago Commission on Human Relations, *Human Relations News of Chicago* newsletters, 1966–1970, PBBF.

8. Mantler, *Power to the Poor*, 49.

9. An excellent account of the color line in Chicago's public schools is Anderson and Pickering, *Confronting the Color Line*, esp. 69–102.

10. Ralph, *Northern Protest*, 18–19; and Don Rose, "Chicago: Tale of Two Cities in One," contraryperspective.com, July 31, 2013.

11. Pastoral letter from the author to his congregation, Mandell Methodist Church, August 20, 1963.

12. *CD*, February 4, 6, and 17, May 16, and June 8, 1964. I am amazed that Jeanne Theoharis omits the impressive numbers of the Chicago school boycotts in her list of significant northern protests in her introduction to *Freedom North*, 1–2.

13. Mantler, *Power to the Poor*, 51.

14. *CD*, July 20, 1965.

15. PBBF: "We Can't Wait" flyer for July 24–26, 1965, events.

16. Drake and Cayton, *Black Metropolis*, 214, 223–28.

17. Ibid., 231–42, 261.

18. Ibid., 218–19.

19. Ibid., 223.

20. Ibid., 265.

21. Ibid., 815.

22. Ibid., 814.

23. Ibid. Drake and Cayton delineate the job ceiling very well; see esp. 223–65 and 288–92. See also Jackson, *From Civil Rights to Human Rights*, 281.

24. Drake and Cayton, *Black Metropolis*, 828.

25. McKee, *The Problem of Jobs*.

26. Branch, *At Canaan's Edge*, 293–99.

27. http://kingencyclopedia.stanford.edu/encyclopedia/encyclopedia/enc_watts_rebelion_los_angeles_1965; Fairclough, *To Redeem the Soul of America*, 303.

28. Fairclough, *To Redeem the Soul of America*, 296.

29. Flamm, "Law and Order," 321.

30. D'Emilio, *Lost Prophet*, 454. Rustin's view probably influenced Dr. King's decision to have Daddy King join him in Chicago to launch Breadbasket by assisting in the recruitment of key black pastors.

31. An excellent account of Dr. King's decision to come to Chicago is in Ralph, *Northern Protest*, 7–42.

32. Hampton and Fayer, *Voices of Freedom*, 300–301.

33. Anderson and Pickering, *Confronting the Color Line*, 172–88; *CD*, January 10, 1966.

34. Jackson, *From Civil Rights to Human Rights*, 282.

35. Branch, *At Canaan's Edge*, 427–29; and Oates, *Let the Trumpet Sound*, 373–75.

36. Ralph, *Northern Protest*, 58–64, including Dr. King quotation in n. 61.

37. Branch, *At Canaan's Edge*, 444.

38. *CD*, March 14, 1966; Chicago Freedom Festival program, PBBF.

39. Oates, *Let the Trumpet Sound*, 379.

40. At this same time a North Side Puerto Rican community experienced its own despair. After police shot Cruz Arcelis on June 12, 1966, the neighborhood suffered an uprising that left sixteen people injured and fifty buildings destroyed. See Mantler, *Power to the Poor*, 56.

41. *CD*, July 7, 1966.

42. *Chicago Daily News*, July 11, 1966. David Garrow rightly mentions "wildly divergent estimates of attendance" in *Bearing the Cross*, 492.

43. *Chicago Daily News* and *CD*, July 11, 1966.

44. Hampton and Fayer, *Voices of Freedom*, 306–7. Coretta King tells the story of that walk with Martin and their children, "Little Bunny got tired, and Andy Young put her on his shoulders and he carried her for a large part of the distance. Of course, I could see her head bobbing up and down on his shoulders as we walked along. And we got to City Hall. . . . Bunny did not get to see City Hall because she was fast asleep, but it was a very special occasion since it was the first time that all of us [the King family] had marched together."

45. *Chicago Daily News* and *CD*, July 11, 1966.

46. An excellent and detailed account of this uprising can be found in Oates, *Let the Trumpet Sound*, 391–96. See also *NYT*, July 16 and 17, 1966.

47. Heise and Frazel, *Hands on Chicago*, 250–51.

48. Most accounts indicate Dr. King was hit on the side of the head by a brick. In *At Canaan's Edge*, Branch states that it was "a palm-sized rock" (510).

49. Author's sermon, August 7, 1966.

50. Ralph, *Northern Protest*, 158–69. Oates, *Let the Trumpet Sound*, 397–400, gives a somewhat different chronology. See also Hampton and Fayer, *Voices of Freedom*, 314–15.

51. Ralph, *Northern Protest*, 170–71.

52. The Summit Agreement affirmed the Fair Housing Ordinance of 1963; required real estate brokers to post the ordinance in a prominent position in their businesses; authorized the Chicago Commission on Human Relations to monitor enforcement; called on the city to seek fair housing legislation at the state level; and called for specific reforms with the Chicago Housing Authority, the Cook County Department of Public Aid, the Urban Renewal Program, and the County Council of Insured Savings Associations. It authorized a housing center, the Leadership Council for Metropolitan Open Communities, to provide information on suitable housing for minority families. *Human Relations News* 8, no. 6 (September 1966).

53. Oates, *Let the Trumpet Sound*, 401.

54. Ralph, *Northern Protest*, 197. SNCC flyer from PBBF.

55. Refusing to accept the summit promises and defying Dr. King, Lucas and his CORE chapter led some two hundred marchers in Cicero on September 4. Local police aided by members of the National Guard kept the angry crowds from any serious confrontations. Ralph, *Northern Protest*, 198–99.

56. Hampton and Fayer, *Voices of Freedom*, 316–19.

57. Anderson and Pickering, *Confronting the Color Line*, 300.

58. Telegram to the author, January 1, 1967, PBBF.

59. Quoted in Ansbro, *Martin Luther King, Jr.*, 162.

60. Niebuhr, *Moral Man and Immoral Society*, xv, 254.

61. Reed, *Depression Comes to the South Side*, 66–76, gives a thorough account of the short-lived "Don't Spend Your Money" campaign. Also, Drake and Cayton, *Black Metropolis*, 84–85; and *CD*, February 18, 1963.

62. Du Bois, ed., "Editorials: Boycotts," in *The Crisis: A Record of the Darker Races* (September 1934), 268–69, quoted in Massoni's "Perspectives on Operation Breadbasket," 3.

63. "Calvin Morris remembers as a teenager in Philadelphia giving up Tastykake, his favorite snack, to honor Sullivan's boycott" (interview with Gordon Mantler in *Power to the Poor*, 262n).

64. Robert H. Brisbane, "Black Protest in America," in Smythe, *The Black American Reference Book*, 569; McKee, *The Problem of Jobs*, 113–36.

65. Garrow, *Bearing the Cross*, 223; Jackson, *From Civil Rights to Human Rights*, 138.

66. *CD*, February 28, 1963.

67. *CD*, March 16, 1963.

68. *CD*, March 12, 1963.

69. The Atlanta Breadbasket story is told in a series of articles in the *CD* in February and March 1963.

70. A delightful story of Daddy King's participation in Atlanta Breadbasket is in Bishop, *The Days of Martin Luther King, Jr.*, 470–71.

71. An interesting forerunner to Breadbasket was the Clergy Alliance of Chicago, 1963–1964. Sources for this account are Ralph, *Northern Protest*, 18, 68, 138; *CD*, August 1963–July 1964; and an interview with Rev. John Porter. He attended several alliance meetings but remained active with the CCCO and then Breadbasket. This Clergy Alliance was interracial and interfaith and followed the Philadelphia model, but it focused on low-key negotiations and moral suasion, hoping to avoid confrontation. The members chose to protect themselves with a "no leader" policy. Beginning with milk, they soon discovered a recalcitrant Bowman Dairy. Some one hundred pastors issued a call from their pulpits requesting parishioners to stop buying Bowman products. Within a few days the Chicago branch of the NAACP announced its support of the jobs campaign.

In response, Bowman's president, Tom Kullman, told *CD*'s Lillian Calhoun, "We'll do the right thing.... We've got lots of Negro drivers and a non-selective hiring policy as well as a Negro supervisor. Look, Honey, just say we'll work this out." Seniority was a major sticking point. The president of Milk Drivers Union, Local 753, claimed, "We've always been fair with our Negro members but our membership would compel us to live up to the seniority provisions of the contract." An Alliance spokesperson replied: "We do not want anybody fired, but the dairy must find a way to improve jobs for Negroes." After weeks of talks the dairy agreed to upgrade three black drivers and hire additional blacks in the office. Parishioners were asked to resume buying Bowman products. Within four months Bowman hired twelve blacks, but no word was given regarding the three promised driver upgrades.

In February 1964, alliance pastors announced a selective patronage campaign against Hawthorn-Mellody. In a *Defender* column, Lillian Calhoun wrote: "The ministers of the Clergy Alliance happily report that their parishioners are giving up a certain dairy's products for Lent. The clergy are sore at a Negro alderman who is trying to crimp the selective patronage campaign because the dairy involved gives free milk on occasion. "He prefers to be given milk," one snorted, "rather than to get jobs so that Negroes can buy milk."

Talks crawled along with little progress. In May, the alliance finally launched direct action against Hawthorn-Mellody with picketers at nine National Tea Stores. Two weeks later twenty stores were picketed. Then, almost overnight the bottom dropped out, and the alliance simply dissolved and disappeared into the night. In her column a few weeks later, Calhoun wrote: "The Clergy Alliance cannot seem to get off the ground. Whatsa matter with all you good Chicago clergymen???"

In retrospect it is clear that the alliance stepped beyond its policy of moral suasion and lost its footing. Certain black clergy aligned with the Silent Six machine aldermen simply pulled the plug on the group. The alliance ignored the ccco, repudiated assistance from the Negro Labor League, and held to its "no leader" policy. They sought naïvely to make no waves while hoping to bring incremental increases in black employment. They were not willing to confront power with power, à la Niebuhr and King, and so faltered in the stretch drive. In sum, it was an enormous amount of energy poured out for a few dozen jobs.

72. John Porter interview, August 22, 2008; *CD*, August 29, 1962, and September 12, 1964. Porter had met King in the late 1950s and had been arrested with him and sixty-eight other ministers in Albany, Georgia, in August 1962. In the fall of 1964, Porter brought together a small band of brothers and sisters into a fledgling sclc chapter. This group met at the church weekly focusing initially on gang violence and job discrimination at the neighborhood's commercial hub, 63rd and Halsted. In a local interview at that time Porter shared dreams for the new chapter: "Few cities in America need to be [as] transformed as Chicago." The answer for our city, Porter declared, is that "Negroes must become more sophisticated in voting. They must register, must vote." His new sclc chapter promoted a "beloved community" attitude, urging families to clean and fix up their homes. The chapter also planned to "register every unemployed person in the area and to provide his name and skills to employers." Under Porter's leadership, the Englewood sclc chapter did steady, low-key organizing over the next three years. In many ways, Rev. Porter anticipated Operation Breadbasket.

73. John Porter interview, August 22, 2008.

74. This ministers cadre included leading black pastors Revs. Clay Evans, John Thurston, Frank Sims, Edmond Blair, and Stroy Freeman; some of Jesse's own cts professors, Drs. Ross Snyder, Franklin Littell, Robert Meyners, and Thomas Ogletree; and Dr. Alvin Pitcher of the University of Chicago, a ccco member. See seminary report of Jesse L. Jackson and David Wallace, "From October to May: A Report to Rev. C. T. Vivian," Urban Training Center for Christian Mission, Chicago, May 17, 1966, 12, quoted in Massoni, "Perspectives on Operation Breadbasket," 5–6.

75. Branch, *At Canaan's Edge*, 62, 84; David Wallace interview, May 13, 2009.

76. David Wallace interview, May 13, 2009; and Jesse Jackson Sr. HistoryMakers interview, roll 9, March 1, 2009.

77. Jesse Jackson Sr. interviews, December 8 and 10, 2008.

Chapter 2. The Team

1. Biographical data for Jesse Louis Jackson, n.d., in W. Alvin Pitcher papers, box 2, folder 5, ucl; Reynolds, *Jesse Jackson*, 36–37.

2. David Wallace interview, May 13, 2009. Timmerman, *Shakedown*, makes the false claim that Jesse flunked out of cts. This is one of numerous exaggerations and distortions in this sensationalist book.

3. Author's recollections and sc Minutes.

4. sc Minutes, February 18, 1966; *CD*, April 12, 1966.

5. Martin Luther King, *Where Do We Go from Here*, 144–46, contains a summary called "Operation Breadbasket—The Five Stages of the Negotiation Process," an internal document probably from the spring of 1968. Our Chicago operation modified the stages used in Atlanta, eliminating the "purification stage" of spiritual preparation for direct action/economic withdrawal and strengthening the structure from loose rotating "call men" to a sc with staff. See Massoni, "Perspectives on Operation Breadbasket," 9.

6. Names assembled by author from sc attendance lists.

7. Jesse Jackson interview, March 5, 2009.

8. Calvin Morris interview, April 14, 2008.

9. Clay Evans interview, August 22, 2008.

10. Ibid.

11. Public statement from Operation Breadbasket and High-Low Foods, Inc., PBBF.

12. Branch, *At Canaan's Edge*, 297.

13. Letter from Rev. David Wallace to James Manning of High-Low, November 12, 1966, PBBF.

14. *Playboy Interview: Jesse Jackson*.

Chapter 3. Early Campaigns

1. Massoni, "Perspectives on Operation Breadbasket," 11.

2. Ibid.

3. David M. Wallace, "From the Fullness of the Earth: The Story of Chicago's Operation Breadbasket," in CTS, *News Register*, November 1966, 16–20.

4. sc Minutes, April 1, 6, 9, and 15, 1966; *CD*, April 11, 1966.

5. *CST*, April 14, 1966.

6. *CD*, April 16, 1966.

7. The active support of the CUL is evidenced by a letter to pastors from Chicago area district superintendents of the Methodist Church, April 25, 1966. They quote in full an urgent letter from CUL's Bill Berry requesting circulation of the new job openings at Certified, which included these closing words, "Please make this announcement at your services and list these positions in your church bulletin. With everybody's help, we can fill these positions and be ready for the next openings." PBBF: Certified.

8. *CD*, April 16, 1966.

9. Massoni, "Perspectives on Operation Breadbasket," 14.

10. Ibid., *CD*, May 14, 1966; letter from Jesse Jackson, May 9, 1966, W. Alvin Pitcher Papers, box 2, folder 1, Special Collections Research Center, UCL; Operation Breadbasket worship/rally bulletin, May 26, 1966, and author's letter to Methodist colleagues, May 24, 1966, both PBBF.

11. *CD*, June 6, 1966.

12. Committee on Demand Problems, May 27, 1966; sc Minutes, May 27and June 3, 1966.

13. PBBF: Notes.

14. *CD*, June 7, 1966.

15. Letter from Jesse Jackson to Breadbasket ministers, June 11, 1966, PBBF.

16. PBBF: Notes; *CD*, June 15, 1966; press release, June 13, 1966, W. Alvin Pitcher Papers, box 2, folder 1, UCL; letter from Jesse Jackson to Breadbasket ministers, June 18, 1966.

17. Letter from Jesse Jackson to Breadbasket ministers, June 23, 1966; sc Minutes, June 24, 1966; *CD*, June 23, 1966; *CST*, June 22, 1966.

18. Letter from David Wallace, July 8, 1966, W. Alvin Pitcher Papers, box 2, folder 1, UCL.

19. *CST*, July 7, 1966.

20. SC Minutes, July 8, 1966; PBBF: Dairy.

21. *CD*, July 20, 1966.

22. Operation Breadbasket press release, July 21, 1966.

23. *CD*, August 16, 1966.

24. PBBF: Pepsi; letter from Jesse Jackson to Breadbasket ministers, August 9, 1966.

25. *CD*, August 30, 1966; SC Minutes, August 25, 1966.

26. Letter from Seven-Up Bottling Co., August 26, 1966, PBBF.

27. SC Minutes, September 16, 1966.

28. PBBF: Seven-Up Bottling Co.

29. SC Minutes, September 30, 1966.

30. Jeremiah 31:31–34.

31. SC Minutes, October 7, 1966.

32. SC Minutes, September 23, 1966.

33. SC Minutes, September 23 and 30, 1966.

34. CCCO *Newsletter*, Fall 1966, PBBF.

35. National Tea, A&P, Jewel Tea, High-Low Foods, Red Star, and Certified. Kroger was not a factor in Chicago. SC Minutes, September 30, 1966.

36. Quoted in McKersie's memoir, *A Decisive Decade*, 156.

37. CCCO *Newsletter*, Fall 1966, 7–8, PBBF; SC Minutes during October 1966.

38. Massoni, "Perspectives on Operation Breadbasket," 24.

39. SC Minutes, November 18, 1966.

40. Ibid.; PBBF: High-Low Foods.

41. PBBF: High-Low Foods

42. *CD*, November 10 and 21, 1966.

43. *NYT*, November 26, 1966.

44. SC Minutes, November 25, 1966; original ad in PBBF.

45. SC Minutes, September–December 1966.

46. SC Minutes, November 11, 1966.

47. SC Minutes, September–December 1966; *CT*, December 10, 1966.

48. PBBF: National Tea; *Chicago Daily News*, December 9, 1966.

49. Jesse Jackson interview, March 5, 2009. We were all shocked in November 1968 to learn that Rev. Billups, who lived on my block near the Gresham church, was found dead in his car in the Kenwood neighborhood. We held his memorial service at Fellowship Baptist, where he had been associate pastor until his death. Testimonies were given by several Breadbasket colleagues and the eulogy by Rev. Evans. His killer was never found.

50. *Newsweek*, December 26, 1966.

51. *CD*, December 19, 1966.

52. *CD*, May 18, 1967.

53. *CD*, November 21, 1967; speech by Al Pitcher, n.d., W. Alvin Pitcher Papers, box 9, folder 6, UCL.

54. Jesse Jackson Sr. HistoryMakers interview, roll 9, March 1, 2006.

55. "Breadbaskets of Freedom—Operation Breadbasket" by Ed Riddick, staff researcher of the Church Federation of Greater Chicago, December 19, 1966, 8–9, PBBF.

56. Jesse Jackson Sr. HistoryMakers interview, roll 9, March 1, 2006.

57. *Newsweek*, December 26, 1966.

Chapter 4. Evolving Campaigns

1. Letter from Rev. Jesse Jackson to Breadbasket ministers, February 10, 1967.

2. Most of this account is based on PBBF: Jewel Food Stores.

3. SC Minutes, March 24, 1967.

4. Ibid., March 31, 1967.

5. Ibid., April 29, 1967.

6. *CST*, April 29, 1967; Operation Breadbasket press release, April 28, 1967.

7. McKersie, *A Decisive Decade*, 157.

8. "Statement of Purpose and Objectives from Operation Breadbasket and Jewel Food Stores," April 28, 1967.

9. The Chicago Merit Employment Committee of the Chicago Association of Commerce and Industry pre-dated Breadbasket as a program to encourage minority employment. Strictly voluntary, it had 350 members as of May 1966. Its strong suit was a report that showed black Americans' work performance was equal to whites in quality of work, attitude, absenteeism, tardiness, and illness and was actually better in turnover. Jewel was an active member of the CMEC, whose motto was "Merit employment isn't just good citizenship. It's good business, too." CMEC brochure and newsletter, ca. February 1966, PBBF; "This Is Our Report," *CST*, June 8, 1966.

10. PBBF: Jewel Food Stores.

11. Ibid.

12. McKersie, *A Decisive Decade*, 155.

13. *CD*, April 25 and May 9, 1967.

14. SC Minutes, March 17, 1967, contain the first mention of consumer clubs: "Many of the Negro businessmen now have their products on the shelves of several stores. The big job is to get those products off the shelves and into customers' homes. Since Negro businessmen cannot afford television, they must use personal contact. All of us can aid . . . by developing consumer clubs within our churches." See also program sheet, "Why Operation Breadbasket Clubs?" April 24, 1967.

15. McKersie, *A Decisive Decade*, 160.

16. SC Minutes, April 28, 1967.

17. Willie Barrow interview, July 24, 2008.

18. Jackie Jackson interview, March 13, 2009.

19. *Consumer Club Guide* containing letter from Rev. Jackson: "What Is Breadbasket?"; "What Has Operation Breadbasket Done?"; an operational chart; "What Is a Consumer Club"; a consumer club organizational chart; captain's instructions; club assignments; suggested agenda; and consumer report form. Appendix 3 in Massoni's "Perspectives on Operation Breadbasket."

20. "Women of Operation Breadbasket" flyer, W. Alvin Pitcher papers, box 1, folder 13, UCL.

21. *Chain Store Age* magazine, May 1968.

22. Jewel Foods, *Flashes* (in-house newsletter), September 5, 1968.

23. Interoffice memorandum from Nate Armstrong, Jewel Foods, August 9, 1968.

24. Letter from Ed Buron, personnel services manager, Jewel Foods, September 27, 1968.

25. PBBF: Jewel Food Stores.

26. "The Church as Leaven and Light," sermon preached at Gresham church, January 26, 1969.

27. Church conference annual report, Gresham United Methodist Church, February 19, 1969.

28. PBBF: Jewel; *CD*, January 18, 1971.

29. SC Minutes over several months in 1966–1967; and PBBF: Great Atlantic & Pacific Tea Company (A&P).

30. "Covenant between SCLC Operation Breadbasket and the Great Atlantic & Pacific Tea Company," PBBF: A&P.

31. Operation Breadbasket immediate [press] release and original covenant, May 26, 1967. PBBF: A&P.

32. SC Minutes, June 2, 1967.

33. *Citizen Newspapers*, June 21, 1967.

34. Parish of the Holy Covenant, annual report, second Sunday after Epiphany 1968, noted: "When the [Breadbasket] leadership called for boycott and picketing of the High-Low stores, Phyllis Whiting, Virginia Lipson and Pastor Robert Harman spent at least two days supporting picket lines at South Side stores."

35. *CD*, June 21, 1967.

36. Ibid.

37. The 1967 Breadbasket successes with Jewel, A&P, and High-Low may have influenced WBBM-TV to announce a special series, *The Opportunity Center*, detailing job openings in the Chicago area. It was produced in cooperation with the Illinois State Employment Service and the CUL. In a letter from WBBM-TV, I was asked to share this information with my congregation. Letter from Edward R. Kenefick, vice president and general manager, WBBM-TV, Chicago, June 7, 1967, PBBF: High-Low Foods; *CD*, July 6, 1967.

38. Report to SC from Committee on Seven-Up, July 11, 1967.

39. Account taken from sermons delivered at Gresham Methodist Church by the author.

40. *Jet*, November 16 and December 7, 1967; *CD*, September 28, November 1, 4, 6, and 7, 1967.

41. *CD*, October 29, December 11 and 17, 1969, January 8, 1970.

42. *CD*, October 13, 1967.

43. *Jet*, November 9, 1967.

44. *CD*, October 24, 1967; *Chicago Courier*, November 4, 1967.

45. *CD*, November 9 and 18, 1967.

46. "Covenant between Operation Breadbasket and Member Stores of the Certified Grocers of Illinois, Inc.," PBBF: Certified Grocers.

47. Ibid.; *CST*, November 18, 1967.

48. PBBF: Certified Grocers.

49. PBBF: Continental Baking Company.

50. Massoni, "Perspectives on Operation Breadbasket," 23.

51. SC Minutes, April 29, May 13 and 20, July 8, and December 9, 1966.

52. Operation Breadbasket press release; letter from Rev. Jesse Jackson to community, business, and religious leaders, both January 21, 1967.

53. *CST*, May 4, 1967.

54. *CD*, May 10, 1967.

55. PBBF: Banking.

56. In addition to the author, these pastors were Revs. Gerald Forshey, John Porter, Richard Lawrence, and Thomas Ogletree.

57. The author speaking to the June 1967 session of the Rock River Annual Conference

of the Methodist Church: "Operation Breadbasket is one of the most creative programs in the Negro community. It is sponsored and run by ministers, an ecumenical body of Negro and white, Protestant and Catholic, men and women, including 6 Methodists on the Steering Committee. The purpose is economic upgrading of the Negro community by increasing job opportunities, job advancement, strengthening Negro business, increasing capital availability in [the] Negro community. It is a self-help program that presents constructive alternative[s] to welfare, hand-outs, gangs, frustration, unrest and crime in the ghetto. While integration is our vision and we are working at it as Methodists in District programs, the ghetto is a reality and will be with us for a long time." PBBF.

58. *1967 Journal and Year Book, Rock River Conference of the Methodist Church,* DeKalb, Illinois, June 4–8, 1967, 85–86 and 222–223.

59. *1968 Journal and Year Book of the Northern Illinois Conference of the United Methodist Church,* DeKalb, June 9–13, 1968, 65, 76, 84–85, 167–70, 337.

60. Ibid.; SC Minutes, June 14, 1968.

61. *1969 Journal and Year Book of the Northern Illinois Conference of the United Methodist Church,* DeKalb, June 9–13, 1969, 88 and 200.

62. "Preliminary Report on Black Banking and Economic Development of the Black Community," Urban Task Force of the Northern Illinois Conference, June 1969, PBBF.

63. *1969 Journal and Year Book,* 93.

64. Correspondence from Rev. Dr. Emery Percell, November 29, 2007.

65. Conversation with Rev. Richard Lawrence, fall 2007.

66. *Journal and Year Book of the Northern Illinois Conference of the United Methodist Church* (1968, 1969, 1970, 1971, 1972).

Chapter 5. Expansion

1. *West Side Torch,* January 20, 1967.

2. In addition to Conway, Boles, Fuller, and Johnson, there were many other key businesspeople in the Breadbasket circle. A list can be found in appendix 2. See also *CD,* March 4, 1967; Negro Businesses Seminar pictorial paper, March 3–4 , 1967, PBBF.

3. McKersie, *A Decisive Decade,* 158–59; Massoni, "Perspectives on Operation Breadbasket," 30–31.

4. McKersie, *A Decisive Decade,* 160.

5. Ibid., 161–68; Massoni, "Perspectives on Operation Breadbasket," 30–32. Massoni and McKersie provide the only descriptions I have read of Breadbasket's Attunement Committee and the development of Breadbasket's business spoke.

6. While I feel that business development replaced jobs as Breadbasket's central mission only gradually during 1967, Gary Massoni placed this shift in early 1967. Massoni, "Perspectives on Operation Breadbasket," 33.

7. "Black Business" poster, n.d., PBBF: Business Spoke.

8. Massoni, "Perspectives on Operation Breadbasket," 43–44.

9. Ibid., 55.

10. *CD,* June 29, 1967.

11. Letter from Dr. King, July 1, 1967, PBBF.

12. *NYT,* July 12, 1967.

13. Author's sermon preached at Gresham Methodist Church, August 6, 1967.

14. www.mlkcelebration.com/speech_where dowego.php; PBBF: King.

15. *CD*, August 19, 1967.

16. sc Minutes, August 25, 1967.

17. This trend is documented in McAdam's *Political Process and the Development of Black Insurgency*, chart 8.5, 209.

18. Jesse Jackson interview, December 8, 2008; Jesse Jackson Sr. HistoryMakers interview, roll 9, March 1, 2009. The charge of extortion was made by Barbara Reynolds in *Jesse Jackson*, 180–83.

19. Jesse Jackson Sr. interviews, December 8 and 10, 2008.

20. The Downhomers included Ben Branch, saxophone; Wayne Bennett, guitar; Dave McCollough, organ; Al Fooks, trombone; and Harold Varner, drums. *CD*, February 12, 1968.

21. Jesse Jackson Sr. interviews, December 8 and 10, 2008; Jesse Jackson Sr. HistoryMakers interview, roll 11, March 1, 2006.

22. *CD*, March 7 and 25, 1968.

23. *CD*, June 3 and July 22, 1968.

24. *CD*, August 19, 1968.

25. *CD*, August 29, 1968.

26. *CD*, September 5, 1968

27. *CD*, August 26, 1968.

28. Calvin Morris interview, April 14, 2008.

29. Joseph, *Black Power Movement*, 189.

30. Breadbasket's role in the black power movement was recognized by an "endorsement of the total program of sclc's Operation Breadbasket" by the Black Power Conference at its third annual meeting in Philadelphia during the last week of August 1968; *CD*, September 5, 1968.

31. Hermene Hartman interview, August 21, 2008.

32. Ibid.

33. pbbf; *CD* articles, June–September 1968.

34. *CD*, June 12, 1969.

35. Branch and Barge, *On the Case*.

36. *CD*, November 25, 1968.

37. Calvin Morris interview, April 14, 2008; Jackie Jackson interview, March 13, 2009.

38. Reynolds, *Jesse Jackson*, 7–8; *CD*, September 2, 1969.

39. Richard Thomas interview, February 10, 2009.

40. *Time*, April 6, 1970, 21.

41. pbbf: Breadbasket.

42. Introduction of Jesse Jackson to the Organization for the Southwest Community annual banquet, St. Xavier's College, December 16, 1967, pbbf.

43. Jesse Jackson Sr. HistoryMakers interview, roll 10, March 1, 2006.

44. Hermene Hartman interview, August 22, 2008.

45. *Stax Fax*, December 1969, 33–35.

46. *CD*, October 4, 1969.

47. *Stax Fax*, December 1969, 31.

48. Two Breadbasket leaders independently told this account to the author, but both wished to remain anonymous. Also see Moore and Williams, *The Almighty Black P Stone Nation*, 119.

49. *CD*, October 8, 1969.

50. *Stax Fax*, December 1969, 36.

51. *CD*, October 6, 1969.

52. Jesse Jackson Sr. HistoryMakers interview, roll 13, March 2, 2006.

53. *CD*, November 14, 1970

54. PBBF.

55. *CD*, November 10, 14, and 16, 1970.

56. Jesse Jackson, "On the Case" column, *CD*, November 7, 1970.

57. Calvin Morris interview, April 14, 1970.

58. Richard Thomas interview, February 10, 2009; "Black Expo '71" booklet, Alice Tregay's personal collection.

59. *CT*, September 30, 1971.

60. Ibid.

61. Ibid.

62. "Black Expo '71" booklet, Alice Tregay's personal collection.

63. Hermene Hartman interview, August 22, 2008; *CT*, October 1, 1971.

64. *CT*, October 4, 1971; "Black Expo '71" booklet, Alice Tregay's personal collection.

65. *CT*, October 10, 1971.

66. *CD*, October 5, 1971.

67. *CT*, October 3, 1971.

68. Hermene Hartman responses, August 17, and interview, August 22, 2008.

69. See www.indianablackexpo.com.

70. SCLC news release, Atlanta, Georgia, January 29, 1968, PBBF.

71. Mantler, *Power to the Poor*, 238.

72. Orientation workshop for ministers leadership training, Miami, Fla., February 19–23, 1968, report, PBBF.

73. Memo on P. Lorillard negotiations by Al Traugott, May 21, 1968, W. Alvin Pitcher Papers, box 5, folder 2, UCL. Traugott was a lay member of the Breadbasket team.

74. *CD*, May 20 and 31, 1968.

75. "Guidelines for the Organization of Breadbasket Outposts," PBBF.

76. Massoni, "Perspectives on Operation Breadbasket," 39.

77. Quoted in Reynolds, *Jesse Jackson*, 140.

78. Breadbasket supporters, including Jesse Jackson, picketed Pepsi's offices in Manhattan. Jesse noted that Pepsi received 25 percent of its income from the black community, but only 6 percent of its employees were black. *NYT*, July 15 and 29, 1969.

79. *NYT*, October 24, 1969.

80. *CD*, October 25, 1969; Calvin Morris interview, April 14, 2008.

81. *CD*, February 9, 1970; Richard Thomas interview, February 10, 2009.

82. *NYT*, October 7, 1971; *CD*, October 20, 1971.

Chapter 6. Interruption

1. Jesse Jackson Sr. HistoryMakers interview, roll 12, March 1, 2006. History has left mostly unrecognized one of the most incredible teams of reformers ever assembled. Over the life of the SCLC, Dr. King brought together a brilliant and courageous staff, including Revs. Ralph Abernathy, Andrew Young, Fred Shuttlesworth, Walter Fountroy, Wyatt Walker, C. T. Vivian, James Orange, Hosea Williams, James Bevel, and Jesse Jackson. It was an awesome group with hundreds of civil rights arrests among them. Staff meetings were legendary for fiery exchanges, with Dr. King often stepping out of the room to reflect and

pray. Doc sought the whole picture, weighing options, looking at costs and the need for allies, and the national and international impact of every action.

Individual staffers had their own strongly held views. At times, given their spontaneous nature, James Bevel or Jesse Jackson acted without authorization. While the SCLC board or staff was in the room talking about breaking an injunction, Bevel would go out and simply break the injunction. As Jackie Jackson tells it, "Bevel and 'Reverend' [as she called her husband] got out of hand, moving ahead and forcing the action." On several occasions the veteran Bevel came to Jesse's aid, defending his actions to King, sometimes before the entire staff. While Bevel or Jesse could be impetuous, inconsistent, and disruptive, Dr. King was their opposite, usually pensive and deliberate. That was the way I experienced him in our SC meetings. Jackie Jackson remembers King as always consistent and having an inner power, a transforming presence. Jesse, on the other hand, would sometimes just burst out, while putting on his socks in the morning, "I am going to Washington and talk with our senators about this!" In spite of their differences, Jackie claims that all three, King, Bevel, and Jesse, were spiritual interpreters, able to draw people to the cause. The staff that Dr. King put together in the SCLC will remain an emblem for social justice teamwork and achievement. Author's memories; interview with Jackie Jackson, March 13, 2009.

2. Jesse Jackson Sr. interviews, December 8 and 10, 2008.

3. Jesse Jackson Sr. HistoryMakers interview, roll 12, March 1, 2006.

4. Author's notes of Rev. Jesse Jackson's sermon, St. James Methodist Church, Chicago, April 6, 1968.

5. Jesse Jackson Sr. HistoryMakers interview, roll 12, March 1, 2006.

6. Ibid.

7. Ibid.

8. Garrow, *Bearing the Cross*, 620.

9. Jesse Jackson Sr. HistoryMakers interview, roll 12, March 1, 2006.

10. All of the quotations from the "Mountaintop" speech in the following paragraphs are from Washington, *Testament of Hope*, 282–84.

11. This diary is based on author's notes, recollections, and sermon manuscripts.

12. John Porter interview, August 22, 2008.

13. Gerald Forshey, "Reflections on the Death of Dr. Martin Luther King, Jr.," n.d., PBBF.

14. Calvin Morris interview, April 14, 2008.

15. Eleta "Cookie" Murray e-mail, November 19, 2008, and phone interview, February 1, 2009.

16. Ibid.

17. Author's meditation, Gresham Methodist Church, April 5, 1968.

18. Author's notes of memorial service for Dr. King, St. James Methodist Church, Chicago, April 6, 1968.

19. Ibid.

20. Ibid.

21. Forshey, "Reflections," PBBF: Breadbasket.

22. PBBF.

23. Author's Palm Sunday sermon, Gresham Methodist Church, April 7, 1968.

24. *CD*, April 8, 1968.

25. *South Suburban News*, April 13, 1968.

26. Abu-Lughod, *Race, Space, and Riots*, 79–119.

27. Forshey, "Reflections."

28. *Atlanta Inquirer*, April 13, 1968.

29. Author's recollections and notes; *CD*, April 10, 1968.

30. Jeremiah 31:31–34.

31. "Summary of Food Distribution to Relief Agencies during Chicago Riots Disaster," provided by Jewel vice president Lee Smith, cover letter, May 9, 1968.

32. Author's Easter sermon, Gresham Methodist Church, April 14, 1968.

33. Annual meeting report, Gresham Methodist Church, April 21, 1968.

34. Branch, *The Last Request*.

35. Calvin Morris interview, April 14 , 2008.

36. sc Minutes, April 26, 1968. Jesse's reference to "split-level" negotiations was new; since the fall of 1966, the sc had incorporated black products and services along with jobs in our demands.

37. "Targets" by Gary Massoni, May 13, 1968, W. Alvin Pitcher Papers, box 5, folder 2, UCL; "Potential Targets for Negotiation" list, Breadbasket file, May 2 , 1968.

38. Dyson, *April 4, 1968*, 171–99.

39. *CD*, April 11 and May 20, 1968.

40. Chappell, *Waking from the Dream*, 3–27.

41. "Press Conference Announcing the Poor People's Campaign," Atlanta, Georgia, December 4, 1967, in Carson, *Papers of Martin Luther King, Jr.*

42. Ibid.

43. Ibid.

44. SCLC Poor People's Mobilization, Chicago, letter, February 23, 1968, PBBF.

45. Undated flyer, PBBF.

46. Fager, *Uncertain Resurrection*, 17–19. This account by eyewitnesses is a thorough and balanced resource.

47. McKnight, *The Last Crusade*, offers a disturbing but convincing account of the impact of the disinformation and disruption orchestrated under COINTELPRO, which undermined the PPC. "Lawless elements of the American surveillance state, especially the FBI, played a major role in the campaign's bafflement and undoing" (26).

48. Fager, *Uncertain Resurrection*, 20–29, 33.

49. *CD*, May 9, 1968; Willie Barrow interview, July 24, 2008.

50. Letter from author to members of the Gresham church, May 22, 1968.

51. Fager, *Uncertain Resurrection*, 49–64.

52. Ibid.

53. Ibid.

54. *CD*, June 1, 1968; *Evening Star* (Washington, D.C.), May 20, 1968.

55. *Evening Star*, May 20, 1968.

56. Letter from Revs. Jackson and Morris and PPC coordinators to Chicago area pastors, June 13, 1968, PBBF.

57. Fager, *Uncertain Resurrection*, 78–85.

58. PBBF: PPC.

59. As printed in the newspaper *Soul Force*, June 19, 1968.

60. Fager, *Uncertain Resurrection*, 113–40.

61. Jesse Jackson Sr. interviews, December 8 and 10, 2008; Jesse Jackson Sr. HistoryMakers interview, roll 14, March 2, 2006.

62. Clay Evans interview, August 22, 2008.

63. Willie Barrow interview, July 24, 2008.

Chapter 7. Breaking the Chains

1. PBBF: A&P.

2. SC Minutes, June 28, 1968.

3. *CD*, July 8, 1968; "Don't Shop at A&P" leaflet, July 1968, PBBF: A&P.

4. *CD*, July 22, 1968; Calvin Morris interview, April 14, 2008.

5. *CD*, July 27, 31, and August 1, 1968.

6. Hermene Hartman responses, August 17, and interview, August 22, 2008.

7. *CD*, August 29 and September 5, 1968.

8. PBBF: A&P.

9. Forshey, letter to Methodist bishop Thomas Pryor, PBBF.

10. Rev. Jackson et al. letter, PBBF: A&P.

11. Author's sermon, "Feeding the 5000," Gresham Methodist Church, September 8, 1968.

12. Proposals for A&P's action, a working draft, September 23, 1968, PBBF: A&P.

13. PBBF: Breadbasket.

14. SC Minutes, September 20 and 27, 1968.

15. *CD*, September 4, 1968.

16. *CD*, September 4, 5, 9, 10, 14, and 16, 1968.

17. Richard Thomas interview, February 10, 2009.

18. Massoni, "Cirilo McSween: On the Occasion of His Passing," November 8, 2008.

19. SC Minutes, October 4, 1968.

20. Author's recollections; *CD* and *Chicago Daily News*, both October 7, 1968.

21. Letter from Al and Carol Traugott to Florence Deppe, October 6, 1968.

22. "Covenant between SCLC Operation Breadbasket and the Chicago Unit, Great A&P Tea Company," October 5, 1968, PBBF: A&P (the full text of the covenant is in appendix 3).

23. Ibid.

24. PBBF: A&P.

25. *CD*, October 12 and 14, 1968.

26. Author's sermon, "Dollars and Donuts," Gresham Methodist Church, November 10, 1968.

27. *CD*, November 20, 1968.

28. SCLC Operation Breadbasket press release, "Breadbasket Blasts CTA Fare Hike," November 20, 1968.

29. *CD*, December 19 and 21, 1968.

30. Gary Massoni memo, February 1, 1969, PBBF: A&P.

31. Rev. Forshey letter, February 19, 1969, PBBF: A&P.

32. Minutes of meeting at A&P general offices on February 18, 1970, taken by Rev. Douglas Walters, PBBF: A&P.

33. *CD*, June 13, 1970.

34. PBBF: A&P file; *CD*, January 9, February 20, and March 18, 1971.

35. *NYT*, December 10, 1970, January 29 and March 12, 1971; RESIST newsletter, Operation Breadbasket, no. 2, February–March 1971.

36. PBBF: A&P.

37. Al Pitcher's archived files contain meticulous handwritten notes, reports, speeches, and memos revealing hours of labor in developing this division as a key support for the black construction industry.

38. PBBF: Construction Spoke Membership Code, n.d. (Pitcher continued to use "spoke" long after the structural change to "division").

39. *CD*, January 30, 1969.

40. Paper delivered by Al Pitcher at Breadbasket retreat, November 1969, in W. Alvin Pitcher Papers, box 6, folder 4, UCL; Construction Spoke report, n.d., box 5, folder 3, ibid.

41. BCA Construction Division Panel Minutes of several meetings during 1970, W. Alvin Pitcher Papers, box 7, folders 1–5, UCL.

42. *CD*, August 3 and 4, 1971.

43. BCA, First Report/Six Month Prospectus, W. Alvin Pitcher Papers, box 5, folder 6, UCL.

44. PBBF: Red Rooster. Gary Massoni believes the campaign originated with Breadbasket and that community groups formed around us. Massoni, "Perspectives on Operation Breadbasket," 52. A completely different beginning is described by Erik S. Gellman in "'The Stone Wall Behind': The Chicago Coalition for United Community Action and Labor's Overseers, 1968–1973," in Goldberg and Griffey, *Black Power at Work*, 117–18. Gellman lists a totally different set of community groups from the ones I list, as found in *CD*, March 3, 1969.

45. A different take on the Red Rooster story can be found in McKersie, *A Decisive Decade*, 168–71. He remembers trying to mediate between Red Rooster's owner, Bernie Hahn, and Breadbasket to no avail, does not recognize the CUCA at all, and adds a fascinating account of intrigue involving Jeff Fort and the Blackstone Rangers. I found no references to his version of the narrative in my notes, the SC Minutes, or the *CD*.

46. SC Minutes, February 28, 1969.

47. *CD*, March 3, 1969.

48. *CD*, March 8, 1969.

49. *CD*, March 5, 1969; Willie Barrow interview, July 24, 2008.

50. *CD*, March 10, 17, and 24, 1969.

51. Ibid.

52. *CD*, March 15, 17, and 20, 1969.

53. *CD*, September 24 and December 1, 1969.

54. The story of this struggle between the trade unions, construction company owners, and city powers, on one side, and the CUCA with its community groups, including major gangs, on the other, from July 1969 to early 1970, is detailed by Erik Gellman in Goldberg and Griffey, *Black Power at Work*, 112–33.

55. *CD*, August 13 and 16, 1969.

56. Sugrue, *Affirmative Action from Below*, 145–73.

57. *CD*, August 28, 1969.

58. *NYT*, September 9, 1969; *CD*, issues of September 1969.

59. *Greensboro Daily News*, October 5, 1969.

60. *CD*, September 11, 1969.

61. *CD*, issues of September 1969; Sugrue, *Affirmative Action from Below*, 171.

62. *CD*, September 22, 1969; *NYT*, September 23, 1969.

63. *CD*, September 29, 1969.

64. *CD*, issues of October–November and December 3, 1969.

65. *CD*, January 13, 1970.

66. Massoni, "Perspectives on Operation Breadbasket," 53.

67. Sugrue, *Affirmative Action from Below*, 172.

68. Theoharis and Woodard, *Freedom North*, chap. 8, "Black Buying Power: Welfare Rights, Consumerism, and Northern Protest" by Felicia Kornbluh, and chap. 2, "The World of the Illinois Panthers" by Jon Rice.

Chapter 8. The Hunger Campaign

1. *CD*, April 14, 1969. Much of the following account relies on excellent coverage by the *Chicago Defender* and is confirmed by my own notes and recollections.

2. *CD*, April 29, 1969.

3. *CD*, May 1, 1969.

4. Jesse L. Jackson, "Human Subsidy: A Position Paper," May 1969, in Massoni, "Perspectives on Operation Breadbasket," appendix 6.

5. Massoni, "Perspectives on Operation Breadbasket," 46–47.

6. Ibid.

7. *CD*, May 10, 1969.

8. *CD*, May 12, 1969.

9. *CD*, May 14, 1969.

10. *CD*, May 15, 1969.

11. Ibid.

12. *CD*, May 19, 1969.

13. *CD*, May 24, 1969.

14. *CD*, May 21, 1969.

15. *CD*, May 28, 1969.

16. *CD*, June 4, 1969.

17. *CD*, June 12 and 16, 1969.

18. *CD*, June 16, 1969.

19. *CD*, June 24, 1969.

20. *CD*, June 28 and July 5, 1969.

21. Hermene Hartman's written responses, August 17, 2008.

22. *CD*, June 30, 1969.

23. Edith Lovejoy Pierce, "Hidden Hunger," carbon copy from poet, in possession of author.

24. *CT*, August 2, 1969.

25. *CD*, August 13, 1969.

26. *CD*, August 21, 1969.

27. Ibid.

28. *CD*, October 22, 1969.

29. Alice Tregay interview, January 27, 2009.

30. *CD*, October 22 and 23, 1969.

31. *CD*, November 11, 1969.

32. *CD*, December 3, 1969.

33. Ibid.

34. Ibid.

35. *CD*, January 10, 12, and 17, 1970.

36. *CD*, February 17, 1970.

37. Jesse Jackson, "On the Case" column, *CD*, February 28, 1970.

38. Ibid.

39. *CD*, March 2, 1970.

40. *CD*, March 12, 1970.

41. *CD*, March 24 and 25, 1970.

42. *CD*, March 26, 1970.

43. *CD*, April 9, 1970.

44. *CD*, March 31, 1970.

45. "Charlie Cherokee Says" column, *CD*, April 1, 1970.

46. *CD*, April 16 and 21, 1970.

47. *CD*, April 29, June 3 and 6, 1970.

48. *CD*, September 9, 1970.

49. *CD*, October 5, 1970.

50. *CD*, October 12, 1971.

51. *CD*, October 19, 1971.

52. *CD*, October 23 and 28, 1971.

53. *CD*, November 1 and 9, 1971.

54. *CD*, November 13, 1971.

Chapter 9. Proliferation

1. *CA*, December 5, 1968.

2. *CD*, November 26, 1968.

3. *CA*, December 5, 1968.

4. *CD*, December 9, 1968.

5. *CD*, December 31, 1968.

6. *CD*, March 19, 1969.

7. *CD*, April 7, 1969.

8. *CD*, April 8, 1969.

9. *CD*, April 9, 1969.

10. Author's sermon, "The Stones Are Crying Out!," Gresham Methodist Church, March 30, 1969.

11. *CD*, December 9, 1969.

12. W. Advertising Agency, *Black Book Directory*, Donald Walker, founder and president, 1970.

13. *CD*, December 2, 1969.

14. *CD*, December 6, 1969.

15. *CD*, November 30, December 2 and 5, 1970.

16. *CD*, December 7, 1970.

17. Jesse Jackson, "On the Case" column, *CD*, December 12, 1970.

18. *CD*, December 26, 1970.

19. *CD*, January 14, 15, and 16, 1969.

20. *CD*, January 17, 1970.

21. *CD*, January 14, 16, and 18, 1971. Chappell devotes a whole chapter on this struggle in *Waking from the Dream*, 91–123.

22. *CT*, April 4, 1971; *CD*, April 5, 1971.

23. Calvin Morris, letter to Breadbasket ministers, March 15, 1968, PBBF.

24. Author's sermon, "Give Us This Day Our Daily Bread," Gresham Methodist Church, March 17, 1968.

25. Calvin Morris interview, April 14, 2008.

26. *CD*, December 5, 1969.

27. Haas, *Assassination of Fred Hampton*, 96–98.

28. *CT*, December 7, 1969; "Charlie Cherokee Says" column, *CD*, December 11, 1969.

29. Author's sermon, Gresham Methodist Church, December 7, 1969.

30. Mantler, *Power to the Poor*, 238, quoting Hampton from *CST*, May 25, 1969.

31. *CT*, December 6, 1969.

32. Haas, *Assassination of Fred Hampton*, 43–45; Mantler, *Power to the Poor*, 229–31.

33. *CD*, December 10, 1969.

34. *CD*, December 27, 1969.

35. *CD*, December 23, 1969.

36. Jesse Jackson interview, March 5, 2009.

37. *CD*, December 15, 1969.

38. E-mail, December 27, 2009, from Rev. John Baggett, then pastor of Woodlawn Methodist Church. He remembers that Breadbasket's Education Division sent its teacher members "to the Woodlawn School of Human Dignity, to be taught the African American Heritage Course. Some courses had more than 100 participants. They were usually conducted over a weekend. For the first time, hundreds of Chicago educators learned of the great civilizations of Africa." The school, sponsored by the Woodlawn Ecumenical Parish, was "under the charismatic leadership of Rev. John Porter."

39. *CD*, October 19, 21, and 22, 1968.

40. *CT*, October 29 and 31, November 2, 1968.

41. The Breadbasket teachers demanded equal budgets in all schools; comprehensive reading and mathematics in black schools; an increased number of black principals and administrators; the utilization of black services and products; certification of all black teachers; a guarantee of equal hiring of teachers, tradesmen, and laborers; free breakfast and lunch programs in every school; and the creation of local parent-student-teacher councils with decision-making power in each black school district. *CD*, April 21 and May 21, 1969.

42. *CD*, April 14 and May 19, 1969.

43. Years later, Dick Gregory stood in the choir room of the Morgan Park United Methodist Church when I was serving there and asked for a Bible before addressing a movement crowd in the sanctuary. Unfortunately for me, there was not a Bible in sight, and before I could come up with a copy he went out to the pulpit and was introduced. He began, "The pastor, Rev. Deppe, has just told me there is not a Bible available. I thought this was a church." The crowd roared.

44. *CD*, July 21 and 23, 1970.

45. *CD*, July 23, 1970.

46. *CD*, July 30 and August 3, 1970.

47. *CD*, August 1, 1970.

48. *CD*, June 24, 1970.

49. Ibid.

50. *CD*, July 29, 1970; Moore and Williams, *The Almighty Black P Stone Nation*, 117–22.

51. *CD*, August 1, 1970.

52. *CD*, August 3, 1970.

53. *CD*, August 4, 1970.

54. *CD*, August 6, 1970.

55. Charles G. Hurst, "Black Focus," *CD*, August 6, 1970.

56. *CD*, August 6, 1970.

57. *CD*, August 19, 1970.

58. *CD*, October 30, 1968.

59. Alice Tregay interview, January 22, 2009; "Guideline for Political Education" booklet, 1970, Alice Tregay's personal collection.

60. *CD*, November 25 and 29, December 2 and 16, 1969.

61. *CD*, January 24, 26, 27, and 31, February 2, 1970.

62. *CD*, February 12, 1970.

63. *CD*, June 18 and 30, 1970.

64. Massoni, "Perspectives on Operation Breadbasket," 50.

65. Ibid.

66. *CD*, November 4, 5, and 7, December 16, 21, and 23, 1970.

67. *CD*, January 4, 1971.

68. *CD*, February 2 and 8, 1971.

69. *CD*, February 11, 23, and 24, 1971.

70. *CD*, April 13, 1971.

71. "Charlie Cherokee Says" column, *CD*, April 12 and 13, 1971.

72. *CD*, May 6, 1971.

73. Branch, *At Canaan's Edge*, 718.

74. *CD*, November 14, 1968.

75. Ibid.

76. Mantler, *Power to the Poor*, 226.

77. Ibid., 227–29. Mantler confirms my view of Breadbasket's lack of coalitional effort and follow-through with the UFW.

78. *CD*, August 4, 1969.

79. Satter, *Family Properties*, 305.

80. *CD*, April 4, 1970.

81. *CD*, April 1970; press release containing April 6, 1970, telegram from Methodist bishop Thomas Pryor to Mayor Richard Daley and Governor Richard Ogilvie, PBBF.

82. Women of Breadbasket was a spoke and later a division in the Breadbasket structure, under the leadership of Rev. Willie Barrow. They were a committed, active, and loyal group of volunteers who could be counted on to picket, monitor stores for bad meat, and participate in any number of programs. Author's notes and recollections.

83. *CD*, August 25, September 14, 15, and 19, 1970.

84. Satter, *Family Properties*, esp. 215–371.

85. *CD*, May 21, 1970.

86. *CD*, May 12, 23, and 25, 1970.

87. *CD*, November 28 and December 10, 1970.

88. *CD*, December 17, 19, and 22, 1970, January 2 and 6, 1971.

89. *CD*, April 26, 1971.

90. *CD*, July and August 1971 issues.

91. *CD*, June 28, 1971.

92. *CD*, October 27 and 30, November 17, 1971.

Chapter 10. Internal Issues

1. SC Minutes, January 6, 1967.

2. Massoni, "Perspectives on Operation Breadbasket," 69–93, reviewed Breadbasket against Weber's three types of authority: (1) rational, organizational, rule-centered, and legal; (2) traditional, established, almost sanctified; and (3) charismatic, "resting on

devotion to the specific and exceptional sanctity, heroism or exemplary character of an individual person." Massoni said that Breadbasket was centered in number 3, the charismatic, with traditions, particularly of the black church, playing a significant role, and yet Breadbasket increasingly and desperately needed some rational, accountable structure for the ongoing operation. Like Massoni, I find Weber's analysis of authority helpful in understanding Jesse's leadership style.

3. Clergy were involved beyond the SC and Saturday Breadbasket, some serving as captains in "Don't Buy" campaigns. There were no clergy divisions on the picket line.

4. Massoni, "Perspectives on Operation Breadbasket," 62.

5. Willie Barrow interview, July 24, 2008.

6. Purposely, I do not appear in many of the snapshots of Breadbasket negotiators and covenant signers because I felt my role as a white participant was supportive and enabling. It was a humbling place to be.

7. SCLC news release, Atlanta, Georgia, January 29, 1968, PBBF.

8. Letter from Calvin Morris to author, November 27, 2007.

9. SC Minutes, March 1, 1968.

10. Ibid.

11. Author's recollections; SC Minutes, March 8, 1968; Calvin Morris interview, April 14, 2008; Massoni, "Perspectives on Operation Breadbasket," 62–63.

12. SC Minutes, March 8, 1968.

13. Jackson, *From Civil Rights to Human Rights*, 303.

14. Ibid., 304.

15. Dr. King took this a step further in his speech the next month to the SCLC's Tenth Anniversary Convention in Atlanta, saying that "communism forgets that life is individual. Capitalism forgets that life is social. And the kingdom of brotherhood is found neither in the thesis of communism nor the antithesis of capitalism, but in a higher synthesis . . . that combines the truth of both." www.mlkcelebration.com/speech_wheredowego.php; PBBF : King.

16. Martin Luther King Jr., "Why We Must Go to Washington," speech delivered at SCLC retreat, Ebenezer Baptist Church, Atlanta, Georgia, January 15, 1968, in King Archives, Atlanta.

17. McKersie, *A Decisive Decade*, 153–73. McKersie has a different take on jobs versus entrepreneurship. He describes Breadbasket as needing to be put "into the historical context of what came to be called 'Black Capitalism'" (154). For him, the central purpose of Breadbasket was economic development. He seems not to know that King's initial vision was jobs and that this was always the focus of the SC. McKersie's excellent but singular work with the Breadbasket businessmen seems to have blinded him to the larger picture. When "black capitalism" surfaced as a phrase from the Nixon administration in 1969, it was rejected by the SCLC's Ralph Abernathy, Jesse Jackson, and Calvin Morris and most of the civil rights leadership across America.

18. PBBF: Directory of Black Businesses, August 1968.

19. SC Minutes, April 26, 1968.

20. In his seminary dissertation, Massoni noted tensions between efforts to follow our structures and rules and spontaneous interventions by Jesse, as in reassigning staff for a newly conceived program. "On the one hand, Breadbasket attempts to become a significant organization which exercises power to achieve particular, concrete results. . . . On the other hand, Breadbasket remains a kind of charismatic movement under the direct, personal control of the leader." Massoni, "Perspectives on Operation Breadbasket," 70.

21. Mantler, *Power to the Poor*, 224, quoting from Garrow, *Chicago 1966*, 306. The words capitalized are exactly as they appeared in Jesse's memo.

22. In this context, I find both Mantler's and McKersie's work flawed in reducing Breadbasket's efforts to the rhetorical slogan "black capitalism." See Mantler, *Power to the Poor*, 224; and McKersie, *A Decisive Decade*, 154.

23. *CD*, January 20, 1969.

24. *CD*, February 18, 1969.

25. *CD*, March 15, 1969.

26. *CD*, April 5, 1969.

27. sc Minutes, April 26, 1968.

28. Calvin Morris interview, April 14, 2008; Jesse Jackson Sr. interviews, December 8 and 10, 2008.

29. *CD*, January 6, 1969.

30. sc Minutes, March 25, 1969.

31. This view was expressed to me in a side comment after the West Side sc meeting.

32. Calvin Morris interview, July 14, 2008.

33. Mantler, *Power to the Poor*, 229, gives a fine analysis of the West Side–South Side divide.

34. Massoni, "Perspectives on Operation Breadbasket," 64.

35. sc Minutes, September 19, 1969.

36. sc Minutes, November 7, 1969.

37. Author's reflections; John Porter interview, August 22, 2008.

38. Letter from Rev. Clay Evans to sc, January 5, 1970.

39. sc Minutes, January 9, 1970.

40. *CD*, January 10, 1970.

41. sc Minutes, January 16, 1970.

42. Letter to author from Gary Massoni, January 29, 1970, pbbf.

43. sc Minutes, March 6 and 13, 1970.

44. sc Minutes, April 3, 1970.

45. sc retreat packet, April 10, 1970, pbbf.

46. Massoni, "Perspectives on Operation Breadbasket," 59.

47. Ibid., 65–67.

48. "This Is Operation Breadbasket" booklet, n.d., pbbf; Richard Thomas interview, February 10, 2009.

49. Willie Barrow interview July 24, 2008; sc Minutes; author's notes.

50. Operation Breadbasket press release, January 6, 1970, in W. Alvin Pitcher Papers, box 6, folder 1, ucl.

51. Memo from Noah Robinson to Dr. Pitcher, n.d., in W. Alvin Pitcher Papers, box 6, folders 1 and 9, ucl.

52. Dr. Alvin Pitcher letter to Noah Robinson, January 23, 1970, in W. Alvin Pitcher Papers, box 6, folder 9, ucl.

53. bca board of directors, August 1970, in W. Alvin Pitcher Papers, box 5, folder 7, ucl; *CD*, January 8, February 4 and 24, 1970; sc Minutes, February 27 and March 13, 1970; author's observations; Calvin Morris interview, April 14, 2008; memo from Noah Robinson to Dr. Pitcher, n.d., in W. Alvin Pitcher Papers, box 6, folder 1, ucl.

54. Comment overheard by author at the sc in early 1970.

55. Letter from Noah Robinson to Wesley Christopherson, president, Jewel Food Stores, July 7, 1970, pbbf.

56. SC Minutes, July 29, 1970.

57. Letter from Noah Robinson to Nate Armstrong of Jewel, August 3, 1970, PBBF: Jewel.

58. Letter from Noah Robinson to Wesley Christopherson, president, Jewel Food Stores, August 10, 1970, PBBF: Jewel.

59. Author's recollection.

60. Memo, "The Detroit Report," from Noah Robinson to Operation Breadbasket, August 31, 1970, PBBF.

61. Ibid.

62. BCA inner-office memo, September 9, 1970, in W. Alvin Pitcher Papers, box 5, folder 6, UCL.

63. CST, December 20, 1970; CD, December 19 and 21, 1970.

64. CD, July 10, August 2, 4, and 16, 1971.

65. Noah Ryan Robinson stayed on in Chicago following the Breadbasket years, establishing a business empire that included several Wendy's franchises. He then joined the El Rukn gang enterprise, which led to his downfall. In El Rukn jargon Noah was known, among other nicknames, as "I Am I Am's Brother." "I Am I Am" was their name for Jesse Jackson, because that's what "he be chatting all the time," a reference to Jesse's "I Am Somebody" recitations. Austin, *Rule 53*, 224–25. In the late 1980s Noah was indicted for skimming $650,000 from his Wendy's restaurants. He was convicted in 1992 and again in 1996 of first-degree murder-for-hire of a boyhood friend and later business partner, Leroy "Hambone" Barber, on January 2, 1986; the attempted murder-for-hire of Denise Rosemond, a witness to the Barber murder, on December 4, 1987; and racketeering with the El Rukn gang's cocaine and heroin operation in several cities as he sought to wrest control of the El Rukn empire from its imprisoned leader, Jeff Fort. He is currently serving concurrent life sentences at the federal prison in Terre Haute, Indiana. CT, September 27, 1996; Moore and Williams, *The Almighty Black P Stone Nation*, 207–8; Austin, *Rule 53*, 225–45.

66. SC Minutes, September 9, 1970.

67. Ministers Division workshop program, October 9, 1970.

68. SC Minutes and notes, October 14 and 28, 1970.

69. Follow-Up Committee report to the SC, October 14, 1970.

70. Massoni, "Perspectives on Operation Breadbasket," part 2, is a perceptive account of the Breadbasket modus operandi based on Max Weber's authority typology and unveils the trials, tribulations, and personal sacrifices of the Breadbasket staff.

71. A barrage of telephone calls to the *Defender* revealed major criticism of their coverage of the rumors; CD, May 31 and June 3, 1969.

72. Comment heard in the SC by the author.

73. CD, April 15 and 16, 1970.

74. CD, April 18 and 20, 1970.

75. CST, April 19, 1971.

76. Ibid.

77. CD, April 19, 21, 27, 28, 1971.

Chapter 11. Decline and Transformation

1. PBBF: Seven-Up, Pepsi, Continental Baking, Certified Grocers, Dean Foods, and High-Low Foods.

2. SC Minutes, June 28, 1968; PBBF: Walgreen.

3. SC Minutes, October 11, 18, and 25, 1968, February 25 and March 26, 1969; e-mail from Rev. Forshey, September 1, 2007, PBBF: Walgreen.

4. Telegram, May 21, 1970, PBBF: Walgreen.

5. Letter to Walgreen, May 28, 1970; letter from Revs. Jackson and Lawrence to area pastors, June 3, 1970, PBBF: Walgreen.

6. Author's sermon, "Hope: Promise of the Covenant," Gresham Methodist Church, June 7, 1970.

7. CD, June 13, 1970.

8. Covenant between SCLC's Operation Breadbasket and Walgreen Drug Stores, June 27, 1970, PBBF: Walgreen.

9. Letter from Ed Buren, manager, Personnel Services, Jewel Foods, to author and Rev. Gerald Forshey, September 27, 1968; and author's recollection of reports to SC. Buren listed Jewel's efforts to promote its programs for the disadvantaged in presentations to business groups in the Chicago area and as far away as California.

10. PBBF: Walgreen.

11. Ibid.

12. Collection of handwritten notes, entitled "Scraps from a Follow-Up Session, Fall, 1970," PBBF: Walgreen.

13. PBBF: Walgreen.

14. CD, June 5, 1971; variations in the capitalization of black/Black are per the original.

15. CD, October 2, 1971.

16. Ibid.; CD, June 5, October 2, and November 20, 1971.

17. PBBF: National Tea; SC Minutes, August 19, 1970.

18. SC Minutes, November 25, 1970; "Do Not Shop at National Foods" flyer, PBBF: National Tea.

19. PBBF: National Tea.

20. Massoni, "Perspectives on Operation Breadbasket," 60.

21. Ibid.

22. RESIST newsletter, December 1970, PBBF.

23. PBBF: National Tea; SC Minutes, January 13 and 27, April 21, 1971.

24. CD, Jesse Jackson, "On the Case" column, June 5, 1971; CD, June 19 and 26, 1971.

25. CD, July 10, 1971; Calvin Morris interview, April 14, 2008.

26. PBBF: National Tea.

27. CD, July 1, 10, and 14, 1971.

28. Richard A. Lawrence, special column, *Eagle Tribune* (Lawrence, Mass.), February 1995, PBBF.

29. Jesse Jackson, "On the Case" column, CD, July 17, 1971.

30. *Eagle Tribune*, February 1995.

31. *Wall Street Journal*, June 23, 1971.

32. CT, July 15, 1971; CD, July 17 and 26, August 14, 1971.

33. "We are three black sisters that are on the picket lines every week. We don't expect any medals, but we do expect our black brothers and sisters to get hep to the facts and join us on those lines. First of all, we are not out there to close stores in the black neighborhoods. One of the main demands is to 'protect' the jobs blacks already have in National Tea. The stores that are closing were programmed to close before Operation Breadbasket started picketing. . . . Do you enjoy eating rotten meat, paying higher prices in the ghetto

than in the suburbs, shopping in unsanitary stores? That's what is happening." Letter to the editor, *CD*, September 25, 1971.

34. Conversation with Richard Lawrence, fall 2007.

35. Jesse Jackson interview, March 5, 2009.

36. *CD*, July 10 and 13, 1971; *CT*, July 11, 1971.

37. Rev. Morris wrote in conclusion: "I can never forget the tireless efforts of people who steadfastly fight for freedom. I sincerely hope that in those efforts I have helped somebody along the way." PBBF: Calvin Morris.

38. "This Is Your Life, Rev. Calvin S. Morris," honorary book in two volumes, property of Rev. Morris.

39. Jesse Jackson, "On the Case" column, *CD*, August 28, 1971.

40. *CD*, August 26, 1971.

41. Calvin Morris interview, April 14, 2008.

42. Thomas Todd came to Northwestern in June 1970 from the U.S. attorney general's Chicago office, where he had set up the first civil rights unit in 1969 and filed a friend-of-the-court brief on behalf of the CBL. Volunteering at Breadbasket, Todd assisted in Jesse's election requirement lawsuit. *CD*, September 11, 1971.

43. *CT*, November 28, 1971.

44. Ibid.

45. Ibid.; Hermene Hartman interview, August 22, 2008.

46. As a pastor, I experienced this same attitude. With Rev. Jackson's leadership and charisma, he received financial support similar to any successful pastor of a large congregation, in this case, Breadbasket. As of this writing, Jesse and Jackie still live in this same house, now considered a modest home in the middle-income neighborhood of South Shore.

47. *CD*, December 1, 1971.

48. *CD*, December 4, 1971.

49. *CD*, December 6 and 11, 1971.

50. Faith Christmas, *Defender* columnist, reporting on comments of Al Johnson at a news conference by the Black Expo executive board; *CD*, December 11, 1971.

51. *NYT*, December 12, 1971.

52. *CD*, December 13, 1971.

53. *CD*, December 13 and 14, 1971.

54. *CD*, December 14, 1971.

55. *CD*, December 14 and 18, 1971.

56. *CD*, December 16 and 18, 1971.

57. *Greensboro Daily News*, December 19, 1971.

58. *CD*, December 20, 1971.

59. Jesse Jackson, "Country Preacher" column, *CD*, December 18, 1971.

60. Jesse Jackson Sr. HistoryMakers interview, rolls 13 and 14, March 2, 2006.

61. *CD*, December 25, 1971.

62. *CD*, December 25 and 28, 1971.

63. *CD*, December 14, 1971.

Afterword

1. Walter Grady interview, April 10, 2008; Seaway National Bank annual report, 2007.

2. *Time* magazine, April 6, 1970.

BIBLIOGRAPHY

Books

Abernathy, Ralph David. *And the Walls Came Tumbling Down: An Autobiography*. New York: Harper and Row, 1989.

Abu-Lughod, Janet L. *Race, Space, and Riots in Chicago, New York, and Los Angeles*. New York: Oxford University Press, 2007.

Anderson, Alan B., and George W. Pickering. *Confronting the Color Line: The Broken Promise of the Civil Rights Movement in Chicago*. Athens: University of Georgia Press, 1986.

Andrews, Kenneth T. *Freedom Is a Constant Struggle: The Mississippi Civil Rights Movement and Its Legacy*. Chicago: University of Chicago Press, 2004.

Ansbro, John J. *Martin Luther King, Jr.: The Making of a Mind*. Maryknoll, N.Y.: Orbis, 1982.

Austin, Andy. *Rule 53: Capturing Hippies, Spies, Politicians, and Murderers in an American Courtroom*. Chicago: Lake Claremont Press, 2008.

Bartley, Numan V. *The New South, 1945–1980: The Story of the South's Modernization*. Vol. 11 of *A History of the South*. Baton Rouge: Louisiana State University Press and Littlefield Fund for Southern History of the University of Texas, 1995.

Bishop, Jim. *The Days of Martin Luther King, Jr.* New York: Putnam's, 1971.

Black, Timuel D., Jr. *Bridges of Memory: Chicago's Second Generation of Black Migration*. Evanston, Ill.: Northwestern University Press, 2007.

Branch, Taylor. *At Canaan's Edge: America in the King Years 1965–68*. New York: Simon and Schuster, 2006.

Carson, Clayborne, ed. *The Autobiography of Martin Luther King, Jr.* New York: Intellectual Properties Management, in Association with Warner Books, 1998.

———. *The Papers of Martin Luther King, Jr.* Stanford, Calif.: Martin Luther King Jr. Research and Education Institute and Stanford University Press, 1992.

Chappell, David L. *Waking from the Dream: The Struggle for Civil Rights in the Shadow of Martin Luther King, Jr.* New York: Random House, 2014.

Chicago Tribune Staff. *The American Millstone: An Examination of the Nation's Permanent Underclass*. Chicago, Ill.: Contemporary, 1986.

City of Chicago, Department of Development and Planning. *Chicago's Black Population*. Chicago, Ill.: City of Chicago, 1975.

Cobb, Charles E., Jr. *On the Road to Freedom: A Guided Tour of the Civil Rights Trail*. Chapel Hill, N.C.: Algonquin, 2008.

Cohen, Lizabeth. *A Consumers' Republic: The Politics of Mass Consumption in Postwar America*. New York: Knopf, 2003.

Countryman, Matthew J. *Up South: Civil Rights and Black Power in Philadelphia.* Philadelphia: University of Pennsylvania Press, 2006.

D'Emilio, John. *Lost Prophet: The Life and Times of Bayard Rustin.* Chicago: University of Chicago Press, 2003.

Drake, St. Clair, and Horace R. Cayton. *Black Metropolis: A Study of Negro Life in a Northern City.* 1945. Reprint, Chicago: University of Chicago Press, 1993.

Dyson, Michael Eric. *April 4, 1968: Martin Luther King, Jr.'s Death and How It Changed America.* New York: Basic Civitas, 2008.

Fager, Charles. *Uncertain Resurrection: The Poor People's Washington Campaign.* Grand Rapids, Mich.: Eerdmans, 1969.

Fairclough, Adam. *Better Day Coming: Blacks and Equality, 1890–2000.* New York: Viking, 2001.

———. *To Redeem the Soul of America: The Southern Christian Leadership Conference and Martin Luther King, Jr.* Athens: University of Georgia Press, 1987.

Findlay, James F. *Church People in the Struggle: The National Council on Churches and the Black Freedom Movement, 1950–1970.* New York: Oxford University Press, 1993.

Finley, Mary Lou, Bernard LaFayette Jr., James R. Ralph Jr., and Pam Smith, eds. *The Chicago Freedom Movement: Martin Luther King Jr. and Civil Rights Activism in the North.* Lexington: University Press of Kentucky, 2016.

Flamm, Michael William. "'Law and Order': Street Crime, Civil Disorder, and the Crisis of Liberalism." PhD diss., Columbia University, 1998.

Frady, Marshall. *Jesse: The Life and Pilgrimage of Jesse Jackson.* New York: Random House, 1996.

Frazier, E. Franklin. *The Negro Church in America.* Published in a single volume with Lincoln, C. Eric. *The Black Church since Frazier.* New York: Schocken, 1974.

Garrow, David J. *Bearing the Cross: Martin Luther King, Jr., and the Southern Christian Leadership Conference.* 1986. Reprint, New York: Random House, 1988.

———, ed. *Chicago 1966: Open Housing Marches, Summit Negotiations, and Operation Breadbasket.* Brooklyn, N.Y.: Carlson, 1989.

Goldberg, David, and Trevor Griffey, eds. *Black Power at Work: Community Control, Affirmative Action, and the Construction Industry.* Ithaca, N.Y.: Cornell University Press, 2010.

Grossman, James R. *Land of Hope: Chicago, Black Southerners and the Great Migration.* Chicago: University of Chicago Press, 1989.

Haas, Jeffrey. *The Assassination of Fred Hampton: How the FBI and the Chicago Police Murdered a Black Panther.* Chicago: Lawrence Hall, 2010.

Hampton, Henry, and Steve Fayer. *Voices of Freedom: An Oral History of the Civil Rights Movement from the 1950s through the 1980s.* New York: Bantam, 1990.

Hartman, Chester, ed. *America's Growing Inequality: The Impact of Poverty and Race.* Lanham, Md.: Lexington, 2014.

Heise, Kenan, and Mark Frazel. *Hands on Chicago: A Fast Moving Report on All 77 Chicago Neighborhood Communities.* Chicago: Bonus, 1987.

Hirsch, Arnold R. *Making the Second Ghetto: Race and Housing in Chicago 1940–1960.* Chicago: University of Chicago Press, 1983.

Hough, Joseph C., Jr. *Black Power and White Protestants*. New York: Oxford University Press, 1968.

Jackson, Jesse L., Sr., Frank E. Watkins, and Roger D. Hatch. *Straight from the Heart*. Minneapolis, Minn.: Augsburg Fortress, 1987.

Jackson, Thomas F. *From Civil Rights to Human Rights: Martin Luther King, Jr., and the Struggle for Economic Justice*. Philadelphia: University of Pennsylvania Press, 2007.

Joseph, Peniel E. *Waiting 'til the Midnight Hour: A Narrative History of Black Power in America*. New York: Holt, 2006.

Joseph, Peniel E., ed. *The Black Power Movement: Rethinking the Civil Rights–Black Power Era*. New York: Routledge, Taylor and Francis, 2006.

King, Coretta Scott. *My Life with Martin Luther King, Jr*. New York: Holt, Rinehart and Winston, 1969.

King, Martin Luther, Jr. *Strength to Love*. New York: Harper and Row, 1963.

———. *Where Do We Go from Here: Chaos or Community?* New York: Harper and Row, 1967.

Lemann, Nicholas. *The Promised Land: The Great Black Migration and How It Changed America*. New York: Random House, 1992.

MacLean, Nancy. *Freedom Is Not Enough: The Opening of the American Workplace*. Cambridge, Mass.: Harvard University Press, 2006.

Mantler, Gordon K. *Power to the Poor: Black-Brown Coalition and the Fight for Economic Justice, 1960–1974*. Chapel Hill: University of North Carolina Press, 2013.

Marable, Manning. *The Crisis of Color and Democracy: Essays on Race, Class and Power*. Monroe, Maine: Common Courage, 1992.

Massey, Douglas S., and Nancy A. Denton. *American Apartheid: Segregation and the Making of the Underclass*. Cambridge, Mass.: Harvard University Press, 1993.

Massoni, Gary. "Perspectives on Operation Breadbasket." Master's diss., Chicago Theological Seminary, 1971.

McAdam, Doug. *Freedom Summer*. New York: Oxford University Press, 1988.

———. *Political Process and the Development of Black Insurgency, 1930–1970*. 2nd ed. Chicago: University of Chicago Press, 1999.

McKee, Guian A. *The Problem of Jobs: Liberalism, Race, and Deindustrialization in Philadelphia*. Chicago: University of Chicago Press, 2008.

McKersie, Robert B. *A Decisive Decade: An Insider's View of the Chicago Civil Rights Movement during the 1960s*. Carbondale: Southern Illinois University Press, 2013.

———. *Minority Employment Patterns in an Urban Labor Market: The Chicago Experience*. Washington, D.C.: U.S. Equal Employment Opportunity Commission, 1969.

McKnight, Gerald D. *The Last Crusade: Martin Luther King, Jr., the FBI, and the Poor People's Campaign*. Boulder, Colo.: Westview, 1998.

Meier, August, and Elliott Rudwick, eds. *Along the Color Line: Explorations in the Black Experience*. Urbana: University of Illinois Press, 1976.

Miller, Robert Moats. *How Shall They Hear without a Preacher: The Life of Ernest Fremont Tittle*. Chapel Hill: University of North Carolina Press, 1971.

Moore, Natalie Y., and Lance Williams. *The Almighty Black P Stone Nation*. Chicago: Lawrence Hill, 2011.

Morris, Aldon D. *The Origins of the Civil Rights Movement: Black Communities Organizing for Change*. New York: Free Press, 1984.

Niebuhr, Reinhold. *Moral Man and Immoral Society*. 1930. Reprint, New York: Scribner's, 1960.

Oates, Stephen B. *Let the Trumpet Sound: The Life of Martin Luther King, Jr.* New York: New American Library, 1982.

O'Conner, Len. *Clout: Mayor Daley and His City*. New York: Avon, 1976.

Pattillo, Mary. *Black on the Block: The Politics of Race and Class in the City*. Chicago: University of Chicago Press, 2007.

Peake, Thomas R. *Keeping the Dream Alive: A History of the Southern Christian Leadership Conference from King to the Nineteen-Eighties*. New York: Peter Lang, 1987.

Ralph, James R., Jr. *Northern Protest: Martin Luther King, Jr., Chicago, and the Civil Rights Movement*. Cambridge, Mass.: Harvard University Press, 1993.

Reed, Christopher Robert. *The Depression Comes to the South Side: Protest and Politics in the Black Metropolis, 1930–1933*. Bloomington: Indiana University Press, 2011.

Reynolds, Barbara A. *Jesse Jackson: The Man, the Movement, the Myth*. Chicago: Nelson-Hall, 1975.

Rustin, Bayard. *Down the Line: The Collected Writings of Bayard Rustin*. Chicago: Quadrangle, 1971.

Salzman, Jack, David Lionel Smith, and Cornel West, eds. *Encyclopedia of African-American Culture and History*. Vol. 4. New York: Simon and Schuster, 1996.

Satter, Beryl. *Family Properties: Race, Real Estate, and the Exploitation of Black Urban America*. New York: Metropolitan, 2009.

Schultz, George. *Final Report on the Status of Minorities and Women in the Department of Labor: Secretary's EEO Task Force*. Washington, D.C.: U.S. Department of Labor, 1971.

Smythe, Mabel M., ed. *The Black American Reference Book*. Englewood Cliffs, N.J.: Prentice Hall, 1976.

Street, Paul. *Still Separate, Unequal: Race, Place, Policy and the State of Black Chicago*. Chicago: Chicago Urban League, 2005.

Sugrue, Thomas J. *Affirmative Action from Below: Civil Rights, the Building Trades, and the Politics of Racial Equality in the Urban North, 1945–1969*. New York: Oxford University Press, 2004.

———. *Sweet Land of Liberty: The Forgotten Struggle for Civil Rights in the North*. New York: Random House, 2008.

Sullivan, Leon H. *Build, Brother, Build*. Philadelphia: Macrae Smith, 1969.

Theoharis, Jeanne F., and Komozi Woodard, eds. *Freedom North: Black Freedom Struggles Outside the South, 1940–1980*. New York: Palgrave Macmillan, 2003.

Timmerman, Kenneth R. *Shakedown: Exposing the Real Jesse Jackson*. Washington, D.C.: Regnery, 2002.

Travis, Dempsey J. *An Autobiography of Black Chicago*. Chicago: Urban Research Institute, 1981.

———. *An Autobiography of Black Politics*. Chicago: Urban Research Press, 1987.

Venkatesh, Sudhir Alladi. *American Project: The Rise and Fall of a Modern Ghetto*. Cambridge, Mass.: Harvard University Press, 2000.

Washington, James M., ed. *A Testament of Hope: The Essential Writings and Speeches of Martin Luther King, Jr.* San Francisco, Calif.: HarperCollins, 1991.

Wilson, William Julius. *The Truly Disadvantaged.* Chicago: University of Chicago Press, 1987.

Magazines, Journals, and Pamphlets

Cahn, Edgar S., S. Stephen Rosenfelt, and Central Staff. *Hunger, USA.* Washington D.C.: New Community Press, 1968.

Elliot, Osborn, ed. "The Negro in America: What Must Be Done: A Program for Action." Special edition of *Newsweek*, November 20, 1967.

Hefner, Hugh, pub. *Playboy Interview: Jesse Jackson.* November 1969.

Hall, Jacquelyn Dowd. "The Long Civil Rights Movement and the Political Uses of the Past." *Journal of American History* 91 (March 2005): 1234–35.

Kelley, Winslow, ed. *The Chicago Theological Seminary Register.* Vol. 62, no. 2. Chicago: Chicago Theological Seminary, 1966.

Llorens, David. "Apostle of Economics." *Ebony* special issue: "Negro Youth in America" (August 1967).

Luce, Henry, III, pub. "Black America 1970." *Time* special issue (April 6, 1970).

Sound and Video Recordings

Adderley, Cannonball. *Country Preacher.* Hayes, Middlesex, England: Capitol, 1970.

Adderley Quintet and SCLC Operation Breadbasket Orchestra. *Operation Breadbasket Orchestra.* 1968–1970. El Cerrito, Calif.: Pewburner Records, 2007.

Branch, Ben. *The Last Request: Ben Branch and the Operation Breadbasket Orchestra and Choir.* Chicago: Chess Records, 1968.

Branch, Ben, and Gene Barge. *On the Case: The SCLC Operation Breadbasket Orchestra and Choir.* Chicago: Chess Records, 1970.

Fleischman, Stephen, Robert Culp, and Frank Reynolds. *Time for Americans: Operation Breadbasket.* Video. New York: ABC News and AHAB Productions, 1969.

INDEX

CPSIA information can be obtained
at www.ICGtesting.com
Printed in the USA
LVOW11s1553120217
523795LV00008B/12/P